THE LIBRARY OF CHRISTIAN CLASSICS

THE LIBRARY OF CHRISTIAN CLASSICS

Volume

VOLUME XXIII

CALVIN:
COMMENTARIES

THE LIBRARY OF CHRISTIAN CLASSICS

Volume XXIII

CALVIN: COMMENTARIES

Newly translated and edited by

JOSEPH HAROUTUNIAN, Ph.D., D.D.

Cyrus H. McCormick Professor of Systematic Theology,
McCormick Theological Seminary, Chicago, Illinois

In collaboration with

LOUISE PETTIBONE SMITH, A.M., Ph.D.

Professor of Biblical History, Emeritus,
Wellesley College, Wellesley, Massachusetts

PHILADELPHIA

THE WESTMINSTER PRESS

Published simultaneously in Great Britain and the United States of America
by the S.C.M. Press, Ltd., London, and The Westminster Press, Philadelphia

First published MCMLVIII

Library of Congress Catalog Card No. : 58-5060

Typeset in Great Britain
Printed in the United States of America

GENERAL EDITORS' PREFACE

The Christian Church possesses in its literature an abundant and incomparable treasure. But it is an inheritance that must be reclaimed by each generation. THE LIBRARY OF CHRISTIAN CLASSICS is designed to present in the English language, and in twenty-six volumes of convenient size, a selection of the most indispensable Christian treatises written prior to the end of the sixteenth century.

The practice of giving circulation to writings selected for superior worth or special interest was adopted at the beginning of Christian history. The canonical Scriptures were themselves a selection from a much wider literature. In the Patristic era there began to appear a class of works of compilation (often designed for ready reference in controversy) of the opinions of well-reputed predecessors, and in the Middle Ages many such works were produced. These medieval anthologies actually preserve some noteworthy materials from works otherwise lost.

In modern times, with the increasing inability even of those trained in universities and theological colleges to read Latin and Greek texts with ease and familiarity, the translation of selected portions of earlier Christian literature into modern languages has become more necessary than ever; while the wide range of distinguished books written in vernaculars such as English makes selection there also needful. The efforts that have been made to meet this need are too numerous to be noted here, but none of these collections serves the purpose of the reader who desires a library of representative treatises spanning the Christian centuries as a whole. Most of them embrace only the age of the Church Fathers, and some of them have long been out of print. A fresh translation of a work already translated may shed much new light upon its meaning. This is true even of Bible translations despite the work of many experts through the centuries. In some instances old translations have been adopted in this series, but wherever necessary or desirable, new ones have been made. Notes have been supplied where these were needed to explain the author's meaning. The introductions provided for the several treatises and extracts will, we believe, furnish welcome guidance.

JOHN BAILLIE
JOHN T. McNEILL
HENRY P. VAN DUSEN

CONTENTS

CONTENTS

PREFACE

In making this selection from Calvin's Biblical Commentaries, our first intention was to use the translations of the Calvin Translation Society. However, it soon became clear that we had to make one of our own. For this there were two very good reasons. The older translation is about a hundred years old, and its style is no longer our own. Calvin's Commentaries were composed by way of either lecture or dictation. Their Latin style, although uneven, has the vividness and directness of the spoken word. It is the style of a master of the language, and it is neither strange nor archaic. Therefore, it seemed to us unjust both to Calvin and to the reader to perpetuate English versions of the Commentaries that are both out of date and to us stilted. We have tried to make a translation which is at once true to the original and in good and vivid present-day English. It is too much to hope that we have succeeded in every passage we have selected. Any translator knows that fidelity in expressing the meaning and feeling of an author in another tongue is a subtle and risky business. We only hope that we have produced a readable translation without doing Calvin undue violence. We wanted the reader to enjoy Calvin as well as understand him. We hope we have met with some, even if uneven, success.

The older translations are from the hands of a number of scholars. Their English styles are different, and not of the same quality. Besides, the exegetical and theological predilections of the several translators have understandably colored their versions of the Latin text. In a selection like ours we would have had to put together, in immediate succession, passages with different styles and different adequacy as translations. This would have produced a book with a garbled and bewildering style. We made a new translation to avoid such an intolerable defect.

We must say a word as to why we offer the reader this particular volume out of the vast body of Calvin's Commentaries. We had no single principle of selection. We took what we liked—rather, a small fraction of what we liked and would have included if we had had the space. We were intent upon giving the reader good specimens of Calvin's way of explaining Biblical texts, to bring out his qualities as an exegete. We wanted to show his concern with literary and historical questions, his understanding of Scripture both as the Word of God and as a human document, his constant preoccupation with the upbuilding of the church. We could not and did not ignore present-day issues in the interpretation of the Bible in theology and practical church life. We did the best we could to include material in which Calvin can be of some help to the church today. We did our selecting with such interests in mind. However, we do hope that this book has a certain continuity which will convey a proper sense of the integrity of Calvin's mind.

Our organization of the material is one of many possible. The one we adopted seemed natural to us. We have not given special chapters to Calvin's teachings on man, sin, the Holy Spirit, eschatology, politics. We had to choose between depth and spread, and we chose depth. We have much more material in hand, and someday we may be able to use it, especially if there is sufficient demand for it.

I wish to express my gratitude to Prof. Louise P. Smith who collaborated with me, especially in preparing the Old Testament passages. Her knowledge of Scripture and Calvin, her patience and good sense, her encouragement, have been invaluable in this laborious undertaking. I am also grateful to the editors and the publisher for their help, and to Mrs. George W. Baird who typed the major part of the manuscript. I wish to thank Rev. Kenneth M. Keeler and the First Presbyterian Church of Santa Fe, New Mexico, for giving me a study where I worked happily for seven months. My thanks are due also to Prof. Calvin Schmitt of the McCormick Theological Seminary Library for the bibliographical help he gave me, and to Prof. Edward A. Dowey, Jr., for his criticisms and suggestions, especially with regard to the Introduction.

JOSEPH HAROUTUNIAN

McCormick Theological Seminary,
Chicago, Illinois

General Introduction

CALVIN AS BIBLICAL COMMENTATOR

IN THESE TRANSLATED SELECTIONS FROM THE
Biblical Commentaries of Calvin, we have tried to produce
a readable version of a representative part of his work in
this field. The Commentaries were translated into English soon
after they were published in the second half of the sixteenth
century. (They were retranslated about the middle of the nine-
teenth century, by the Calvin Translation Society, Edinburgh,
and have been reprinted in this second version.) They were also
translated immediately into French and somewhat later into
Dutch and German. Calvin's Commentaries profoundly influenced the churches of the Reformed tradition; and there can
be little doubt that a renewed interest in them and study of them
would not only contribute to a better understanding of Calvin,
but would also have a profound influence on the mind and life
of the church today. Our primary interest in preparing this
volume has been to present Calvin as a Biblical commentator,
with the hope that many will be induced to turn to the Commentaries themselves in search of the light Calvin throws upon
the meaning of the Scriptures.

We concur in the judgment of many before us that Calvin
was, for various reasons, a unique and extremely illuminating
commentator. His education as a humanist, his extensive knowledge of the work of other interpreters of the Bible, his classical
and patristic erudition, his insights as a Reformer and churchman, and his exegetical competence and grasp of the Biblical
mind—all these make him an endlessly fresh and eye-opening
interpreter.

I. The Quality of the Commentator

Calvin's Commentaries and sermons fill volumes 23–55 of his *Works* (in *Corpus Reformatorum*[1]); and the Commentaries by themselves fill forty-five volumes in English: thirty on the Old Testament, fifteen on the New Testament (in the series of the Calvin Translation Society).

The grandeur of this achievement becomes all the more evident when we remember that these Commentaries were the work not of a detached scholar, but of a Reformer whose days were filled largely with pastoral work both in the church and in the state. His multiple activities and preoccupations in the latter capacity, especially in the light of his delicate and sickly physical condition, leave one amazed at the diligence and perseverance which made Calvin's literary output (fifty-nine volumes in his *Works*) possible. One must not forget the several versions of the *Institutes*, his numerous tracts and thousands of letters. Calvin believed not only in the Word of God, but also in human words as means of promoting the gospel and serving the church.

The Commentary on Romans, the first, was published in 1540. The latest, Joshua (1564) and Ezekiel, chs. 1–20 (1565), were published after Calvin's death. In between came the great Commentaries on Genesis, the four last Books of Moses (Harmony), the Psalms, Isaiah, Jeremiah, and Lamentations, Ezekiel, and the Minor Prophets (Calvin preached on the other books such as Deuteronomy, Job, and Samuel, but he did not lecture on them). There were also the Commentaries on all the books of the New Testament, except II John and III John and Revelation. The Harmony of Exodus-Deuteronomy (four volumes in English) and the Harmony of the Gospels (three volumes) deserve special mention as astonishing works of organization, both of narrative and of topics. They are, in fact, convincing evidence of Calvin's grasp of Scripture as a whole and in detail. It is impossible to single out the greater Commentaries. Each is valuable for the insights it gives into the Word of God contained in it. One has only to consult Calvin on a few given passages of Scripture to recognize that he is indeed a teacher without an equal. Calvin comments with the conviction that any passage of Scripture he may examine contains a Word of God full of God's wisdom, applicable to the

---

[1] *Opera*, in *Corpus Reformatorum*, ed. by G. Baum, E. Cunitz, E. Reuss, vol. 59, pp. 451–482, contains a list of Calvin's publications during his lifetime.

condition of his hearers and readers in one respect or another. This conviction enables him to respond to the Bible with a vitality and intelligence which certainly go into the making of the mass of interesting material contained in the Commentaries from one end to the other. So it is that in spite of the occasional dips, one is aware of walking through on a high road, with solid pleasure and frequent excitement of illumination.

Most of the Old Testament Commentaries were delivered as lectures. Calvin spoke slowly and quietly, so that his words could be recorded fairly accurately by his students and more exactly by his secretaries. Afterward he went over what had been taken down, corrected it, and allowed it to be published with proper dedications to friends and persons of importance in England and elsewhere.

It is important to remember that these lectures were delivered at the Academy, which provided education to the children of Geneva, and attracted students of theology by the hundreds from France, England, Scotland, Holland, and elsewhere. Some of the greatest Protestant theologians of the day were trained in this Academy. But the majority of those who attended his lectures went to their several countries to work, and often to suffer, for the establishment and the progress of the Reformed faith. What these men needed was clear, sure, and strong grasp of Scripture doctrine, available for the new churches or gatherings of Protestants in their own lands, surrounded by hostile forces and in constant peril. Calvin commented for the upbuilding of these people and the churches they came from and went to.

He began his lectures always with the prayer, "May the Lord grant that we study the heavenly mysteries of his wisdom, making true progress in religion to his glory and our upbuilding." The closing prayer was longer, and in it Calvin laid before the Lord the special needs of the faithful as the Scripture just studied had revealed them.

The Scripture passage was read in the original language, then translated into Latin.[2] Calvin's Latin translation is apparently his own; in the classroom, it was made directly from the text. He was of course as familiar with the Vulgate as most modern English translators are with the Authorized Version, and like

[2] There was often a desire to include the Hebrew in the publication, but to keep the cost of the volumes as reasonable as possible, this was not always done. But see the Amsterdam edition of 1667.

the modern translators, he enjoyed making improvements.[3] His wording is said to be closest, in the Old Testament, to the translation of Leo Jud, printed at Zurich in 1543 (reprinted 1545 and 1557[4]); but it does not seem so close as to suggest actual dependence. For example, in Gen. 1:6 Jud's translation runs, *Dixit quoque Deus sit expansio*; Calvin's, *Et dixit Deus sit extensio*.

What Hebrew text he used is apparently uncertain. Available, besides the Brescia edition used by Luther, were the Soncino (1488), the Bomberg editions, printed at Venice (1518–1526), and three editions of Münster, printed at Basel (1534, 1536, 1546). None of them differed significantly from the Brescia edition. The Complutensian Polyglot, finally published in 1521, was used by Beza (according to Delitzsch) and presumably was available to Calvin.

Calvin's opponents have minimized his knowledge of Hebrew (*Il n'en connoissoit gueres que les caracteres*[5]), but the Commentaries themselves offer sufficient evidence to the contrary. He deals repeatedly with disputes over the roots from which words were derived, and with various grammatical constructions. Further, he has a real sense of Hebrew style and uses it frequently as a guide to interpretation.[6] He recognizes fully the importance of "synonymous parallelism." He takes for granted the relative antiquity and accuracy of the Masoretic Hebrew in comparison with the Septuagint and the Vulgate, and he therefore uses them both along with the Targum, Theodotian, and the church fathers, much as he uses the commentaries of his own contemporaries, as aids to the interpretation of the text, not as independent authorities.

While translating the New Testament, Calvin has both the Vulgate and Erasmus before him. But he does not hesitate to make his own rendition. This statement could be substantiated from almost every other page of the New Testament Commentaries. One or two examples will suffice. He translates εὑρίσκομαι as *inveniam* ("that I may find"), against Erasmus' *reperior* and the Vulgate's *invenior*; and he justifies his rendition by saying "as Budaeus[7] (the great Hellenist) shows by various examples" (on Phil. 3:9). Erasmus translates ἀλλά μᾶλλων

---

[3] For strong objections to the Vulgate, see *Tracts* (Edinburgh edition), vol. 3, pp. 76 f., or *Opera*, vol. 7, pp. 411 f.

[4] King, John. Preface to Genesis, Edinburgh ed., pp. xv-xvi.

[5] Footnote of an article by Tholuck in the English volume on *Joshua*, Edinburgh ed., p. 348.

[6] See pp. 157, 310, 365, 396.   [7] See note 32.

εὐχαριστία, of Eph. 5:4, aₒ *sed magis gratiarum actio,* "but rather by giving thanks greatly." Calvin prefers Jerome's *sed magis gratia.* He admits that the Greek word usually means "thanksgiving," but he thinks the present context requires that it be translated as *gracious.*

As to the New Testament text, Calvin clearly uses that of Erasmus. But references to ancient and more recent "manuscripts" show that he was not satisfied simply to follow even an authority like Erasmus.

Erasmus' influence on Calvin as critic and exegete was far-reaching. The former's insistence upon the necessity of knowing the original languages of the Bible[8]; his principle that the more obscure passages of the Bible should be interpreted with the help of those which are clear[9]; his plea for understanding the Bible in its "natural, or historical and grammatical" sense, and spiritually, that is, for moral edification[10]; his view of the Bible as having been written under the direction of the Holy Spirit (*Ut enim Spiritus ille divinus, mentium apostoliarum moderatur*) without a forced uniformity as to content[11]; his conviction that various and divergent accounts and teachings in the Bible do not diminish its authority and saving power[12]; his critical attitude with regard to the authorship of certain books, and his independence in relation to patristic interpreters, including Jerome; his dictum: *In fontibus versetur oportet, qui vellit esse vere theologus*—"Every man who would be a true theologian must return to the sources"[13]—all this, together with the example of free and competent examination of Scripture he sets in his emendations and annotations, are written large in Calvin's Commentaries. (How much of this agreement is to be credited to the direct influence of Erasmus on Calvin and how much to the humanistic classical training which Calvin had received is of course debatable.)

Calvin divides his text conveniently, so that he may be able to deal with a story or topic as a whole. After explaining a given passage in general, he then proceeds to discuss specific verses, phrases, and words, which he repeats sometimes in Latin and sometimes in the original. As he proceeds, he uses Latin rendi-

---

[8] *Opera Omnia,* 10 vols., ed. by J. Clericus, Leyden, 1703–1706, vol. 5, pp. 77–78. [9] *Ibid.,* p. 131.
[10] *Ibid.,* vol. 3, pp. 1026, 1029, 1034.
[11] *Ibid.,* vol. 6, p. 13, on Matt. 2:7.
[12] Berger, Samuel, *La Bible au seizième siècle,* Paris, 1879, p. 78.
[13] *Ibid.*

tions of the text which are not the same as those first given. His mind is on the original Hebrew or Greek and not on a Latin version, whether his own or another's.

As the occasion demands, Calvin goes into details in discussing a geographical and historical point. He appeals to classic authorities; to Jewish, pagan, Christian writers of antiquity, like Josephus, Pliny, and Jerome; and he quotes the best authorities of his own day. But he is brief and to the point. He weighs evidence, expresses an opinion, and moves on. It is seldom that he loses himself in detail and turns aside from his main purpose (as he does on Gen. 15:2, where his discussion of *mesek, sagah, shuk,* and Damascus must have bored all but the hardiest students). After details have been dealt with, he returns to the meaning of the whole passage, often giving a summary of its teaching, or stating the central theme and applying it to the need of the church and of his hearers and readers. He had a habit, which must have brought reassurance to his students, of marking the end of the treatment of a passage by saying, "Now we have [*tenemus*] the prophet's meaning."

He paraphrases frequently, clarifying statements and ideas for the duller students. One can imagine the quick dipping of quill pens in the ink whenever the class heard "as if he were to say" (*acsi diceret*), followed by the repetition of a text in his own words. Often he projects his mind into those of his hearers, and takes up a line of thought which is of special practical concern to them. It is surprising how often he does the same for a present-day reader. One can hear the soft-spoken lecturer occasionally shaking up the unconcerned with well-aimed and adroit thrusts, and waking them up to the relevance of the Word of God to their own and their churches' condition. The Word applied, and Calvin was eminently resourceful in pointing this out to the mind of the not too bright student. The occasional belaboring of the obvious must no doubt be attributed to Calvin's concern with what we would call "average mentality." He can also make his point clear by an occasional flash of humor: "the uproar made by a fallen leaf,"[14] the suggestion that he might wear a military uniform to class,[15] the comment on bracelets and nose rings[16] or the asses' ears.[17] Calvin was never boisterous, but he certainly had wit and could be witty— a good but rare quality in a commentator!

Characteristically, his worst term of condemnation for any

[14] See p. 322.   [15] See pp. 353. f.
[16] On Ezek. 16:12.   [17] See p. 80.

interpretation is "frigid," by which he means not so much "remote" or "lifeless" as lacking in the power to give living faith to the church; on the other hand, his favorite word of praise is "solid," a sound and sure foundation for the church's faith. Eight years separated the printing of the Isaiah Commentary and that on the Minor Prophets. A comparison of Calvin's treatment of Isa. 2:4 with that of Micah 4:2 (written eight years later) shows him addressing himself to different specific situations. And yet it also reveals the continuity of his thought in his primary concern with the upbuilding of the church.

With all this practical concern with the "progress" of his students and of the churches, Calvin was a conscientious historical critic. His comments did not degenerate into the undisciplined exhortation which often goes with "practical preaching." He neither practiced nor encouraged irresponsibility toward "the genuine sense" of Scripture. The students were to know what the author of a given text meant by what he said, and any "spiritual" meaning other than one derived from the author's intention was at once misleading and unedifying. Calvin said bluntly of Ezek. 17:1–2, "The prophet's discourse cannot be understood without a knowledge of the history [behind it]." Calvin's concern with history will be dealt with later.[18] Here we point it out as an essential part of his work as a lecturer, contributive rather than irrelevant to the hearing of God's Word.

Calvin's refusal to be diverted from his main purpose is clear also in his use of classical and early Christian literature. The list of classical references is a long one. Cicero appears most often (sixteen times in the Pentateuch Harmony alone); but there are quotations from all the better-known Latin authors (Horace, Juvenal, Seneca, Terence, Cato, Quintilian, Virgil, Plautus, Suetonius, Tacitus, Livy, Pliny), and from the Greek authors (Homer, Euripides, Xenophon, Ovid, Aristophanes, Epicurus, Plutarch, and Aesop). He quotes Plato and Aristotle with respect. He admires Plato's wisdom and piety, but objects to the "angelology" of Platonism (II Peter 1:4, Col. 2:18, etc.). He quotes Aristotle on the distinction between anger and hatred (from "The Second Book on Rhetoric"), and refers with approval to his saying that the tongue should be an image of the understanding (Gal. 5:19, I Cor. 14:11). In the field of law, he speaks of Portius' law, Flavian law, the laws of Sempronius, and Valerius' law (Acts 16:35, 22:25, I Tim. 1:10). Herodotus,

18 See "Calvin as Historian," pp. 29–31.

Pliny, Gellius, Homer all contributed a discussion of the giant Og in Deut. 3:4. It is not always possible to tell whether Calvin is depending on his own memory of a quoted passage, or on a collection of quotations such as the *Adagies* of Erasmus. Calvin was admired by his friends and feared by his enemies as a most learned man. But he never makes a display of his erudition and it seldom interferes with a forthright presentation of the meaning he saw it and with his communication with his hearers and readers.

The same holds for his use of ancient Christian literature. Hundreds of references in the Commentaries, quotations, approving and disapproving discussions make it obvious that Calvin had an extensive and masterly knowledge of Augustine, Jerome, and Chrysostom. He obviously learned a great deal from all three, and depended upon the latter two, as well as on Josephus, for his knowledge of Biblical times and places. But his knowledge is not limited to these giants. He makes apt reference, with frequent quotations, to Tertullian and Cyprian; to Irenaeus and Origen; to Cyril of Jerusalem, Epiphanius, Basil, Gregory Nazianzen, Hilary, Lactantius, and Ambrose of Milan; to Eusebius and Socrates, the historians; to Pope Leo I, Gregory the Great, and Bernard of Clairvaux. But again, the fathers are consulted for the help they may provide for understanding Scripture; they do not interfere with his exposition of it.

Calvin was grateful to contemporary commentators like Melanchthon, Bucer, Bullinger, and others (on Romans[19]). But the use he makes of their works keeps a consistent pattern. No references are given to exhibit his own learning. However, his comments show that he had read and pondered over the works of his contemporaries. Ecolampadius,[20] he says, interprets rightly and prudently, but one needs leisure to read his work (Dan. 9:25). He quotes approvingly and supports by his own argument Luther's designation of Ps. 132:14 as "the bloody promise," but he disagrees with Luther on Dan. 8:22-23; "Luther indulging his own thoughts too freely refers this to the masks of Antichrist." He gives high praise to Bucer in the

---

[19] See Epistle to Simon Grynaeus, below.

[20] 1482-1531. He was born in Weinsberg in the Palatinate. He went to Bologna to study law but ended studying theology in Heidelberg. In 1515 he became cathedral preacher in Basel, and after a period in Germany, in 1522 he returned to Basel, after which his name was associated with that of Zwingli and with the Protestant Reformation. He was well versed in "the new learning" and was respected both as exegete and as theologian.

Preface to Psalms,[21] but he says of him elsewhere (Preface to Romans) that he is too prolix for busy men to read, and too profound to be understood by the simple, and that because of the incredible fecundity of his mind, he does not know where to stop.

Calvin declares (and truly) that he does not expend words refuting contrary opinions unless he knows the faithful are troubled by them.[22] Most of his arguments therefore are with the "papists" and the Anabaptists. There are uncomplimentary references to "the doctors of the Sorbonne." Jewish commentators are usually treated as a group and dismissed as blind to the relation between the Old Testament and Christ. He uses their judgment frequently on details, especially the meaning or derivation of words. Kimchi he mentions by name and calls him "the most correct interpreter among the rabbis" (Ps. 112:5).

It is ironical that Calvin in spite of his frequent references to "the blindness of the Jews" was himself attacked, especially by the theological faculty of Wittenberg, as "a Judaizer." A pamphlet against his method of interpreting Scripture, which was published in 1593, bore the horrendous title "Calvin Judaizing, that is, the Jewish Glosses and Corruptions by which John Calvin did not Fear to Corrupt the most Luminous Passages of Sacred Scriptures and its witness to the Glorious Trinity, the Deity of Christ and of the Holy Spirit, including the Predictions of the Prophets on the Coming of the Messiah, His Birth, Passion, Resurrection, and Sitting at the Right Hand of God, in a Detestable Fashion. A Refutation of the Corruptions is Added." The reason for such attacks was of course Calvin's insistence on attending to the "genuine sense" of Scripture.[23] He despised the allegorical method of interpreting Scripture, which had provided Christians with their favorite means of twisting the Bible into a religious book of their own liking. In insisting upon the original meaning of a text, he deprived the orthodox, even among Protestants, of many of their traditional proof texts. He even undermined the traditional doctrine of Biblical authority. But he taught the Protestant ministry how to read their Bible, and to understand it as the Word of God to the churches—which is the utmost a commentator can do.

Calvin published his Commentaries to give his readers insight into the Word of God and to point out its relevance to

[21] See p. 54 (and cf. p. 75).
[22] See Autobiographical Sketch, p. 57.
[23] Pp. 28f. .107 f., 140 f., 353, 366 f. But see also on Deut. 13:1, John 11:58.

their own life and situation. To this end he cultivated accuracy, brevity, and lucidity. He achieved his purpose to a degree that has aroused the admiration and gratitude of generations of readers. And in this day, as Prof. James Everett Frame of Union Theological Seminary of New York used to say, a man who would understand his Bible will do well to have Calvin's Commentaries within easy reach.

Here we must not fail to point out that every salient point of Calvin's theology is discussed, and is often more briefly and clearly and persuasively presented, in the direct statements of the Commentaries than in the sustained and usually technical arguments of the *Institutes*. We hope that our selections on faith, providence, Jesus Christ, and so on, will help the reader to correct many an impression he has received either by dipping into the *Institutes* or by secondhand acquaintance with Calvin. We ourselves were repeatedly and pleasantly surprised by what we found in these Commentaries: we hope the reader will find the same instruction and pleasure.

II. THE PREPARATION OF THE COMMENTARIES

In the main, the Old Testament Commentaries were delivered as lectures, and the New Testament Commentaries were dictated at home. We owe an enormous debt to Calvin's friends and secretaries who wrote down his lectures and sermons, and took dictation at his home.[24] Among these special mention must be made of Jean Budé, the son of the great humanist Guillaume Budé, and his brother-in-law Charles de Jonvillers, both of whom were refugees from France and lived on Calvin's street. They worked tirelessly with him in the preparation of the Commentaries on Jeremiah and Lamentations, on Ezekiel, Daniel, and the Twelve Minor Prophets, which occupy seventeen volumes in English translation. They have left us firsthand accounts of the way Calvin's Commentaries were composed and made ready for publication.

Budé wrote of the beginning of the work: "When some years ago that most learned man, John Calvin, at the advice and request of friends, undertook to explain the Psalms of David in the School, some of us his hearers began to take notes in our own way, for our own private study, according to our own judgment, and at will. But aroused by what we heard, we began to think how unjust it would be to a great many people, and to the whole

[24] Doumergue, Emile, *Jean Calvin*, vol. 3, pp. 592 f.

church, if the benefit of such lectures were to be restricted to a few people. We did our best to take down the lectures word for word. Without wasting time, I joined myself with two zealous brothers for this purpose; and it happened by God's grace that our effort was not without success. For, when we put our several notes together, and wrote out the lectures, we found that little had escaped us, and that we could fill the gaps without much trouble. Calvin himself is our witness that this is what happened in the first undertaking in which our abilities were put to the test. All the hearers [of the lectures] will readily acknowledge that we followed the same procedure far better in taking down the lectures on Hosea; for by this time we were more skillful at our job through much repetition and long practice." [25]

And we have the following, from Charles Jonvillers, on the preparation of the Commentary on Ezekiel:

"On February 13, 1563, Calvin began to expound Ezekiel in the Public School; even though he was constantly afflicted by various serious diseases, and had either to be carried to the lecture hall in a wooden chair, or arrive perforce on a horse; for his frail body had become so worn out that there was hardly any strength left in him. And yet, for a whole year after that February, the virulence of his disease did not keep him from discharging his responsibilities of preaching and lecturing.

"Finally, in February of the following year, when he had finished chapter twenty (except for four verses), he was forced to stay at home and almost continuously in bed. Still, even while his mind had to carry the burden of his illness, he was constantly thinking, or dictating; and he often kept writing, so that it is hardly credible how much he accomplished even when he could not leave his house because of bad health. Among other things, he corrected diligently the greater part of these lectures, as is evident from the copy with his notations, which I have saved with care along with the rest." [26]

A passage from The Life of John Calvin, by Nicolas Colladon, a minister and friend of Calvin, gives us a glimpse of the latter at work:

"About the month of September (1558), he was attacked by a prolonged and dreadful fever; and while it lasted, he was forced, to his great regret, to stop both reading and preaching. But he did not cease to work at home, in spite of the remonstrances of those around him that he spare himself. At this very

[25] Opera, vol. 42, pp. 191–192.
[26] Ibid., vol. 40, proleg. See Edinburgh edition of Ezekiel, p. xlvii.

time he revised and improved his Commentary on Isaiah, which had already been printed in the year 1551. Besides, at this time his lectures on all the Minor Prophets were printed; for previously there had been only a separate printing of his lectures on Hosea. It may be that when he was seized by the fever he had already read all the Minor Prophets, and there were only two or three lectures on Malachi left. However, since the printer was nearby, Calvin, wanting to avoid publishing an imperfect work, worked over his lectures in his own rooms and dictated them to several persons who were able to be present. Thus these lectures, as well as the others, were taken down from his mouth, and printed like the rest. He worked in his room because it was winter and he had the fever; and it was not good for him to go outside."[27]

Again, according to Colladon: "Calvin on his part did not in the least spare himself. He worked much harder than his strength and health could bear. Every other week he preached one sermon a day.[28] Three times a week he lectured on theology. He was present at every meeting of the consistory, and made all the remonstrances. Every Friday, at a discussion on Scripture, which was called the congregation, what he added after the main speaker was like a lesson in itself. He did not fail to visit the sick, to give pastoral advice, and to do an endless number of things that went with the ordinary exercises of his ministry. Aside from the usual activities, he was greatly occupied with the faithful in France. He instructed, exhorted, counseled, and comforted them in the midst of persecution, as well as interceded for them, or had others do it when he thought there was a way."[29]

After describing Calvin's excellent memory, Colladon goes on to say: "It is not that he had much time to prepare his lectures, for even though he would have preferred to do so, he had no leisure for it. And for a truth, most of the time he did not have one whole hour for preparation. . . . I will add still another evidence for his [remarkable] memory: If, while he was dictating, someone came in to speak to him and stayed a half hour, or even an hour, most often he would remember

---

[27] *Ibid.*, vol. 21, pp. 87–88.
[28] According to Doumergue, Calvin "often preached twice a day; he gave lectures; he spoke before the congregation every week. He spoke before the consistory every week. He spoke before the council. How often a week?" (*Jean Calvin*, 6, p. 73). See also F. W. Kampschulte, *Johann Calvin*, 2, p. 375. But this writer is dependent to a large extent upon Colladon, whom we have been quoting.
[29] *Opera*, vol. 21, p. 66.

where he had left off, and would go on from there as though nothing had happened, whether he was dictating letters, or a commentary, or something else. . . .

"He slept very little. Even though this meant he was less than energetic, it did not keep him from being ready for work and the fulfillment of his duties. On the days when he was not to preach, he would stay in bed and at five or six o'clock would ask for a number of books, so that he might dictate with someone writing down his work. If it was his week, he was always ready to go up into the pulpit. When he returned home, he went to his bed and lay down on it with his clothes still on, and taking some book, continued his labors. . . . So it is that he dictated most of his books in the morning, working continually and in a very happy state of mind."[30]

III. Calvin as Renaissance Humanist

1. Calvin's "Literalism"

Calvin's exegetical method and procedure were the product of a century of classical humanism, first in Italy, but later especially in Northern Europe. Humanists, such as Lorenzo Valla[31] (1407–1457), Guillaume Budé[32] (1467–1540) and Erasmus[33] (1466–1536), had in common a zeal for recovering

---

[30] *Ibid.*, pp. 108–110.

[31] Lorenzo Valla was a learned, boisterous, and fearless scholar. He is famous for his exposure of "the Donation of Constantine," which was supposed to have established the supremacy of Rome in the church and over Italy and Western Europe. He was an accomplished Latinist, a rigorous textual and historical critic, and a general nuisance for the tradition. But he escaped the inquisition because of powerful friends including two popes (Nicholas V and Calixtus III).

[32] Calvin called Budé "a matchless ornament and crown of literature, by whose contribution today our France lays claim to the palm of erudition" (O. Breen, *John Calvin: A Study on French Humanism*, p. 114). He refers to Budé often (I Cor. 4:13, II Cor. 1:13, Phil. 2:9, John 2:5, 6:7, etc.) as an authority on the languages and civilization of Greece and Rome. *De asse at partibus eius* of Budé was held in highest esteem as a source book on the subject. He was critical of the church and defended the primacy of Scripture and the cross for salvation, but he refused to join "the Lutherans." His family later found their way to Geneva. (See Josef Bohatec, *Budé and Calvin*, Graz, 1950, for a classic discussion.)

[33] Erasmus requires no special discussion here. His relation to the Reformation has inspired a literature that is copious and readily available. See Preserved Smith, *Erasmus*, 1923; Albert Hyma, *The Youth of Erasmus*, Ann Arbor, 1931; Margaret M. Phillips, *Erasmus and the Northern Renaissance*, London, 1949; Louis Bouyer, *Autour d'Erasme*, Paris, 1955.

the literature of Greece and Rome, and for publishing reliable versions of the old classics. They loved the wisdom and style of the ancient writers, and drank up their sayings for new insight into a virtuous and happy life. These men, and many others like them, were fine linguists and critics, with whom it was axiomatic that the establishment of the best possible text of a writing was the first step toward understanding it. They compared manuscripts and authorities, and assumed the responsibility of producing their own editions of the classics. Calvin, who was trained in the humanistic method, and admired Budé and Erasmus greatly, took it for granted that before commenting on any passage in Scripture, he had to ascertain what the author of it actually said.

The so-called literalism of Calvin is directly related to the Renaissance scholars' desire to get at the original and "genuine" meaning of a text. Reformers, like Luther, Bucer, and Zwingli, as well as Calvin, who were all indebted to Erasmus and the humanistic method, agreed that the *natural* meaning of a statement was to be preferred to one arrived at by way of allegorizing or supplying a meaning other than the *literal*. This method was a commonplace among humanists, who applied it to Greek and Roman writings earlier than to the Bible. Allegory was contrary to the humanistic canon of interpretation; and "literalism," that is, the desire to get at an author's own mind, was of its essence.

So we find Calvin bent upon establishing what a given author in fact said. He criticized the church fathers, especially Augustine, Chrysostom, and Jerome, for dealing too subtly with the texts, for allegorizing and speculation; even though he obviously takes their understanding of the Bible more seriously than he does that of the humanists.[34] He complains repeatedly that even while Augustine's remarks on a given passage are good, they are irrelevant to the purpose of its writer (on Rom. 8:28, John 1:16). Allegorizing was misunderstanding, and misunderstanding was the evil a scholar had to avoid by all means.

Neither the humanists nor Calvin meant by the literal meaning necessarily an unspiritual meaning. The natural interpretation of a passage for them was one that did justice to the *intention* of the author. When Calvin protested against allegorizing, he was protesting not against finding a spiritual meaning in a passage, but against finding one that was not there. The Word of God written for the upbuilding of the church was of course

[34] See pp. 107 f., 307 (cf. 327), 311, 334, 370.

spiritual, but in the primary sense of leading to the knowledge of God and obedience to him. Calvin's "literalism" establishes rather than dissolves the mystery of the Word of God, provided for the Christian's help and comfort.

2. *Calvin as Historian*

As a disciplined humanist, Calvin recognized that the Biblical writers, for example the prophets, wrote for their own times and situations. In this sense, Calvin is a confirmed "historicist." When Isaiah, or Hosea, or Jeremiah, or a psalmist speaks he speaks for the benefit of God's people or the church in his own day. The Holy Spirit does indeed speak by them, prophesying the Messiah, and for the future church. Calvin can say that Isaiah foresaw the glory of Christ (on John 12:45). But he habitually looks at the prophecies quoted in the New Testament, not from the position of the prophet, but from that of the apostles or Evangelists who "applied" them to their own situation. Even while he assumes that the New Testament writers wrote as dictated and directed by the Holy Spirit, as a commentator he is concerned with the way they dealt with the Old Testament; and he speaks of their activity as applying [*traho, apto*], both in the active and in the passive.[35] His basic conviction in this matter, put in practice throughout his Commentaries, is that the Old Testament applied to the situation of the early church, especially to the mission of Christ, and that the Bible as a whole applies to the situation of the church in his time. So, he is interested in the way the New Testament writers applied prophecy to their own history after Christ. In fact, in the Old Testament itself, the exodus from Egypt is more than an incident in the past. It is a parable of the life of Israel, and we might add, of human life in general. The same is true of the mission of Christ, and his cross. Calvin was profoundly impressed with the analogy between Christ's destiny and that of the church in his time. Thus he saw a profound continuity between the Old Testament and the New, and between both and the events of his day (on Matt. 3:3).

To Calvin, the ultimate end of the Bible is the Kingdom of Christ, his reign over the people of God, and their faithfulness and obedience to him. This end was seen in the Old Testament dimly, or as he likes to say, *umbratile*, in a shadowy way. It was only right that when Christ came, the Evangelists should have

[35] See p. 91.

applied the prophecies to him; for the words fitted him and his work far better than they did David, or Cyrus, and their works. Commenting on Matt. 27:35, he says that the statement of Ps. 22:18, *They parted my garments among them, and did they cast lots upon my vesture,* applies better to Christ than to David who was speaking of himself only by way of metaphor. The same according to Calvin is true of Ps. 118:22, *The stone which the builders rejected, the same is become the head of the corner* (Matt. 21:42). Christ himself applies Jer. 7:11, *But you have made it a den of robbers,* to his own situation, when he cleanses the Temple (Matt. 21:13).

As a critic Calvin recognized in the Bible a natural working of the human mind which is not always too clear or too apt. Commenting on I Peter 3:14, *And be not afraid of their terror, neither be troubled,* he goes so far as to accuse Peter of misconstruing Isaiah (ch. 8). But he excuses Peter on the ground that he was only referring to the prophet for a purpose of his own, and not explaining "every word used by the prophet." He says that when Paul quoted Ps. 68:19, in Eph. 4:8, *When he ascended up on high, he led captivity captive, and gave gifts to men,* he actually changed the wording of the psalm, even though "he can hardly be said to have departed from the substance." But he believes that Paul did not actually quote the psalm; he "used it as an expression of his own, adapted to the matter on hand." Paul more than once gets into difficulties by using "the Greek translators" (on Heb. 10:5, 38), and at least once one cannot tell what prophet he is quoting from (on I Cor. 15:54). When Stephen says in Acts 7:16 that the patriarchs were taken to Shechem and buried in a sepulcher bought by Abraham, he clearly contradicts Gen. 50:13, Josh. 24:32. Calvin refers to Jerome's statement that the pilgrim Paula saw the tombs of the twelve patriarchs in Shechem. But he is not convinced. He says that perhaps Moses was using "synecdoche," that is, Joseph stands for the patriarchs; or that perhaps Luke was following an old tradition. He ends the discussion with, *Quare hic locus corrigendus est.* Hence this verse must be corrected! (See also on Josh. 24:32, Gen. 46:8, 47:31.) He also admits that when Luke made Paul speak Hebrew in Jerusalem, he may have been mistaken. Calvin thinks Paul spoke the common language of the day—Aramaic (Acts 22:2). He thinks Mark is less accurate than Luke about Easter morning (on Mark 16:1), and that Matthew's version of Jesus' denunciation in ch. 23:24 is defective (*defecta est oratio apud Matthaeum*). Even Christ himself does not quote Isaiah exactly, but applies his words to his own purpose (on Matt. 15:7).

3. The Reliability and Inspiration of the Bible

Calvin studied the Bible as a book composed by human beings, according to the interests of the authors, and he followed the practices familiar to critics of literature. In this his humanism is obvious. But he also was a humanist of the bent of Lefèvre d'Étaples,[36] Erasmus, or Bucer, when he put his method to a theological use. Calvin was not interested in the Bible as a merely human product. His critical study was inspired by a profound and powerful desire to get back, through texts and versions, to "the oracles of God." If some humanists went back to the classical authors for new wisdom on man, Calvin, with the other Reformers, went back to the Bible for the wisdom of God.

It is important to remember that the Bible was to him above all the Word of God spoken for the edification of the church. This explains his willingness to admit many unsolved problems of detail, even while he insists that the writers of the Bible were the *mouthpieces of God*. He sees that the Evangelists differ one from another in many a detail (on Matt. 22:2), but he insists that they agree on the main points of a story or parable. Where there is a question of numbers, as of women and angels at the resurrection, he points to the writers' unconcern for exact information in such matters and draws the reader's attention to the gospel or law. In fact, he sets aside a discrepancy of a thousand, between an account of Moses (Num. 25:90) and that of Paul, by remarking that the Biblical writers cared no more than the ancient Romans for numerical minutiae (on I Cor. 10:8). Paul was concerned to warn the church at Corinth against idolatry. What mattered was the reliability of

---

[36] Lefèvre d'Étaples (1450–1536) visited Italy (in 1492, 1500) and brought to France new zeal for classical learning. In 1512 he published a commentary on Paul's epistles, and pleaded for the study of Scripture as "the unique means of approaching Him who works all things in all" (A. L. Herminjard, *Correspondence des Reformateurs*, col. 1, p. 6). In 1517 he was denounced by the Sorbonne for denying that Mary Magdalene, Mary the sister of Lazarus, and "the sinful woman" were the same. After 1520 he became the center of a lively reform movement including the Bishop of Meaux and the king's sister, Marguerite d'Angoulême. In 1523 he translated the Gospels into French, and continued translating the Bible until 1530. He died a fugitive at Nérac in 1536.

the Bible with regard to the word of God and the promises of God, and not factual accuracy on detail.

The humanists believed in the wisdom of the classics, feeding their minds on the sayings (of which they made collections) of the ancient philosophers; but they did so not for mere factual accuracy, but for the edification of their age. There is a suggestive analogy between the humanist attitude toward the classics and Calvin's toward the Bible. The Word of God spoken by the Spirit was the word of salvation and every blessing that goes with it. One had to believe in it and receive it with gratitude. It was worthy of the most diligent investigation. So one did one's best to understand the Bible, and to discover its consistency as the Word of God. A man had to attend to the chief business on hand. What we have in the Bible is the wisdom of God, a "Christian philosophy," a way of life that will enable us to live and die well in a world where the devil rages and perils are always at hand. Indeed the humanistic method required that one deal with questions of time, place, and authorship raised by the texts; but one also had to be prepared to leave them unsettled, and go on to the main point, to what was said of God's glory and man's duty.[37]

Calvin knew that there were variant versions of the Bible, but he did not know—nobody knew—in his time, that there were various traditions behind the Biblical literature. Today we recognize that "contradictions" in the Bible are due to "date, authorship, and composition." But our way was not open to Calvin. Both assuming the inerrancy of the Spirit and knowing the ways of the human mind, Calvin did his best to harmonize contradictory statements. But even where he failed, he was satisfied that the intention of the Spirit in dictating "the oracles of God" was fulfilled; that the Word of God for the guidance of the church had been properly received and set down for the benefit of God's people.

Calvin indeed insisted that the Spirit "dictated" the oracles of God. But such dictation did not so much establish the authority of the Bible as give us the Word of God for the upbuilding of the church and the benefit of the Christian in particular situations. Since the Holy Spirit spoke by the prophets, God himself spoke; so, when men read the Bible, they attend to their God. But what is their business but to listen to him and to hear him for obedience? So it is that the Christians read the whole of the Bible as the Word of God: not to believe

[37] See the Preface to the Commentary on Hebrews.

God spoke *because* the Bible tells us he does, but that as they read the Bible, God himself may speak to their condition. The authority of the Bible is to Calvin the authority of God revealing himself and speaking to a Christian's specific need; and the inspiration of the writers of the Bible is presupposed in God's self-revelation to the Christian who reads it.

Calvin's doctrine of the authority of Scripture is discussed at length by theologians and church historians. Unfortunately, too many of them rely on sections of the *Institutes*, and fail to test the conclusions they draw by the content of the Commentaries themselves.[38]

Calvin, of course, accepts the whole Bible as the Word of God and he uses terms like "dictation" and "amanuensis of the Holy Spirit." In his Commentaries he shifts back and forth between God and the prophet as the speaker in the same way in which the prophets alternate the first and third person in their oracles. But those who see in such phrases a doctrine of inerrant Scripture and exact verbal inspiration forget that Calvin himself had a good deal of experience in dictating to secretaries and to students, and then correcting the results. God, the Holy Spirit, is of course inerrant, and the Word of God given by the Spirit was formulated to serve best the needs of God's church. But the human instruments, being men, were certainly not perfect. And they did remain men. Isaiah remained a great poet and Ezekiel indulged in wearisome repetitions. Calvin made no assumption of a succession of miracles to eliminate every slip.[39]

Calvin trusted the fidelity of those to whom God had entrusted his Word more than he trusted the care of the Jewish rabbis who supplied the vowel points. More fundamentally, he trusted the providence of God to provide his chosen in all ages with needful instruction. He himself seldom emends (but see

---

[38] Cf. Davies, Rupert E., *The Problem of Authority in the Continental Reformers*, London, 1946. Exceptions are Emil Kraeling, *The Old Testament Since the Reformation*, Harpers, 1955, and the section in *The Interpreter's Bible*, vol. 1, pp. 124–126, by John T. McNeill. See also Henri Clavier, *Étude sur le Calvinism*, Paris, 1936, especially pp. 103 f. Dr. Edward A. Dowey maintains that Calvin assumes the traditional views of the inerrancy of the Bible even while he comments upon it as the work of human beings (*The Knowledge of God in Calvin's Theology*, 1952, pp. 90 f.). This position, which seems correct, has been debated, and it does not alter our thesis that the ground of the authority of the Bible for Calvin was not inerrancy, but God who speaks by it. For a fine discussion of the subject, see "The Reformer's Use of the Bible," by Paul L. Lehmann, in *Theology Today*, October, 1946. See also Kemper Fullerton, *Prophecy and Authority*, ch. 7.

[39] But see on Jer. 36:4–6, 28, and Dowey, *op. cit.*, pp. 90 f.

Ezek. 16:43); however, when he discusses emendations suggested by others, he dismisses them, not on the ground of impiety, but because of the better sense he can find in the Masoretic text (e.g., Ezek. 14:4). Inerrancy is not for Calvin the basis for the authority of Scripture.

Calvin uses the doctrine of inspiration against the Church of Rome.[40] The Bible is the Word of God as over against the word of man as found in the papacy. His contention is that the Spirit spoke by the prophets and not by the pope or the Roman Church. The fathers could be wrong and often were; the councils could be wrong and often were; the tradition and the canon law could be and often were wrong. Over against all these, the Bible could not be and was not wrong. So when the fathers, the councils, or the tradition in general oppose the Bible, the Bible is right, and all the rest are wrong.

But the things at issue between Rome and the Reformers were not the incarnation of our Lord, or his resurrection, or any miracle or prophecy. They were not the number of Israelites who came out of Egypt or the genealogies of Matthew and Luke. They did not even have to do with "the date, authorship, or composition" of the books of the Bible. All such questions, which have agitated men from "the age of reason" to our own day, were not the points at issue. Therefore, the question of verbal infallibility and plenary inspiration, with the relevant questions having to do with "science and religion" or "faith and reason," were not at issue. The issue was a proper exposition of the Christian faith: the grace of God, sin, justification, the ministry, and the sacraments; in short, the gospel. The heart of the Bible to Calvin as to Luther is Christ—the anticipation of Christ and the witness to Christ, Christ's own work and his relation to the people of God.[41] This is where the inspiration of the writers is crucial. Witness to Christ is the reason for inspiration, as it is also the reason for the work of the Spirit in the church. The Spirit spoke by the prophets about Christ! And as he spoke about Christ and all that is relevant to our salvation by him, he spoke with absolute authority. The Church of Rome had corrupted the gospel. The gospel in its purity was to be found in Scripture. This purity of the gospel was the work of the Spirit, who had dictated the gospel, as found throughout the Bible, to the writers.

At a later time, inspiration meant infallibility with regard to miracles, predictions, and sundry accounts of matters of fact.

[40] *Institutes*, Bk. I, ch. 7.   [41] See pp. 61 f., 93 f., 101, 104 f., *et al.*

For the "fundamentalists," the test of belief in inspiration has been an acceptance of factual statements that seem contrary to natural process, or others that seem to involve contradiction. A grain of historical sense should suggest that Calvin was neither liberal, nor orthodox, nor neo-orthodox; even though all these can claim him in one respect or another. He was liberal in his determination to understand the Biblical writers historically. He was orthodox in his belief that the Bible was "dictated" by the Spirit. He was "neo-orthodox" in making Christ who came to save sinners central to the whole Bible.

4. Knowledge of God

The language of the Spirit is the language of human beings, and even while it is dictated, spoken, it is dictated or spoken not in an alien tongue with an alien logic but in the familiar tongue of man with its common logic. However, the speech of the Spirit is a heavenly discourse, concerning God and his benefits, spoken not to satisfy our curiosity as to his "essence," but that we may know his power.[42] The language of the Bible is intended not to disclose God as he is in himself, but as he is toward us. He is toward us, not as an informant first but as a Savior, with his power. To know God in fact is to know above all his power; and we know his power in the faithfulness, peace, joy, the spiritual gifts, we receive from him. God's power and Word go together. According to Calvin, God's power is spiritual and the Spirit of God, who is witness to God's power above all, speaks a spiritual language which is accommodated to our understanding by the use of our common language.

There is a knowledge that gives a man power over the thing known; the knowledge of the Christian man is the opposite of this. By the knowledge of God the Christian subjects himself to God's power. The latter knowledge differs from "the speculative," which Calvin considered incongruous with the Christian's relation to God. We know God, not to use him, but to worship and obey him. Therefore we know, not God's essence (as we know the essence of an object), but his grace and will by and for worship and obedience. This knowledge is one adapted to our role as creatures, and one sufficient for this role; not more and not less than we need to believe in God and obey him. It is knowledge first and last of God's love exercised toward us; a knowledge carrying with it a certainty all its own by the same

[42] See below, pp. 141, 176.

acting of God; but one in which "facts" as read in the Bible act as "signs" of God's spiritual power, and establish the sovereignty of God as God by pointing to him whose "being" is hidden from the mind of man.[43]

There is of course a singular congruity between the sign and the thing signified: as between the resurrection and the victory of God over sin and death; or between the ascension and the return of the Son to the right hand of the Father. But prior to the congruity we discern, there is the congruity of God's own doing, as established by the Holy Spirit. If we recognize the signs as signs, it is because the Spirit gives us light as an aspect of God's redemptive work. When we put Calvin's doctrine of inspiration in its proper context, and remember the unique way in which Biblical language is to him a signification of God's love and power as present in the church, we realize that Calvin used the Bible neither as an authoritarian nor as an anti-authoritarian, neither as a Hodge nor as a Sabatier; the Bible was to him the vehicle of God's power first, and secondly of our knowledge of Him.

5. *Knowledge of Man*

Calvin's belief that the Bible is God's Word, and his discipline as a humanist, are not sufficient for explaining his greatness as a commentator. What indeed is it that keeps a reader of these volumes of Commentaries interested, as he proceeds chapter after chapter, verse after verse? The variety in the treatment of the texts of course does a great deal to prevent boredom. But the positive interest of the reader is maintained by Calvin's constant concern with the light that the texts throw upon the life of man in its many aspects and its tantalizing depth. The *Institutes* begin with the proposition that the knowledge of God and the knowledge of man are inseparable one from the other, and that they together constitute the only true and solid wisdom (*vera demum ac solida sapientia*).[44] Here in the Commentaries Calvin makes full use of this principle. The stories of "holy men" like Abraham, Moses, David, Jeremiah, Peter, Paul, and Jesus himself become occasions for illuminating comments upon humanity and its ways. Calvin does not, any more than the Biblical writers, apologize for God's elect. Aware of God's faithfulness and grace, he gives the reader "realistic" insights into the characters he depicts and helps him to under-

---

[43] See pp. 59–63, 270 ff., 356, 366 ff.   [44] The first sentence of the *Institutes*.

stand himself as well as his fellow men. Thus it is that the Commentaries remain endlessly and perennially interesting. And the fact that Calvin sees all things ultimately in the light of the gospel gives his wisdom a special quality which we might well characterize as "Christian understanding." He knows that the wisdom of the Bible is not the wisdom of the "philosophers."[45] But to him it is wisdom, presented to us by the Holy Spirit himself, as wisdom without which we would have only our folly. It is clear that this conviction kept Calvin's ardor and his thought alive and made him a superb commentator on the Bible.

The Bible contains a definite perspective upon human life. Calvin appropriates it, and uses it freely and variously for an understanding of man. Calvin's interpretation of this perspective may well appear to some readers as "pessimistic." In the light of God's wisdom, men seem to be given to folly which produces in turn the miseries writ large in their history. The failings of patriarch, king, and apostle, not to mention those of God's people in general, are set down impressively in the Bible, and Calvin does not fail to point them out. He points out the infidelities, rebellions, cowardices, and malefactions of men which have brought contempt for God and misery upon themselves. History is tragic; but it is neither hopeless nor futile. Universal though evil is, men act as responsible beings, under the mercy as well as the judgment of God, who is wise and knows what he is doing. Calvin entertains neither Stoic fatalism nor humanistic "faith in man." He repudiates both fatalism and "free will" because he sees history as the drama of God's sovereign dealings with sinners, for their salvation and the fulfillment of God's purpose. Thus history is suffused, as Jonathan Edwards would say, "with a divine and supernatural light"; in it the Spirit speaks with the might of the living God toward faith and a godly life. So, the miseries of men are seen in the context of God's mercy and faithfulness, even his judgment and wrath co-operating with his Fatherly benevolence, toward the pre-destined purpose of his self-disclosure to men as illumined by Jesus Christ who is God manifested in the flesh.

IV. INTERPRETER FOR THE SUFFERING CHURCH

In Calvin's mind there was a profound and prevailing continuity between Christ and the church: between the experience

[45] See pp. 127, 131, 279, 313, 341, 389.

of Christ and the experience of God's people, whether in days of the "fathers," or in the early Christian church, or in his own day. There is hardly a Biblical account of the trials and tribulations of the godly that does not occasion a lively discussion from Calvin's pen. He never fails to see Christian life *sub specie crucis*. The prophets were persecuted, and Christ was crucified. Christ's disciples were persecuted, and so were the Christians in the early church; so also were Christians in England, Scotland, Germany, Italy, Spain, Holland, Eastern Europe, and especially in Calvin's own country, France. News of the tortures, exiles, executions from these lands came to Calvin both by letter and by word of mouth from the many who sought refuge in Geneva. He spent much time and effort helping the refugees in the city, and writing letters of comfort and encouragement to Christian people in hopeless situations abroad.[46] Geneva itself was an object of ecclesiastical hatred and political machination, and in danger of invasion. Within the city there were rebellions, divisions, and all manner of restiveness. The fact is that all through his ministry Calvin's mind and soul were preoccupied with the sufferings that were the lot of the Protestants among whom he labored and for whom he was called upon to provide instruction, guidance, and encouragement; sufferings for which there often was no human help.

Calvin appropriated the sufferings of God's people depicted in the Bible for the evangelicals in Europe and for himself. It is hardly possible, as we read his comments on Noah, David, Job, Jeremiah, or on the disciples of Jesus, to escape the truth that they all are vivified by their profound appropriateness to his condition.[47] Calvin turns again and again to the inescapable and bewildering fact that in this world the disciples of Christ have suffered far more grievously than the wicked who have abused and oppressed them. So it had been in the past; so it was in his own day; so it was in his own person. He suffered physically as well as mentally all his days. He lived under cares and contentions which gradually killed him at the age of fifty-six. The image of Calvin as a stern and insensitive puritan overlord does not bear examination. He not only felt the afflictions of his fellow evangelicals, but also commented upon them constantly both as an interpreter of the Bible and also as a "theologian." It is quite possible and even necessary to see Calvin's

[46] See *Letters of John Calvin*, ed. by Jules Bonnet, 4 vols. It has an excellent index.
[47] See especially the Autobiographical Sketch, pp. 51, 55–57.

work as a whole in the light of the wrongs that were perpetrated against the faithful throughout his ministry. It is no exaggeration to say that if one overlooks the mystery of the world's animosity to the gospel and to those who adhere to it, one is bound to misunderstand Calvin profoundly and to misconstrue his work both as a thinker and as a man of action. The following discussion of particular doctrines from this point of view is intended to give the reader a helpful clue to Calvin's mind. It is not meant to be a complete exposition, nor is it meant to obscure Calvin's primary concerns with the "honor of God," justification by faith alone, obedience to God in man's total life, and so on, which are essential for understanding his theology. We have not dwelt upon these latter emphases in Calvin because they are commonplaces of all adequate expositions of his work.

1. *The Providence of God*[48]

The suffering of the righteous confronts us directly with the providence of God; and the doctrine of providence was constantly on Calvin's mind and to it he made a peculiar contribution. It was traditional in medieval theology to write on "providence and free will." The providence of God, although welcome as providing for man's necessities, was a stumbling block in so far as it made man's own freedom doubtful. So the main interest of the philosophical theologians was to reconcile God's providence with man's freedom and responsibility. Now, all this is changed by Calvin. He finishes his comments on Acts 20:32 with the characteristic and blunt statement: "Since Scripture teaches that we have sufficient help in God's power, let us be mindful that only they are strong in the Lord who renounce their free will and lean upon him who alone, as Paul confesses rightly, is able to build up." When people suffered dungeon and exile, yea, were at the brink of death in the hands of irresistible foes, it was irrelevant and futile to reconcile providence with the free will of man. These victims of oppression were not free against the combined power of church and state. The only proper question under the circumstances was, "What did God intend by their suffering?" What these people needed to know was that God was "at the helm" and that neither torture nor death came upon them without the providence of God

---

[48] For the following sections, the reader is referred to the chapter corresponding to the following topics.

who was their Father. They were comforted, not by the knowledge of their freedom, which they did not have, but by faith in the sovereignty of God the Father which Calvin would not let them forget.

When Calvin took up the other matter of providence in relation to human wickedness, he insisted upon man's sin (as in the case of Judas), and upon the subtle tyranny of Satan over human beings (Matt. 26:14). But once again he insisted upon the proposition that no evil is perpetrated apart from God's providence and his use of it for his glory and the good of his people. Even as a sinner, a man could receive hope and courage from the faith that his own wickedness was under God's providence and would further, in spite of himself, God's glory.

We are not concerned here with justifying Calvin against his detractors. The point is that his doctrine of providence grew out of his preoccupation with the sufferings of "the elect," and can be stated and understood properly in that context. "Since Scripture teaches!" In a way, it is quite unwarranted to claim that Scripture *in toto* denies man's freedom in so far as he is a responsible being. Calvin himself does not deny, in fact he insists upon, the doctrine of man's responsibility (on Matt. 11:21). But he is far from wrong in the insight that Scripture is a celebration of God's peculiar sovereignty as God and Father, and was written above all by men who set themselves to instill courage and hope among God's troubled people, declaring God's control over the affairs of men and the hope of the fulfillment of his purpose through all the vicissitudes of human existence. In any case, Calvin's doctrine of providence, with all the thought he spent upon it, means that whether we are good or evil, whether we live or die, we are God's.

The subject of providence requires a discussion of miracles. To Calvin, the miracles of the Bible were in a class by themselves. They were the work of God the Father, in praise of Christ and for the sake of the church; and the knowledge of them was the work of the Spirit. They were to Calvin the means with which God revealed himself to his people. They were strictly "signs" in the sense of the Gospel of John. God worked them not to inflame man's taste for miracles in general, but as vehicles of his grace suitable for human apprehension. What made a miracle a sign was the Word of God. A miracle without the Word was to Calvin a prodigy which even the Pharaoh's magicians could perform (Ex. 7:12). It proved, not God's grace, but his judgment which blinded the people and made them deaf to God's word. Calvin recognized no sure way to discriminate between a sign and an imposture except by the Word of God as illumined by his Spirit (on I John 4:1 f.).

Calvin was aware that men are always gaping for miracles (on John 11:18). The more they feel their weakness before the powers of nature, the more they look for a supernatural power that will enable them to overcome the evils caused by nature and the climax of these evils in death. The miraclemongers care, not about the Kingdom of God, but about their convenience and their belly (on John 6:26). They have no taste for the cross, and therefore they debase the power of Christ with their "hope of gain." Calvin knew all this as a permanent temptation in the church. He insisted, therefore, repeatedly and strongly that miracle and doctrine go together (on Matt. 24:23, Mark 16:20), and refused to identify God's power with the working of miracles (on I Thess. 1:4), holding that the Word of God is superior to miracles (on John 4:48, 20:31). Christians languished and died in prisons without any miracle to enable them to escape. These people lived, not by miracles, but by the Word of God, by their faithfulness to Christ. What they had available was not the hope of physical escape, but the greater miracle of faithfulness and joy. Therefore, Calvin received the Biblical miracles as signs of God's power; but he knew the same power by the preaching of the gospel, by the miracle of weak men made strong, both as to those who preach and as to those who hear (on Mark 16:20).

2. Predestination

Calvin's doctrine of predestination is a complex matter, and is above all directed against the Roman Church, in support of "justification by faith."[49] But here it is necessary to keep in mind the persecution of the Protestants in his day. As in Scripture, so in Calvin's mind it was no small comfort that the sufferings of the church were predestined according to the will and the purpose of God.[50] Predestination meant to Calvin, as to Paul, that the sufferings of the Christians were no accident in the history of mankind. The unfolding of history was the realization of God's purpose which went back to the beginning. The doctrine of predestination for Calvin was bound up with the

[49] See pp. 197 f., the *Institutes*, Bk. III, chs. 21–24. The position of these chapters in the *Institutes* is itself revealing.
[50] See especially on Rom. 8:28–30, pp. 306 f.

doctrine of history as the continued fulfillment of God's purpose. There had been, there was, and there was to be nothing fortuitous, nothing apart from God's intention, nothing that originates from man's will and caprice. Jesus Christ had been called and predestined by God for his mission, together with his suffering and cross. His gospel, scoffed at and rejected by the world, was no novelty. It had been in God's purpose and was promised in prophecy through the ages. So as age followed age, fulfillment followed fulfillment, all according to God's own eternal purpose.

Calvin's doctrine of predestination was inspired by the need of the Protestant churches for a knowledge of the continuity between the gospel they believed and for which they suffered, and the *promises of God* made from the beginning and through the ages. Like the early church, like evangelist and apostle, the Reformer took great pains to establish the antiquity of the gospel he preached. A church under persecution was plagued with profound doubts. Excommunicated ex-Romanists, subject to enemy power, deprived of home and goods, in exile and at death's door, these poor people who lived in anxiety and despair, subject to miseries from which even the dregs and criminals of society were exempt, had nothing to sustain them except the promises of God. They were invited by Calvin to turn their eyes to Abraham and Moses and Noah and David, to the great deliverance of God, to the mysterious workings of his "secret purpose," to the manifestations of his wisdom and power, rooted in his eternal purpose and his predestined end— all established in Jesus Christ crucified, risen, ascended, and at the right hand of God the Father Almighty. If one abstracts the doctrine of predestination *before* the ages from the *promises* of God made by creation and fulfilled through the ages since, one does violence to Calvin's mind on this matter (see especially on II Tim. 1:9–10, Titus 1:2).

This introduction is not the place for a full exposition of such a complex and profound doctrine as predestination. We are interested only in indicating that Calvin's version of this doctrine cannot be understood properly except in relation to the suffering church. For instance, it is common to think of predestination as deterministic (on Rom. 9:17). Determinism means that one fact arises from one or more others by way of a natural necessity and that one can discover how one situation determines another. But one does not study the condition of the Christians in this world and arrive at an understanding of predestination. There is no open and comprehensible explanation of God's ways with his people one by one. God's purpose remains God's secret, and he alone can justify his deeds among men. So, God's predestination remained a mystery to Calvin, and was affirmed not as a doctrine of determinism arrived at by observing "the causes and connections of things," but by fixing the mind and heart upon the Word of God, upon Christ and the history of God's people. Determinism has nothing to do with the mystery of evil. On the contrary, it explains the mystery away. Predestination as Calvin understands it is inseparable from that same mystery and the very ground of courage for living with it.

3. *Faith and Reason*

Calvin refused to "explain" to himself or to others the workings of God's purpose in the fearful destiny of the believers in the world. On the other hand, the triumph of Christ, his ascension and sitting at God's right hand, were the immovable signs of God's sovereignty and thus the certainty of the fulfillment of God's predestined purpose. Predestination therefore meant to Calvin hope in a world where "determinism" could have produced only despair. This hope Calvin received from Scripture, and he was determined to let Scripture rule his mind and keep it within the bounds of sanity.

But the Word and promise of God made no sense to the carnal mind. The Word of God was both a stumbling block and a foolishness, and the flesh recoiled from it. There was no way of verifying it while believers were tortured and murdered all around him. There was no way of justifying the ways of God in this world except by faith.

Faith which is the proper work of the Spirit must rely upon and draw its strength from the promise of God in Christ and Scripture. It has no mandate to supersede the Word of God. And this is so because faith is to believe in God's love and care for his people in the midst of their humiliations and sufferings. But this love and care we know, not by our cogitations upon "the facts of life," but by adhering to God's word in the Bible. "Reason," which confronts us with the injustices and cruelties of this world, cannot attain to a certain knowledge of God's beneficence. The usual rational arguments for God's justice and mercy, based upon the observed workings of God's providence, even though Calvin himself used them, gave him no "certain knowledge." There was no use trying to make sense of the suffering of the elect by deep or high thinking. Therefore, the primacy of faith in our knowledge of God became established as a fixed point in Calvin's theology.

But faith did not solve the problem raised by reason to reason's satisfaction. The Spirit did not open to him the "secret counsel" of God, because in fact Scripture itself confronted him with this secret counsel, rather than removed its secrecy. Faith, therefore, could not, any more than reason, penetrate to a knowledge of God as he is in himself. Faith was a gift of God whose main function was to create in man a certain knowledge of God's goodness toward us. The miracle of faith was the miracle of joy in the midst of suffering. The knowledge of God given by the Word and the Spirit was a knowledge which occurred and became established with the joy of partaking in the cross of Christ. If the Christians not only bore their cross, but also rejoiced in bearing it, it was by the doing of God's own Spirit who regenerated them, made them new creatures. The doctrine of the Spirit comes to life in Calvin's theology, because he recognized that the comfort and joy of Christians at their cross is the work of the living God who "spoke by the prophets."

Faith is the knowledge of God's goodness toward his suffering people, and not a vague and general sense of the divine. Calvin did not deny that the carnal mind has a confused and idolatrous awareness of God. But he knew that a natural knowledge of God, without his self-revelation in Christ crucified and risen, by the inward working of his Spirit, is no match whatsoever against the machinations of the devil and the cruelty of men. He knew that human cogitation, without God's illumination and power, is helpless before the monstrous evils which proclaim the power of Satan and his reign of darkness and death. Calvin knew this, and felt it adequately. He knew the misery of this body of death, and he knew also that a mind conjoined with this body must inevitably be overwhelmed by a life that is in fact a shadow of death (on II Cor. 4:11–12). Sufferings of this life act as portents of death, and before death, says Calvin, "all the powers of men succumb with terror" (on II Cor. 1:8). Calvin was deeply impressed, doubtless in himself as in others, with the elemental desire to live and the shrinking of the flesh from its destruction (on II Cor. 5:1, Gal. 2:20, II Tim. 4:7). He knew how brave men are away from danger, and how they turn into trembling leaves when they meet it (on John 18:17). This was no academic matter with him. He knew it as a common human reality. And he knew that in the jaws of hell, it is only the Lord who gives true courage. "Let us, therefore," he says, "learn to be strong nowhere but in the Lord" (*ibid.*).

4. *Jesus Christ*

The Commentaries contain numerous and weighty statements that we know God in Christ. Commenting on I Peter 3:21, Calvin says, "Hence all cogitation on God apart from Christ is an immense abyss which immediately swallows up our whole mind." In another place, speaking of the knowledge of God among the Athenians, he says that "the Lord allowed the men of Athens to fall into extreme madness" (on Acts 17:16). Abyss, labyrinth, madness: such were words which came to Calvin's mind when he considered man's knowledge of God apart from Christ. For those who have taken up their cross for the gospel's sake, there is no knowledge of God's goodness except in the knowledge of the crucified and risen Christ.

In the context of the Christian life, Christ's mediatorship was to Calvin a continuing experience as well as a historical event. That God had revealed himself as Father in a man who was tempted and suffered, who exercised his Sonship by the death of the cross, was at the center of the gospel to multitudes of Christians who suffered and were tempted under their cross. Calvin's Christ was nothing if he was not the Comforter of the church, the source of the Christian's courage and hope, and his power of endurance.

This explains two of the characteristic emphases of Calvin: the humanity and the Kingship of Christ, perhaps his Kingship and humanity, as two focuses of his mediatorship. No one after Paul in the history of the church, so far as we know, made so much of the ascension of Christ and his sitting at the right hand of the Father, as did Calvin. There is nothing more joyful for a Christian than to know that Christ crucified is at God's right hand as the King and comfort of his people, reigning over the church, interceding with the Father for his people, protecting and watching over them in their tribulations. Hence in Calvin's thought the death, resurrection, ascension of Christ, issue in his sitting at God's right hand as the climax of his own mission; from it they derive their whole glory as elements of the gospel. The sitting at the right hand is also the source of all the benefits that Christians receive from God the Father. It is not too much to say that if one takes away Christ at God's right

hand, the whole gospel as addressed to the suffering church falls
to pieces, because the Christians are left without their Christ,
and therefore without their God. Hence, there is no image so
alive in Calvin's mind as that of the Son seated next to the
Father. Calvin insisted upon the ascension of the same Christ
who lived and died for us. The Christ who sits at God's right
hand is not a spirit who is ignorant of our flesh. He has gone
from us to lift our minds up to our God and his heaven. So it is
that he gives us his spiritual gifts, by the Spirit, of courage and
hope in the midst of our trials. Thus it is that he is at once "the
vicar of God" (on Mark 16:19) and our brother.

Calvin was as little concerned with the divine "essence" of
Christ as he was with the essence of God in general. It is the
divine power and grace of Christ that he finds of decisive importance for the church. He of course never denied, he emphatically affirmed, the union of divine and human natures in
Christ. By the standard of the Church fathers, he was orthodox
enough. But the words "essence" or "nature" belonged to con-
texts of thought that were not his own. He had no stomach for
the kind of metaphysical reflection that is required by the
mind's desire to penetrate to God's or Christ's essence. The
main point of Calvin's insistence on the deity of Christ was that
he was the agent of our salvation. Commenting on Col. 1:15, he
insists that Christ is "the image of the invisible God," not only
by virtue of his essence, but also as one in whom God makes
himself known to us. We know nothing about Christ's divine
nature apart from what he has done and continues to do for
us. And he has done and continues to do his work as a human
being and our brother. Our brother is our King, and our King
is our brother. This situation is stated properly in terms, not
of essence, but of God's saving work; provided we bear in mind
with Calvin that the one and the same saving work was at once
the Father's and the Son's by the Spirit.

Calvin's eloquent comments on the events of Christ's life and
death as recorded in the Gospels are clearly intended to show
the Christians that they are suffering after their King and par-
ticipating in his life. Here the deity of Christ in no wise vitiates
his authentically human experience of temptation and "Passion." Calvin pays his tribute to orthodoxy by reminding himself that the Son of God put on humanity and shared our life
freely and voluntarily. He even shows a predilection for the
notion that he was "God clothed in human flesh" (on Luke
19:41), or "manifested in the flesh" (on John 1:1, I Tim. 3:16).

"And yet, in Christ we see the infinite glory of God united with our polluted flesh so that they become one" (on I Tim. 3:16). Calvin's concern for the encouragement of the church led him not only to emphasize Christ's common humanity but also to present it as a state of creaturely weakness. The human nature of Christ was not that of Adam before the Fall! He was no ideal and splendid specimen of humanity such as man is supposed to have been before he sinned (Augustine[51]). He had "our polluted flesh"; our flesh with all its susceptibilities and pains. When he was slapped, or whipped, or finally nailed to the wood, he did not look down upon the proceedings as a bemused god or hero; he suffered as suffer the believers who are tormented by their persecutors.

It is quite evident that the orthodox understanding of the two natures of Christ, as involving a divine and a human essence, and even a divine and a human consciousness, was, to say the least, awkward in relation to Calvin's concern with Christ's role as mediator—especially with Christ as the head of a church engaged in mortal combat with evil. It is hardly too much to say that Christ's divinity meant to Calvin above all that he, with the Father, was the source of the Christian life and its blessings (on II Thess. 2:16). He insisted that the Biblical statements concerning Christ's relation to God are, as it were, not metaphysical but soteriological or "operational." They refer to his work, to what he is to us and for us. God himself we know by his saving work; and as this saving work is done by Christ, we know *him* as God.[52]

5. *The Christian Life and the Last Things*

About the Christian life we need not say much in this place. We have cited Calvin extensively on this subject in our selections. Here we shall consider his so-called otherworldliness.

Calvin's emphasis on self-denial can be understood and interpreted rightly only if we keep in mind that there is in fact no victory over the power of death without a denial of the self which works by sin and despair. A man has to know the death of Christ by his own death, and know the resurrection of Christ by the miracle of the victory over death within him; and such

[51] *City of God*, Bk. XII, pars. 9 f., Bk. XXII, pars. 12 f.
[52] Niesel, Wilhelm, *The Theology of Calvin*, The Westminster Press, 1956, tr. by Harold Knight.

knowledge is inseparable from the warfare in which he is subject to temptation and harassment under the assaults of Satan.
Calvin speaks of an inner and an outer mortification. The first
has to do with the struggle against sin or unfaithfulness; the
latter with the struggle against the powers of this world (on II
Cor. 4: 10). It is quite evident that these two go together, since
the temptation to deny our Lord rises in the midst of fear of the
evils to which men expose themselves in the hands of men when
they set out to obey God and cleave to Christ.

Calvin knew no antidote to defeat and ruin except to raise
our minds to heaven. To him, a Christian walked on earth, but
his life was hid in heaven. He spoke with obvious passion against
attachment to this world, and exhorted Christians to renounce
it in favor of heaven. In a sense, nothing is so essential to his
theology as the opposition between heaven and earth, and the
insistence that Christians, with their minds and hearts, leave
the earth and go up to heaven.

But Calvin wanted Christians to lift their minds to heaven
because Christ is there, and it is from there that he reigns over
the church in the world. He says explicitly that heaven, where
God is, and Christ is, is "above all the heavens." It is not the
heaven we see and in which the stars shine (on Heb. 9:24).
Calvin is not concerned with it except as the abode of God and
Christ, and the origin of our salvation; so that, to turn the mind
to heaven means to turn it to Christ at God's right hand: to
turn to him for strength against tribulation and for victory over
evil. We must turn to "heaven" for victory on earth.

On the other hand, to turn away from the earth is to Calvin
to mortify the sinful flesh which shrinks before warfare with
evil and the suffering it entails. To renounce the world is to
renounce Satan and all his evil works. It is hard to be faithful
to the gospel while the flesh rebels against the privations and
oppressions which it would avoid at the expense of treachery to
Christ and his gospel. In short, Calvin's insistence upon self-
denial and world renunciation must be understood in the context of the Christian warfare and in the light of the sheer
necessity of dying to sin if one is to live to Christ. It has nothing
to do with ascetic contempt for the created world, or with an
otherworldliness which seeks a heaven because it despairs of
this world in general. Calvin had only love and respect for the
world as God's creation for the use and enjoyment of man.[53]

Calvin turns the attention of the Christian not only upward

[53] See pp. 124, 347, 349 f., 355, 356.

but also toward the future. Hope, for Calvin, is at the heart of the Christian life. He sets before his readers "the blessed and immortal rest of heaven" as the hope that will enable them to suffer death with patience, and even to desire eagerly what they fear (on Luke 12:50). With Paul, he argues that if there be no resurrection of the dead, Christians, who are sheep meant for slaughter, are the most miserable of men (on I Cor. 15:19). He regards the present life of the Christians, with all its travail and groanings, as unfulfilled unless our redemption culminates in the resurrection and "eternal felicity."

But the new life in Christ is itself by a resurrection from the dead (on John 5:21). When Paul says that the Spirit of God "shall also quicken your mortal bodies," according to Calvin he means "everything left in us that is subject to death. . . . From this we gather that here he speaks not of the last resurrection which shall be in a moment, but of the continuous working of the Spirit, by which he gradually destroys the remnants of the flesh and restores a heavenly life in us" (on Rom. 8:11). In his comments on Acts 2:19, he identifies *the great day of the Lord* not with the last things, but with "the whole Kingdom of Christ" and the trials of the church. He does not postpone the destruction of death prophesied by Paul to the end, but speaks of it as having already occurred, as already realized in the deliverance of the Christians from the power of death (on I Cor. 15:26). The Day of Judgment is even now anticipated in the present dread and terror deep in the lives of the ungodly, and in the present joy and exultation of the believers (on Rom. 2:5). The coming of Christ itself is anticipated when Christians obey God and "vie one with another in imitating him" (on Heb. 10:7); when Christians, in the extremity of their sufferings, call upon him, and he comes to them with power and help (on Matt. 19:23); when he consummates his present reign with a complete revelation of his authority in all the earth (on Matt. 25:31). Calvin speaks of the last things as a full manifestation of what is now hidden or obscure.

He even, as we say, demythologizes the prophecy "Heaven and earth shall pass away," by calling upon Christians to raise their faith "above heaven and earth," to Christ in God's heaven (on Matt. 24:35). He calls upon them so to meditate upon the last things as to receive patience and perseverance in their trials (on I John 3:2). Their life is to be a waiting, without any clairvoyance as to time and seasons. They are to live every day as though it were their last (as it might well have been under the cross), in the hope of Christ's coming, by which they are to be comforted by Christ (on Heb. 10:25). Calvin was well aware of the absurdity of the Christians' situation, and knew very well how foolish the Christians' hope looked from the outside. But he also knew that the hope which grows within the Christian life, from it and into it, has its own peculiar rationale, and flourishes in spite of external circumstances, because it is the work of Christ and his Spirit. In this way, the eschatological statements of the Bible, with their several "metaphors" (on I Cor. 15:52, Heb. 10:26–27), illuminate the life of the Christians, as well as point to their ultimate destiny with God. But here one must remember Calvin's concern with the present responsibilities of Christians and his whole ethical concern to which we have devoted a long chapter.

Introductory Selections from Calvin

THE TEXT

I. Autobiographical Sketch from the Dedicaton of the Commentary on the Psalms

IF THOSE WHO READ THIS COMMENTARY, WHICH HAS cost me much labor, derive some benefit from it, I should like to have them know how greatly I have been helped [in writing it] through those relatively mild conflicts by which the Lord has trained me. My own experience not only aided me in applying to our present situation the teaching I gathered [from the Psalms], but also opened the way to an intimate understanding of the mind of those who wrote them. It gave me no little help in understanding the complaints of David, the greatest of the psalmists, about the evils which the church suffered at the hands of those who were supposed to be its members, for I myself had had the same or similar experiences with enemies within the church. I differ so much from David since I lack the many virtues which distinguished him, and I labor so much under the corresponding faults, that I am ashamed to compare myself to him. But although as I read the records of his faith, endurance, ardor, zeal, and sincerity, the difference between us often made me groan, yet I found especial help for myself when I saw in the Psalter as in a mirror both the requirements of my calling and how ceaselessly [David] fulfilled them. . . .

It goes without saying that my own position is far below David's. And yet, as he was elevated from the sheepfolds to the highest position of authority, so God took me also from obscure and small beginnings and honored me with the office of herald and minister of the gospel. My father intended me as a young boy for theology. But when he saw that the science of law made those who cultivate it wealthy, he was led to change his mind by the hope of material gain for me. So it happened that I was called back from the study of philosophy to learn law. I followed my father's wish and attempted to do faithful work in this field; but God, by the secret leading of his providence, turned my course another way.

First, when I was too firmly addicted to the papal superstitions to be drawn easily out of such a deep mire, by a sudden conversion He brought my mind (already more rigid than suited my age) to submission [to him]. I was so inspired by a taste of true religion and I burned with such a desire to carry my study further, that although I did not drop other subjects, I had no zeal for them. In less than a year, all who were looking for a purer doctrine began to come to learn from me, although I was a novice and a beginner.

Then I, who was by nature a man of the country and a lover of shade and leisure, wished to find for myself a quiet hiding place—a wish which has never yet been granted me; for every retreat I found became a public lecture room. When the one thing I craved was obscurity and leisure, God fastened upon me so many cords of various kinds that he never allowed me to remain quiet, and in spite of my reluctance dragged me into the limelight.

I left my own country and departed for Germany to enjoy there, unknown, in some corner, the quiet long denied me. But lo, while I was hidden unknown at Basel, a great fire of hatred [for France] had been kindled in Germany by the exile of many godly men from France. To quench this fire, wicked and lying rumors were spread, cruelly calling the exiles Anabaptists and seditious men, men who threatened to upset, not only religion, but the whole political order with their perverse madness. I saw that this was a trick of those in [the French] court, not only to cover up with false slanders the shedding of the innocent blood of holy martyrs, but also to enable the persecutors to continue with the pitiless slaughter. Therefore I felt that I must make a strong statement against such charges; for I could not be silent without treachery. This was why I published the *Institutes*—to defend against unjust slander my brothers whose death was precious in the Lord's sight. A second reason was my desire to rouse the sympathy and concern of people outside, since the same punishment threatened many other poor people. And this volume was not a thick and laborious work like the present edition; it appeared as a brief *Enchiridion*. It had no other purpose than to bear witness to the faith of those whom I saw criminally libeled by wicked and false courtiers.

I desired no fame for myself from it; I planned to depart shortly, and no one knew that I was the writer [of the book]. For I had kept my authorship secret and intended to continue to do so. But Wilhaim Farel[1] forced me to stay in Geneva not so much by advice or urging as by command, which had the power of God's hand laid violently upon me from heaven. Since the wars had closed the direct road to Strasbourg, I had meant to pass through Geneva quickly and had determined not to be delayed there more than one night.

A short time before, by the work of the same good man [Farel], and of Peter Viret,[2] the papacy had been banished from the city; but things were still unsettled and the place was divided into evil and harmful factions. One man, who has since shamefully gone back to the papists, took immediate action to make me known. Then Farel, who was working with incredible zeal to promote the gospel, bent all his efforts to keep me in the city. And when he realized that I was determined to study in privacy in some obscure place, and saw that he gained nothing by entreaty, he descended to cursing, and said that God would surely curse my peace if I held back from giving help at a time of such great need. Terrified by his words, and conscious of my own timidity and cowardice, I gave up my journey and attempted to apply whatever gift I had in defense of my faith.

Scarcely four months had passed before we were attacked on the one side by the Anabaptists and on the other by a certain rascally apostate who, relying upon the secret aid of certain important people, was able to give us much trouble. Meanwhile, internal dissensions, coming one upon another, caused us dreadful torments.

[1] Guillaume Farel (1489–1565), was like Calvin, a Frenchman. He was one of the circle of Reformers who gathered around Bishop Briconnet at Meaux near Paris. When, after much struggle in which Farel was active, the Reformed faith was established in Geneva in 1535, he was the leader of the church and induced Calvin to work with him. He was ousted with Calvin in 1538, and returned with him in 1541; but he left in 1542, and in 1544 settled in Neuchâtel. He remained Calvin's close friend, and died a year after Calvin in 1565 in Metz.

[2] Pierre Viret (1511–1571), Swiss-born Reformer, helped Farel in Geneva and stayed in the city when Farel and Calvin were expelled (1538–1541). Thereafter he worked in Lausanne, his birthplace, and also lectured on the New Testament in Bern, until he was ousted in 1559 and returned to Geneva. After a checkered career in France and much controversy with French Catholics, he died at Orthez (south of Bordeaux) in 1571. He was an extensive and respected writer as well as an effective preacher. Unfortunately he has not been studied fully or properly.

I confess that I am by nature timid, mild, and cowardly, and yet I was forced from the very beginning to meet these violent storms. Although I did not yield to them, yet since I was not very brave, I was more pleased than was fitting when I was banished and forcibly expelled from the city.

Then loosed from my vocation and free [to follow my own desire], I decided to live quietly as a private individual. But that most distinguished minister of Christ, Martin Bucer,[3] dragged me back again to a new post with the same curse which Farel had used against me. Terrified by the example of Jonah which he had set before me, I continued the work of teaching. And although I always consistently avoided public notice, somehow I was dragged to the imperial assemblies.[4] There, whether I wished it or not, I had to speak before large audiences.

Afterwards the Lord had pity on the City of Geneva and quieted the deadly conflicts there. After he had by his wondrous power frustrated both the criminal conspiracies and the bloody attempts at force, I was compelled, against my own will, to take again my former position.[5] The safety of that church was far too important in my mind for me to refuse to meet even death for its sake. But my timidity kept suggesting to me excuses of every color for refusing to put my shoulder again under so heavy a burden. However, the demand of duty and faith at length conquered, and I went back to the flock from which I had been driven away. With how much grief, with how many tears, and in how great anxiety I went, God is my best witness. Many faithful men also understood my reluctance and would have wished to see me released from this pain if they had not been constrained by the same fear which influenced me.

It would make too long a story to tell of the conflicts of all sorts in which I was active and of the trials by which I was tested. I will merely repeat briefly what I said before, so as not to offend fastidious readers with unnecessary words. Since

[3] Martin Bucer (1491–1551) was the Protestant Reformer in Strasbourg, where Calvin stayed for three years (1538–1541) when he was forced out of Geneva. A man zealous for Christian unity, he had considerable influence upon Calvin, especially during this early period in the latter's activity. He commented extensively upon the Bible, and did his best-known work on the Gospels. His commentary on Romans was published in Strasbourg in 1536, shortly before Calvin began to work on his own. See Henri Strohl, *Bucer: humaniste chrétien*.

[4] At Worms in 1540 and at Regensburg in 1541, where the Catholics and the Protestants entered into futile discussions on reunion.

[5] See John T. McNeill, *The History and Character of Calvinism*, 1954, ch. 11.

David showed me the way with his own footsteps, I felt myself greatly comforted. The holy king was hurt more seriously by the envy and dishonesty of treacherous men at home than he was by the Philistines and other enemies who harassed him from the outside. I also have been attacked on all sides and have had scarcely a moment's relief from both external and internal conflicts. Satan has undertaken all too often in many ways to corrupt the fabric of this church. The result has been that I, who am a peaceable and timid man, was compelled to break the force of the deadly attacks by interposing my own body as a shield.

In all these five years certain men have had too great an influence, and a part of the common people who were corrupted by their alluring propaganda have been seeking unrestrained license. We therefore had both to oversee discipline and to fight without intermission. For the ruin of the church was a matter of no account to profane men and despisers of heavenly doctrine who desired and obtained power to gain every indulgence they dared. Some were driven mad by famine and hunger, and certain others by insatiable ambition or shameful greed for profit; and they all were ready to ruin themselves and us by mixing everything up rather than to [allow us to] maintain order. They were at it a long time, and I think made use of every tool forged in Satan's workshop. The only possible way to end their wicked plots was to destroy the men themselves by a shameful death—a spectacle which grieved me very much. For although they deserved any possible punishment, I would rather have had them live safe and unharmed. And they could have done so, if they had not been wholly impervious to wise counsel.

This five-year trial, hard and burdensome enough to me, was made still worse torture by the ill will of those who never ceased to attack me and my ministry with vile slanders. Many were so blinded by their desire to abuse me that their effrontery became shamefully outspoken. Others were saved by their own craft from conviction and ignominious exposure. But when anyone repeats an offense of which he has been accused a hundred times and acquitted, the indignity of it all is hard to bear.

Because I assert that the world is governed by the hidden providence of God, insolent men rise up and say that I make God the author of sin—a futile and baseless slander which would come to nothing of itself if it did not find eager listeners. Envy or spite or ingratitude or wickedness so rules men that they recoil from no lie, however absurd and monstrous. Others strive to overturn the eternal predestination by which God distinguishes the reprobate from the elect; others undertake the defense of free will. And not ignorance so much as a kind of perverse zeal brings many adherents to these factions.

When one suffers trials at the hands of professed enemies, one can bear them. But when people who hide under the name of brothers, those who not only eat the sacred bread but also serve it to others, and who boast loudly that they are heralds of the gospel—when these carry on such wicked warfare, how detestable it is! It is of this kind of thing that David most rightly complains, when he says, *The man of my peace and he who ate bread with me has lifted his heel against me* (Ps. 41:10); and also, *My companion and associate who used to go with me to the temple of God, with whom I took sweet counsel, he like an enemy has handed me over to the wicked* (Ps. 55:14).

Some men have spread frivolous rumors about my treasures; others about my enormous power. Others have talked about my sumptuous table. Does a man live in the lap of luxury when he is content with meager food and plain clothing; when he requires no more frugality from the poorest folk than he himself practices? As for my authority, I wish I could hand it over to them! They measure my power by the amount of my labor, by the weight of work that wears me down. How much money I have, my death will show—if there are any whom I cannot convince while I am alive. But I admit that I am not "poor," because I desire nothing beyond my actual needs.

These inventions, although they have no basis in fact, are believed among many people because the majority think that the only way to cover up their shame is to mix black with white. They think the best guarantee of impunity and license would be the end of the authority of the servants of Christ. In addition there are the *mockers at feasts* of whom David complains in Ps. 35:16: not only the plate lickers but those who hunt the favor of the powerful with false denunciations. I have become used to swallowing insults for so long that I am almost insensitive; yet as their insolence increased I could not help feeling some bitter pricks.

And as though it were not enough for me to suffer the inhumanity of neighbors, a throng of evil-driven men from the frozen sea [Germany] stirred up (*accenderet*) against me a storm I have no words to describe. I am still speaking of internal enemies of the church, proud proclaimers of the gospel of Christ, who because I do not accept their crass explanation of [the Lord's Supper as] devouring the flesh of Christ, are roused against me more violently than my open enemies. Here also I can associate myself with David, *While I seek peace, they rush to war* (Ps. 120:7). Moreover they all show great ingratitude when they attack on the flank and the rear a man who is laboring in defense of the common cause, and deserves their support. Certainly, if they possessed the slightest human sympathy, their great hatred of me would be placated by the fury the papists pour upon me and the way they attack me.

But this also was David's experience. He deserved well of his people, yet he was hated by many, as he laments in Ps. 69:4: *They hate me without a cause. . . . I returned what I did not rob.*[6] When I was assailed by the undeserved hatred of those whose duty it was to help me, I received no small comfort from knowing of the glorious example [set by David].

Now these experiences were a very great help to my understanding of the Psalms, since, as I read, I was going through well-known territory. And I hope my readers will realize that when I discuss David's thoughts more intimately than those of others, I am speaking not as a remote spectator but as one who knows all about these things from his own experience.

I have striven faithfully to make the value of this treasury [of the Psalms] available to all the faithful. And even though I have not accomplished what I had desired, I deserve some thanks for my attempt. All I ask is that each reader judge my labor justly and honestly by its fruits and the profit he finds in it. Certainly, as I said, when a man reads my book, he will see that I did not seek to give pleasure unless I also gave help.

I have kept throughout to a simple method of teaching; and to avoid all ostentation, I have refrained for the most part from the refutation of others, which readily provides much opportunity for plausible showing off. I have not mentioned opinions opposed to mine except where there was danger that my silence would leave my readers doubtful or perplexed. I realized, of course, that many would have been more attracted and tickled if I had included a varied mass of ostentatious and glittering material. But nothing meant more to me than to consider the upbuilding of the church.

May God who gave me this purpose also guarantee its success.

Geneva, August 10, 1557.

[6] Calvin's wording.

II. Preface to Olivétan's New Testament

Epistle to the Faithful Showing that Christ Is the End of the Law[7]

To all those who love Christ and his gospel, Greetings.

God the Creator, the most perfect and excellent Maker of all things, who had already shown himself more than admirable in their creation, made man as his masterpiece, to surpass all other creatures. Man is endowed with a singular excellence, for God formed him in his own image and likeness, in which we see a bright refulgence of God's glory. Furthermore, man would have been able to continue in the state in which he was formed, if he had been willing to bow down in humility before the majesty of God, magnifying him with deeds of grace; not to seek his glory in himself, but knowing that all good things come from above, always to turn his mind on high and to glorify the one and only God to whom belongs the praise.

But the wretched man, wanting to be somebody in himself, began incontinently to forget and misunderstand the source of his good; and by an act of outrageous ingratitude, he set out to exalt himself in pride against his Maker and the Author of all that is excellent in him. For this reason, he went down in ruin and lost all the dignity and superiority of the state in which he was first created; he was despoiled and divested of all his glory and deprived of all the gifts which were his; and this, to confound him in his pride and to constrain him to understand what he was unwilling to do voluntarily: that he was by himself nothing but vanity, and would never have been anything else except with the help of the Lord of power.

Therefore, seeing that God's image and likeness was thus defaced, and man was without the graces which God in his

---

7 This preface to Pierre Robert Olivétan's translation of the New Testament, which has had a lasting influence upon the French versions of the Bible, was written in 1534, about a year after Calvin's conversion. We have translated it and put it here in the beginning of this volume because it is his first statement of faith as a Protestant and an eloquent defense of it. Erasmus wrote a similar preface to his New Testament, and so did Lefèvre d'Étaples. For the latter, see Herminjard, *op. cit.*, vol. 1, pp. 132 ff. (No. 69). See also Nos. 1, 49, 79, 202 in the same work. We regret that space did not permit us to include at least his "Epistle of Exhortation" (No. 69) in this selection. For Erasmus' preface see *Opera Omnia*, 1704, vol. 5, pp. 137 f. This was translated into English in 1529, 1540. Again we regret leaving this preface out! The title at the head of Calvin's preface appeared at the beginning of Bibles and New Testaments printed in Geneva and elsewhere after 1543. The present text, from the *Opera*, C. R. 9, pp. 791 f., contains additions Calvin made after 1534.

goodness had bestowed upon him, God began to hold man in abhorrence and disavowed him as his handiwork. Since he had put man there and ordained [his life] for his own enjoyment and pleasure in him, as a father with his beloved child, He now held him in contempt and abomination. Whereas before everything in man pleased him, it now gave him displeasure; everything that he would have loved, now aroused his wrath; everything that he had contemplated with the good will of a father, he began to detest and to look at with regret. In short, the whole man with all that he had, his deeds, his thoughts, his words, his life, wholly displeased God, as though man were a special enemy and adversary of God; so much so that God repented of having made him. After having been thrown into such a confusion, man was fruitful in his cursed seed, to beget descendants like himself; that is, vicious, perverse, corrupt, void, and deprived of all good, rich and abundant in evil.

Still, the Lord of mercy, who not only loves but is himself love and kindness, being ready in his infinite goodness to love him who deserved no love, did not altogether destroy men, or overwhelm them in the abyss of their iniquity. But on the contrary, he sustained and supported them gently and patiently, giving them time and opportunity to return to him and to apply themselves again to that obedience from which they had turned aside. And even though he disguised himself and kept silent, as though he wished to hide himself from them, leaving them to go after their desires and the yearnings of their lusts, without law, without order, without any correction of his Word, he nevertheless has given them notice enough [of his presence] to move them to seek, feel, and find him, and to know him and honor him as is his due.

For he has raised everywhere, in all places and in all things, his ensigns and emblems, under blazons so clear and intelligible that no one can pretend ignorance in not knowing such a sovereign Lord, who has so amply exalted his magnificence; who has, in all parts of the world, in heaven and on earth, written and as it were engraved the glory of his power, goodness, wisdom, and eternity. Saint Paul has therefore said quite rightly that the Lord has never left himself without a witness; even among those to whom he has not sent any knowledge of his Word. It is evident that all creatures, from those in the firmament to those which are in the center of the earth, are able to act as witnesses and messengers of his glory to all men; to draw them to seek God, and after having found him, to meditate upon him and to render him the homage befitting his dignity as so good, so mighty, so wise a Lord who is eternal; yea, they are even capable of aiding every man wherever he is in this quest. For the little birds that sing, sing of God; the beasts clamor for him; the elements dread him, the mountains echo him, the fountains and flowing waters cast their glances at him, and the grass and flowers laugh before him. Truly there is no need for long searching, since everyone could find him in himself, because every one of us is sustained and preserved by his power which is in us.

Meanwhile, in order to reveal his infinite goodness and kindness more fully among men, he was not content to teach all men as we have just described; but he made his voice to be heard especially by a certain people, whom he elected, by his good will and free grace, from among all the nations of the earth. These were the children of Israel, to whom he showed himself clearly by his Word, and declared to them by his marvelous works what he intended them to know. For, he drew them away from subjection to Pharaoh the king of Egypt, under whom they were held down and oppressed, to deliver them and set them at liberty. He accompanied them night and day in their flight, as one more fugitive in their midst. He fed them in the desert. He made them to possess the Promised Land. He gave victories and triumphs to their hands. And as though he were nothing to the other nations, he willed expressly to be called the God of Israel, and to have Israel called his people, on condition that they would recognize no other Lord and receive none else as their God. And this alliance (covenant) was confirmed and handed down by authentic instruments of testament and testimony given by himself.

Nevertheless, these people, all of whom shared in the experience of their cursed race, showed themselves to be true heirs of the wickedness of their father Adam. They were unmoved by all these remonstrances [of God], and did not listen to the teaching by which God admonished them. The creatures that had the glory and magnificence of God stamped upon them were of no help to the Gentiles, and failed to make them glorify him to whom they testified. And the Law and the Prophets did not have the authority to lead the Jews in the right way. All have been blind to the light, deaf to admonitions, and hardened against the commandments.

It is true enough that the Gentiles, astonished and convinced by so many goods and benefits which they saw with their own eyes, have been forced to recognize the hidden Benefactor from whom came so much goodness. But instead of giving the true God the glory which they owed him, they forged a god to their own liking, one dreamt up by their foolish fantasy in its vanity and deceit; and not one god only, but as many as their temerity and conceit enabled them to forge and cast (*feindre et fondre*); so that there was not a people or place which did not make new gods as seemed good to them. Thus it is that idolatry, that perfidious panderer, was able to exercise dominion, to turn men away from God, and to amuse them with a whole crowd of phantoms to which they themselves had given shape, name, and being itself.

As for the Jews, even though they received and accepted the messages and commandments which their Lord sent them by his servants, they have nonetheless intemperately falsified the faith before him, turned carelessly away from him, violated and despised his law, hated it, and resisted walking in its ways. They have become strangers to the house of God and run as dissolute men after other gods, worshiping idols after the manner of the Gentiles, contrary to the will of God.

Wherefore, if God were to approach his people, whether Jew or Gentile, a new covenant was needed: one which would be certain, sure, and inviolable. And to establish and confirm it, it was necessary to have a Mediator, who would intercede and come between the two parties, to make concord between them; for without this, man would have had always to live under the ire and indignation of God, and would have had no means of relief from the curse, misery, and confusion into which he was snared and had fallen. And it was our Lord and Savior Jesus Christ, the true and only eternal Son of God, who had to be sent and given to mankind by the Father, to restore a world otherwise wasted, destroyed, and desolate.

Also from the very beginning, the world was not without the hope of recovering the loss suffered in Adam. For even Adam, in spite of his incontinency after his ruin, was given the promise that the seed of the woman would crush the head of the serpent; which is to say that Jesus Christ born of a virgin would strike down and destroy the power of Satan.

After that, this promise was renewed more fully to Abraham, when God told him that all the nations of the earth would be blessed in his seed. This meant that from his seed would come Jesus Christ according to the flesh, by whose blessing all men of every land would be sanctified. And the same promise was renewed to Isaac, in the same form and in the same words; and after that it was announced often, repeated and confirmed by the testimony of the various prophets, so as to state plainly, and most reliably, of whom Christ was to be born, at what time, in what place; what afflictions and death he was to suffer, and with what glory he was to rise from the dead; what was to be his Kingdom, and to what salvation he was to bring his own.

In the first place, it is foretold for us in Isaiah, how he was to be born of a virgin, saying: Behold, a virgin shall conceive and shall bear a son, and you shall call his name Immanuel (Isa. 7:14). The time is described for us in Moses, when good Jacob says, The scepter shall not be taken from the line of Judah, nor the government from his hand, until the coming of the One who is to be sent; and the same is the expectation of the nations (Gen. 49:10). And this was verified when Jesus Christ came into the world; for the Romans, after having divested the Jews of all government and rule, had, thirty-seven years before [the coming of Christ] ordained Herod king over them, whose father was Antipater the Edomite and his mother an Arabian; he was therefore a foreigner. It had happened sometimes before that the Jews had been without a king; but they had never before been left as they were now without counselors, rulers, and lawgivers. Another numbering [of the time of Christ's birth] is given in Daniel, by the reckoning of the seventy weeks (Dan. 9:24). The place of his birth was given us clearly by Micah, who said, And thou Bethlehem Ephrata, thou are the least among the thousands of Judah; but from thee shall come for me the One who shall reign over Israel; and his coming shall be for all the days of eternity (Micah 5:2). As for the afflictions he was to bear for our deliverance and the death he was to suffer for our redemption, Isaiah and Zechariah have spoken of those matters fully and with certainty. The glory of his resurrection and the nature of his Kingdom, and the grace of the salvation he was to bring to his people—these things were fully treated by Isaiah, Jeremiah, and Zechariah.

Such promises, declared and testified to by these holy men who were filled with the Spirit of God, have been the comfort and consolation of the children and elect of God, who have nourished, supported, and sustained their hope in these promises, waiting upon the will of the Lord to show forth what he had promised. Many kings and prophets among them have desired greatly to see its accomplishment, never ceasing all the while to understand, in their hearts and spirits by faith, the things they could not see with their eyes. And, God has confirmed his people in every possible way during their long waiting for the great Messiah, by providing them with his written law, containing numerous ceremonies, purifications, and sacrifices, which were but the figures and shadows of the great blessings to come with Christ, who alone was the embodiment and truth of them. For the law was incapable of bringing anyone to perfection; it only presented Christ, and like a teacher spoke of and led to him, who was, as was said by Saint Paul, the end and fulfillment of the law.

Similarly, many times and in various seasons, God sent his people kings, princes, and captains, to deliver them from the power of their enemies, to govern them in peace, to recover their losses, to give them flourishing reigns, and by great prowess to make them renowned among all the other peoples. He did all this to give them a foretaste of the great miracles they were to receive from this great Messiah, who was to be endowed with all the power and might of the Kingdom of God.

But when the fullness of time had come and the period foreordained by God was ended, this great Messiah, so promised and so awaited, came; he was perfect, and accomplished all that was necessary to redeem us and save us. He was given not only to the Israelites, but to all men, of every people and every land, to the end that by him human nature might be reconciled to God. This is what is stated plainly in the next book (the New Testament), and set forth there openly. This book we have translated as faithfully as we were able according to the truth and the style of the Greek language, to enable all Christians, men and women, who know the French language, to understand and acknowledge the law they ought to obey and the faith they ought to follow.[8]

It is to declare this thing (reconciliation), that the Lord Jesus, who is its foundation and substance, has ordained his apostles, whom he has charged and commanded to publish his grace to the whole world. And the apostles, in order to discharge their duty properly and plainly, not only have taken pains and shown diligence in fulfilling their embassy by the preaching of the word by mouth, but they have also followed the example of Moses and the prophets, and have left an eternal remembrance of their doctrine by reducing it to writing; in which they have first told the story

---

[8] Instead of this passage, the treatise of 1543 and all the editions of the Bible that reproduce it contain the paragraph which follows in the text.

of the things the Lord Jesus did and suffered for our salvation,
and then shown us its value, what profit we gain from it, and how
we are to receive it. This whole collection is called the New
Testament, and is called such in relation to the Old, etc.

And this book is called the New Testament in relation to the
Old, which, in so far as it had to be succeeded by and related to
the New, and was shaky and imperfect in itself, was abolished
and abrogated. It is the new and the eternal, which will never
grow old and fail, because Jesus Christ is its Mediator. He has
ratified and confirmed it by his death, by which he has accomplished full and complete remission of all sins (prevarications)
which remained under the first testament.

Scripture is also called gospel, that is, new and joyful news,
because in it is declared that Christ, the sole true and eternal
Son of the living God, was made man, to make us children of
God his Father, by adoption. Thus he is our only Savior, to
whom we owe our redemption, peace, righteousness, sanctification, salvation, and life; who died for our sins and rose again
for our justification; who ascended to heaven for our entry
there and took possession of it for us and [it is] our home; to be
always our helper before his Father; as our advocate and perpetually doing sacrifice for us, he sits at the Father's right hand
as King, made Lord and Master over all, so that he may restore
all that is in heaven and on earth; an act which all the angels,
patriarchs, prophets, apostles did not know how to do and
were unable to do, because they had not been ordained to that
end by God.

As the Messiah had been promised so often in the Old Testament by the many testimonies of the prophets, so also Jesus
Christ was by sure and certain testimonies declared to be the
One, and none other, who was to come and was to be waited
for. For the Lord God has made us so completely certain in
this matter, by his Word and his Spirit, by his angels, prophets,
apostles, and even by all his creatures, that nobody is in a
position to contradict it without resisting and rebelling against
God's power. In the first place, the eternal God has testified to
us by his voice itself (which is without doubt irrevocable truth),
saying, Behold my well beloved Son, in whom I am well
pleased; hear him (Matt. 9:7). And as Saint John says, the
Holy Spirit himself is our great witness in our hearts (I John
5:1). The angel Gabriel, sent to the Virgin Mary, said to her:
Behold, you shall conceive in your womb, and shall bear a Son,
and shall call his name Jesus; for he shall be great and shall be

called the Son of the Most High. And the Lord God shall give him the throne (*le siege*) of his father David, and he shall reign forever in the house of Jacob; and there shall be no end to his Kingdom (Luke 1:32–33). This same message was given in substance to Joseph; and later also to the shepherds, who were told that the Savior was born, who was Christ the Lord (Matt. 1:20–21; Luke 2:10–11). And this message was not only brought by an angel, but was confirmed by a multitude of angels, who all together glorified the Lord and announced peace upon earth. Simeon the Just confessed it nobly in the spirit of prophecy: and taking the little child in his arms, he said: Now, O Lord, let thy servant depart in peace according to thy word. For my eyes have seen thy salvation, which thou hast prepared in the presence of all peoples (Luke 2:29–31). John the Baptist also spoke of him as was fitting, when he saw him coming to the river of Jordan, and said, Behold the lamb of God; behold him who takes away the sins of the world (John 1:29). Peter and all the apostles have confessed, testified, preached all the things which belong to salvation, of which the prophets had foretold that they would be accomplished in Christ the true Son of God. And those whom the Lord has ordained to be witnesses down to our own age have amply demonstrated the same by their writings, as their readers can see well enough.

All these witnesses come together into a unity so well, and they are of one accord among themselves so fully, that it is easy to recognize in such agreement most certain truth. For there could not be such harmony in lies. Besides, it is not only the Father, the Son, the Holy Spirit, the angels, the prophets and apostles that bear witness to Jesus Christ; his own wonderful works show forth his most excellent power. The sick, the lame, the blind, the deaf, the mute, the paralytic, lepers, lunatics, demoniacs, and even the dead raised by him have carried the emblems of his power. By his power, he has given life; in his name, the works he has had given him to do were sufficient witnesses to him (John 10:25). Besides, even the wicked and the enemies of his glory were constrained by the very force of truth to confess him and to acknowledge something [of his glory]: for instance, Caiaphas, Pilate, and his wife. I do not care to bring up the witness of the devils and unclean spirits, seeing that Jesus Christ rejected them.

In short, all the elements and all the creatures have given Jesus Christ the glory. At his command, the winds ceased, the raging sea subsided, the fish brought two drachmas in his belly, the stones (to render him witness) were broken to pieces, the veil of the Temple was torn in the middle, the sun was darkened, the graves were opened, the many bodies were restored to life. There has been nothing in heaven or on earth which has not witnessed that Jesus Christ is God, Lord and Master, and the great Ambassador of the Father sent here below to accomplish the salvation of mankind. All these things were announced, manifested, written, and signed in this Testament, by which Jesus Christ has made us his heirs in the Kingdom of God his Father, and declares to us his will (like a testator to his heirs) that it [his Testament] be put into execution.

Furthermore, we are called to this inheritance without respect for persons; male or female, little or great, servant or lord, master or disciple, cleric or lay, Hebrew or Greek, French or Latin—no one is rejected, who with a sure confidence receives him who was sent for him, embraces what is presented to him, and in short acknowledges Jesus Christ for what he is and as he is given by the Father.

In the meantime, all we who bear the name of Christians, male or female, shall we permit ourselves to dishonor, to conceal, and to corrupt this Testament, which is so rightly ours, without which we could not pretend any right to the Kingdom of God, without which we should be ignorant of the great blessings and promises which Jesus Christ has given us, of the glory and beatitude he has prepared for us? We do not know what God has commanded or forbidden us; we cannot tell good from evil, light from darkness, the commandments of God from the ordinances (constitutions) of men. Without the gospel everything is useless and vain; without the gospel we are not Christians; without the gospel all riches is poverty, all wisdom, folly before God; strength is weakness, and all the justice of man is under the condemnation of God. But by the knowledge of the gospel we are made children of God, brothers of Jesus Christ, fellow townsmen with the saints, citizens of the Kingdom of Heaven, heirs of God with Jesus Christ, by whom the poor are made rich, the weak strong, the fools wise, the sinners justified, the desolate comforted, the doubting sure, and slaves free. The gospel is the Word of life and truth. It is the power of God for the salvation of all those who believe; and the key to the knowledge of God, which opens the door of the Kingdom of Heaven to the faithful by releasing them from sins, and closes it to the unbelievers, binding them in their sins. Blessed are all

they who hear the gospel and keep it; for in this way they show
that they are children of God. Woe to those who will not hear it
and follow it; because they are children of the devil.

O Christians, men and women, hear this and learn. For surely
the ignorant man shall perish in his ignorance, and the blind
who follows another blind man will fall into the ditch with him.
There is but one way to life and salvation, and that is faith and
certainty in the promises of God which cannot be had without
the gospel; for by hearing it and knowing it living faith is provided, together with sure hope, and perfect love for God and a
lively love toward our neighbor. Where then is your hope, if
you contemn and scorn to hear, see, read, and retain this holy
gospel? Those who have their affections fixed upon this world
chase with every means whatever they think will bring them
happiness, without sparing labor, body, life, or reputation. And
all this is done in the service of this wretched body, which has a
life so vain, miserable, and uncertain. When it is a question of
life immortal and incorruptible, of beatitude eternal and
immeasurable, of all the treasures of Paradise, shall we not
endeavor to pursue them? Those who give themselves to the
mechanical arts, however low and mean these may be, expend
pain and labor to learn and know them; and those who aspire
to a reputation of greatest excellence torment their minds day
and night, to understand something of the human sciences,
which are nothing but wind and smoke. Should we not then
much more be employed and diligent in the study of this divine
wisdom, which passes beyond the whole world and penetrates
as far as the mysteries of God, which it has pleased him to make
known by his holy Word!

What then shall estrange and alienate us from this holy
gospel? Shall injuries, curses, disgrace, and want of worldly
honor? But, we know well that Jesus Christ has traveled the
same road which we have to follow, if we would be his disciples;
that we must not refuse to be despised, mocked, humiliated, and
rejected before men. For it is thus that we shall be honored,
prized, glorified, and exalted in God's judgment. Will there be
banishments, proscriptions, privation from goods and riches?
But we know that if we shall be banished from one country, the
whole earth is the Lord's, and if we be thrown out of the earth
itself, nonetheless we shall not be outside of his Kingdom. [We
know] that when we are despoiled and impoverished, we have a
Father who is rich enough to nourish us; even that Jesus Christ
was made poor, so that we might follow him in his poverty.

Will there be afflictions, prisons, tortures, torments? But we know by the example of Jesus Christ that this is the way to arrive at glory. Finally, will there be death? But death does not do away with a life that is worth having.

In short, if we have Jesus Christ with us, we shall come upon nothing so accursed that he will not turn it into a blessing; nothing so execrable that it shall not be made holy; nothing so evil that it shall not turn into our good. Let us not lose our comfort when we see all earthly powers and forces against us; for the promise cannot fail, that the Lord on high will hold in mockery all the assemblings and efforts of men who would conspire against him. Let us not be desolate, as though all hope were lost, when we see true servants of God die and perish before our eyes. For it was said truly by Tertullian, and so it has been approved and shall be until the consummation of the age, that the blood of the martyrs is the seed of the church.

And we have a still greater and a more sure consolation, when we turn our eyes away from this whole world and set aside all that we can see before us, to wait with patience for the great judgment of God, by which in one moment all the machinations of men against him shall be struck down, brought to nought, and overturned. This shall be when the Kingdom of God, which we now see in hope, shall become manifest; when Jesus Christ shall appear in majesty with his angels. It shall then be that the good and the evil shall be present before the judgment seat of this great King. Those who have remained firm in this testament, who have followed and kept the will of this good Father, shall be at his right hand as his true children, and shall be blessed with the fulfillment of their faith, which shall be eternal salvation. And since they were not ashamed to own and confess Jesus Christ, when he was despised and condemned before men, they shall also share in his glory, and shall be crowned with him in eternity. But the perverse, rebellious, and condemned, who have despised and rejected this holy gospel, and similarly those who for the sake of holding on to their honor, riches, and high estate have been unwilling to be humbled and made low with Jesus Christ; who for fear of men have cast aside the fear of God and like bastard [sons] disobeyed this Father—these shall be on the left hand; they shall be executed and cast out; for the reward of their unfaithfulness, they shall receive eternal death.

Therefore, when you hear that the gospel presents you Jesus Christ in whom all the promises and gifts of God have been accomplished; and when it declares that he was sent by the Father, has descended to the earth and spoken among men perfectly all that concerns our salvation, as it was foretold in the Law and to the Prophets—it ought to be most certain and obvious to you that the treasures of Paradise have been opened to you in the gospel; that the riches of God have been exhibited and eternal life itself revealed. For, this is eternal life; to know one, only true God, and Jesus Christ whom he has sent, whom he has established as the beginning, the middle, and the end of our salvation. He [Christ] is Isaac, the beloved Son of the Father who was offered as a sacrifice, but nevertheless did not succumb to the power of death. He is Jacob the watchful shepherd, who has such great care for the sheep which he guards. He is the good and compassionate brother Joseph, who in his glory was not ashamed to acknowledge his brothers, however lowly and abject their condition. He is the great sacrificer and bishop Melchizedek, who has offered an eternal sacrifice once for all. He is the sovereign lawgiver Moses, writing his law on the tables of our hearts by his Spirit. He is the faithful captain and guide Joshua, to lead us to the Promised Land. He is the victorious and noble king David, bringing by his hand all rebellious power to subjection. He is the magnificent and triumphant king Solomon, governing his kingdom in peace and prosperity. He is the strong and powerful Samson, who by his death has overwhelmed all his enemies.

It follows that every good thing we could think or desire is to be found in this same Jesus Christ alone. For, he was sold, to buy us back; captive, to deliver us; condemned, to absolve us; he was made a curse for our blessing, sin offering for our righteousness; marred that we may be made fair; he died for our life; so that by him fury is made gentle, wrath appeased, darkness turned into light, fear reassured, despisal despised, debt canceled, labor lightened, sadness made merry, misfortune made fortunate, difficulty easy, disorder ordered, division united, ignominy ennobled, rebellion subjected, intimidation intimidated, ambush uncovered, assaults assailed, force forced back, combat combated, war warred against, vengeance avenged, torment tormented, damnation damned, the abyss sunk into the abyss, hell transfixed, death dead, mortality made immortal. In short, mercy has swallowed up all misery, and goodness all misfortune. For all these things which were to be the weapons of the devil in his battle against us, and the sting of death to pierce us, are turned for us into exercises which we can turn to our profit. If we are able to boast with the apostle, saying, O hell, where is thy victory? O death, where is thy sting? it is because by the Spirit of Christ promised to the elect, we live no longer, but Christ lives in us; and we are by the same Spirit seated among those who are in heaven, so that for us the world is no more, even while our conversation is in it; but we are content in all things, whether country, place, condition, clothing, meat, and all such things. And we are comforted in tribulation, joyful in sorrow, glorying under vituperation, abounding in poverty, warmed in our nakedness, patient amongst evils, living in death.

This[9] is what we should in short seek in the whole of Scripture: truly to know Jesus Christ, and the infinite riches that are comprised in him and are offered to us by him from God the Father. If one were to sift thoroughly the Law and the Prophets, he would not find a single word which would not draw and bring us to him. And for a fact, since all the treasures of wisdom and understanding are hidden in him, there is not the least question of having, or turning toward, another goal; not unless we would deliberately turn aside from the light of truth, to lose ourselves in the darkness of lies. Therefore, rightly does Saint Paul say in another passage that he would know nothing except Jesus Christ, and him crucified. And such knowledge although mean and contemptible to the mind of the flesh is nevertheless sufficient to occupy us all our lives. And we shall not waste our time if we employ all our study and apply all our understanding to profit from it. What more would we ask for, as spiritual doctrine for our souls, than to know God, to be converted (*transformez*) to him, and to have his glorious image imprinted in us, so that we may partake of his righteousness, to become heirs of his Kingdom and to possess it in the end in full? But the truth is that from the beginning God has given himself, and at present gives himself more fully, that we may contemplate him in the face of his Christ. It is therefore not lawful that we turn away and become diverted even in the smallest degree by this or that. On the contrary, our minds ought to come to a halt at the point where we learn in Scripture to know Jesus Christ and him alone, so that we may be directly led by him to the Father who contains in himself all perfection.

Here, I say once again, is enclosed all the wisdom which men can understand, and ought to learn in this life; which no angel,

9 This paragraph is not in the 1535 preface. It appears for the first time in the treatise of 1543 (C. R. 9, 815).

or man, dead or living, may add to or take away from. This is where we ought to stop and put a limit to our understanding, mixing nothing of our own with it and refusing any doctrine whatever which might be added to it. For anyone who undertakes to teach one other syllable beyond what is taught us in it, ought to be accursed before God and his church.

And you kings, princes, and Christian lords, who are ordained of God to punish the wicked and to uphold the good in peace according to the Word of God—to you it belongs to have this sacred doctrine, so useful and needful, published, taught, and understood in all your lands, realms, and lordly domains, to the end that God may be magnified by you, and his gospel exalted; because by right it is his due that all kings and kingdoms obey him in all humility and serve his glory. Remember that sovereign Empire, above all kingdoms, principalities, and lordships, was given by the Father to the Lord Jesus; and he is to be feared, held in awe, and honored by everyone, great or little. Remember[10] what was foretold by the prophets: that all the kings of the earth would render him homage as their superior, and would adore him as their Savior and their God; let this come true in you. And remember that it is no dishonor for you to be subject to such a great Lord, as though in this way your own majesty and high place would be reduced and become as nothing; for it is the greatest honor you may lawfully desire, to be known and regarded as the officials and lieutenants of God. It is unthinkable that Jesus Christ, in whom God wills to be glorified and exalted, should not have dominion over you; and in fact it is reasonable enough that you should be the ones to give him this pre-eminence, provided your own power is founded in him alone. Otherwise what an ingratitude it would be that you should want to shut out him who has established you in the power you possess, and maintains and keeps you in it! What is more, you ought to know that there is no better foundation, nor one firmer, for keeping your domains in true prosperity, than to have him as Chief and Master, and to govern your peoples under his hand; and that without him they [your domains] can be neither permanent nor endure for long, but shall be accursed of God and shall consequently fall down in confusion and ruin. Since God has thus given you the sword in hand for governing your subjects in his name and by his authority; since he has done you the honor of giving you his name and

---

[10] See previous note for this passage and the next paragraph.

title; since he has sanctified your position above those of others, to make a portion of his glory and majesty reflected in it—let each one of you engage himself by his own hand to magnify and exalt him who is God's true and glorious image, in whom he fully represents himself to us. Moreover, to do this, it is not enough merely to confess Jesus Christ, and to profess to be his own, so that you have the title without the truth and reality of the matter; you must give place to his holy gospel and receive it with obedience and humility. This is an office every man must fulfill; but it belongs to you especially to see to it that the gospel is heard, to have it published in your lands, in order that it may be known by the people who have been committed to your charge; in order that they may know you as servants and ministers of this great King, and may serve and honor him, by obeying you under his hand and under his guidance.

This is what the Lord requires of you through his prophet, when he calls you the guardians of his church. For this tutelage and protection is not a matter of enlarging the riches, privileges, and honors of the clergy, which makes them high and haughty, living in pomp and in all dissoluteness, contrary to their proper estate; much less is it a matter of maintaining the clergy in their pride and inordinate displays; it is rather a matter of seeing to it that the entire teaching of the gospel is kept in its purity and truth; that the Holy Scriptures are faithfully preached, read, and perused; that God is honored according to the rule given us in them, and the church is well governed; that all which is contrary to the honor of God, or to the good government of the church, be corrected and repressed; so that the Kingdom of Jesus Christ may flourish by the power of his Word.

O you who call yourselves bishops and pastors of the poor people, see to it that the sheep of Jesus Christ are not deprived of their proper pasture; and that it is not prohibited and forbidden to any Christian freely and in his own language to read, handle, and hear this holy gospel, seeing that such is the will of God, and Jesus Christ commands it; for it is for this cause that he has sent his apostles and servants throughout the whole world; giving them the power to speak in all tongues, so that they may in every language preach to every creature; and he has made them debtors to the Greeks and the barbarians, to the wise and the simple, in order that none might be excluded from their teaching. Surely, if you are truly their vicars, successors, and imitators, it is your office to do the same, watching over the flock and seeking every possible means to have everyone instructed in the faith of Jesus Christ, by the pure Word of God. Otherwise, the sentence is already proclaimed and put down in writing, that God will demand their souls at your hands.

It is the will of the Lord of lights by his Holy Spirit, by means of this holy and saving gospel, to teach the ignorant, to strengthen the feeble, to illumine the blind, and to make his truth to reign among all peoples and nations, to the end that the whole world may know but one God and one Savior, Jesus Christ; one faith, and one gospel. So be it.

III. Epistle to Simon Grynaeus on the Commentary on Romans

John Calvin, to Simon Grynaeus,[11] a most illustrious man.

I remember that three years ago we had a friendly talk about the best way of expounding Scripture. The method which you liked best, I myself approved most of all others. We both felt that the chief virtue of an interpreter consists in clarity combined with brevity. And indeed, since about the only business he has is to lay open the mind of the writer he has set out to explain, the more he leads the reader away from it, the more he deviates from his own purpose and is sure to wander out of the bounds. We expressed the desire that, from among all those who are today engaged in aiding [the cause of] theology with this kind of work, someone would come forward who would strive for simplicity and would write so as not to discourage his readers too much with long-winded expositions. At the same time, however, I know that not everybody agrees with us in this matter; and that those who do not accept [our views], have good arguments on their side. Still, I cannot budge from my love of brevity. Of course, since it happens that there is a variety of disposition among men, and different people find pleasure in different things, let everyone, in this case also, enjoy his own judgment, provided that he does not try to make it a law for everybody else. Let us not, on our part, repudiate or condemn the labor of those who are more wordy and expansive in their expositions of the Sacred Books. But let them in return do

---

[11] Simon Grynaeus (1493–1541), Swabian scholar, professor of Latin and Greek in Heidelberg, left for Basel in 1529 to succeed Erasmus. He lectured on Greek and later on the New Testament. He took part in the preparation of the First Helvetic Confession and attended the Conference of Worms in 1540. As the above dedication and other letters make clear, Calvin had a great admiration for this linguist, exegete, and theologian.

the same to us, even though they may think our [exposition] is too compressed and concise.

I simply could not resist trying my hand at something along this line, which might be of benefit to the church of God. I am not sure that I have succeeded in doing what we thought was desirable; nor did I hope as much when I began. But I did make the effort to discipline my style, so that one could see I was aiming at the ideal we set down. How far I have succeeded, it is not for me to decide; I leave it to you and others like you to judge.

I can indeed see that many people will be offended by my undertaking and condemn me because of all things I have dared to try [my ability] on this epistle of Paul. Since men of excellent learning have already labored at expounding it, it is unbelievable that any room is left for others to produce something better. And I must say that even though I hoped my labor would produce some good results, I was at the beginning deterred by this very consideration. I was afraid that, if I set my hand to this task after so many excellent workmen, I would incur the reputation of temerity.

There are commentaries on this epistle by many ancient and many modern writers. Indeed they could not have labored at a better task; because when anyone understands this epistle, the way is open before him to an understanding of the whole of Scripture. I do not need to say anything about the ancient [interpreters] whose piety, erudition, saintliness, and age invest them with such authority that we should not condemn anything we have received from them. As to those who are living, nothing will be gained by mentioning all of them by name. I will speak my mind about those who have labored zealously and done outstanding work [in the field]. Philip Melanchthon,[12] by his singular learning and industry, and the power of his competence in every kind of intellectual discipline has shed much light on this epistle; more than all who came before him. But he evidently set himself to examine closely only those matters which were worthy of his own attention; he stopped with these, and deliberately passed by a great deal which cannot but trouble the ordinary mind. Then comes Bullinger,[13] who also received

12 1497–1560. German Reformer and friend of Martin Luther. His annotations on Romans were published in 1529 and his commentary in 1532.
13 Heinrich Bullinger (1504–1575), a Swiss Reformer, was the successor of Zwingli in Zurich. His commentary on Romans and the other epistles of the New Testament was published in 1537.

much praise; and that rightly, because he has combined simplicity with learning, and for this he has been highly approved.
Finally there is Bucer[14] who, by his tireless labors, has just about
said the last word. He is a man (one of us) of exceptionally
profound learning, with an immense knowledge of many subjects, endowed with an extraordinarily lucid mind; a great
reader, possessor of other qualities, many and various, in which
nobody today can surpass him, few can equal him, and he
excels most people; and beyond all this, he deserves special
praise because I can think of nobody who has turned to the
exposition of Scripture with equal diligence and [desire for]
precision. I submit, therefore, it never entered my head to com-
pete with such men, as this would have been a most impudent
rivalry; nor did I want to grab for myself the smallest part of
the praise which belongs to them. Let them have the blessing,
and favor, and authority, which all good men acknowledge they
deserve. But I hope this much will be conceded to me: nothing is
so perfect among men that those who come after them will find
no room for refining and clarifying it, and adding to its beauty.
As for myself, I do not dare to say anything except that I
thought my work might perhaps be of some use; and that I
undertook it for no other purpose than to promote the common
good of the church.

To this end, I hoped that when I wrote in my own way, no
[charge of] odious rivalry would be pressed against me, as I was
at first afraid it would be. Philip succeeded in what he set out
to do: to clarify to the utmost what is essential. He had no intention of preventing others from doing what must not be neglected;
and he did omit much because he was occupied with the things
that come first. Bucer is too prolix to keep the interest of busy
people; his [thoughts] are so high that the lowly and those
whose attention is not the best are in no position to understand him. Whenever he deals with any subject, his unbelievably
forceful and fecund mind brings up so many things that he does
not know how to take his hand off the paper (*tabula*). Therefore,
because Melanchthon has not dealt with everything, and Bucer
has written too much to be read through in a short time, my
intention does not in the least look like rivalry with them.

And yet, I wondered for some time whether I would do
better to make some gleanings from these other men, so as to be
able to put together something to help those of mediocre mentality; or whether I should compose a complete commentary,

[14] See note 3, p. 54.

in which I would have had to repeat much that has been said before by all or at least by some of them. But these men often differ among themselves, which gives much trouble to readers who are not very acute, causing them to hesitate with whom they should agree. Therefore, I thought I would not regret my labor if I could point out the best interpretation, and thus relieve those whose judgment is not sufficiently strong from the trouble of judging; especially since I was determined to compress and be succinct, so that my readers would waste no time, and would learn, by reading my work, what is in [the books of] the others. In short, I vowed not to give just cause for the complaint that much [of my work] has been superfluous.

As to its usefulness, I shall say nothing. However, men of good will who read it have acknowledged having benefited from it more than I dare modestly promise in so many words.

It is only right that I should be excused when I at times disagree with others and differ from them. [I know that] we must have such reverence for the Word of God that we do not, so far as it is possible, set it against itself with our contradictory interpretations. I dare not think how much damage is done to its majesty, especially when we do not treat it with great discernment and sobriety. And, if to contaminate anything dedicated to God involves a great crime, anyone who handles the most sacred thing in the world with unclean or incompetent hands ought not to be endured.

Therefore, it is sacrilegious audacity rashly to turn Scripture this way and that (as we please), and to fool with it as though it were a game; many people have been doing this very thing long enough.

But we ought always to remind ourselves that even those who have not been wanting in zeal for piety, and have handled the mysteries of God with conscience and sobriety, have not always agreed among themselves. God has in no instance honored his servants with such blessing as to endow them with full and perfect knowledge of every subject; and doubtless his reason for this has been to keep them humble and desirous to keep in communication with their brothers. It is of course highly desirable that we should constantly agree in our understanding of Scripture passages. But there is no hope for such a thing in this life. Therefore, we must do our best neither to be pushed by a desire for novelty, nor to deprecate others through envy; neither to be aroused by hatred, nor to be goaded by ambition; rather, we should do only what is necessary, our aim being nothing else than to make progress, disagreeing only for reasons which are honorable. When we follow this rule in our interpretation of Scripture, there will be less license with regard to the essentials of our religion, in which principally God would have his own of one mind. The readers will easily see that I have tried to do both [to make progress and to maintain unity].

But because it is not proper that I state or establish the value of my own work, I am happy to leave criticism to you. Since everybody defers to your judgment in many things, I also, who have been intimate with you and know very well the kind of man you are, owe you deference in everything. Familiarity has a way of diminishing respect, but as men of learning know very well, in your case, it greatly increases esteem. Farewell.

Strasbourg, November 18, 1539.

I

The Bible

THE TEXT

1. The Word of God

I spake not unto your fathers . . . concerning burnt offerings or sacrifices. But this thing I commanded them, saying, Obey my voice. Jer. 7:22–23.

We know that from the beginning God desired spiritual worship, and that he has not changed his nature. Today he approves nothing but spiritual worship, for he is Spirit. But equally under the law, he wished to be worshiped with a sincere heart. . . . That is why the prophets speak harshly of sacrifice. This clear statement removes all ambiguity: God sets obedience against sacrifice (even though sacrifice was a part of obedience).

Now we can continue with the content of the teaching, holding firmly to the principle that true religion is founded upon obedience. Unless God sheds light for us from his Word, there is among us not true religion, but mere sham and superstition. This is how we can distinguish true religion from superstition: when the Word of God directs us, there is true religion; but when each man follows his own opinion, or when men join together to follow an opinion they hold in common, the result is always concocted superstition.

After we grasp the principle that God cannot be worshiped unless we listen to his voice, we must consider, as I said, what God's voice prescribes to us. Since he is Spirit, he demands the sincere love of the heart. And we know also how he has revealed to us that he desires us to put our confidence in his free kindness; that he wishes us to depend wholly on his Fatherly compassion; that he wishes us to call upon him for help, and to offer to him the sacrifice of praise.

But his delight is in the law of the Lord; and in his law doth he meditate day and night. Ps. 1:2.

This verse does not simply declare (as I have said elsewhere) that those who fear God are blessed; it equates religion with the study of the law. It teaches that God is rightly worshiped only if his Word is obeyed. Therefore, men are not free to model a religion, each after his own idea. The standard for religion must be taken from God's Word.

The law only is mentioned here: but we are not to suppose that the rest of Scripture is ignored, since all of it is really an interpretation of the law and so is included under that title. The prophet is commending the law with its supplement. Indeed, as I just said, the faithful are here urged to read The Psalms.

But the first thing required of the faithful is *delight in the law of the Lord*. These words show us that compulsory or slavish worship is not at all acceptable to God. Only those who come happily to the study of the law, who enjoy its teaching, who think nothing more worth-while or pleasanter than to make progress in it, are qualified students of the law.

From this love of the law comes constant meditation on it, as the prophet immediately adds. Only those inspired by this love can devote themselves to its constant study.

He will teach us of his ways, and we will walk in his paths. Micah 4:2.

Here in a few words the prophet defines true worship of God. For it would not be enough for the nations to come together to one place to confess that they are worshipers of one God if they did not also show real obedience. True obedience depends on faith, as faith depends on the Word. It is, therefore, especially worthy of note that the prophet here sets God's Word in the center to show us that religion is founded on obedience in faith, and that God can be worshiped only when he himself teaches his people and tells them what they ought to do. When God's will is revealed to us, we can truly adore him. When the Word is taken away, some form of worship of God remains, but there is no real religion which could please God.

Hence we conclude that the church of God can be established only where the Word of God rules, where God shows by his voice the way of salvation. Therefore, until true doctrine sheds its light, men cannot be gathered in one place to constitute the true body of the church. Clearly, then, where the teaching is corrupt or is despised, there is no religion approved by God.

Men can, indeed, take God's name boastfully on their lips;

but before God, there is no religion except what is measured by the rule of the Word. It follows then that there is no church which is not subject to God's Word and is not ruled by it. The prophet here defines both true religion and the way in which God gathers his church.

He will teach us of his ways. Here we have a third point. God is robbed of his right and honor when men usurp the power of teaching. For it belongs to God alone to teach his people. There were at that time priests and prophets. But Micah here reduces both to their proper place and shows that the right and the office of teaching belong to God alone. It is clear that God claims this work for himself, to prevent us from wavering and from being pulled around by different teachers; to keep us in simple obedience to his Word, so that he alone may rule over us. In a word, God is not God and head of the church, if he is not the chief and only teacher.

Now when the prophet says that God will *teach* us *his ways,* this must mean that he will show the nature of his ways; he means, "The perfect wisdom of the people is to know what pleases God and what his will is." This is all I need to say.

There follows: *Let us walk in his ways.* By this clause we are warned that God's teaching is not theoretical, as they say, but full of energizing power. When God speaks, he does not only intend men to know that what is announced by him is true; he also requires their obedience. We shall be truly taught by God only if we *walk in his ways.*

For it is silly for us to wag our ears like asses, and confess God with mouth and lips only. Men truly progress in God's school when they form their lives by his teaching, when they have their feet ready to walk, to follow wherever he calls.

If ye will not hearken to me to walk in my law, which I have set before you, to hearken to the words of my servants the prophets whom I sent unto you. Jer. 26:4–5.

The prophet here sums up briefly the teaching which he was commanded to bring to the people. There is no doubt that he used many words whenever it was necessary; but here he holds a few words to be enough to state what he has been told. He declares that unless the Jews begin to listen and to follow the law, and unless they obey the prophets, the final destruction of the Temple and the city is at hand. This is the sum of what he teaches here. But we should note the details.

By the words *unless you hear and walk in my law,* God shows that his chief demand is for obedience. . . . We see that the one and only specific rule for living devoutly, rightly, holily, and perfectly is to surrender ourselves to God's piloting. This is his only command.

But what follows should also be noted: *that you walk in my law.* For here God testifies that his will is not ambiguous, for in his law he has stated what is right. If God should descend from heaven a hundred times, he would reveal nothing we need to know in addition to what he has said. His law is perfect wisdom. If he had said only *hear me,* men could evade by declaring themselves ready to be taught by him. God checks these hypocrites by saying that there will be no word from him other than that they should follow his law. And for the same purpose he adds *which I have set before your eyes.* This phrase means that there is nothing obscure or uncertain about the teaching of the law. As Moses said (Deut. 30:19), *I call to witness today heaven and earth that I have set before your eyes life and death;* and in another place (Deut. 30:14), *The word is in your heart and your mouth*—that is, God takes every excuse away from you. There is no reason for uncertainty after he has spoken plainly to you and explained fully what is necessary.

Here is the refutation of that impious popish blasphemy which prattles that not only the law but even the gospel is obscure. But Paul claims that the gospel is plain *except to those who are perishing* (II Cor. 4:3); over them a veil is thrown because they deserve to be blind (II Cor. 3:14–15). But, as we see, Jeremiah here affirms that the law, even though it is less clear than the gospel, is set plainly before the eyes of all, and that all may learn from it exactly what pleases God and what is right.

Now we must consider carefully the statement which follows in the next verse; for it unquestionably belongs with the previous one. God demands nothing except that men obey his laws, and yet he wishes his servants, the prophets, to be heard: *That you may hear the words of my prophets whom I send to you* (he uses the second person, *you*). Here there seems to be a kind of inconsistency. For if the law of God is sufficient, why is hearing the prophets added to it? But the two commands are really in perfect agreement. The law alone must be heard, and with it the prophets who continually interpret it. For God did not send his prophets to correct the law, to change something in it, to add to it or subtract from it. There was an inviolable decree *neither to add nor take away* (Deut. 12:32). What then was the purpose of prophecy? Truly, it was to explain the law more and more fully, and also to fit it to the immediate need of the people. Since, then, the prophets do not invent any new teaching, but are faithful interpreters of the law, God is not combining here two separate commands. He wishes his law and his prophets to be heard simultaneously. The majesty of the law does not lessen the authority of the prophets. For the prophets uphold the law; they in no way subtract anything from it.

So this passage teaches that all those who reject the daily exercise of learning the Scriptures are godless men and quench, so far as it is within their power, the grace of the Spirit. In our day there are many of the Anabaptists[1] who act in this way, rejecting all teaching. They say this [Scripture] is "the letter," and they dream that the Holy Spirit is injured when men attend to "the letter." And some dare to utter uglier blasphemies. They say that all the Scripture we need is the two commands, "Fear God" and "Love your neighbor."

But as I have already said, we must consider how it is that God has spoken through the law, and whether [it is not true that] our way to him would have been blocked had he not explained his will more clearly through the prophets; for it is through the prophets that God adapts to our need whatever might seem to us remote and of no concern to us. Surely since God gave his law and then added to it his prophets, it is obvious that anyone who rejects God's prophets puts no real confidence in God's law. So today those who scorn to go to school to Christ and to train themselves in listening to the Word, really mock God himself and judge both the law and the prophets—and even the gospel itself—as without value.

Therefore, this passage is of the highest importance. God wishes his law to be our guide and rule, and he binds it to his prophets.

But the word of the Lord endureth forever. And this is the word which by the gospel is preached unto you. I Peter 1:25.

The prophet teaches us, not what the Word of God is in itself, but how we are to think of it. Since man has emptied himself of life, he must look for it outside of himself. And Peter tells us on

---

[1] Anabaptists is a loose and derogatory term applied to radical sects of the Reformation era. Calvin was especially opposed to them; not so much because they opposed infant baptism as because they claimed revelation beyond Scripture and because they advocated a complete separation of church and state.

the authority of the prophet, that God's Word alone possesses the energy and efficacy to bestow upon us whatever is solid and eternal. For the prophet knew that our lives have no stability except in God, and except as he communicates it to us by his Word. Since man's nature is in itself perishing, the Word himself invests it with eternal life, and restores it by a new creation.

And this is the word declared to you. Peter first warns us that when the Word of God is mentioned, we do wrong to imagine something far away, up in the air or in heaven beyond; for the Lord himself has shown it to us. What then is the Word of God which gives us life; what but the law, the prophets, and the gospel? Anyone who wanders away from this revelation will find, instead of God's Word, nothing but Satan's impostures and madness. Therefore, we must keep carefully in mind that godless and devilish men have a crafty way of pretending to honor God's Word, when they turn us away from the Scriptures; like that dirty dog Agrippa,[2] who praised the eternity of God's Word to high heaven, and at the same time heaped mockery on the prophets and the apostles; in his deceitful way, he covered the Word of God with derision.

In short, as I have already told you, nothing is said here of a Word shut up in God's bosom. We have to do with the Word which came forth from God's mouth and was given to us. So once again, we are to acknowledge that God's will is to speak to us by the mouths of the apostles and prophets, and that their mouths are to us as the mouth of the only true God.

Therefore, when Peter says, *the word which has been declared to you,* he means that we must not look for the Word of God anywhere except in the preaching of the gospel; and that we cannot know the power of its eternity except by faith. But we do not believe unless we know that the Word was destined for us.

And, behold, the Lord stood above it, and said, I am the Lord God of Abraham thy father and the God of Isaac. Gen. 28:13.

Here is the third point which I said must be noted. Silent visions are cold, and the Word of God is the breath which gives them life. The symbol of the ladder is a less important adjunct, with which the Word of God illustrates and embellishes itself

---

[2] Heinrich Cornelius Agrippa von Nettesheim of Cologne (1486–1535). A man in the stereotype Renaissance style. He was a Neoplatonist and worked at "occult philosophy." His unorthodoxy and skepticism aroused the ire of the Catholics, and the Protestant Reformers regarded him as a heretic and a charlatan.

for the sake of greater clarity—not for greater authority. Hence we judge the papal sacraments to be frivolous, since in them the voice of God is not heard for the upbuilding of souls.

We should note, therefore, that whenever God showed himself to the patriarchs, he *spoke*; for a silent vision would have left them dangling in uncertainty.

By the name *YHWH*, Jehovah, God proclaims that he alone is the maker of the world, and that Jacob must seek for himself no other gods. But because in itself God's majesty is incomprehensible, he adds immediately, adapting himself to the capacity of his servant, that he is the God of Abraham and Isaac. It is necessary to believe that the God whom we worship is he who alone is God; but when our minds seek to attain his height, they faint at the very start. We need to cultivate moderation and sobriety, and we should not attempt to know more of him than he reveals to us. He himself, in his great kindness, accommodates himself to our little mold, and he leaves out nothing which helps toward our salvation.

When he says that he had made a special covenant with Abraham and Isaac, and proclaims himself as their God, he calls his servant Jacob back to the real beginning of faith and keeps him within the eternal covenant. This is the holy bond of faithfulness by which all the sons of God are bound together. They hear the same promise of salvation, from the first to the last, and they agree together in one hope.

All Scripture is given by the inspiration of God, and is profitable for doctrine, for reproof, for correction, for instruction in righteousness; that the man of God may be perfect, thoroughly furnished unto all good works. II Tim. 3:16–17.

All Scripture, or the whole of it; both phrases mean the same. He now continues with his praise of Scripture which had been much too brief. He commends first its authority, and then the usefulness which proceeds from it. He asserts its authority by teaching that it is inspired by God. If this is the case, men should receive it reverently and without further argument. Our religion is distinguished from all others in that the prophets have spoken not of themselves, but as instruments of the Holy Spirit; and what they have brought to us, they received by heavenly commission. Any man then who would profit by the Scriptures, must hold first of all and firmly that the teaching of the law and the prophets came to us not by the will of man, but as dictated by the Holy Spirit.

Somebody may object: But how do we know all this? I answer, the selfsame Spirit revealed both to the disciples and to the teachers (*doctorem*) that the author of the Scriptures is God. Neither Moses nor the prophets brought to us by chance the things we have received at their hands; they spoke as moved by God, and testified with confidence and courage that God's very mouth had spoken. The same Spirit who made Moses and the prophets certain of their calling, has now testified to our own hearts that he used them as his servants for our instruction. It is not surprising that many have doubts as to the author of Scripture. For, even though the majesty of God is displayed by it, only those illumined by the Spirit have the eyes to see what should be evident to all men, but in fact is seen only by the elect. So, the first point is that we treat Scripture with the same reverence that we do God, because it is from God alone, and unmixed with anything human.

And is profitable. The second part of this praise of Scripture follows from the first; that it contains the perfect rule of a good and happy life. He means that Scripture is useful because it is free from the kind of corruption which comes with the abuse of God's Word by sinful men. Thus he indirectly rebukes those woolly-headed men who feed the people with empty speculations as with wind. For this reason, today, we ought to condemn all those who make it their business not to build up the people but to arouse them with questions which are as childish as they are clever. Whenever men come to us with such clever trifles, we must repel them with the principle that the Scripture is for upbuilding. Consequently, it is unlawful to handle it as a useless thing. God gave us Scripture for our good, and not to satisfy our curiosity, or to indulge our desire for showing off, or to give us material for babble and fable. Therefore, to use Scripture rightly is at all times to profit by it. . . .

That the man of God may be whole. Whole means perfect, in the sense of unmutilated. He asserts simply that Scripture is adequate and sufficient for our perfecting. Therefore, anyone who is not satisfied with Scripture, hopes to know more than he needs or than is good for him. But now comes a serious objection. Since Paul means by Scripture the Old Testament, how are we to believe that it makes us perfect? If the Old Testament makes us perfect, then the apostolic additions are superfluous. I answer that, as to substance, the apostles added nothing. The writings of the apostles contain nothing that is not simply a natural explanation of the law and the prophets, together with a straightforward presentation of what they contain. Therefore, Paul's praise of the Old Testament was not wrong. And since its teaching is understood more fully and shines more brightly now that the gospel has been added to it, must we not hope that the value of Scripture, of which Paul speaks, shall be all the more displayed, if only we will try living by it and take hold of it?

Beloved, believe not every spirit, but try spirits whether they are of God; because many false prophets are gone out into the world. I John 4:1.

Many, as I said before, are so troubled by the discords and wranglings in the church that, in their dismay, they run away from the gospel. But the Spirit prescribes an altogether different way: that believers be watchful not to accept any doctrine lightly and without judgment. We should be careful not to be offended by the variety of opinion in the church; we should rather discriminate between teachers, with the Word of God as our only norm. It is enough to make it our rule not to listen indiscriminately to everyone that comes along.

I take the word *spirit* as a metaphor, as meaning a man who claims the gift of the Spirit, so that he may assume the office of a prophet. Since nobody ought to speak in his own name, we must not trust those who do not speak as instruments of the Spirit. The prophets spoke with authority because God himself honored them with this title, and in so doing, set them apart from all other men. These men were called spirit because they gave utterance to the oracles of the Spirit, and by their ministry represented God's own person. They offered nothing out of their own heads, neither did they come forth among the people in their own names. They were given this high title, in order that their own insignificance might not take away from the reverence that is due to the Word of God. God has willed it that we always receive his Word from the lips of men, as though he himself had appeared from heaven.

But now Satan interferes. He not only places false teachers among the people, so as to corrupt the Word of God, but he also calls them prophets, so that the people fall [into error] all the more easily. These arrogant pseudoprophetic windbags are in the habit of snatching an honor which God bestowed upon his own servants. The apostle uses the word *spirits* purposely, to keep us from being deceived by those who pretend falsely to speak in God's name; for in our own day we see many who are stupid enough to be so overcome by the mere title of "the church," that they take sides with the pope, and would be damned forever rather than raise a finger against his authority.

It should be noticed that the apostle did not deny outright the claim of these men to be prophets. He might have said simply that they ought not to be believed. When these false teachers lyingly claimed that they had the Spirit, he let them have their way; only he warned that their claim was both fictitious and foolish unless they could come forth with the reality of prophecy. It is silly to be so taken in by a high-sounding title that one does not even dare to see if there be anything behind it.

Try the spirits. Since not everyone who calls himself a prophet is one, the apostle says here that he should be put to a test; not only by the church at large, but also by individual believers. But the question arises, Where do we get our discernment? When some say that we should judge men's words by the Word of God, they are right so far; but that does not settle the matter. I admit readily that men's teachings should be tested by the Word of God. But the truth is that without the good sense we receive from the Spirit, it helps us little or nothing to have the Word of God in our hands; for its meaning is bound to escape us. For instance, gold is tested with fire or touchstone; but only by those who know how to do it. What use is fire or touchstone to the ignorant? In the same way, we are fit to judge only when we receive discretion from the Spirit and are guided by him. Since we could not follow the apostle's precept, unless the power of judging were added to it, certainly the godly shall not be left without the Spirit of sound judgment, provided they seek him from the Lord. But it is also true that the Spirit will lead us to true discretion only when we bring all our thoughts under subjection to the Word of God; for, as we said above, it is, so to speak, our touchstone, which should be most precious to us, since it is the only source of sound teaching.

But here comes a difficult question. If everyone has a right to be a judge and arbiter in this matter, nothing can be set down as certain; and our whole religion will be full of uncertainty. I reply that we must test doctrines in a twofold way: private and public. By private testing, each one establishes his own faith, and accepts only the teaching which he knows to be from God. For our conscience cannot find security and peace except in God. Public testing of doctrine has to do with the common consent and polity of the church. Since there is a danger that fanatical men may rise up and boast rashly that they have the Spirit of God, believers should seek a remedy by coming together and reasoning their way to an honest and godly agreement. The old proverb is right when it says, "So many heads, so many minds." Therefore, it is a marvelous work of God that, overcoming all our perversity, he makes us of one mind, and unites us together in a pure unity of faith.

Knowing this first, that no prophecy of Scripture is of any private interpretation. II Peter 1:20.

Here Peter begins to teach how our minds must be prepared if we would make proper progress in Scripture. There is in this verse a word which may mean one of two things. If you read it ἐπηλύσεως, as some do, it means an impulsion. But if you read it ἐπιλύσεως, as I do, it means interpretation. In either case, almost all agree that we should not rush at reading Scripture rashly, trusting our own wits; because the Spirit who has spoken by the prophets is his own interpreter.

This explanation contains a true, godly, and useful doctrine. The only way to read the prophets to advantage is to set aside the mind of the flesh and to submit to the authority of the Holy Spirit. It is godless profanity to set up our own acumen as capable of understanding Scripture, which contains mysteries of God hidden to our flesh and sublime treasures of life which are far beyond our powers. This is why we say that the light which shines in it comes only to the lowly.

But the papists are foolish when they conclude that no private interpretation by an individual is valid. They abuse Peter's testimony, in order to give their councils alone the right to interpret Scripture. But this is childish. When Peter speaks of private interpretation, he does not refer to individuals; neither does he forbid them to interpret Scripture. He means that it is not godly for them to come out with something out of their own heads. Even if all men in the world were to agree and be of one mind, the outcome would still be *private*, of their own. The word *private* is here set against divine revelation; for the believers, illumined inwardly by the Holy Spirit, know as truth only what God says by his Word.

However, I think the simpler meaning of Peter's statement is that Scripture is not of men, or by the initiative of men. You will never come to it well prepared to read it, unless you bring reverence, obedience, and teachableness with you. But reverence comes from the knowledge that it is God who speaks to us and not mortal men. Therefore, Peter in the first place urges us to believe without doubting that the prophecies are God's oracles; which means that they were not set in motion by men's own action.

What comes next means the same thing. The holy men spoke as they were moved by the Spirit of God; that is, they did not babble out fables, moved by their own impulse and as they willed. In short, the first step in right understanding is that we believe the holy prophets of God as we do him. The apostle calls them *holy men of God* because they performed faithfully the task which was laid upon them; and in this service, they were surrogates for the person of God. Peter says they were *moved*, not because they were bereft of their own minds (as the Gentiles imagined their prophets to have been during their "enthusiasm"), but because they did not dare to say anything of their own. They followed the Spirit as their guide and obeyed him to such an extent that their mouths became his temple, and he ruled in them.

The Jews answered him, We have a law, and by our law he ought to die, because he made himself the Son of God. John 19:7.

The Jews explain that they are pursuing Christ out of regard for the law, and not from passion or hatred. For they realize that they are being indirectly held in check by Pilate. Knowing that Pilate is ignorant of the law, they as much as say to him: "We have a right to live according to our customs. Our religion does not suffer a man to give himself airs as the Son of God." Besides, this accusation was not groundless; but they were altogether wrong in the deduction they made [from the law]. The general thesis was, of course, correct. It was not right for any man to assume divine honor; and anyone who took for himself what is God's alone, was worthy of death. Their error was that they applied the law to Christ; for they did not consider with what praise Scripture itself had predicted the Messiah. If they had done so, they would have inferred readily that he was the Son of God. Thus it is evident that having started with a true principle, they were led by bad reasoning to a false conclusion.

Let us be warned by this example to distinguish carefully between general doctrine and the particular inferences we make from it. This we should do for the sake of inexperienced and simple people who, when deceived by some pretended truth, reject even the fundamental doctrines of Scripture; and there is too much of this kind of thing going on in our world today. Let us, therefore, be careful to shun fallacies, so that truth may remain inviolate and faith in Scripture may be not overthrown.

If I have told you earthly things, and ye believe not, how shall ye believe, if I tell you of heavenly things? John 3:12.

Christ concludes that if Nicodemus and his like do not make progress in the knowledge of the gospel, it is their fault. He shows that since he has come down to earth itself, he is not to be blamed if not everybody learns his doctrine properly. It is too common a vice among men that they want to be taught in a subtle and ingenious way: hence most of them are very happy with deep and abstruse speculations; for the same reason, many do not think much of the gospel: in it they do not find the kind of pompous discourse with which they like to fill their ears. They do not care to sink so low as to waste their time with the rude and lowly teaching of the gospel. But, it is most stupid not to honor the Word of God, because he has lowered himself to the level of our ignorance. When we find God prattling to us in the Bible in an uncultivated and vulgar style, let us remember that he does it for our sake. Anyone who presumes or pretends to be offended by the condescension of God so that he will not submit to God's Word, is a liar. Anyone who cannot bear to lay hold of God as he comes down to him will still less soar up to him beyond the clouds.

Some explain *earthly* things as the ABC of spiritual truth, and speak of self-denial as the first step in godliness. But I prefer the view of those who think this phrase has to do with Christ's way of teaching. For even though Christ's discourse as a whole was heavenly, he spoke plainly, as it were in an *earthly* way. Furthermore, this is not true of one discourse only. In this verse, Christ's habitually simple and popular way of teaching is contrasted with ambitious men's addiction to speech that is full of pomp and splendor.

And thou, Bethlehem, in the land of Juda, art not the least among the princes of Juda; for out of thee shall come a governor, that shall rule my people Israel. Matt 2:6.

There is no doubt that the scribes quoted the words of this passage (Micah 5:2) in their own tongue, faithfully, as found in the prophet. But Matthew was satisfied to refer to it. Because he wrote in Greek, he followed the commonly accepted reading of it. From this place and others like it, we can readily gather that Matthew did not compose his Gospel in Hebrew. Moreover, one must always notice that when the apostles quote a Scriptural testimony, they do not give it word for word, and sometimes depart quite far from its language; they nevertheless accommodate it (*accommodare*) in a fitting and proper way to their own purpose. Let the readers always keep in mind the purpose of the Evangelists in bringing forward passages of Scripture, so that they will not insist upon dwelling upon mere words, but will be content with the fact that the Evangelists never torture Scripture into a false meaning, and apply (*aptare*) it properly to a genuine use. Since the latter intended to feed infants and novices in the faith with milk, because these were as yet incapable of taking solid food, there is no reason why the children of God should have scruples against a diligent and exact inquiry into the contents of Scripture, so that the taste offered them by the apostles may lead them to the fountain [of God's Word].

2. The Old and the New Testaments

Now all these things happened unto them in examples: and they are written for our admonition, upon whom the ends of the world are come. I Cor. 10:11.

Now he repeats that all these things happened to the Israelites to serve us as types, examples by which God sets his judgments before our eyes. I am aware that others philosophize more subtly over these words; but I think I have understood the mind of the apostle when I say that by these examples, as by painted pictures, we are taught what judgment is waiting for idolators, fornicators, and others who treat God with contempt; they are living images which present God to us as angry with such sins. This explanation, besides being simple and valid, has the advantage of shutting the mouth of those madmen who twist this passage to prove that the people in old times were given nothing but [empty] shadows. First they assume that the people of Israel were only a figure [form without content] of the church: and from this they conclude that everything God promised and did among them, every good, every punishment, was a mere figure of that which was to become actual after the coming of Christ. This is but a pestilential madness, an atrocious injury to the holy fathers, and a more atrocious injury to God. The people [of Israel] was a figure of the Christian church; but it was itself the true church; its condition was a sketch of our own; but as such it had even at that time the proper character of the church. The promises made to it anticipated the gospel, so as in fact to include it; its sacraments served as figures of our own, but even in that age the inherent efficacy of their presence made them true sacraments. In short, those who used rightly the doctrines and the signs given them were endowed with the same spirit of faith as we ourselves. These words of Paul, therefore, give no support to those insane people who would have it that the things done at that time were types in the sense of unreal and empty shows. Nay, more, as we have explained, they teach us plainly that these types are pictures which depict events useful for our admonition.

They were written for our admonition. This second phrase clarifies the former. It was not for the sake of the Israelites, but for ours, that these things were kept in remembrance. It does not follow that punishments they suffered were not real warnings from God and valid for their own correction; and yet when God exercised his judgments at that time, he intended that there should be a perpetual remembrance of them for our instruction. What use is history for those who are dead? And what good is it to the living, except as they are warned by the example of others, and come to their senses? And now, the apostle confesses the principle with which all believers should agree: that there is nothing put forth in Scripture which it is not profitable to know.

Upon whom the ends of the world are come. τέλη elsewhere means mysteries; and perhaps that meaning would not be unsuitable for this passage. However, I follow the common rendering, because it is simpler. He says that the end of all the ages has come to pass among us and all things are fulfilled and come to a head in this age, because it is now the fullness of time. For the chief end toward which the law and all the prophets looked is the Kingdom of Christ.

But this statement of Paul contradicts the popular opinion that God, under the Old Testament, was more rigid, always armed and ready to punish wickedness; that now he has begun to be lenient, and ignores [evil] much more readily. Our living under the law of grace is interpreted to mean that we have a God who is much more easy to please than the God of the ancients. But what does Paul say about all this? If God punished them, he will not spare us any more than he did them. Away then with the error of those who reason that God is now less strict in exacting the punishment of crimes! I must confess that, since the coming of Christ, God's goodness has been poured upon men more strikingly and in more abundance; but how does this change the impunity of the wicked who abuse his grace? Only, we must notice that today God punishes differently. For, as formerly God showed his Fatherly love to the godly with great outward blessings, he showed his wrath with severe bodily punishments; now, on the other hand, in the fuller revelation which we have, it is not often that he inflicts visible punishments: nor does he send physical punishment immediately even upon the wicked. About this matter you will find a great deal in our *Institutes*.[3]

Of which salvation the prophets inquired and searched diligently, who prophesied of the grace that should come unto you: searching what, or in what time, the Spirit of Christ which was in them did signify. I Peter 1:10-11.

Peter sets high the value of salvation, by referring to the prophets who had been intent upon it with all their zeal; since the prophets sought for it with burning hearts, he regards it as a thing of great and singular excellence. And the goodness of God toward us is all the greater and shines all the more brightly, because much more has been revealed to us than was sought after by the prophets so long and so eagerly.

At the same time, Peter establishes the certainty of salvation from its very antiquity, because from the very beginning of the world it has received the true witness of the Holy Spirit.

These two things must be kept clearly in mind. He affirms that more is given to us than to the ancient fathers; and by this comparison, he magnifies the grace of the gospel. Further, what is preached to us concerning our salvation cannot be suspected of novelty, because the Spirit, by the prophets, has borne witness to it through the ages. Therefore, when he says that the prophets sought and searched ceaselessly, he refers not to their teachings or writings, but to the inner yearning which agitated them. He deals with their public activity in what follows.

If we would understand the particulars of the verse more clearly, we need to break it down into several parts. First, when the prophets prophesied of the grace which Christ exhibited to us by his coming, they were anxious to know the time of full

[3] Bk. II, ch. 11, par. 3.

revelation. Secondly, the Spirit of Christ foretold, through them, the true state of the coming reign of Christ, partly as they already discerned it, and partly as they looked forward to it in hope; they predicted that both Christ and his universal body were destined to enter into glory by way of many sufferings. Thirdly, the prophets as they received God's revelation ministered to us more than to their own age; because the things of God revealed to them by way of obscure images were exhibited in their solid reality in Christ alone. In the fourth place, the gospel, in which the Spirit himself speaks, contains not only a clear confirmation of prophetic teachings, but also a much fuller and plainer explanation of them. For the salvation to which he pointed through the prophets from afar off, he now presents to us openly and as it were to our very eyes. The last statement [in this passage] adequately confirms the marvelous glory of the salvation promised us in the gospel, since even the angels who enjoyed the vision of God in heaven, burned with the desire to see it. And what all this amounts to is that Christians, raised to such a height of blessedness, ought to overcome all the obstacles which the world sets before them; for what [suffering] is there that is not mitigated by such an incomparable blessing?

Of which salvation. But did not the fathers have the same salvation in common with us? Why then does he say that the fathers inquired, as though they did not have what is now offered to us? The answer is easy; in my view, salvation means the clear and visible manifestation of it which we have in the coming of Christ. These words of Peter mean nothing else than those spoken by Christ: *Many kings and prophets have desired to see the things which you see, and have not seen them. Blessed therefore are your eyes,* etc. (Matt. 13:17). Since the prophets had only a small taste of the grace which Christ brought to us, their desire turned rightly toward a different manner of revelation. When Simeon saw Christ, he made ready for death with a calm and peaceful spirit; which shows that he was previously anxious and disquieted. Such was the state of all believers [before Christ].

He indicates how [the fathers] searched, when he adds the phrase, *in what,* or *in what manner of time.* The difference between the law and the gospel is that, under the former, there is a veil interposed, which kept the fathers from seeing the nearness of the things which are set before the eyes of us [who live under the gospel]. Nor was it indeed proper that when Christ, the Son of Righteousness, was yet absent, the fullness of light should have shined as at noontime. But though it was necessary for the fathers to stay within their prescribed limits, yet they were not rash when they sighed with desire for a closer sight of salvation. Even while they yearned for the speedy coming of salvation, and for a sight of it, their eagerness did not keep them from waiting with patience so long as it pleased God to delay it.

Also we have a more sure word of prophecy; whereunto ye do well that ye take heed, as unto a light that shineth in a dark place, until the day dawn, and the day-star rise in your hearts. II Peter 1:19.

Also we have. Here he teaches that the truth of the gospel is certain because it is founded upon the oracles of the prophets; and he does this so that those who embrace the gospel may be free of doubt and subject themselves totally to Christ. For anyone who wavers in this matter cannot but be lax in his spirit.

We have may refer to himself and other teachers, as well as to their disciples. The apostles regarded the prophets as surety of their own teaching; the believers also found the confirmation of the gospel in the prophets. So, I am inclined to the view that the apostle is speaking of the whole church, and including himself in it. Still, he is speaking particularly of the Jews, who were familiar with the doctrine of the prophets. In my opinion, this is why he says that the gospel is *more sure.* Those who understand this comparison as establishing the superiority of the gospel to the prophets do not pay enough attention to its context. It is tortuous to make this phrase mean *more sure* than the words of the prophets, because the gospel is in fact the fulfillment of the promises which God made to them concerning his Son. It is enough to establish the truth of the gospel in two ways: by God's own high and solemn praise and approval of Christ, and by the fact that all the prophecies of the prophets were made with regard to Christ.

On the other hand, anyone can see immediately how absurd it is that the word of the prophets should be *more sure* than any other word spoken by the mouth of our Holy God! First, the authority of God's Word is from the beginning and always the same. Secondly, the coming of Christ established it more firmly than ever, as The Epistle to the Hebrews tells us at length. But it is not hard to untie this knot. The apostle is speaking to his own people, who were passionately attached to the prophets, so that the teaching of the latter was beyond controversy among them. Since there was no doubt among the Jews that whatever the prophets taught was from the Lord, we should not be surprised at Peter's saying that word of the latter was *more sure*. Therefore, here the question is not whether the prophets deserve to be believed more than the gospel. Peter was pointing out the great deference the Jews paid to the prophets, whom they accepted without question as servants of God, and in whose school they had been educated from their very childhood. . . . We must remember that Peter was speaking to these people. He was not instructing ignorant novices who knew only the rudiments [of the faith]. He had previously testified that his hearers had already received the precious things of the faith and had been confirmed in the truth which he was presenting to them. Surely such a people could not have been said to be in the gross darkness of ignorance. . . . Therefore, as the context makes it clear, Peter was speaking to these men; and this statement was necessarily made to believers who had received Christ's name and were made partakers of the true light. I, therefore, extend this darkness spoken of by Peter to the whole of our lives, and interpret [this statement to mean] that the *day* will *shine* upon us only when we see face to face what now we see in a mirror and darkly. Of course, Christ, the Sun of Righteousness, does shine in the gospel. But, until we are brought out of the prison of the flesh and taken up to heaven, our minds shall at all times be in part occupied by the darkness of death.

In short, Peter warns that so long as we walk in this world, we need the teaching of the prophets for a directing light; because without this light we can do nothing but live in darkness and go astray. He is not, therefore, separating the prophets from the gospel; he tells us that they shine for us to show us the way. His point is that throughout the whole course of our life we ought to be directed by the Word of God, because otherwise we shall be enveloped on all sides with the darkness of ignorance. The Lord does not shine upon us unless we see by his Word as our light.

This passage is significant in that it tells us how God directs us. The papists have it always on their tongue that the church cannot err. They forget the Word and pretend to be guided by the Spirit. Peter, on the contrary, claims that all those who disregard the light of the Word are buried in darkness. Therefore, if you do not want, of your own will, to lose yourself in a labyrinth, do your very best to avoid rejecting the guidance of the Word even in the smallest matter. The church cannot follow God as its guide, unless it observes this rule. With this statement

Peter condemns all the wisdom of men, in order that we may learn not to seek the true rule of understanding in our own minds. Without the Word, there is nothing left for us but darkness.

It is worth noting that here he speaks of the clarity of the Scripture. For his eulogy would be false, unless Scripture were apt and able to show us the way clearly and certainly. Anyone, therefore, who opens his eyes with the obedience of faith shall know by experience that Scripture has not been called *light* in vain. It is indeed obscure to the unbelievers; but those who are given up to destruction blind themselves. The blasphemy of the papists is damnable, when they pretend that the light of Scripture merely dazzles the eye. This is their way of keeping the simple people from reading it. But, of course, we need not wonder that the proud, inflated with the wind of a perverse self-confidence, cannot see the light with which the Lord favours only those who are humble as a child (Matt. 11:25). David praises the law of God in a similar vein (Ps. 19 and 119).

But the hour cometh, and now is, when the true worshipers shall worship the Father in spirit and in truth. . . . John 4:23.

Now there follows the second part, which has to do with the annulling of the cultic laws. When Christ says, *the hour is coming,* or *is come,* he teaches that the Mosaic order is in no way permanent. When he says, *the hour now is,* he puts an end to the ceremonies, and in this way declares that the time of training is now over. Still, he puts his approval on the Temple, the priesthood, and all the rites that went with them, in so far as these were useful in the past (Heb. 9:10). Besides, in order to show that God does not wish to be worshiped [exclusively] either in Jerusalem or on Mount Gerizim, he appeals to a higher principle: namely, that a true worship of God must be done in the spirit; from which it follows that men may call upon him in all places.

But we must first ask why and in what sense the worship of God is called spiritual. If we are to understand this, we must know the difference between the spirit and external forms as the difference between shadow and reality. The worship of God is said to be in the spirit, because nothing can take the place of the inward faith of the heart, which makes us call on God, or of purity of conscience and self-denial, by which we may give ourselves to the obedience of God as holy sacrifice.

From this arises another question: Did not the fathers, while under the law, worship God spiritually? I answer that since God is always the same, from the very beginning of the world, he could not have approved any kind of worship except the spiritual, which alone is compatible with his nature. Moses himself bears abundant witness to this, when he declares the end of the law to be none other than that his people cleave to God in faith and a pure conscience. In fact, the same thing is expressed in even a more telling way by the prophets, when they inveigh against the hypocrisy of the people who thought they could satisfy God by killing their sacrificial beasts and making a big show of it. There is no need to produce the many proofs, which are found everywhere, the most significant of them being Psalm 50; Isaiah 1, 58, 66; Micah 5; Amos 7.

However, even though the worship of God under the law was spiritual, since it was hidden under a multitude of external ceremonies it had the taste of something carnal and worldly. This is why Paul speaks of ceremonies as *flesh* and *beggarly elements of the world* (Gal. 4:9). In the same way, the writer of The Epistle to the Hebrews says that the ancient sanctuary, with its appendages, was *earthly* (Heb. 9:1). Thus we say properly that the cult of the law was spiritual in substance, but with respect to its form somewhat carnal and earthly. Therefore, the whole apparatus of the cult, the reality of which is now manifest, was a thing of shadows.

Now we see what the Jews had in common with us, and how they differed from us. In every age, God desired to be worshiped by faith, prayer, acts of thanksgiving, purity of heart, and innocence of life; and at no time was he pleased with other sacrifices; but under the law there were various additions made, and the Spirit and truth were covered over and hidden. Now that the veil of the Temple is torn, nothing is hidden or obscure. We also today have some external exercises of piety, which we need because of our inaptitude: but they are characterized by sobriety, and do not obscure the naked truth of Christ. In short, what was shadowy to the fathers, we now have openly and clearly.

For if the blood of bulls and of goats . . . sanctifieth to the purifying of the flesh, how much more shall the blood of Christ, who through the eternal Spirit offered himself without spot to God, purge our conscience from dead works, to serve the living God? Heb. 9:13-14.

This passage has led many people astray, because they have forgotten that it has to do with sacraments, which have a spiritual meaning. They have talked about the cleansing of the flesh, such as was practiced by the heathen, who tried to blot out infamous crimes by offering some sacrifice of expiation. Such an interpretation of this passage is the height of profanity: for it is an insult to God that we should limit his promises to merely secular or civic matters. Moses teaches often that when sacrifice is offered properly, iniquity itself is expiated. Therefore, the doctrine of our faith is spiritual. The ultimate purpose of all sacrificial killing was to lead us to Christ; it was a testimony to the salvation of our souls in Christ, which alone is eternal. Therefore, how could the apostle have spoken of "the purification of the flesh" except in a spiritual, or sacramental, sense? If even the blood of beasts was a symbol of true purification, so that it did cleanse in a sacramental way, how much more shall Christ, who is the truth, not merely testify to purification by external rites, but rather establish its reality in our consciences! So the argument of this verse is from the sign to the reality signified by it; for the effectiveness of reality takes precedence by far over the validity of the sign.

Through the eternal Spirit. Now he shows clearly that the death of Christ is to be understood not in terms of outward act, but of the power of the Spirit. Christ suffered as a man. If his death has the power to save us, it is by the efficacy of the Spirit; for the sacrifice which brought us eternal expiation was more than a human act. And the apostle calls the Spirit eternal, to teach us that the reconciliation which He works is itself eternal. . . .

By the works of death we may understand either works which produce death, or works which are the fruit of death. Since the life of the soul is bound to God, those who are by sin alienated from him are to be regarded as dead.

But let us consider the end of our purification, which is the service of the living God. We are washed by Christ, not immediately to bury ourselves once again in filth, but so that our purity may serve the glory of God. Besides, the apostle teaches us that nothing from us will please God, unless we are purged by the blood of Christ. Since before we are reconciled with God we all are enemies to him, all our works are worthless before him. Therefore, the beginning of the true worship of God is reconciliation. Besides, since no act of ours is pure, free from all spot, it cannot please God; it must, therefore, be purified by the blood of Christ which blots out all our spots. And, of course, the contrast between dead works and the living God is beautiful.

Whereupon neither the first testament was dedicated without blood. For when Moses had spoken every precept to all the people according to the law, he took the blood of calves, and of goats, with water, and scarlet wool, and hyssop, and sprinkled both the book and all the people, saying, This is the blood of the testament which God hath enjoined unto you. Heb. 9: 18–20.

The apostle wants us to attend not to words but to the substance of what is being said. He has found the word *testament* in the Greek language in which he is writing. Since the [Hebrew] word for *covenant* often becomes *testimony* in Greek, he takes advantage of this fact, and turns it to his own use. He eulogizes God's covenant as a testimony, which is one way of speaking of it; and why not, since angels from heaven and so many gifted men on earth, that is, all the holy prophets, apostles, and a multitude of martyrs, have been witness to it, and at the last, the Son of God himself has sponsored it? Hence there is nothing absurd in the apostle's use of the word *testament*. It is true that the Hebrew word *toude* does not in fact mean covenant; but since nothing which the apostle says is inconsistent with it, we must not be tied down to the exact meaning of the word.

The apostle says that the Old Testament was dedicated with blood; this he takes as a warning to the people that it was effective and stable only by the interposition of death. But he denies that the blood of beasts was a valid confirmation of the eternal covenant. This becomes clearer when we consider the rite of sprinkling enjoined by Moses, as described in our text. The apostle tells us, in the first place, that the covenant was sanctified, not because it was in itself profane, but because nothing is so sacred that the people would not profane it by their own impurities, unless it were restored by God himself. Therefore, the dedication was on men's account, and only because they were unclean.

He then adds that the tabernacle with all its vessels, and also the Book of the Law itself, were sprinkled. By this rite the people were taught that God cannot be sought, or found, for salvation, and neither can he be worshiped truly, unless faith at all times uses the requisite blood. It is only right that we should find the majesty of God dreadful, and the way to it a hopeless labyrinth, unless we know that he turns to us with favor through the blood of Christ, and that through this same blood we have an easy access to him. Therefore, all worship is unclean and wicked unless purified by the sprinkling of the blood of Christ.

The tabernacle stood for a visible image of God. The vessels of the ministry set aside for the service of God were symbols of true worship. But since they were without blood useless for salvation, it is evident that unless Christ himself appears with his blood, we have no part in God. Even doctrine itself, in spite of God's constant will [to save us], is without power or benefit, unless sanctified with blood. Our verse makes this perfectly clear.

I know that others understand this passage differently. They say that the tabernacle is the body of the church; and the vessels, the faithful whom God uses in his service. But my view of the matter is far more suitable. Whenever the people called on God, they turned to the sanctuary; and it was a common saying that when they appeared in the Temple, they stood before the face of the Lord.

This is the blood of the testament. . . . This means that the testament is not ratified without blood, and that the blood works no expiation without the testament. Therefore, the two must go together. We see that the symbol was added after the law was explained: for what is a sacrament unless the Word come before it? Therefore, the symbol is an accessory to the Word. And mark you, the Word was not murmured as a magical incantation, but spoken with a loud and clear voice, because it was meant for the people, so that the words of the covenant, *which God has commanded you*, might ring out. Therefore, it is a perverse misuse of the sacrament, and an ungodly corruption of it, when no one hears the exposition of God's commandment, which is, as it were, the very soul of the sacrament. Therefore, the papists who separate the sign from a true understanding of its substance have nothing left but the dead letter.

Moreover, this passage warns us that we receive God's promises only when they are confirmed by the blood of Christ. All God's promises are Yea and Amen, as Paul testifies in II Cor. 1:20, only when by the blood of Christ they are inscribed on our hearts as a seal; for, we hear God speaking to us only when we see Christ offering himself as a pledge in what is said to us. If we could only get it into our heads that the Word of God we read is written not so much with ink as with the blood of the Son of God; or that when the gospel is preached, his own blood is poured with the voice we hear—we would pay far more attention and that with far greater reverence. The sprinkling spoken of by Moses was a symbol for the reality which we have just explained.

Of course, all this (which the apostle tells us) is not contained in the words of Moses. Moses does not tell us that either the Book or the people were sprinkled. He does not tell us that the sprinkling included the goats, or the scarlet wool, or the hyssop. We cannot even be sure that he sprinkled the Book, even though we may guess that he probably did so, since he brought it out before the people after the sacrifice, when he bound them to God by a solemn compact. As for the rest (the goats, the scarlet wool, the hyssop), it seems to me that the apostle has thrown them together as several kinds of offering having the same expiatory purpose. And after all, there is nothing absurd in this, since he was dealing with the general question of purification under the old covenant. What matters is that the whole thing was done with blood. As to the sprinkling with hyssop, and scarlet wool, it doubtless represented the mystical sprinkling by the Spirit. We know that hyssop has a singular power to purify and make clean. Therefore, Christ in turn sprinkles us with his Spirit, to wash us with his blood; to convert our minds to true repentance; to make us clean of the lusts of our depraved flesh; and to make us beautiful with the hues of his own wonderful righteousness. Indeed, it was not for nothing that God commanded this practice of sprinkling. Let us remember the words of David in Ps. 51:7, *Sprinkle me, O Lord, with hyssop, and I shall be clean.* That is enough for anyone who is minded to philosophize soberly.

3. THE LAW AND THE GOSPEL

Do not think that I will accuse you to the Father; there is one that accuseth you, even Moses, in whom ye trust. John 5:45.

It is a mistake to think that this verse sets the office of Moses against that of Christ; even though it is the peculiar function of the law to convict unbelievers of sin. This was not the intention of Christ; it was rather to disarm the hypocrites who gloried in Moses with a false reverence. It is like telling the papists today that the holy doctors of the church, behind whom they hide, are their worst opponents. Besides, this verse teaches us that our boasting in Scripture does us no good unless we worship the Son with the true obedience of faith; for, in the last day, all those whom God shall raise as witnesses to Christ shall come forth to accuse us. When Christ says that his hearers hope in Moses, he does not accuse them of superstition, or of thinking that Moses was their Savior. He is rather pointing out the folly of their taking refuge in Moses, as though they had his backing in their wicked and arrogant rebellion.

This is he, that was in the church in the wilderness with an angel which spake to him in Mount Sinai, and with our fathers: who received the lively oracles to give unto us. Acts 7:38.

Who received living oracles. Erasmus translates this as "the living word"! But those who know their Greek must agree that I have given a better rendition of what Stephen said; for oracles have more majesty than words. What I say is words, but what comes out of the mouth of the Lord is an oracle. Besides, these words of Stephen are intended to establish the authority of Moses' teaching, and to impress upon the people that Moses spoke only what was from God; from which it followed that in rebelling against Moses, they had rebelled not against him but against God; hence, their effrontery was obviously all the more brazen. (And, in general, the right way to establish [true] doctrine is for men to teach nothing they have not been commanded from God.) For, how could any man have dared to look down on Moses, who, as the Spirit says, had a right to be believed because he explained to the people faithfully the doctrine which he had received from God!

But someone may ask, Why does he call the law a "living word"? Such praise may seem to fit poorly with Paul's statement that the law is minister of death and works wrath, and that it makes us to sin (II Cor. 3:7). If anyone understands "the living word" to mean a word that is valid and effective in spite of men's contempt for it, I will not contradict him; but on my part, I interpret "living" as that which is active. Since the law is the perfect rule of a godly and holy life, and sets forth the righteousness of God, it is rightly thought of as the doctrine of life and salvation; and it is to this that Moses bears witness, as he swears by heaven and earth, when he presents the law to the people as the way of life and death. In the same way, in Ezekiel, chapter 20, God complains that the people have violated his law which is good, and his precepts concerning which he had said, *Any one who does them, shall live in them.* The law, therefore, contains life in itself. If anyone prefers to interpret "living" as efficacious and full of power, I shall not object too strenuously.

When Paul calls the law the minister of death, he speaks of a characteristic which it has contingently, because of the corrupt nature of man. The law itself does not produce sin; it finds sin in us. It offers life to us; but we, being evil, derive nothing but death from it. Hence, the law works death only in relation to man. In this verse, Stephen refers to something more than the bare commandments of the law; he speaks of the teaching of Moses as a whole, which includes the promises God has made freely, and therefore Christ himself, who alone is the life and salvation of men.

And ye have not his word abiding in you: for whom he hath sent, him ye believe not. John 5:38.

We profit from the Word of God only when it takes root in us, and is so fixed in our hearts that it remains there. Christ denied that the Jews possessed the heavenly doctrine, because they did not receive the Son of God who is proclaimed everywhere in it. And he rejected them with good reason. God did not speak through Moses and the prophets for nothing. His only purpose in speaking to Moses was that he might call everyone to Christ. Therefore, it is clear that those who repudiate Christ are no disciples of Moses. After all, how can the Word of life be and remain in anyone who pushes aside life itself? How does any man hold to the teaching of the law when he does his best to extinguish the Spirit of the law? For the law without Christ has nothing solid about it, and in fact avails us nothing. Therefore, progress in the Word of God goes with a right knowledge of Christ.

Search the Scriptures; for in them ye think ye have eternal life; and they are they which testify of me. John 5:39.

As we have pointed out, Christ's previous statement that the Father is his witness in heaven, applies also to Moses and the prophets. Now Christ explains the matter more clearly by saying that the Scripture itself is his witness. He again attacks the stupidity of those who declared loudly that the Scriptures gave them life, while they treated them as dead letter. He does not judge them because they sought life in the Scriptures; the Scriptures were given to be used for this purpose. But the Jews thought the Scriptures gave them life when they had no sense of their true meaning, and had even put out the light of life in them. How can the law make alive, when Christ alone gives it life?

Moreover, this passage teaches us that if we would know Christ, we must seek him in the Scriptures. Anyone who imagines Christ as he will, gets nothing but a mere blur (*umbratile spectrum*). So, we must first hold that Christ is known rightly nowhere but in Scripture. If this be so, our chief purpose in reading the Scriptures must be to arrive at a right knowledge of Christ. Whoever turns aside from this aim, even though he wear himself out with learning all his life, will never arrive at truth; for what wisdom can we attain apart from the wisdom of God? Moreover, since we are commanded to seek Christ in the Scriptures, he declares that our zeal in this matter shall not be in vain; for the Father himself testifies that in them he shall certainly reveal his Son to us. Many are deprived of this blessing, because they neglect reading the Scriptures, or do it cursorily and superficially. But it deserves utmost attention that Christ himself commands us to probe deeply into this hidden treasure. It was sheer apathy that led the Jews, who had the law in their very hands, to abhor Christ. The glory of God shone brightly in Moses, but they put up a veil and darkened it. In this place, Scripture means obviously the Old Testament. It is not true that Christ appears first in the gospel. It is rather that after the witness of the Law and the Prophets, he appeared in the gospel for everyone to see.

But if thou wilt enter into life, keep the commandments. Matt. 19:17.
Some ancients, and the papists after them, have misinterpreted this verse so as to make Christ promise that if we observe the law we shall have eternal life. Christ was not talking about what man can do; he was answering a question as to right conduct or what the law defines as righteous. Certainly, God gave his law as the way of a right and holy life, which includes righteousness. It is not for nothing that Moses made the statement, *Anyone who does these things, shall live by them*; again, *I call heaven and earth to witness that today I have put before you life.* Therefore, it cannot be denied that the keeping of the law is righteousness, and that anyone who keeps it perfectly, obtains life. But, since we all are destitute of the glory of God [righteousness], in the law we find nothing but a curse; there is nothing left for us to do but to fly to a righteousness which shall be given us freely. Therefore, Paul presents us with two kinds of righteousness: of the law and of faith; the former he makes to consist in works, and the latter in the mere grace of Christ.

From this we gather that the reply of Christ was correct. He had first to answer the young man who asked about the right thing to do; for no man is righteous before God unless he satisfies the law (which is impossible). He did this in order that the young man might acknowledge his inability, and look to faith for help. Therefore, I admit that since God has promised the reward of eternal life to those who keep the law, it would be right, if it were not for the weakness of our flesh, for us to follow this way [to expect life through our good works]. But Scripture itself teaches us that we must be given what we cannot acquire through our own merit. If anyone object that it is frustrating to be confronted with righteousness through obedience to the law, if nobody has it in him to achieve it, I answer that the law is only the beginning of this matter, and that it is by no means futile if it leads us to pray for righteousness. For this reason, where Paul says that those who do the law are justified, he also denies that anyone can be justified through the law (Rom. 2:13; 3:9-10).

This passage abolishes all the fictions which the papists have invented in order to obtain salvation. Their error is not merely that by their good works they want to bind God, and make him grant them salvation as a matter of debt; but also that when they gird themselves to do good, they set aside the teaching of the law, and become intent upon fictions which they call their "devotions." In this way, they not only repudiate the law of God, but also far prefer their human traditions. But what else does Christ say, except that God approves only of that worship which he himself has prescribed? For, obedience is better to him than all slaughtered sacrifice. So then, let the papists be occupied with their silly traditions; if anyone would be serious about ordering his life so as to live in obedience to Christ, let him devote his whole attention to obeying the commandments of the law.

Who hath also made us able ministers of the new testament, not of the letter, but of the spirit; for the letter killeth, but the spirit giveth life. But if the ministration of death, written and engraven in stones, was glorious, . . . which glory was to be done away, how shall not the ministration of the spirit be rather glorious? For if the ministration of condemnation be glory, much more doth the ministration of righteousness exceed in glory. For even that which was made glorious had no glory in this respect, by reason of the glory that excelleth. II Cor. 3:6-10.

Paul had before touched upon the comparison between the law and the gospel; now he pursues the matter further. However, the occasion for this argument is not certain; was it that he saw some Corinthians make a perverse use of the law, or was it something else that started him? For my part, I see no evidence that false apostles were comparing the law with the gospel. I think it is more probable that he had in mind chatterboxes whose lifeless rhetoric had the kind of glitter which swept the Corinthians off their feet. He wanted to show the latter that the chief glory of the gospel and the chief praise of its ministers is the power of the Spirit. It seems to me that he embarked upon the following comparison of the law with the gospel because it was a good way of proving his point.

However, there is no doubt that by the letter he meant the Old Testament, as by the word Spirit he means the gospel; for, when he calls himself a minister of the new covenant, he also adds immediately that he is a minister of the Spirit; and it is in this connection that he contrasts *the letter* with *the Spirit*.

We must now look into the reason for his use of these words. Origen's invention in this matter has become well established as truth: that the letter means the grammatical and genuine meaning of Scripture, or as they say, the literal; and that Spirit means the allegorical meaning, which is commonly called the spiritual. Thus, through the centuries, it has been commonly accepted and passed around that here Paul has provided us with a key for the allegorical interpretation of Scripture. But nothing was further from his mind. By the word *letter* Paul means preaching which is external and does not reach the heart; by *Spirit* he means teaching which is alive, which works mightily in the souls of men by the grace of the Spirit. *Letter*, therefore, means literal, that is, dead and ineffective preaching, which is heard only by the ear. *Spirit*, on the other hand, means spiritual teaching, which is not merely a matter of mouthing words, but rather has the power to penetrate the soul and bring it to life. Paul had in mind the verse from Jeremiah which I cited before; there the Lord says that his law had been given by word of mouth, and that it had neither lasted long, nor had it been received by the people with their hearts; therefore, he promises the Spirit of regeneration in the reign of Christ, who will write the gospel, that is the new covenant, in their hearts (Jer. 31:31). Now, it is Paul's boast that this prophecy has been fulfilled in his preaching. He would have the Corinthians know that the bombast of the loud mouths amounts to nothing, because it lacks the power of the Spirit.

Now let us consider if, under the Old Testament, God spoke merely with an outward voice, or if he did not speak inwardly by his Spirit to the hearts of the godly. I answer, in the first place, that Paul here has in mind the peculiar function of the law. In so far as God worked by his Spirit, he did so not by the ministry of Moses, but by the grace of Christ. As we learn from John 1:17, the law was by Moses, but grace and truth by Jesus Christ. Of course, all that time, the grace of God was not inactive; but also, clearly enough, it did not work by the law. Moses' part was done when he gave the way of life, with the threats and promises. Paul calls the law *letter* because in itself it is dead preaching; and he calls the gospel "Spirit," because its ministry is alive and makes alive.

Secondly, I answer that Paul is speaking of the law and the gospel not in general, but in so far as they are opposed one to the other. Even the gospel itself is not always *Spirit*. Still, when it comes to a comparison between the two, one must say truly and properly that the nature of the law is such that it teaches the *letter*, without penetrating beyond the ear; on the other hand, it is the nature of the gospel to teach spiritually, because it is the instrument of the grace of Christ. God has ordained it so, for it has pleased him to reveal the power of the Spirit more through the gospel than through the law; and it is the Spirit alone that can teach the spirits of men. . . .

For the letter kills. First Origen, and then others, distorted this phrase badly, to give it a corrupted meaning; and so arose the most pernicious error that Scripture is not only useless but even harmful unless it is turned into elaborate allegories. This error became a source of much evil. It not only gave license for corrupting the true meaning of Scripture, but also led to the notion that the more unprincipled the allegorizer, the more expert he was as interpreter of Scripture. So, many of the ancients threw the sacred Word of God around as though it were a tennis ball. In this way, the heretics too were unbridled and found occasion to trouble the church. Now, anybody could do anything, and many did; there was no madness so absurd or so great but it could be practiced in the name of some allegory. Even good people were caught, and invented many false notions, because they were deceived by their fondness for allegory. . . .

But if the ministration of death. He now magnifies the dignity of the gospel so much the more, by insisting that God has conferred great honor upon the law, which is as nothing in comparison with the gospel. The prestige of the law was established by many miracles. But Paul touches upon one: namely, that Moses' face was bright with such splendor as to dazzle the eyes of all those around him—a splendor which was a symbol of the

glory of the law. So he argues from the lesser to the greater, and
presents the glory of the gospel as all the more magnificent since
it is far superior to the law. First, he calls the law the ministry
of death; secondly, he says that the doctrine of the law consisted
in *letter*, and was done with ink; thirdly, that it was written on
stones; fourthly, that it was not to last forever, but was temporary and meant to pass away; in the fifth place, once again
he calls it the ministry of condemnation.

To make the antithesis complete, he should have used the
same number of points on the opposite side with regard to the
gospel; but he calls the latter simply the ministry of the Spirit,
and of righteousness, which is to remain valid at all times. In
terms of words, the comparison is not carried through; but as to
the substance of the matter, what he says is adequate, for he has
already said that the Spirit gives life; and further, he has pointed
out that now men's hearts take the place of stones and inner
disposition takes the place of ink.

Let us now examine briefly the characteristics of the law and
the gospel. But let us remember that the point at issue is neither
the whole of the teaching we find in the Law and the Prophets,
nor the experience of the fathers under the Old Testament; but
rather the peculiar function of the ministry of Moses [or the
law]. The law was chiseled upon stones; therefore, its teaching
was one of the letter. This defect of the law had to be corrected
by the gospel, since, the law having been consigned to tablets
of stone, it could not but be breakable. The gospel, therefore, is
a holy and inviolable covenant because under God it was hewed
out by the Spirit. It follows that the law was the ministry of
condemnation and death; for when men were told their duty,
they also heard that anyone who does not satisfy God's justice
is cursed, and ends in sin and death. Therefore, men get
nothing from the law but condemnation, for in the law God
demands his due, but does not confer the power to pay it
properly. The gospel, on the other hand, which regenerates
us and reconciles us with God through the free forgiveness of
sins, is the ministry of righteousness, and consequently, of life
itself.

But now arises the question: If the gospel be to some a deadly
odor of death, and if Christ be the rock of offense and the stone
of stumbling set for the ruin of many, why is it that the law alone
is blamed for what it has in common with the gospel (II Cor.
2:16, Luke 2:34, I Peter 2:8)? If one answers that the gospel
does not work death in itself, or that it is the occasion rather

than the cause of death, since its own nature is to save all men, one does not get rid of the difficulty, because the same is true of the law. Moses himself argued that he set life and death before the people (Deut. 30:15); and Paul also said, in Rom. 7:10, that the law is turned into a source of ruin for us, not because it is evil but because we are wicked. Therefore, since neither the law nor the gospel leads to condemnation in itself, our knot is still with us.

My answer is that, in spite of all this, there is a great difference between the law and the gospel. Even though the gospel is an occasion for condemnation to many, it is rightly regarded as the doctrine of life, because it is the means of regeneration and offers us free reconciliation with God. The law, on the other hand, even though it prescribes the rule of a good life, does not change the heart for a righteous obedience; and in declaring eternal death to sinners, it can do nothing but condemn them. To put it another way, it is the function of the law to uncover the disease; it gives us no hope of its cure. It is the function of the gospel to bring healing to those who are without hope. The law, in so far as it leads men to put their confidence in it, consigns them necessarily to death. The gospel, on the other hand, leads us to Christ and thus opens the gate to life. Thus, in one word, the property of the law by which it kills, even though not essential to it, is permanent and inseparable from it; for, as the apostle says elsewhere, all those who remain under the law are subject to the curse (Gal. 3:10). On the other hand, it is not true of the gospel that it kills always, because in it the righteousness of God is revealed from faith to faith; and, therefore, it is the saving power of God to all those who believe (Rom. 1:16-17).

It remains to consider the last contrast made by the apostle when he says that the law was for a time, and to be abolished, whereas the gospel is for perpetuity. There are many reasons why the ministry of Moses was for a season. Shadows had to cease with the coming of Christ. But the statement applies beyond the shadows, to the Law and the Prophets until John (Matt. 11:13). It means that Christ put an end to the ministry of Moses, in all that was peculiar to it and apart from the gospel. Finally, in Jer. 31:31-32, the Lord bears witness to the weakness of the old covenant because it was not inscribed upon the hearts of men. I interpret the abolition of the law mentioned in this place as referring to the whole of the old covenant in so far as it was opposed to the gospel; and that includes the Law

and the Prophets until John. The context of the present statement requires this interpretation. Paul is not arguing only about
the ceremonies; his point is that the Spirit of God exercises his
energy far more powerfully under the gospel than he did long
ago under the law. . . .

This is no denial of what is said above, but rather a confirmation of it; for Paul means that where the gospel appears, the
glory of the law is extinguished. As the moon and the stars,
which have light enough to illumine the whole earth, disappear
before the splendor of the sun, so also the law, whatever glory
it might have in itself, is as nothing before the refulgence of the
gospel. Hence, it follows that we cannot magnify enough, or
treat with too much reverence, the glory of Christ which shines
in the gospel, as the brightness of the sun shines in its rays. It is
in bad taste, and a foolish profanation of the gospel, when the
power and majesty of the Spirit, which draw the minds and
hearts of men to heaven, are withheld from the people.

*But their minds were blinded: for until this day remaineth the same
veil untaken away in the reading of the old testament; which veil is
done away in Christ. But even unto this day, when Moses is read, the
veil is upon their heart; nevertheless, when it shall turn to the Lord, the
veil shall be taken away. Now the Lord is that Spirit; and where the
Spirit of the Lord is, there is liberty.* II Cor. 3:14-17.

He puts the whole blame upon them [the Jews]; for it was
because of their blindness that they were unable to benefit from
the teaching of the law. . . .

He now gives the reason for their continued blindness in the
midst of light. The law in itself is a source of light: but we enjoy
its brightness only when Christ appears to us in it. The Jews
do all they can to turn their eyes away from Christ: it is therefore not surprising that they see nothing, since they will not
turn to the Sun. This blindness on the part of God's chosen
people, especially since it has lasted so long, should warn us
that we ought to rely upon God's favors toward us, and not be
lifted up with pride. (On this, see Rom. 11:20.) And let the
reason for blindness given in this passage keep us from a contempt of Christ, which exposes us to the awful vengeance of God.
In the meantime, we should learn that there is no light in the
law, or even in the whole Word of God, without Christ who is
the Sun of Righteousness.

But when it shall have turned to the Lord. So far, this passage has
been seriously misunderstood; both the Greek and the Latin

interpreters[4] have thought that it refers to Israel. But Paul is speaking of Moses. He had said that when the Jews read Moses, a veil was thrown over their hearts. Now he continues that as soon as their heart is turned to the Lord, the veil shall be taken away. Who cannot see, as I said, that when he speaks of Moses, he is speaking of the law? Since Christ is the end (or fulfillment) of the law, the Jews ought to have accepted the truth that the law refers them to Christ; when they shut out Christ, they turned the law in another direction. Since in reading the law they wandered aimlessly, the law itself has become to them a complicated thing, like a labyrinth; and it will remain such until it is turned toward its fulfillment, who is Christ. If the Jews seek Christ in the law, God's truth will appear to them clearly; while they continue to seek wisdom without Christ, they shall lose their way in darkness and never arrive at the true meaning of the law. What is said of the law applies to the whole of Scripture: when it is not directed toward Christ as its one aim, it is tortured badly and twisted.

The Lord is the Spirit. This passage also has been interpreted badly, so as to make Paul mean that Christ is of a spiritual essence; people do this by tying it up with John 4:24, where we read *God is a Spirit.* As a matter of fact, this statement has nothing to do with Christ's essence; it simply points out his office. It goes with what Paul said above: namely, that the teaching of the law is literal, not only dead but also a source of death. Conversely, he now calls Christ the Spirit of the law, which means that the law is living and life-giving only in so far as it receives the breath of Christ. When the soul is united with the body, there is a living man, endowed with intelligence and perception, competent for living behavior; take the soul away from the body, and what do you have but a useless corpse, empty of all sensibility?

This verse is of particular value; for it tells us how we are to reconcile the praises with which David commends the law to us (in Ps. 19:7-8: "the law of the Lord converts the soul, enlightens the eyes, and imparts wisdom to babes," and other statements like it) with Paul's statements which apparently contradict them: that the law is the ministry of sin and death, which only kills (II Cor. 3:7). When Christ gives life to the law,

---

[4] When Calvin speaks roundly of Greek and Latin interpreters, he means primarily Chrysostom, Jerome, and Augustine, whose works were continually before him. But he knew many of the other fathers of the ancient church (see Introduction, p. 22).

David's praises apply to it; when Christ is taken away, the law is altogether as Paul describes it. Therefore, Christ is the life of the law.

Where the Spirit of the Lord. Now Paul describes the way Christ gives life to the law, which is, by giving it his Spirit. The meaning of the word *Spirit* here is not the same as it is in the previous verse. There it means soul, and is used as a metaphor for Christ; here, it refers to the Holy Spirit himself, who is the gift of Christ to us. In regenerating us, Christ brings the law itself to life, and reveals himself as the fountain of life. He acts like the human soul, which is the source of all human vitality. Therefore, Christ is (so to speak) the soul of all beings; not as their essence, but by the action of his grace. Of, if you prefer it, Christ is the Spirit because he makes us alive by the vivifying power of his Spirit.

And of his fullness have we all received, grace for grace; for the law was given by Moses, but grace and truth came by Jesus Christ. John 1:16-17.

Now John embarks upon the mission of Christ, which contains the abundance of all blessings, for there is not a thing belonging to our salvation which we need seek elsewhere. God indeed is the fountain of life, and righteousness, and power, and wisdom; but he is a fountain hidden and inaccessible to us. All these blessings are presented to us in Jesus Christ in all fullness, so that we may look for them in him. And he is ready to make them flow upon us, if by faith we build the proper pipeline. In short, in every part of this sentence John makes but one point, namely, that we must not look for any good outside of Christ. First, he makes it clear that we are utterly destitute and empty of all spiritual good. For if Christ himself abounds, it is to fill our emptiness, to relieve our poverty, and to satisfy us who are hungry and thirsty. Secondly, the writer warns us that no sooner do we turn away from Christ than we look in vain for a single drop of good; because it was God's will that every good should reside in him. Therefore, we find men and angels dry, the heaven empty and the earth sterile, when we try to have a part in God's gifts by any means but Christ. In the third place, he assures us that we shall want nothing whatsoever if we draw upon the fullness of Christ, which is in every respect so rich that we shall never be able to drain it off. John includes himself with all men, not because of modesty, but to make it clear that no one is excepted.

There is some doubt as to whether John speaks of mankind in general or only of those who, after Christ's coming in the flesh, have shared more fully in his blessings. It is certain that those who lived under the law drew from the fullness of Christ. But since John distinguishes between the time before the Advent and the time after, he is more probably speaking of the new abundance of good which Christ at his coming brought with him. We know that when Christ appeared in the flesh, the benefits which were enjoyed in a limited way under the law were, so to speak, scattered abroad with a full hand; so that we have more than enough. This does not mean that each and every one of us is superior to Abraham in the grace of the Spirit. I am speaking of the greater extent to which God now distributes his gifts, and of the way and manner in which he does it. John's purpose in emphasizing all men's poverty with regard to the good offered us richly in Christ, was to invite his disciples to him the more persuasively. At the same time, it would not be absurd to extend the meaning of this statement further. In fact, the context itself justifies us in adding that all the fathers, since the beginning of the world, have drawn every good they have enjoyed from Christ. Since Moses gave them the law, they received grace from another hand. But I have already stated the interpretation I prefer: which is that John compares us with the fathers, in order to impress upon us the riches of the gift we have in Christ Jesus.

And grace for grace. Augustine's exposition of this verse is well known.[5] He says that the continued blessings of God, and finally life eternal itself, are not rewards due us because of our merits, but acts of divine generosity with which by grace God rewards what we do and crowns his own gifts to us. All this is intelligently said; but it has nothing to do with this verse. We would get its simple meaning if we took ἀντί in a comparative sense, which would give us the statement: All the graces alike which God showers upon us come to us from the same source (which is Christ). This verse might also be taken to point out that grace is given us for salvation, which is the completion of grace. But I myself agree with those who believe that it refers to the graces which are poured out in Christ, and over us like water upon a dry land. But, even while we receive these graces from Christ, he does not act as God (who is the source), but

[5] The anti-Pelagian writings, *De gratia et libero arbitrio*, ch. 21, and *De correptione et gratia*, ch. 41. See also his *Tractates on the Gospel of John*, No. 3, Sec. 9.

rather as the channel through which the bountiful Father pours
them upon us. So it is that he was anointed for our sake, to
anoint us all with him: wherefore, he was called Christ and we,
Christians.

For the law came by Moses. Here he anticipates a likely objection. The Jews had such a high regard for Moses that they would
admit nothing as true if it differed from his teaching. The
Evangelist, therefore, shows how inferior the ministry of Moses
was to the power of Christ. At the same time, this comparison
sheds no little light on the authority of Christ. Since there was
no deference the Jews did not pay Moses, the Evangelist points
out that what he brought was little when compared with the
grace of Christ.

Another difficulty was that the Jews thought they received
from the law what is not given us except in Christ. Therefore,
the Evangelist contrasts the law with grace and truth, and
implies that both were lacking in the law. *Truth*, in my judgment, indicates a fixed and firm stability in things. By grace I
understand the spiritual fulfillment of the things which the law
contains as mere letter. And these two words may be said to be
figures of speech with the same meaning: namely, that the truth
of the law consists in the grace which was exhibited in Christ.
It does not much matter whether these two words are put
together or separated one from the other, for either way the
sense of the statement is the same. This much is certain: according to John, the law contained the shadowy image of the
spiritual goods which we find in Christ; from which it follows
that when the law is separated from Christ, nothing is left but
empty forms. This is why Paul said that the law is shadows,
Christ the substance (Col. 2:17). But we must not imagine that
the law gives us only falsehood; because even though the law in
itself is dead, Christ himself is the soul of the law and makes it
alive. Still the question here has to do with the power of the
law apart from Christ; and the Evangelist asserts that without
Christ the law is nothing but a shadow, without substance and
without power. This *truth* consists in the fact that through Christ
we obtain a grace which is not available through the law. By
grace in general, I understand the free forgiveness of sins and the
renewal of the heart. With this word John states briefly the
distinction between the Old and the New Testaments (which
was done more fully in Jer. 31:31), and includes in it all that
has to do with spiritual righteousness. But this righteousness
consists of two parts: namely, that God is reconciled to us freely,

not imputing our sins to us; and that he has engraved his law within us and renewed us by his Spirit for obedience to it. It follows that the law is expounded wrongly and falsely when it keeps us to itself and even prevents our access to Christ.

4. EXAMPLES OF EXEGESIS

Then was fulfilled that which was spoken by Jeremy the prophet, saying, In Rama there was a voice heard, lamentation, and weeping, and great mourning, Rachel weeping for her children, and would not be comforted, because they are not. Matt. 2:17–18.

It is certain that the prophet was describing the destruction of the tribe of Benjamin as it occurred in his time (Jer. 31:15). He had already predicted the destruction of Judah, to which had been attached half the tribe of Benjamin. He put this mourning in dead Rachel's mouth by way of personification (prosopopoeia), which is very effective in rousing the feelings. Jeremiah did not use rhetoric merely to embellish his speech. He did it because there was no way to correct the stupidity and hardheartedness of the living, except by calling the dead out of their graves, to weep over the chastisements of God which most people laughed at.

Since the prediction of the prophet had already been fulfilled, Matthew did not take it as a prophecy of what Herod was going to do; rather he meant that with the coming of Christ there was to be a recurrence of the affliction which the Benjamites suffered many centuries before. He wanted to meet an objection which might have troubled and shaken the believers' minds: for how could one hope to be saved by a man because of whom, and at whose very birth, there had been a massacre of infants? It was surely a dark and dreadful omen that the birth of Christ kindled a flaming fire of such fury as we do not meet even in wars of greatest cruelty! But as Jeremiah promises a restoration after the slaughter of the people down to the infants, so Matthew argues that in spite of Herod's wholesale murder, Christ would surely come forth as the Redeemer of the nation. We know that in the same chapter of Jeremiah (31), mourning is followed by tender words of comfort. For immediately after the mournful complaint come the words: "Refrain thy voice from weeping, and thine eyes from tears; for thy work shall be rewarded, and there is hope at the end," etc. Such then was the likeness between the former calamity suffered by the tribe of Benjamin and this latter one [which occurred under Herod]; and they both

were preludes to the restoration of well-being which was soon
to follow.

*And he came and dwelt in a city called Nazareth: that it might be
fulfilled which was spoken by the prophets, He shall be called a Nazarene.*
Matt. 2:23.

Matthew does not derive "Nazarene" from "Nazareth," as
though there were a real and certain and etymological connection between the two words. What we have here is a mere
allusion. *Nazir* means holy and devoted to God, and is otherwise
derived from *nazar*, which means to separate. It is true that the
Hebrews called a certain flower (or rather, the insignia of the
royal diadem) a *nazar*. But there is no doubt that Matthew used
the word as meaning *holy*. We read nowhere of the Nazarenes
as flourishing; but we do read, as in Num. 6:4, that they were
consecrated to God as prescribed by law. We are, therefore, to
understand Matthew's statement as follows: Although it was
fear that drove Joseph to a corner of Galilee, God had a higher
purpose; for Nazareth was ordained to be Christ's home, so
that he might bear the name of Nazarene which was rightly
his.

But it might be asked what prophet gave this name to Christ;
for there is in fact no such testimony in Scripture. Some think
it is enough to answer that Scripture often calls him holy; but
this is a poor solution of the problem. Matthew, as we have
seen, emphasizes the word Nazarene, and by it refers to the
ancient Nazarenes, who were considered especially holy. He as
much as says that the holiness foreshadowed in the Nazarenes,
as selected firstfruits before God, was perfected in the person
of Christ.

But we must still face the question as to where the prophets
gave this name to Christ. Chrysostom,[6] who was unable to un-
ravel the knot, settled the matter by saying that many books of the
prophets have perished. But this is a careless answer. For even
though the Lord punished his ancient people by depriving them
of a part of Scripture, or suppressed those parts which were of
lesser importance, nothing has been lost since the coming of
Christ. People have been misled on this point by a passage in

[6] John Chrysostom (347–407), the bishop of Constantinople, was a man
much after Calvin's heart. He was a powerful preacher who aimed at
reform. He practiced "lucidity and brevity" in his voluminous Biblical
homilies and commentaries. He was a brave critic of the mighty both in
the church and in the state. He made many enemies and ended in exile.

Josephus,[7] where he says that Ezekiel left behind two books. But Josephus may have been referring to Ezekiel's prophecy of the new Temple and new Kingdom, which is obviously distinct from his former prophecies, and amounts to a new book. In any case, we still have safe and sound all the books which were extant in Matthew's time, and they are preserved in good condition. Therefore, somewhere we should come across his citation from the testimony of the prophets.

I think Bucer's judgment with regard to this matter is the best. He thinks we find the reference we need in Judg. 13:5.[8] This verse has to do with Samson, who is called deliverer in so far as he prefigured Christ; and the salvation which came by his hand and ministry was a shadowy prelude to the fullness of salvation which was exhibited to the world in the Son of God. Anything good said about Samson in Scripture must by right be transferred to Christ. If anyone prefers it that way, Christ is the original exemplar, and Samson is the inferior copy (antitype). We must understand that when Samson was invested with the honors due to the person of the Savior, the titles which adorn that high and truly divine office were intended not for him but for Christ. The fathers had only a taste of that grace of redemption which we who are in Christ have received in full.

It is easy to see why Matthew spoke of *prophets* in the plural: The Book of Judges was composed by a number of prophets. But I think that the reference to *the prophets* in this place has a wider significance. For, the patriarch Joseph, who was called a Nazarene by his brothers, was a temporal savior of the church; he was in many respects a type of Christ, and even his living image (Gen. 49:26, Deut. 33:16). God, therefore, intended that the high dignity conferred upon Joseph should have reappeared in the person of Samson, who therefore received the title Nazarene. In all this, it was God's purpose to provide for the training of the faithful: to fix their hearts upon the Redeemer to come, who was set apart from all men, to be the firstborn among many brothers.

---

[7] Flavius Josephus (A.D. 37–95?), Jewish antiquarian and historian, has put all subsequent historians of the Bible in his debt. His two books, *On the Jewish War* and *Jewish Antiquities*, have been "primary sources" for our knowledge of events, places, parties, etc., having to do with the New Testament. Calvin seems to have had his works before him as he dictated his New Testament Commentaries at home.

[8] Bucer's *In sacra quatuor evangelia, enarrationes perpetua*, 1536, on Matt. 2:23.

And they crucified him, and parted his garments, casting lots: that it might be fulfilled which was spoken by the prophet, They parted my garments among them, and upon my vesture did they cast lots. Matt. 27:35.

It is quite certain that it was the custom of the soldiers to divide the spoils of a condemned man among themselves; even though it was perhaps unusual to cast lots for a seamless coat. So, nothing happened to Christ that did not happen to all condemned men. And yet this story deserves utmost attention. The Evangelists present us with a Christ stripped naked of his clothes, to impress upon us that by his nakedness we are covered with riches which adorn us before God. The Son was stripped by God's will, to clothe us with his righteousness and an abundance of all wealth. So it is that whereas before our rags and filth made us unfit for heaven, now we all can appear with God's angels, in his presence, boldly and without fear. Christ himself let the soldiers tear his seamless coat in pieces, like beasts at their prey, to enrich us with the riches of his victory.

Moreover, as Matthew says, this happened in fulfillment of David's prophecy, *They divided my garments among them* (Ps. 22:18). This bitter complaint is a metaphor, and its language is figurative. But as applied to Christ, its meaning is, as we say, literal; for it states a matter of fact. By *garments*, David means his wealth and honor; he means that he had been a prey to his enemies, who had in his own lifetime and under his very eyes despoiled his house of everything he possessed, and gone so far as to ravish his wife. When he writes that his garments were divided by lot, he is using a metaphor to express the cruelty of his enemies.

Since David was an image and foreshadowing of Christ, he was endowed with the Spirit of prophecy, and predicted the sufferings of Christ. We must not forget that when the soldiers robbed Christ of his garment, they did this outrage according to signs and tokens indicated a long time before. When we see this, we are no longer troubled by the scandal Christ's nakedness causes to the carnal mind. We now understand that he suffered everything rightly and properly as the Redeemer, and as prophesied and declared by the Spirit.

II

The Knowledge of God

THE TEXT

In the year that king Uzziah died I saw also the Lord sitting upon a throne, high and lifted up, and his train filled the temple. Above it stood the seraphims: each one had six wings; with twain he covered his face, and with twain he covered his feet, and with twain he did fly. And one cried unto another, and said, Holy, holy, holy, is the Lord of hosts: the whole earth is full of his glory. And the posts of the door moved at the voice of him that cried, and the house was filled with smoke. Then said I, Woe is me! for I am undone; because I am a man of unclean lips, and I dwell in the midst of a people of unclean lips: for mine eyes have seen the King, the Lord of hosts. Isa. 6: 1–5.

We may ask how Isaiah could see God who is spirit and is therefore not visible to bodily eyes. Since the minds of men are incapable of mounting to the infinite height of God, how can man apprehend God under any visible form? But we must realize that whenever God revealed himself to be seen by the fathers, he never appeared as he is in himself but as he could be understood by human minds. Since men crawl on the ground, or at least dwell far below the heavens, there is no absurdity in the statement that God descends to them in order to turn upon them, as though he used a mirror, some reflected rays of his glory. Therefore Isaiah was shown a form of a kind which enabled him with his own understanding to taste the inconceivable majesty of God. This is the reason that he attributes a throne, a robe, and a bodily appearance to God.

From this passage we may derive the valuable assurance that whenever God gives any sign whatever of his presence he is in truth present with us. He does not play a game with such meaningless shapes as men use when they impiously distort him with their inventions. Since the vision was in no way a false

symbol of the presence of God, Isaiah is right in asserting that
he saw God. Similarly when John is said to have seen the Holy
Spirit in the form of a dove, the name *Spirit* is transferred to the
symbol and there is nothing false in the statement. John did
not indeed see the essence of the Spirit, but he did have certain,
clear, and unambiguous evidence that the Spirit of God dwelt
in Christ.

In the second place we may ask, Who was that Lord? John
(ch. 12:41) teaches that he was Christ; and this is true because
God never revealed himself to the fathers except in his eternal
Word, his only-begotten Son. Yet, in my judgment, it is wrong
to restrict this vision to the person of Christ, since the prophecy
refers rather to God without any differentiation. Nor does the
use of the name *'adonai* (Lord), which may seem more appropriate to Christ, support the restriction, for it is often used
simply for God. Here then God is meant. Yet it is correct to
say that Isaiah saw the glory of Christ, because Christ was the
image of the invisible God.

Sitting upon a throne the prophet could have found no better
image than that of a judge to impress the Jews with the majesty
of God. And later we shall hear the severe sentence which the
Lord pronounces from his judgment seat. But we should not
suppose that the prophet deliberated about the way in which he
should depict God. He described faithfully the form which was
disclosed and exhibited to him.

We may wonder whether the prophet was led into the Temple, or whether the whole vision appeared to him in his sleep.
Many arguments are offered on both sides, but they leave us
uncertain. If he was not in the Temple, the revelation could
have been given him at home or in a field, where other prophets
received their visions.

His extreme parts (extrema) filled the temple. Almost all interpret
as "the fringes of his garments," although the word may equally
well refer to the edges of the throne, to emphasize its great size,
which was as large as the whole Temple. The purpose of the
statement in any case is to attribute to God a grandeur beyond
any human form.

The vision had the more authority because it appeared in
the Temple. God had promised that he would meet his people
there, and the people expected his voice to come from there, as
Solomon had said at the dedication. Therefore, in order that
the people might know that this vision came from the God
whom they daily invoked, in whom they were boasting without

warrant, it was granted to the prophet in the Temple. For thus no little assurance was given them that this was not the speech of any mortal man but a heavenly oracle pronounced by the God whose name they used so presumptuously whenever they wished to obtain something more for themselves. . . . The prophetic word was harsh and hateful, and it greatly needed confirmation. So it is not unusual for the prophets to say that God speaks from his Temple, his sanctuary.

Seraphim. After the statement that God had appeared to him, full of majesty and glory, he adds that angels were standing near God; and he calls them *seraphim* because of their fiery zeal. Although the derivation of this word [from *saraph, burn*] is known, various explanations of it are offered. Some say they are called *seraphim* because they burn with the love of God; others, because they are swift like fire; others, because they shine. Whatever may be the reason, the description shows us the radiant splendor and the boundless majesty of God, so that we learn to understand and hold in reverence his matchless and immeasurable glory.

Many think there were two seraphim, corresponding to the two cherubim above the Ark of the Covenant. I like this idea, but I do not dare to affirm what is not stated in the text. However, in general, descriptions like this one use symbols which were familiar and well known to religious people; and this may well be the case with this prophecy. So I accept the guess of two as probable, leaving open the possibility of more; for Daniel saw not two angels but myriads.

Six wings. This figure has a meaning: the wings so placed represent a mystery which God did not wish left wholly hidden.

The two wings with which the angels fly represent simply the swiftness and readiness with which they carry out God's commands. Since this analogy is very obvious, only contentious men will raise objections.

The two wings with which they covered their faces show clearly enough that not even angels can endure the full glory of God, and so they shade their eyes as we do when we wish to look at the sun. But if angels cannot endure God's majesty, how great is the rashness of men who try to penetrate it! Let us learn then that we ought to limit our inquiries to what is within our capacity and fitting for us, so that our understanding may soberly and modestly taste what is beyond our powers. The angels do not cover their faces so completely that they have no joy in the sight of God (and they can still see to fly without deviating from their course). So we also should behold God, but only so far as our nature can bear.

It is more difficult to interpret the two lower wings. Some think the feet of the angels were covered so as not to touch the earth and become unclean as human feet do. For whenever we walk we pick up dirt and filth, and so long as we wander on earth we are always contracting some contagion or other. The believing are then warned that they will have no dealings with angels until they have risen and are no longer tied to earth. Some give this explanation, but I agree more with others who think that the purpose of these wings is the opposite of the upper ones. As with the upper wings the angels cover their faces lest they be annihilated by the splendor of God, so also they have the lower wings by which they themselves are hidden from our sight. But if it is true that the faint beams of divine glory shining out from the angels cannot be seen by us without destroying us, how can we behold God's most glorious and splendid majesty which overwhelms all sense? Let men learn that since they cannot even look at the angels, they are very far from the perfect knowledge of God. This seems to me the better interpretation, but I do not exclude the others.

They were crying. When we read that the angels are busy proclaiming the glory of God, we know that their example is presented for our imitation. For the holiest service of all that we can offer God is to occupy ourselves in praising his name. Such adoration links us with the angels, so that even while we sojourn on the earth we are yet joined to the citizens of heaven and somewhat resemble them. But if there is to be true harmony between all the chords of the angels and our own, we must strive earnestly that there may be a correspondence between the praise of God with our tongues and all the actions of our lives. This aim will be achieved at the last if we keep our eyes fixed as steadily as possible on the glory of God.

Holy, holy, holy. The ancients used this passage when they wished to prove against the Arians that there are three persons in the one divine essence. I do not reject this interpretation, although if I were dealing with heretics I should prefer to use clearer evidence. . . . And although I do not doubt that the one God in three Persons is here meant by the angels (for certainly God cannot be praised without honoring Father, Son, and Holy Spirit together), yet I think clearer passages should be used in defending our faith, lest we incur the ridicule of heretics. Surely the repetition proves rather the unwearied zeal of the seraphim;

the prophet meant that the angelic song has no end, for God's holiness furnishes to them and to us an inexhaustible theme.

The whole earth is full. The fullness could refer to the fruits and the living creatures with which God so abundantly fills the earth, and the meaning would then be that the glory of God shines out in the enticing variety of the beauty of the earth, which is evidence of his Fatherly love. But a simpler and truer interpretation is that the glory of God fills the whole world or extends to all the quarters of the earth. Here, in my judgment, is an implied contradiction to the foolish self-conceit of the Jews who thought that the glory of God did not exist apart from them, and wished to confine it to the Temple. This latter meaning is consistent with the prophecy of the destruction of the Jews which follows. For access to the church of God was open to the Gentiles who were to take the place left empty by the Jews.

And the posts shook. This tremor is a sign that it was not a human voice which the prophet heard. For no human voice can shake foundations and pillars. God did not intend that the authority of his words should have been recognized by the prophet alone; he meant it to be sanctified to all posterity, for all generations, and without ceasing. By this trembling we are led to realize that this voice of God is valid for us today; when he speaks we tremble. For if inanimate objects and dumb creatures are shaken by it, what must we do, who have feeling, smell, taste, and understanding, in order to obey his word devoutly and reverently?

Woe is me: for mine eyes have seen. The prophet's reaction is not surprising. The whole carnal man must be reduced to nothingness that he may be renewed by God. For how does it happen that men live, or rather think they live, and are puffed up with vain confidence in their shrewdness and power? Only because they do not know God. Before he reveals himself to us we think ourselves to be not men, but rather gods. But when the Lord appears to us, then we begin to sense and realize what sort of beings we are. Humility arises from and consists in this: that man claim nothing more for himself and depend wholly on God.

This passage and others like it must be carefully considered. It was customary for the ancients, whenever they saw God, to speak in this way: "I am undone. It's all up with me." Before our minds seriously approach God, our life is an empty sham. We walk in shadows in which it is hard to distinguish true from false. But when we come into light, the difference is clear and easy to know. When God comes to us, he brings light with him, and we see our emptiness. . . . But does the sight of God really bring death to men? It seems absurd that the sight or nearness of God should destroy life of which he is origin and giver. I answer that it does this contingently, since death results from our fault and not from the nature of God. For death is already in us, but we do not perceive it except when it is contrasted with the life of God. This truth the prophet clearly and certainly knows.

Thus saith the Lord, Let not the wise man glory in his wisdom, neither let the mighty man glory in his might, let not the rich man glory in his riches. But let him that glorieth glory in this, that he understandeth and knoweth me, that I am the Lord which exercise loving-kindness, judgment and righteousness, in the earth: for in these things I delight, saith the Lord. Jer. 9:23–24.

From the second part of this passage we learn that men are stripped of all their glory, not to leave them groveling in their own shame, but to clothe them with another that is better. For God does not take pleasure in men's shame. But since men claim for themselves more than is good for them, and even intoxicate themselves with self-flattery, God takes away from them their false glory. After they have learned that whatever they think they possess, either by nature, or their own efforts, or through other creatures, is a mere phantom, then they may seek true glory.

In understanding and knowing me. Although the prophet means the same thing by both verbs, he does not use the two without a reason. When men belittle the knowledge of God, they must be warned that to know God is the sum of perfect wisdom. Jeremiah wishes to correct a perverse error under which the whole world suffers. Today all sorts of subjects are eagerly pursued; but the knowledge of God is neglected. We see with what zeal everyone follows his own interests, while scarcely one man in a hundred deigns to devote half an hour a day to the knowledge of God. And from pride arises men's second mistake: they think the knowledge of God to be a common possession. So we see why the prophet used two verbs to name the same thing: he wanted to arouse greater zeal in men, since he saw that all were so lazy in the pursuit of this knowledge. Yet to know God is man's chief end, and justifies his existence. Even if a hundred lives were ours, this one aim would be sufficient for them all. But, as I said, men despise the thing which should be preferred above all else.

Afterwards he adds *that I am the Lord doing mercy and judgment and justice*. God wishes to be so known. He alone is exalted; yet he comes down, so to speak, within our sight. The words which follow must be carefully considered. If God had said only, *that I am the Lord*, this would have been a complete doctrine; but it would not have been sufficiently clear ... for men would think it enough to confess that there is one God. Therefore we must carefully note these words: God does *mercy, judgment, and justice*. We see today among the papists the name of God rashly flaunted aloft. There is no one of them who will not reiterate again and again that he worships God. But meanwhile they all profane the name of God. They rob God of his honor and distribute the spoil to the dead. This passage shows that the name of God by itself is of no importance when it is emptied of its true content.

The true knowledge of God is not only to know him as the maker of the world, but also to be persuaded that the world is directed by him, and further to know the nature of that direction. He does mercy and judgment and justice.

Moreover, the first thing to know about God is that he is kind and forbearing. For without God's forbearance, what would become of us? It is true and right that the knowledge of God should begin with the assurance that he is merciful towards us. For what use would it be to us to know that God is just unless we already know his mercy and his free kindness? But we know God by also knowing ourselves, for these two things are bound together; and if anyone scrutinizes himself, what will he find but reason for despair? As often as the thought of God's justice comes into our minds, we should shudder and despair. Truly all would flee from God unless he attract them by the sweetness of his grace. Therefore it is with good reason that Jeremiah, when he ordered men to glory in the knowledge of God, gave the highest place to God's compassion, and then added judgment and justice.

The Lord God is truth (Those who translate *God of truth* do not attend to the syntax of the Hebrew, for that would need to read *'elohē 'emeth*); *God himself is life and the king of the ages*. Jer. 10:10 (Calvin's wording).

Here the prophet exalts and triumphs in God's name, and speaks of him as having overthrown and destroyed the falsehoods of the nations. He exposes their gross errors and shows up the wisdom of the world as absolutely worthless, because they stupefy themselves with [the worship of] wood and stone.

He exalts the glory of God magnificently, by saying: *For the Lord is God*; that is, the nations worship their gods by telling fables about their powers and falsely inventing many miracles. For, when we examine everything honestly, it becomes certain that there is only one God; and all the gods of the nations vanish of themselves. This is what the prophet means: God is sufficient to destroy all the falsehoods of the nations. When his majesty comes forth, its splendor is such that all others which receive the admiration of the world are reduced to nothingness. After this, he speaks of *truth*; then he opposes truth with vanity. Before he had said that wood is vanity; now he says, *Eternal God is truth*; which means that He has no need to take on colors. The idols of the nations are painted, dressed up, decorated; but all such images are empty show. *Jehovah*, on the other hand, is Lord; that is, he does not in any way change; he desires nothing which he does not possess, and his own perfection carries all authority.

God, then, *is truth*; and *God is life*. After the prophet has declared that in the essence of the one God there is true and substantial glory, he adds another certitude which he derives from the experience of men: *God is life*. For although God is in himself incomprehensible to us, he not only sets his glory before our eyes, but even offers himself to our touch, as Paul says (Acts 14:17). For Paul knew that God can be found by touch, even by men who are blind. Although the blind are deprived of sight, yet when they walk around a hall, they find the way out by touch, or they locate by touch the door out of a room, and when they wish to go in again they find the door. And Paul says that we have no need to go outside of ourselves, for whoever searches himself will find God within. For, *in him we live, move, and exist* (Acts 17:28). Hence if we raise the objection that God is beyond our comprehension, and that we cannot rise to the height of his glory, yet certainly *life* is in us. If life is in us, then so is evidence for God. Who is foolish enough to say that he lives of himself? Since men do not create their own life but obtain life precariously from another, it follows that God dwells in them.

Now the prophet, after he has spoken of the essence of God, comes down to his activity. And surely this is the true knowledge of God—not to speculate in the air as the philosophers do when they argue, but to know by experience that there is one God. How do we know? Because we exist; not, strictly, *exist*, but *subsist* (*live in*). And if we *live in*, truly that in which we live must be taken into account. And, to speak accurately, our *subsisting* will be found to be within the one God. Whence it follows that the life of man is an excellent index to the only God.

God therefore *is life* and *the king of the ages*. First the earth was founded, and since then the years follow one another; in this cycle, there is great variation from one year to another yet there is regular and right order in their procession. Who will not recognize the glory of God in this ordering of the world? Therefore the prophet called God *king of the ages*.

And ye shall know that I am the Lord, when I have wrought with you for my name's sake, not according to your wicked ways, nor according to your corrupt doings, O ye house of Israel, saith the Lord God. Ezek. 20:44.

Here God declares that his glory will be especially manifest when, solely for his name's sake, he has compassion freely upon the desperate and lost. And Paul, in the first chapter of Ephesians, especially praises God's gracious kindness when he calls the compassion with which God honors his elect, the glory of God κατ' ἐξοχην.[1]

Now the glory of God includes more than his compassion. *As thy name, so is thy praise through all the countries of the earth* (Ps. 48:10). God deserves no less to be glorified when he destroys the wicked than when he takes pity on his people. But Paul calls God's especial glory the undeserved kindness with which he embraces his chosen whom he has adopted. So God says here, *You will know that I am the Lord when I deal with you for my name's sake, and not according to your crimes.*

Moreover, since God wishes his glory to shine pre-eminently in his free mercy, we must conclude that those who obscure his compassion or minimize it, or attempt to reduce its greatness to nothing, are the most hardened and open enemies of his glory.

And we know that the teaching of the papacy aims in that direction. For in it, God's free kindness lies buried, or is hidden in a fog, or has wholly vanished. For they set forth *merits* of various sorts which they oppose to God's grace. And they

---

[1] The phrase κατ' ἐξοχην occurs in the New Testament only once, Acts 25:23, but the sense agrees with the emphasis in Eph., ch. 1. This is one example among many to prove that Calvin relied largely on his prodigious memory to provide him with the material needed for his Commentaries. The mistake here illustrates both the extraordinary range of his memory and its occasional fallibility.

divide merits into *preparations*, good works by which they gain God's favor; and *satisfactions*, by which they escape the penalties they would otherwise pay; and finally they add the *interposition* of the saints (as they call them). They invent for themselves a host of patrons and then devise countless other things for no other purpose than to keep the glory of God from being seen by men, or at most to allow only a few sparks to glow dimly. When we see the whole papal organization moving in this direction, we know that they are openly opposing God's glory, and that all who defend those abominations are worse than sworn enemies of God's glory.

As for ourselves, let us learn that God cannot be known as Savior unless we accept from him what is essential to our salvation. For if we wish to keep accounts of what we give and what we receive, or to make any claim whatever, we reduce his glory. And so far as in us lies, we throw away the inestimable privilege which the prophet here extols.

Therefore let us strive to know God through this Word. He deals with us according to his great mercy and compassion, that is, *for his name's sake*, and not according to our wrongdoing. But if these words were spoken to the ancient people because they had returned to the Land of Canaan, how much more today, when the Kingdom of Heaven lies open, God's free kindness deserves to be praised! Today, when he openly calls us to himself, to heaven, to the hope of the blessed immortality which is given us through Christ!

[This was Calvin's last lecture. His closing prayer was:]

Grant, Almighty God, since we have already entered in hope upon the threshold of our eternal inheritance, and know that there is a mansion for us in heaven since Christ, our head and the first fruits of our salvation, has been received there, grant that we may proceed more and more in the way of thy holy calling until at length we reach the goal, and so enjoy that eternal glory of which thou givest us a taste in this world by the same Christ, our Lord. Amen.

And he built there an altar, and he called the place El Beth-el. . . . *And God went up from him in the place where he talked with him.* Gen. 35:7, 13.

Now we know why the holy fathers had to have their own altar, distinct from those of other nations. It was to bear witness that they worshiped not the various gods who were recognized everywhere in the world, but a God of their own.

For although God is worshiped in the heart, yet external confession is the inseparable accompaniment of faith. And there is no one who does not know how helpful it is to us to be roused to the worship of God by external aids.

If anyone objects that this altar looked no different from the others, I answer that the actual difference was very great. Others built altars, rashly and with thoughtless zeal, to unknown gods. Jacob bound himself always to the Word of God. No altar is legitimate unless it is consecrated by God's Word. Jacob's worship excelled that of others simply because he did nothing without the command of God.

In calling the place *God of Bethel*, he may seem to be too bold; and yet the faith of the holy man is praiseworthy at this point also, and that rightly, since he keeps himself within the limits set by God. The papists are stupid when they claim to honor humility by exhibiting dull moderation. Humility deserves praise truly when it does not seek to know more than the Lord permits. But when he descends to us, adapting himself to us and prattling to us, he wishes us also to prattle back to him. And true wisdom is to embrace God exactly as he adapts himself to our little measure. Thus Jacob does not dispute with learned arguments about God's essence, but according to the oracle he has received he brings God near and makes him accessible to himself. Because he opens his mind to the revelation his prattling and his simplicity are, as I said, pleasing to God.

Today, when the knowledge of God shines clearer, and when God in the gospel has undertaken the role of nurse, let us learn to yield our minds to him. Let us remember that he came down to us to raise us up to him. He does not adopt an earthly fashion of speech to keep us at a distance from heaven, but rather as a means of raising us up to heaven.

Meanwhile we must keep to this rule of interpreting [Jacob's action]: since the altar was commanded by a heavenly oracle, the building of it was truly and duly a work of faith. Where the living voice of God does not sound, pomp and ceremony, however elaborately observed, are like empty phantoms. So, we should see that papacy is so much wind.

God's *ascent* is like his descent. For God who fills heaven and earth does not change location. He is said to come down to us when he shows us a sign of his presence suited to our littleness. He *ascended from* Jacob when he disappeared from his sight or when the vision ended.

By this way of speaking, God shows us the value of his Word

which is always near us, as witness to his grace. Because of the great distance between us and his heavenly glory, he himself came down to us through the Word. This he did wholly and finally in the person of Christ; and Christ by his ascent into heaven has so elevated our faith that by the power of his Spirit he dwells always with us.

And the light shineth in darkness: and the darkness comprehended it not. John 1:5.

It may be objected that Scripture in many places calls men blind, and that the blindness to which they are condemned is a matter of common knowledge—that all men's reasoning is a miserable business and comes to nothing. Where do all the labyrinths of error in the world come from [the objector will continue], if not from the fact that when men follow their own minds they land in vanity and lies? So long as men are without the light, the knowledge of Christ's divinity, mentioned above by the Evangelist, is extinct among them.

The Evangelist anticipates this objection, and cautions us first that we must not judge the light given to man in the beginning by his present condition, because in man's present corrupted and degenerate nature, light has been turned into darkness. Nevertheless, he denies emphatically that the light of intelligence is entirely extinct, because some sparkling bits of light keep darting out of the deep and heavy darkness of the human mind.

And the darkness comprehended it not. Even though, through the feeble bit of light left in men, the Son of God has always invited them to himself, the Evangelist tells us that this has not done any good, because "they saw but did not see." After man was alienated from God, his mind was oppressed by such ignorance that any light left in him was quenched and useless. This is proven daily by our experience. Still, even those who are not regenerated by the Spirit of God enjoy some rationality; which shows that man was made not only to breathe but also to understand. But it is none the less true that men do not come to God by way of their own reason; neither do they in this way get near to him, because all their intelligence is but vanity. Whence it follows that the salvation of men is hopeless unless God come to their aid with a new help. For even while the Son of God pours out his light upon them, they are so dull that they do not know the source of it; on the contrary, carried away by their own sickly and depraved imaginations, they only become insane.

The chief parts of the light which remain in our corrupt natures are two: first, everyone has a certain seed of religion implanted in him; and secondly, every man's conscience is capable of distinguishing good from evil. But then, what happens except that religion degenerates into a thousand chimeras of superstition; and consciences pervert every act of judgment, so that one cannot tell vice from virtue? In short, natural reason can never guide men to Christ. Even though prudence teaches men to regulate their lives, and though they are born capable of the arts and sciences, the whole thing vanishes and leaves nothing behind.

Further, it ought to be clear that the Evangelist is speaking only of man's natural endowments, and does not touch upon regenerating grace. The Son of God possesses two distinct powers: the first is known from the structure of the world and the order of nature; the second is the power by which he renews and restores our fallen nature. Since he is the eternal Word of God, the world was created by him and it is by his power that all retain the life they have received. By him also, man was adorned with the gift of the singular imprint of intelligence; and although by his defection he lost the light of intelligence, he still sees and understands, so that what he has naturally by the grace of the Son of God is not completely abolished. But since he has darkened the light which he retains by his stupidity and wickedness, it is necessary that the Son of God take on a new office, that of mediator, and restore the ruined man by the Spirit of regeneration. Therefore, those who confuse the light of which the Evangelist speaks with the gospel and the doctrine which deals with our salvation, philosophize absurdly and in an irrelevant manner.

That was the true Light, which lighteth every man that cometh into the world. He was in the world, and the world was made by him, and the world knew him not. John 1:9-10.

The true light here is not opposed to the false. The Evangelist meant to distinguish Christ from all others, so that no one would think He has the light in common with men and angels. The distinction is made to point out that whatever is bright in heaven and on earth derives its splendor from another; Christ on the other hand is himself light, and his brightness is his own, filling the whole world with his radiance; and there is no other source or cause of light. He is called the true light because it is his nature to illumine.

Which lighteth every man. The Evangelist insists on this chiefly because he wants to base his teaching that Christ is the light upon the effects which he produces in us and in our experience. He might have argued more subtly by saying that since Christ is the eternal light, his radiance is inborn and not derived from another. But he turns our attention to our common experience. The argument is that since Christ makes all of us to share in his light, we should honor him alone as the *Light.*

Now this passage is usually explained in two ways. Some restrict *every man* to those who, having been regenerated by the Spirit, partake of the life-giving light. Augustine gives the example of a schoolmaster who, if he has the only school in a town, is said to be everybody's teacher, even though many may not go to his school. Some people understand the statement that Christ enlightens everyone in the sense that no one can boast of having received the grace of the light of life otherwise than from him. But since the Evangelist speaks in general of all those who have come into the world, the next explanation pleases me better: namely, that rays from this light are diffused in all of mankind, as I have already said. We know that men, above all other living beings, have the singular superiority of having been endowed with reason and intelligence, and that they have engraved in their consciences the ability to discriminate between right and wrong. There is therefore no one who is without some intuition of the eternal light. But there are fanatics who are somehow insane enough to twist and torture this passage, and to infer from it that the grace of illumination is offered equally to all. But let us remember that this statement has to do with the common light of nature which is far inferior to faith. For no man will ever, with all the sharpness and perspicacity of his mind, penetrate to the Kingdom of God. It is the Spirit of God alone who opens the gate of heaven to the elect. Further, let us remember that the light of reason which God gave men is obscured by sin; so that in the deep darkness of dreadful ignorance and the abyss of errors there are hardly any sparks which are not utterly put out.

He was in the world. He accuses men of ingratitude because they had so blinded themselves as not to know the cause of the light they enjoyed. This is true of every age. For even before Christ appeared in the flesh, he displayed his power everywhere. Therefore those daily effects he produces ought to shake people out of their torpor. What is more absurd than to draw water from a running river, and not to think of the fountain from which the river flows? Wherefore, there is no just excuse for the world's ignorance of Christ before he appeared in the flesh; it was due to their apathy and wickedness, because he has always been present among them with his power. In short, Christ was at no time so absent from the world that men might not have been aroused by his light and have raised their eyes to him. It follows that the blame is theirs.

Let not your heart be troubled: Ye believe in God, believe also in me. John 14:1.

This might be taken as imperative: "Believe in God, and also believe in me." But the other reading is more exact, and has been more generally accepted, as I have pointed out. Here we find that the way to stand fast is to let our faith rest in Christ and to recognize that he is all ready to come to our help with outstretched arms. One might wonder, however, why he puts faith in God first. Maybe he should have told his disciples that having believed in him, they should believe in God: for Christ is the very image of the Father, and we should fix our eyes first on him. Besides, he descended to us so that our faith, starting with him, might ascend to the Father. But Christ has something else in mind. All confess that we ought to believe in God. This is a fixed axiom to which all subscribe without controversy. Yet there is hardly one in a hundred who really believes it; not so much because the sheer majesty of God is too distant from us, but because Satan puts every kind of cloud between us and God, so as to keep us from the vision of God. So it is that our faith vanishes even while it seeks our God in his heavenly glory and inaccessible light. Our own flesh comes up spontaneously with a thousand fancies which turn us away from a right apprehension of God.

Christ therefore presents himself to us as the proper object of our faith. If we direct our faith to him, it will immediately find certainty and rest. He is Immanuel, who responds within us to our inquiring faith. It is a basic article of our faith that if we do not wish to go around and around endlessly, we must direct our faith to Christ alone. If our faith is not to waver in the midst of temptations, it must be fixed on him. And this is the evidence of faith that we never allow ourselves to be torn away from Christ and the promises we have in him. The papal theologians dispute, or rather chatter a great deal, about the object of faith; but they leave Christ out, and mention only God. Those whose knowledge comes from their writings must needs waver with the least breath of a breeze. Proud men are ashamed of the lowliness of Christ; therefore they fly to the incomprehensible deity of God. But faith seeks to attain heaven only by submission to Christ, whose countenance seems to reveal a lowly God; and it finds no stability unless it find support in the weakness of Christ.

If ye had known me, ye should have known my Father also; and henceforth ye know him, and have seen him. John 14:7.

This confirms what we have already said; namely, that the curiosity by which people, not content with Christ, seek God in devious byways is at once stupid and harmful. They admit that there is nothing better than the knowledge of God. But when he is near them and speaks to them as a friend, they wander around looking high and low, and search for him beyond the clouds because they are too proud to see him nearby. Christ therefore reproaches his disciples because they do not know that God has been revealed to them fully in him. "I see," he says, "that so far you have not known me rightly because you have not seen the living image of God in me."

And henceforth. He adds this not only to tone down his reproach, but also to accuse them of ingratitude and apathy because they have not done justice to the Father's gift through him. He says it in praise of his teaching rather than of their faith. What he means, therefore, is that they would even now see God, if they would only open their eyes. But by *"see,"* he means the certainty of faith.

Then they said unto him, Where is thy Father? Jesus answered, Ye neither know me, nor my Father: if ye had known me, ye should have known my Father also. John 8:19.

Instead of doing them the honor of a direct reply, he reproaches them briefly for their ignorance and their complacency. They asked about the Father; and yet, here was the Son before their eyes, and they, seeing, did not see. It was, therefore, the just punishment of their pride and impious ingratitude that when they despised the Son of God who was there for everyone to see, they had no access to the Father. How can any mortal being rise to the height of God except he be raised there by the Son's own hand? Moreover, God has lowered himself in Christ to the mean condition of man, so as to stretch out his hand to him; and do not those who reject God's approach to them deserve to be excluded of heaven?

Let us then know that it was said to us all: anyone who does not begin his way to God with Christ, must wander, as it were, in a labyrinth. It is not for nothing that, as we read elsewhere, he is called the image of the Father. Besides, all those who storm heaven like giants, without Christ's help, are deprived of any right knowledge of God. Anyone, on the other hand, who turns his mind and all his senses to Christ is led directly to the Father. The Apostle therefore is not deceiving us when he says that in the mirror of the gospel we see God clearly in the person of Christ (II Cor. 3:18). And certainly the priceless reward of the obedience of faith is that a man who humbles himself before Christ rises above all heavens and penetrates the mysteries which the angels witness and adore.

Now they have known that all things whatsoever thou hast given me are of thee. For I have given unto them the words which thou gavest me, and they have received them, and have known surely that I come out from thee, and they have believed that thou didst send me. John 17:7–8.

Here we are told the chief thing about faith: which is, so to believe in Christ that our belief rests not in an apprehension of the flesh, but rather in the contemplation of his divine power. When he says, "*They knew whatever thou gavest me as from thee,*" he means that believers recognize all they have as divine and from heaven. And certainly, unless we apprehend God in Christ, we are bound to be always wavering.

He now declares that men have this knowledge when they receive what he teaches them. But anyone who thinks that his doctrine is from man, or that it is from this earth, will not acknowledge that its author is God. Hence he says, *The words which thou gavest me, I gave them.* And when he says that he taught as he received from God, he speaks as the mediator or the servant of God. He refers to God as his Father because he is in the lowly state of the flesh, and has concealed his divine majesty under the form of a servant. At the same time, we must hold on to John's initial testimony that, in so far as Christ was the eternal Word of God, he had always been one God with the Father. The point here, therefore, is that Christ was to his disciples a faithful witness to the Father; that, since the Father himself had spoken in the Son, their faith had its foundation in the sole truth of God. Moreover, he points out that if they accepted his words, it is because he has given them an effective revelation of the name of the Father by the power of the Spirit.

And have known surely. He repeats with other words what he has already touched upon. The statement that Christ came from the Father and was sent by him means the same thing as that whatever he has is from the Father. In short, faith ought to look at Christ rightly, not to know him in his flesh and humiliation, but to rise to a knowledge of his divine power; for thus it becomes established that he has in himself God and whatever is God's. It is important to notice that in the former clause the Evangelist uses the word *to know*. In the latter, *to believe* takes its place. We are thus warned that we can know nothing of God rightly except by faith. But there is such certainty in faith as to justify our calling it knowledge.

But if I do, though ye believe not me, believe the works; that ye may know, and believe, that the Father is in me, and I in him. John 10:38.

He puts faith after knowledge, as though it were of a lower order, because he has to do with unbelieving and wrongheaded men, who will not yield unless they are overcome and forced by experience. Such rebels insist that they must know before they believe. And our God indulges us to the extent of preparing us for faith through a knowledge of his works. However, true knowledge of God and of the secret of his wisdom comes from faith, because the obedience of faith opens to us the gate of the Kingdom of Heaven.

And this is life eternal, that they might know thee the only true God, and Jesus Christ, whom thou hast sent. John 17:3.

He now enlightens the elect in the true knowledge of God; and in so doing, he declares the way in which we receive life. He does not here deal with the ultimate enjoyment of life which is our hope, but rather with the way men attain life. If we are to understand this statement rightly, we must first realize that unless God, who alone is life, illumine us, we are all dead. Where, therefore, he has shone, we possess him by faith; and at the same time enter into the possession of life. This is why the knowledge of him is truly and properly said to be saving. Almost every word of Christ in this place is weighty. We are not concerned here with just any kind of knowledge of God, but with the knowledge which transforms us into the image of God, and the beginning and the end of it is faith; rather it is the same as that faith by which, ingrafted into the body of Christ, we are made to partake of the divine adoption and are made heirs of heaven.

And Jesus answered and said unto him, Verily, verily I say unto

thee, except a man be born again, he cannot see the kingdom of God.
John 3: 3.

By this statement, he means, "So long as you lack what is
first in God's Kingdom, it does not impress me that you call me
Master. For the first step into the Kingdom of God is that you
become a new man." This sentence is so weighty that we must
look into each part of it separately. To see the Kingdom of God
is to enter it, as we shall soon see from the context. But those
who identify the Kingdom of God with heaven are mistaken;
the Kingdom means rather the spiritual life, which begins in
this life by faith, and in which we grow daily as we progress in
a constant faith. This statement means that no one truly belongs
to the church and is counted among God's children, unless he
first becomes a new man. This verse shows briefly how one
begins the Christian life. It also teaches us that we are born
exiles and complete strangers to the Kingdom of God and that
we are perpetually at war with it, until he makes us other than
we are by a new birth. This verse therefore applies universally
to the whole human race. If Christ had said to one man or to a
few that they could not enter heaven except by being born
again, we might imagine that he referred only to certain people.
But this is not the case. He was speaking of all men, without
excepting any. The wording conveys no impression of limita-
tion. It is a universal statement which means that all those
who are not born again, cannot enter the Kingdom of
God.

Moreover, being born again means not the improvement of
a part but the renewal of the whole of one's nature. It follows
that there is nothing in us that is not corrupted. If we must be
renewed part and whole, it follows that this corruption is spread
throughout our being. Of this we shall soon speak more fully.
Erasmus, following Cyril's[2] opinion, has translated the adverb
ἄνωθεν incorrectly as "from above." I confess that the meaning
of this word in Greek is unclear. But we must remember that
Christ spoke with Nicodemus in Hebrew; and in Hebrew, this
word is not ambiguous. There was no reason why Nicodemus
should have been deceived and shrunk from the prospect of a
physical second birth. Therefore, he understood Christ's words

---

[2] Cyril of Jerusalem (ca. 315–386) tried vainly to keep to a middle way
in the Arian controversy. After a career of conflict, of exile and return, he
enjoyed four years of peace until his death. He is most famous for his
Catechetical Lectures to the Illumined (The Library of Christian Classics, The
Westminster Press, Vol. IV). See Lecture II, 4 f.

well enough as meaning that, unless a man be born again he is not reckoned as belonging to God's Kingdom.

For I desired mercy and not sacrifice, and the knowledge of God more than burnt offerings. Hos. 6:6.

This passage is especially important because it was cited twice by the Son of God (Matt. 9:13 and 12:17). . . . For a better understanding of the prophet's meaning, we must first notice that under the terms *sacrifice* and *burnt offerings* the outward worship of God and all formal ceremonies are included. The part is put for the whole (synecdoche). The same is true of the word *chesed*, *mercy* or *kindness*. There is no doubt that the prophet is setting faith or devotion to God and love of neighbor in opposition to all external ceremonies.

I desire mercy (or "compassion pleases me") *more than sacrifice, and the knowledge of God more than burnt offerings.* Here the knowledge of God is certainly to be understood as faith or devotion to God. Since hypocrites think that they worship God properly when they use many rites, both clauses must be read together. It is faith with kindness that pleases God. Faith by itself cannot please him, since without love of neighbor there is no faith. And kindness alone would not be enough. If a man refrains from doing injury to others and does not harm his brothers, but is blasphemous and despises God, certainly his humanitarianism would be of no account.

So we see that these two clauses cannot be divided, for to give the right sense to the prophet's words love of God must be joined with love of neighbor. . . .

Further, it is important to notice that faith is called knowledge of God. This makes it clear that faith is not some cold and empty formula. When God's will is revealed to us and we so far accept it that we can honor and serve him as Father—that is faith. The knowledge of God is a necessity of faith.

Then spoke Jesus again unto them, saying, I am the light of the world: he that followeth me shall not walk in darkness, but shall have the light of life. John 8:12.

It is a most beautiful praise of Christ that he is called the light of the world. With this statement, we who are by nature blind are offered a remedy, by which we are snatched and freed from darkness and made to share in the true light. This blessing is not offered to this or that individual only; Christ declares himself the light of the whole world. By this universal statement, he takes away the distinction not only between the Jew and the Greek, but also between the learned and the ignorant, the distinguished and the common people.

But first we must inquire as to why it is needful to seek after this light. Men will not turn to Christ for light until they know this world as darkness and themselves so profoundly blind. Let us know, therefore, that when our minds see the way we obtain this light in Christ, we are all condemned as blind, and whatever light we have from elsewhere is judged as darkness and a deep night. Christ here refers not to what he has in common with others, but to that which is his own and his alone. Whence it follows that apart from him there is not a spark of true light. Every other brilliance is like lightning which merely dazzles the eye.

In the beginning God created the heaven and the earth. Gen. 1:1.

In the beginning. To interpret *the beginning* as meaning Christ is too frivolous. Moses meant simply to say that the world at its beginning was not the finished product we see today, but was created an empty chaos of sky and earth. . . .

By the word *create*, he shows that something was made which did not before exist. For he does not use the verb *yatsar* which means shape or form, but *bara'*. What he means is that the world was created from nothing.

This refutes the futility of those who imagine that formless matter was always in existence and who get nothing more from Moses' statement than that the world was fitted with a new look, clothed with form which it had previously lacked. This is the general opinion of unbelievers to whom only an obscure report of God's truth has come. Men usually mix God's truth with alien inventions. But it is absurd and most intolerable that Christians should labor to adopt this stinking error (as Steuchus[3] does). Therefore, the first article of the creed is: The world is not eternal, but was created by God. . . .

God. The word *Elohim*, which Moses uses, is plural, and it is customary to conclude that here the three Persons in the Godhead are specified. But this does not seem a solid proof for so great a truth, and I do not agree with it. Rather readers should be warned to be on their guard against false glosses of this kind.

[3] Augustinus Steuchus or Agostino Steucho (1496–1549) was an influential Roman churchman and director of the Vatican Library. He was a philosopher and a scholar. He wrote *De perennia philosophia* and many works on Biblical antiquities and literary exegesis.

They think that here they have evidence to prove against the Arians[4] the divinity of the Son and Spirit. But meanwhile they involve themselves in Sabellianism.[5] For immediately afterwards Moses adds that *God (Elohim)* spoke, and that *the Spirit of God brooded upon the waters.* If you would see three Persons [in this verse, you will not succeed, because] you will find here no distinction between them. . . .

It seems to me sufficient to understand the plural as expressing the powers of God which he exercised in creating the world. I recognize that although the Scripture often recounts many divine powers, it always calls us back to the Father, his Word, and the Spirit. But those who twist what Moses is saying of God himself into a reference to the three Persons are presenting us with absurdities. I set it down as indisputable from the context that this passage names God and includes by implication the power of his eternal essence.

[4] Arius of Alexandria in the fourth century denied that the Son was of the same essence as the Father. He made of Christ a divine being of secondary rank. The term "Arian" was later used loosely to include Unitarians who asserted that Jesus was man only.

[5] The Sabellians declared that Father, Son, and Holy Spirit represent aspects or functions of God. They thus denied the three Persons of the Trinity and consequently the reality of the humanity of Jesus. Both Arianism and Sabellianism are recurrent under various labels in Western Christianity.

III

Jesus Christ

THE TEXT

1. The Mediator

Jesus Christ the same yesterday, and today, and for ever. Heb. 13:8.
The only way to continue in the right faith is to keep to the
foundation and not to turn away from it a single inch. If a man
does not hold on to Christ, his wisdom is mere folly, even
though he comprehend heaven and earth; for all the treasures of
heavenly wisdom are contained in Christ. Therefore, this is a
remarkable verse, because from it we see that there is no other
rule of true wisdom except to set our whole minds on Christ
alone. And, since the writer had to do with the Jews, he teaches
that Christ has at all times in the past reigned as he does today,
and that he will reign till the end of the world as he has reigned
to the present time. *Yesterday*, he says, *today*, and *the same also
forever*; by these words he means that Christ, who is now manifested to the world, has reigned from the beginning of the world,
and that, when we come to him, we must go no further.
Yesterday, therefore, includes the whole duration of the Old
Testament. The word is used to establish that, even though the
gospel has been preached but recently, this does not justify
jumping to the conclusion that it will soon disappear; in fact,
Christ has been revealed recently for the very purpose that men
might know him from that time on and ever after. From this it
is evident that the apostle is speaking not of Christ as he is in
eternity, but of our knowledge of him, which the godly have
always had, and which is at all times the foundation of the
church. Of course it is true that Christ was, before he revealed
his power. But about what is the apostle speaking? I say that in
this verse he is speaking not of Christ's being but, so to say, of
his quality (or of how he acts towards us); the question is not
his eternal presence before the Father, but what men have

known of him. Moreover, even though, with regard to external form and manner, Christ was manifested differently under the law and in our time, the apostle nonetheless speaks truly and properly when he says that the faithful have always had their eyes fixed upon Christ.

The sun of righteousness shall rise to you who fear my name, and with healing in his wings; and you will go forth and leap like well-fed (or fattened) young bulls. Mal. 4:2. (Calvin's wording.)

Now the prophet directs his words to the faithful. Up to this point, he had been threatening the hypocrites who arrogantly claimed holiness for themselves alone, although they had never ceased to provoke God's anger. Now, as I said before, he is addressing the others when he says *shall rise to you.* He distinguishes those who fear God or worship him purely from the multitude with which he has so far been disputing.

The antithesis is important. Although the people as a whole had been infected with the general disgrace, God had kept a few untouched by it. He had been contending with the majority of the people; now he gathers the chosen apart by themselves and promises that for them Christ will be the author of true salvation. We know that the faithful would be terrified at God's threats of punishment and would almost cease to breathe, if God did not soften the severity of his condemnation. Whenever he announces punishment to sinners, most of them either laugh, or become angry, or else pay no attention at all. So it happens that the wicked continue securely in their crimes, while God thunders. But the faithful are terrified at one word from him and would be wholly discouraged if God did not bring some remedy.

Therefore the prophet softens the harshness of the preceding threat, as if to say that he had not proclaimed the terror of Christ's coming with the purpose of filling their hearts with fear. Its dreadfulness did not concern them; he had described it only to frighten the wicked.

This, then, is what he means: "Come near, you who fear the Lord, for I have a different word for you. The Sun of Righteousness will rise and will bring healing in his wings. Let those perish who despise God, who even fight against him and wish to hold him in subjection to themselves. But you, lift up your heads and wait patiently for that day. In the hope of it, endure all misfortunes calmly."

Now we come to the high point of the verse. There is no

doubt that Malachi here calls Christ *the Sun of Righteousness*, and the words appear especially appropriate when we consider how the situation of the fathers differed from our own. God always gave light to his church, but the full light was brought by Christ; as Isaiah also taught (60: 1 ff.), *The Lord will shine upon you and the glory of God will be seen among you.* This is fulfilled only in the person of Christ. *Then behold shadows will cover the earth . . . and the Lord will shine upon thee*; and also, *There will be no sun and moon by day or night, but God alone will shine.* All these passages show that the name of *sun* is appropriate to Christ because God the Father shines upon us so much more brightly in his person than formerly in the law and all the additions to the law.

For the same reason Christ calls himself the light of the world. Not that the fathers wandered like blind men in a mist, but that they had to be content with the light of early dawn or with the moon and stars. We know how obscure the teaching of the law was, so that it is truly called a "shadow." But when the heavens were finally opened by the gospel, then indeed did the sun rise; and when the risen sun gives light the full day comes. It is Christ's true office to give light. Therefore John begins by saying that the true light was from the beginning and lights every man coming into the world; and that the light itself shines in darkness. For some sparks of reason remain in men even when they have become blind by Adam's Fall and the corruption of their nature.

But Christ is fittingly called light in relation to the faithful whom he has rescued from their natural blindness and has raised up to be ruled by his Spirit. This is the meaning of *sun* when the name is given metaphorically to Christ. He is called *sun* because without him we can only wander and go wrong, but when He leads us we keep on the right road; as he says, *Who follows me does not walk in darkness.*

It must be noted that this promise is not restricted to the physical presence of Christ, but refers also to the gospel; as Paul says, *Wake, you who sleep, and rise from darkness and Christ will give you light* (Eph. 5: 14). Every day, Christ enlightens us by his teaching and his Spirit; and although we do not see him with our eyes we know by experience that he is our sun.

Further, he is called in the Hebrew *sun of righteousness*, that is *perfection of justice*, either because in him nothing will be incomplete or because the righteousness of God will be seen in him. But in order to comprehend the light which we enjoy through him and which comes to us from him to shine upon us, we must keep our eyes not on temporary advantages but on the spiritual life. This is the one requirement. Christ acts as our sun, not to direct our hands and feet in earthly actions, but to bring to us the light which shows the road to heaven and the direction by which we come to a happy and eternal life.

Also we must note that this spiritual light connot be separated from righteousness. In what sense is Christ our sun? Because he rescues us from the shame of the world and transforms us to the image of God. This is the force of the word *righteousness*.

The prophet adds *healing in his wings*, calling the rays of the sun *wings*. This metaphor has much charm, because it is taken from nature itself and is beautifully suited to Christ. For we know that nothing is more health-giving than the sun's rays. We should be overcome in a short time—even in one day—by evil smells, if the sun did not cleanse the earth of its refuse. Without the sun, we could not breathe.

Also we feel a lift of the spirit at sunrise. For night is like a burden to us, and when the sun sets we feel a heaviness in all our limbs. But in the morning, even the sick are encouraged and feel some change just from the effect of the sun's nearness, because it does indeed bring healing in its wings.

But the prophet is here saying more than that a bright sun in a clear sky brings health. There is also an implicit contrast between storm clouds and fair, clear weather. In good weather we feel much more alive—I mean all men, both sick and well. There is no one who does not get some sense of revival from a clear sky; but when the weather is cloudy even the strongest of us feel some discomfort. In this sense, Malachi says that healing will be in the wings of Christ, although we must still bear many ills.

If we think back to the history of those times, we realize that the condition of the people was most miserable. The prophet now promises them a change, [a time] when the restoration of the church will bring them joy. We see then how he understands the healing in Christ's wings. Christ will disperse the darkness, and bring back from behind the clouds a serene sky, giving courage to the minds of the faithful.

To call the faithful *those who fear God* is an ordinary usage in Scripture; for, as we have said, the center of righteousness and holiness is the worship of God. But here something new is expressed. It is the mark of true religion that men submit themselves to God although he is not seen, and although he does not speak face to face, and does not openly show his hand holding the scourge. When men willingly honor God's glory and acknowledge the world to be ruled by him and themselves to be under his authority, then they give true evidence of religion. This is what the prophet means by *fear my name*. Those who *fear the name* of God, do not desire to bring him out of heaven, nor do they demand obvious signs of his presence; they are content to show their faith by adoring and serving God, although they do not see him face to face, but only in a mirror or a riddle, or through his righteous and powerful judgments and the other great acts which he presents to our eyes.

After saying that the sun of righteousness will rise for the Jews, Malachi adds that this will give them joy. As sadness oppresses the faithful when they are without Christ, or think him to be far away, so his favor is their greatest happiness and a solid delight. Therefore the angels proclaiming Christ's birth to the shepherds began, *Behold I give you tidings of great joy.* And although the metaphor may seem harsh, the prophet has a good reason for saying that the Jews will be like *fattened calves.* He is describing an unbelievable change and he must put it before them in vivid terms, to give them the greater hope.

A contrast is implied in the verb *go out.* Their anxiety had long held them captive; now there would be freedom to go out. When things change for the better with us, we show the joy of our hearts openly to others, and seek a stage on which to express our feelings. Now we can see why the prophet says the Jews will *go out.* They have before been shut in by hard times. Now God will grant them room for lively rejoicing. So Paul says (II Cor. 3:17), *Where the Spirit of the Lord is, there is liberty.*

And he dreamed, and behold, a ladder was set up on the earth, and the top of it reached to heaven: and behold, the angels of God were ascending and descending on it. Gen. 28:12.

Behold a ladder. Here we have the description of a vision in which form and content are closely related. God showed himself perched upon a ladder, the ends of which touched heaven and earth. And angels were using it to go back and forth between heaven and earth.

The ladder is taken by some Jewish commentators as a symbol of divine Providence which includes both heaven and earth under its direction. This interpretation is not satisfactory, for God would have given a more suitable symbol.

But for us who hold the truth that the covenant of God was founded on Christ and that Christ was always the same eternal image of the Father and revealed himself to the holy patriarchs, nothing in this vision is perplexing or ambiguous. For men are separated from God by sin, although his power fills and sustains all things; and we do not see the line of communication which draws us towards him. Rather there is between us such a gulf that we flee from him, believing him to be hostile to us. The angels who are assigned the guardianship of the human race do not deal with us in a way which makes us familiar with their nearness and reveals it to our senses.

It is Christ alone who joins heaven to earth. He alone is Mediator, reaching from heaven to the earth. He it is through whom the fullness of all heavenly gifts flows down to us and through whom we on our part may ascend to God. . . . Therefore, if we say that the ladder is a symbol of Christ, the interpretation is not forced. For the metaphor of a ladder is most suited to a Mediator through whom the service of angels, righteousness, and truth, and all the spirits of holy grace descend to us step by step. We, on our part, who are firmly fixed not only upon the earth but in the abyss of the curse, and are submerged in hell itself, through him climb up to God.

Moreover the God of hosts tops the ladder because the divine fullness dwells in Christ, who therefore reaches heaven. For although all power was given by the Father to Christ's human nature, yet he would not be the support of our faith if he were not God manifest in the flesh. The fact that the body of Christ is finite in no way prevents his filling the heavens, since his grace and power is spread over all. To this Paul bears witness when he says that Christ ascended to heaven to fill all things.

Those who translate 'al as near wholly distort the meaning [of this verse], for Moses wished to say that full deity dwelt in Christ. In fact, Christ does not so much come to us as become encumbered with our nature to make us one with him.

Confirmation of the ladder as a symbol of Christ is found also in this consideration (and nothing has been more fully agreed by all): God sanctified his eternal covenant with his servant Jacob in his Son. And incalculable joy comes to us when we hear that Christ who excels all creation is joined to us. Indeed the majesty of God, plainly shown in his Son, must inspire terror so that every knee bows to Christ, all creatures pray to him and adore him, and all flesh is silent before him. Yet at the same time Christ shows himself to us as friendly and gentle, and he makes known to us by his descent that heaven is open to us and the angels are made our companions; with them we

have a brotherly communion, because our common Head took
his place on earth.

The angel which redeemed me from all evil, bless the lads. Gen.
48:16.

Jacob joins the angel to God as an equal. He worships him
and asks from him the same things he asked from God (v. 15).
If you take this verse as a reference to an ordinary angel, the
words are absurd. ... It is necessary to understand them of
Christ, who is intentionally given the title of *angel* because he has
been the perpetual Mediator. Paul testifies that He was the
leader and guide of the journey of his ancient people [through
the wilderness].

Christ had not yet been sent by the Father to take on our
flesh that he might come nearer to us; but he was always the
link joining men to God, and God did not reveal himself otherwise than through him. Therefore he is rightly called *angel,
messenger*. ... For there has always been between God and man
a distance too great for any communication to be possible
without a mediator.

But although Christ has appeared in the form of an angel, we
must hold to what is said in Heb. 2:16; he did not put on the
nature of an angel and become one of the angels, as he did
become true man. When the angels are clothed with a human
body, they do not become men.

Moreover we are taught by these words that the true gift of
Christ to us is that he guards us and rescues us from all evils.
And we must therefore take heed that our faithless forgetfulness
does not bury this gift, which has been shown to us more clearly
than it was formerly to the saints under the law. For Christ
proclaimed openly that the faithful are given into his custody
and that no one of them will perish. Therefore trust in his
guardianship ought to flourish better in our hearts, and we
ought to celebrate it with fitting praise. And also we should be
roused to seek primarily the help of our best Guardian.

His help is indeed especially necessary for us today. For if we
think over all the dangers which surround us, we can find
scarcely a day on which we were not rescued from a thousand
deaths. And how does this happen except that we are under
the care of God's Son, who took us over from his father's hand
to watch over us.

... The first tabernacle was yet standing, which was a figure for the

times then present, in which were offered both gifts and sacrifices, that could not make him that did the service perfect, as pertaining to the conscience. . . . But Christ being come as a high priest of good things to come, by a greater and more perfect tabernacle, not made with hands, that is to say, not of this building; neither by the blood of goats and calves, but by his own blood he entered in once into the holy place, having obtained eternal redemption for us. Heb. 9:8–9, 11–12.

The Greek word for *figure* is παραβολὴ, which in my judgment is about the same as ἀντίτυπον. The apostle means that the Tabernacle was a secondary exemplar which corresponded to the original; as the picture of a man ought to correspond to himself, so that when we see it we are immediately reminded of him.

Besides, when he says that the first Tabernacle was a likeness *for that time,* he means that it was valid so long as the external observances were in force. In this way, he restricts its use to the period of ancient law. This is almost the same as what he says soon after: that the ceremonies were in effect until the time of reformation (under the gospel). . . .

As pertaining to conscience. This means that the ancient gifts and sacrifices could not penetrate the soul so as to make it truly holy. Some use here the word *perfect,* which I do not reject; but I think *sanctify* fits the context better.[1] But, if the reader is to understand the words of the apostle, he had better watch the contrast between the flesh and the conscience. What the apostle does is to deny that the legal sacrifices cleansed inwardly and spiritually those who performed them; and the reason he gives for his denial is that all the rites of the first Tabernacle were of the flesh or carnal. Then what good were they? There is a common notion that they were intended to teach people honesty and good manners. But those who think this way forget the promises which were added to these observances. Therefore we must reject their invention. It is all wrong and absurd to think that the flesh itself was justified by these rites, as though they were good only for the cleansing and purity of the body! The apostle's judgment is that they were earthly symbols which failed to penetrate to the soul. They were testimonies to perfect holiness, even though they neither contained it nor could confer it on men. They were helps given to the faithful, which laid hold of their hands and led them to Christ, to seek in him what was lacking in the symbols.

But, someone will ask, Why did the apostle show so little

[1] Notice the contrast with the King James Version.

respect for sacraments instituted by God, treating them with contempt, and going even so far as to rob them of all power? He did so, because he was thinking of them as they are when separated from Christ. We know that considered in themselves, they are niggardly elements of this world, as Paul himself called them (Gal 4:9). . . .

But Christ being come an high priest of good things to come, by a greater and more perfect tabernacle, not made with hands . . .

He now presents us with the reality behind the symbols of the law, in order to turn our eyes to it. For, anyone who believes that the things foreshadowed [in the law] have been revealed truly in Christ, will no longer hold on to the shadows. He will embrace the substance in all its solid reality.

Nevertheless, we must see carefully and in detail how he compares Christ with the ancient high priest. He has already said that the high priest alone entered the sanctuary once a year, carrying blood with which to expiate sins. Christ is like the ancient high priest, in that He alone is honored with this dignity and office; but he is different in that he brings with him gifts which are eternal and establish his priesthood forever. Secondly, the ancient high priest and our own are alike in that they both entered the Holy of Holies through the sanctuary; but they differ in that Christ alone entered heaven by way of the temple of his own body. Even though the Holy of Holies was opened to the high priest once a year for a solemn performance of expiation, this was only a poor figure for the matchless [self-] offering of Christ. Indeed, they both went in. But the one entered into an earthly place; the other, into heaven, forever, even to the end of the world. Both offered blood, but there is all the difference in the world between blood and blood; the ancient high priest offered the blood of cattle, Christ offered his own. They both made expiation; but the one made under the law was ineffectual and had to be repeated each year; Christ's expiation kept its vigor forever, and is the source of our salvation in eternity. Hence, every word of the apostle is heavily weighted. Some change *Christ being come* to "Christ being nearby." But this does no justice to the apostle's thought. What he means is that after the Levitical priests had performed their office, at a fixed time they were removed, and Christ was chosen in their place. But this is obvious from ch. 7 of this epistle.

Of good things to come means of things eternal. As μέλλων καιρὸς is set against τῷ ἐνεστήκοτι, so future goods are opposed to the present. In short, the priestly work of Christ brings us to the heavenly Kingdom of God, and makes us to partake in spiritual righteousness and eternal life: therefore, no good comes from looking for something better. We need not go beyond Christ, because he himself possesses all that we need, and he will fill us.

And for this cause he is the mediator of the new testament, that by means of death, for the redemption of the transgressions that were under the first testament, they which were called might receive the promise of eternal inheritance. Heb. 9:15.

He concludes that there is no further need for another priest, because Christ himself fulfills this function under the New Testament. Besides, he does not claim the title of Mediator for Christ to let others share it with him; on the contrary, he contends that when this office was attached to Christ, all other mediators were repudiated. . . . He confirms this more fully when he states specifically how Christ discharged the office of the Mediator by the intercession of his death. If this happened only in Christ, and in no one else, it follows that he alone is the true Mediator. . . .

Now, if anyone asks whether the sins of the fathers were forgiven under the law, the answer is the same as I gave before: they were forgiven, but through the benefit of Christ; in terms of the physical acts of expiation, we must always hold and maintain that they remained guilty. For this reason, Paul says that the law is a handwriting against us (Col. 2:14). When a sinner came forward, confessing openly that he had done evil before God and killed an innocent animal, he admitted that he was worthy of eternal death. And what did his victim do for him except that by it he sealed his own death as it were by his own handwriting? In short, only those who looked at Christ found peace in the forgiveness of sins. If looking to Christ only takes away sins, those who remain under the law do not find freedom. David himself declares, *Blessed is the man to whom sins are not imputed* (Ps. 32:2); but if a man is to share in this blessing, he must, setting aside the law, fix his eyes on Christ; for if he stays with the law, he is not set free from guilt.

For he shall grow up before him as a tender plant, and as a root out of a dry ground; he hath no form nor comeliness, and when we shall see him, there is no beauty that we should desire him. Isa. 53:2.

This statement turns our minds to what we said before:

namely, that Christ at the beginning [of his life on earth] is to show neither splendor nor beauty before men, but before God he will nonetheless be highly exalted and beloved. Hence we see that the glory of Christ must not be judged by human eyes. What the holy books teach about him must be understood by faith. Therefore, the phrase *before him* is to be contrasted with the human senses which cannot grasp the wonder of Christ.

The prophet used a similar metaphor in ch. 11:1: *a branch will come from the trunk of Jesse*. He compared the house of David to a dry trunk with no strength in it and no beauty; and he did not name the royal house, but Jesse whose name by itself was obscure. Here he adds *in desert ground*, by which he means that Christ's strength will come not like a tree from the humidity of the soil, but from outside the ordinary course of nature.

Those who philosophize from this passage about the Virgin Mary, supposing that she was called desert ground because she conceived from the Holy Spirit and not from man's seed, are beside the point. For the passage deals not with the birth of Christ but with his whole reign. It states that he will be like a branch growing from dry ground, which is not expected to reach the right size.

We should think of the whole history of his planting, of the men whose work he has used, of the small beginnings of the church and of the many adversaries who oppose it. Then we can easily see that all things happened as predicted. What kind of men were the apostles who could subdue so many kings and nations by the sword of the Word? Are they not deservedly compared to branches in a desert? The prophet is describing the ways by which the Kingdom of Christ was founded and established, so that all men may not judge it by human reason.

The ugliness which he next mentions ought also to be understood not only of the person of Christ who was despised by the world and condemned to a shameful death, but of his whole reign. For that reign has had, in men's eyes, neither beauty nor splendor nor magnificence. In fact, it has nothing which could by its appearance attract men or charm their eyes. And although Christ rose from the dead, the Jews think of him always as crucified and dishonored, and look on him with disgust and contempt.

But he was wounded for our transgressions, he was bruised for our iniquities: the chastisement of our peace was upon him; and with his stripes we are healed. Isa. 53:5.

In order to counteract the offense which people might take, the prophet repeats the reason for Christ's great suffering. The sight of the cross of Christ offends many so long as they consider only what their eyes see, and pay no attention to the purpose. But all offense is certainly taken away when we understand that by this death our sins are atoned for, and salvation is won for us.

Chastisement of our peace. Some think this is called *chastisement of our peace* because men feel so secure and remain so stupefied in their evil ways that Christ's suffering was required to move them. Others apply *peace* to conscience. Christ suffered that we might have a quiet conscience; as Paul said (Rom. 5:1), *We, justified through Christ by faith, have peace with God.*

But I take it simply as reconciliation. Christ paid the price of our chastisement, that is, the chastisement due to us. By him, God's anger, which was inflamed against us, was appeased. The peace in which we are reconciled came from him who is the Mediator. Thus we have the general doctrine that we are freely reconciled to God because Christ paid the price of our peace.

This doctrine, indeed, the papists confess, but then they restrict it to original sin; as if after baptism there were no more place for free reconciliation, and satisfaction were to be made by our merits and works. But the prophet here is not treating of a single aspect of forgiveness; he extends God's forgiving kindness through the whole course of our lives. Therefore the doctrine cannot be attenuated or restricted to any specific time without great sacrilege. ... Our prophet teaches plainly that the penalty for our sins was transferred to Christ. What then are the papists claiming for themselves but equality with Christ and a share in his authority as his partners?

With his stripes. Again we are recalled to Christ, called to flee to his wounds if we wish to regain life. Here he is set in contrast to us. In us are only destruction and death; in Christ alone is life and safety. He alone brings us a remedy. He provides health for us by his weakness, and wins our life by his death. He alone satisfies the Father; he alone reconciles us to him.

We could say many things here about the fruit of Christ's suffering, but our task is to interpret, not to preach; and we must be content to state the plain meaning [of the verse]. Let each one of you take comfort for himself from this passage and fit its use to his own need. For these words were spoken not only publicly to all, but to each man individually.

All we like sheep have gone astray; we have turned every one to his own way, and the Lord hath laid on him the iniquity of us all. Isa. 53:6.

In order to impress on our minds the greatness of the blessing given us in Christ's death, he shows us how great is our need for healing. For unless we realize our own helpless misery, we shall never know how much we need the remedy which Christ brings, nor come to him with the fervent love we owe him. But as soon as we know ourselves to be lost and realize our own wretchedness, we rush eagerly to seize the remedy, which otherwise we should hold in contempt. To know the true flavor of Christ, we must each of us carefully examine ourselves, and each must know himself condemned until he is vindicated by Christ. No one is exempt. The prophet includes *all*. If Christ had not brought help, the whole human race would perish. . . .

The prophet makes the comparison with sheep, not to lighten our guilt, as if straying were a minor misdemeanor; but to teach more plainly that it was the work of Christ to gather those who were scattered like foolish animals.

By adding *each* to the general statement including all men, he appeals to every individual to ponder whether this is not true of himself. For we are little moved by a generalization unless each one of us separately feels that it applies to him. Therefore let every one of us rouse his own conscience and take his place before God's tribunal. Then will each one of us know his own bankruptcy.

Next the prophet declares more plainly what this wandering is: every one has followed the way of his own choice; he has chosen to live as it pleased him. This means that there is only *one* way of living rightly; and if any man turn away from it, he can find nothing but ways which send him in the wrong direction. He is not speaking so much of actions as of our nature itself, which always sends us wandering. For if by natural instinct or wisdom we could bring ourselves back to the road and escape from error, we would have no need for Christ. But we all by ourselves perish unless we are freed by Christ our Savior. The more we trust our own wisdom and industry, the more quickly we rush to ruin. Here the prophet has shown us what sort of creatures we should be if Christ had not redeemed us. And all are included in the same condemnation. There is no one who is righteous; no one who understands; no one who inquires of God. All have gone astray and become unprofitable. There is none who does well, not one, as Paul said more at length (Rom. 3:10).

And the Lord hath laid on him. Here we have a beautiful anti-thesis. In ourselves we are scattered, in Christ we are collected; by nature we go astray and are driven headlong to destruction, in Christ we find the road by which we are led to the gate of salvation. Our sins overwhelm us; but they are transferred to Christ, in whom we are acquitted. When we were perishing, separated from God and hastening to hell, Christ took upon himself the filth of our iniquities and rescued us from eternal destruction. (This refers of course only to the punishment of sin, for he was free from all guilt.) Let each one of us weigh his own sins carefully, that he may truly taste the grace [of Christ] and begin to see the fruit of his death.

He shall see the travail of his soul, and shall be satisfied: by his knowledge shall my righteous servant justify many; for he shall bear their iniquities. Isa. 53:11.

Isaiah continues the same theme. Now he declares that Christ, after he has suffered, will see the reward of his death in the salvation of men. For, to *He will see*, we must add the "fruit" or the "result" [of his labor]. These words are full of comfort. For Isaiah could not have expressed better the greatness of Christ's love for us than by saying that his delight will be in our safety; that he will be content with the fruit of his labor, like a man whose one wish and longing has been fulfilled. No man is *satisfied* except when he obtains the one thing he has most desired; then he disregards all else and is content with it alone.

Afterwards the prophet shows the way or method by which we may rightly appreciate the force and efficiency of Christ's death and realize its fruit. The way he shows is *the knowledge of him.* I admit that the word *da'ath* can be read passively or actively, as *knowledge of him* or *his knowledge*. Whichever way we take it, it is easy to see what the prophet means. However insolently the Jews may quibble and in spite of their objections, we need not twist the meaning of what is here said plainly: that Christ alone is both master and author of man's justification.

The work of Christ is stated in the words *He will justify many*; which mean that in the school of Christ, men are not merely taught about justification; they are made just by what he has done for them. And this is the difference between justification by law and justification by faith. For although the law shows what it is to be righteous, as Paul says, it cannot produce right-eousness; and experience shows the same thing. The law is for us a mirror showing us our own unrighteousness. But the way to obtain righteousness, as taught by Christ, is simply to know him; and this is faith. In faith we lay hold on the benefit of his death and find full rest in him.

The philosophers have given many excellent rules by which they think righteousness may be established; but they cannot give righteousness to anyone. For who by their rules has achieved the good life? And it is of little help to know what righteousness is, if we remain without it.

But let us leave the philosophers aside. The law itself, which contains the most perfect rule of life, could not, as we said, confer righteousness. Not that there was anything lacking in the law; Moses declared that he set before the people good and evil, life and death. But because of the corruption of our nature, the law was not enough to insure righteousness. Even as Paul taught (Rom. 8:3), the defect was in our flesh, not in the law. When the law speaks, nature drives us in the opposite direction, and our desires break out with the greater force, like untamed wild elephants, against God's command. Thus the law *works wrath* rather than righteousness. The law holds all guilty, and by exposing sin takes away from men every excuse. Therefore we must seek another way to righteousness: the way which is in Christ, whom the law itself set forth as its fulfillment.

The righteousness of the law said, *Who does these commandments, shall live in them* (Lev. 18:5). But none did them. Therefore there had to be another righteousness; one that Paul taught, from Moses himself: *The word is near, in your mouth and in your heart; this is the word of faith which we preach* (Rom. 10:8). It is this doctrine that justifies us—not the bare doctrine, but because it offers us the fruit of Christ's death, by which our sins are forgiven and we are reconciled to God. For if by faith we grasp this gift, we are counted as righteous before God.

The prophet expresses this teaching clearly and shows its meaning. For these two clauses belong together: *He will justify by his doctrine* or *by the knowledge of him*, and *He will bear our iniquities*. He made atonement for us once for all; but now, by the teaching of the gospel, he is inviting us to accept the fruit of his death. Therefore the death of Christ is the substance of the doctrine that he justifies us. Paul adhered closely to the prophet's word when he taught that Christ was offered as sacrifice for us, so that in him we might become the righteousness of God; to which he added that Christ is our advocate, and urged us to be reconciled to God (II. Cor. 5:20).

My righteous servant. The prophet teaches that Christ justifies us not only as God, but also as man, since he won righteousness for us in his flesh. For the words are not *my son* but *my servant*. Therefore, let us not think of Christ only as God, but let us study his human nature in which he practiced the obedience by which we are forgiven before God. For this, the sacrifice of himself which he offered, is the foundation of our salvation. As he himself said, *I consecrated myself for them that they themselves might be holy* (John 17:19).

Therefore will I divide for him a portion with the great, and he shall divide the spoil with the strong; because he has poured out his soul unto death: and he was numbered with the transgressors; and he bore the sin of many, and made intercession for the transgressors. Isa. 53:12.

Here the figure is changed to one drawn from the customary celebration of military triumphs, where the leaders are generally received and honored with a magnificent exhibition of the spoils of victory. So Christ like a strong and noble general triumphs over his conquered enemies. The second clause has the same meaning as the first, for such repetition is usual in Hebrew. Those whom he first calls *great* he next calls powerful or *strong*. Those who translate *rabbim* as "many" in my opinion misinterpret the prophet's meaning. There is only this difference between the two clauses: in the first, God states what he will give to Christ; the second adds that Christ will rejoice in the gift. Christ rejoices not for his own sake but for ours, since he gives the fruits of his victory to us. For us, Christ conquered death, the world, and the devil.

He prayed for the transgressors. It is Christ's prayer to the Father in our behalf which ratifies the forgiveness won for us by his death. Therefore this addition is essential. In the old law the priest, who did not come to the altar without the blood of sacrifice, prayed there for the people; and so he foreshadowed what was fulfilled in Christ. For first Christ offered the sacrifice of his body, and poured out his blood to pay the penalty which we owed. Then to make the atonement effective, he performed the work of advocate and made intercession for all who in faith accepted for themselves his sacrifice. To this he testified in the words written for us by the hand of John: *I pray not for these only, but for all who believe in me by their word* (John 17:20). If we are to be numbered with the faithful, let us not doubt that Christ suffered for us and that even now we receive the fruits of his death.

2. THE PERSON OF CHRIST

And thou, Lord, in the beginning hast laid the foundation of the earth: and the heavens are the works of thine hands; they shall perish, but thou remainest. . . . Heb. 1:10–11.

At first this testimony may seem not to fit the case of Christ, since it has to do with the creation of heaven and earth. But this whole passage has to do with the glory not of God but of Christ. It is true that the psalm is a celebration of God's majesty, and makes no mention of Christ. I admit this. At the same time, it is clearly a public praise of God's Kingdom, and everything that is said in it fits Christ very well. For, where are the following prophecies fulfilled except in Christ: "Thou shalt arise and have mercy on Zion, that the nations may fear thy name, and all the kings of the earth thy glory"; or again, "When the people shall be gathered together, and the kingdom, to serve the Lord." Where except in Christ are we to look for this God by whom the whole world shall be united in one faith and worship of God? All the rest of the psalm fits the person of Christ; among other things, because he is the eternal God, the Creator of heaven and earth, everlasting and changeless; therefore, high and lifted up in majesty, and set apart from all that has been created. David declares that the heavens shall pass away; but some get around this statement by making him say, "should the heavens pass away," as though he had made no positive assertion. But what reason is there for such a strained exposition? After all, we know that everything comes to an end. And why do even the heavens yearn and travail with hope for a renewal, unless they are marked for destruction? Besides, the eternity of Christ affords no small comfort to the believers who, according to the psalm, shall participate in it as Christ communicates himself and all his riches to his body.

And now, Father, glorify thou me with thine own self with the glory which I had with thee before the world was. John 17:5.

He declares that he has no desire except for what is his own; that he only wants to be seen in the flesh with the glory which was his before the world was made; or, more plainly, that the divine majesty which was eternally his might shine in the person of the Mediator and in the human flesh he has put on. This is a striking passage which teaches us that Christ is not an upstart and temporary God. For as his glory was eternal, so he himself always was. Add to this that there is here a distinction made

between him and the Father; which means that he is not only
God eternal but also the eternal Word of God begotten of the
Father before all ages.

*Philip findeth Nathanael, and saith unto him, We have found him,
of whom Moses in the law, and the prophets, did write, Jesus of
Nazareth, the son of Joseph.* John 1:45.

Many argue deeply about Christ, but they get so subtle and
involved that they can never find him. So it is with the papists
who refuse to call Christ the son of Joseph. They are particular
about his name: but yet they so empty him of his power, that
in Christ's place they have a ghost. Were it not better to babble
crudely with Philip and hold on to the real Christ, rather than
with clever and high-sounding talk end up with only a fiction?
There are many poor dunces today who, even though they speak
as rude and ignorant men, teach Christ much more faithfully
than the theologians of the pope, with their deep speculations.
So we are warned that when we hear simple and ignorant men
speak inaptly, we should not take offense and reject them, provided they lead us to Christ. However, we must seek pure knowledge from the Law and the Prophets, in order that we may
not be driven away from Christ by falsehoods invented by men.

*Labor not for the meat which perisheth, but for that meat which
endureth unto everlasting life, which the Son of Man shall give unto you;
for him hath the Father sealed.* John 6:27.

He confirms the first part of this verse by saying that the
Father has appointed him for this end (to give us an imperish-
able food). The ancient fathers tortured and misused this verse
in order to prove the divine essence of Christ; as though *sealed*
here meant that Christ bore the stamp of the Father. But he
speaks here, not subtly of his eternal essence, but of his mandate
and mission in our behalf, and of what we are to hope and expect from him. By an apt metaphor, he refers to the ancient
custom of sealing with a ring, which made an agreement
authoritative and binding. Christ's intention is to declare that
his task was imposed upon him by the Father, and that the
appointment of the Father is as a seal engraved upon him. In
this way, he emphasizes that all he has is from the Father. In
short, it is not for everybody to feed souls with incorruptible
food, when Christ comes forth with the promise of so great a
blessing. He adds that he has God's approval and has been sent
to us with God's own seal as the mark of his mission.

I and my Father are one. John 10:30.

He sets out to meet the mockery of the wicked, who claimed that he was in no position to protect his disciples, since he did not possess God's power. He, therefore, testifies that his business and the Father's are one; which means that the Father will never deny his help to him or to his sheep. The ancient fathers misused this verse when they brought it up as proof that Christ is ὁμοούσιος (of one essence) with the Father. Christ is not here arguing that he is one substance with the Father, but that he is of one mind with him; which means that whatever Christ does has behind it the power of God.

Believest thou not that I am in the Father, and the Father in me? *The words that I speak unto you I speak not of myself.* John 14:10.

These words refer not to Christ's divine essence, but to the manner of revelation. For, as to his secret deity, Christ is known to us no better than the Father. He is rightly called the express image of God, for the Father revealed himself totally in the Son: but in the sense that God's unbounded goodness, wisdom, and power appeared in him. Therefore, the fathers were not wrong when they found in this verse a basis for asserting the divinity of Christ. Still, since Christ is here speaking not of what he is in himself, but of what he is toward us, it is a question of power rather than of essence. The Father therefore is said to be in Christ because the fullness of Divinity dwells in him, and manifests his power in him. On the other hand, Christ is said to be in the Father, because by his divine power he shows that he is one with the Father.

The words which I speak to you. He proves by the effects of his words that we should seek God nowhere but in him. He contends that his teaching, which is heavenly and truly divine, is evidence and the brilliant reflection of God's own presence. If anyone objects that the prophets also were sons of God, because, inspired by the Spirit, they spoke in a divine manner, so that God was the author also of their teaching—the answer is easy. We should consider the content of their teaching: the prophets send their disciples to someone else; Christ on the other hand holds them as his own. We must keep in mind what the apostle says in the first chapter of Hebrews: namely, that God spoke by the mouth of his Son from heaven; whereas he spoke by Moses, as it were, from the earth.

Ye have heard how I said unto you, I go away and come again unto you. If ye loved me, you would rejoice, because I said, I go unto the Father; for my Father is greater than I. John 14:28.

This passage has been variously distorted. The Arians, in order to prove that Christ is beneath (second to) God, objected that he is less than the Father. The orthodox fathers, in order to cut such calumny short, said that this statement refers to Christ's human nature. Even though the Arians abused this statement wickedly, the answer given by the fathers was neither right nor relevant. It is a question neither of the human nature of Christ nor of his eternal divinity, but of mediation between us and God because of our own weakness. Since it is not given to us to go up to the height of God, Christ came down to us in order to raise us there. Rejoice, he says, because I return to the Father; because this is the ultimate destination at which you yourselves ought to aim. With these words he does not show how he differs from the Father; he tells us that he descended to us, to unite us with God. Unless we arrive at this point, we remain stranded midway. Unless he lead us to God, we only imagine a mutilated Christ, cut into half.

Of a similar import is I Cor. 15:24, where Paul says that Christ will turn over the Kingdom to God and the Father, that he be all in all. Obviously, Christ does reign not only in his human nature, but as God manifest in the flesh. How then will he put aside his Kingship? Plainly, the divinity which we now discern only on the face of Christ will then be seen openly and conspicuously in him as his. The only difference is that Paul is here referring to the ultimate and perfect manifestation of divine brightness, whose rays began to shine when Christ ascended to heaven. To make the matter more plain, let us speak more bluntly. Here Christ does not compare the divinity of the Father with his own; neither does he compare his human nature with the divine essence of the Father. But rather, he contrasts his present state with the glory of heaven where he was soon to be received again. What he means is, "You want to keep me in this world, but it is better that I ascend to heaven." So therefore let us see Christ emptied of the flesh, that he may lead us to the fountainhead of blessed immortality. He is our leader, not in order to raise us to the sun or to the moon, but to unite us with God the Father.

Jesus answered, and said unto them, Though I bear record of myself, yet my record is true: for I know whence I came, and whither I go: but ye cannot tell whence I come, and whither I go. John 8:14.

Though I testify. Christ answers that the authority of his witness is sufficient as the ground for faith, because the status (*persona*) he bears is very different from that of a private man picked out of a crowd of common people. He sets himself apart from the common run of men by saying that he knows where he comes from and where he is going. What he means is that although we must suspect an ordinary man who pleads his own cause, and although our own laws warn us not to believe a man who speaks on his own behalf, we are not to apply such reservations to the Son of God who has a pre-eminence above the whole world. Christ, who has the privilege from the Father to bring all men in line (*ordo*) by his mere word, must not be reckoned as of the order (*ordino*) of men.

I know whence I came. By these words he discloses that he is not of this world, but has come from the Father; and that for this reason it is foolish and wicked to subject his teaching, which is from God, to human standards. These people treated him with contempt because he had put on our lowly flesh and was among them in the form of a servant; therefore, he turns their attention to the future glory of his resurrection, in which his divinity, now hidden and unknown, was to shine forth in all its proper glory. The lowly position of Christ among them should not have prevented the Jews from submitting to the unique Ambassador of God, who had been promised shortly before in the law itself.

When he says that he knows and they do not know, he means that their unbelief does not in the least take away from his glory. Besides, since he has given the same testimony to us, faith ought to despise all the chicaneries and vicious outcries of wicked men; for, if it is founded upon God, it is far above the loftiness of the world. Moreover, if the majesty of his gospel is to remain before us, we need to see him always in his heavenly glory; we need so to hear him speaking in the world that we may keep in mind where he came from and what sovereignty he has obtained, now that his work as ambassador is finished. For, as he humbled himself for a season, so he now sits at the right hand of the Father, that every knee may bow to him.

And the word which ye hear is not mine, but the Father's which sent me. John 14:24.

No matter how great, therefore, the mad insolence of the world, let us follow the teaching of Christ which rises high above heaven and earth. When Christ denies that the word is his own, it is for his disciples' sake. He means that the Word is not from man, and that he teaches by the authority of the Father. Still we know that since he is the eternal wisdom of God, he is the foundation of all doctrine; and all prophets since the beginning have spoken by his Spirit.

And the Word was made flesh. John 1:14.

The Evangelist has already spoken of Christ's coming. He now tells us he came putting on our flesh and showing himself openly to the world. He touches briefly upon the ineffable mystery that the Son of God put on human nature. Even though brief, he is astonishingly clear. At this point, some mad people amuse themselves with frivolous subtleties and make fools of themselves. They say, The Word is said to have been made flesh in the sense that God conceived the Son in his own mind and then sent him into the world as a man; as though the Word were I do not know what sort of shadowy image. But we have shown that the statement refers to a real hypostasis in the essence of God.

By saying "flesh," the writer expresses himself more forcibly than if he had said *He was made man.* He means to state that the Son of God, for our sakes, left the height of his heavenly glory and humbled himself to a state at once low and abject. When Scripture speaks of man with contempt, it calls him *flesh.* In spite of the vast distance between the spiritual glory of the Word of God and the stink of our filthy flesh, the Son of God stooped so low as to take upon himself this same flesh which is subject to so many miseries. *Flesh* here means not, as so often with Paul, our nature corrupted by sin, but mortal men in general. Still, it refers to our nature with disdain as frail and perishing; so we read in Scripture in Ps. 78:39, *Thou art mindful that they are flesh,* and in Isa. 40:6, *All flesh is grass.* (There are other passages of this kind.) At the same time, however, we must notice that this is a figure of speech: [flesh] which is one part of man, stands for him as a whole. Therefore Apollinaris[2] was foolish to fancy that Christ put on a human body without the soul.

Now my soul is troubled. . . . John 12:27.

At first this verse seems to differ greatly from the preceding

---

[2] Apollinaris (d. 392) taught that Christ had a human body and the life of a man, but that in him the rational soul or mind was replaced by the λόγος. Thus he represented Christ as neither God nor man, but a mixture (μίξις) of the two. He was repudiated, but orthodoxy was permanently infected by him.

discourse. There he showed more than heroic courage in exhorting his disciples not only to undergo death, but to face it willingly and eagerly whenever needful. But now he shrinks from death and seems to go soft. However, here we do not read anything that does not agree with the believers' own experience. If scoffers laugh at this, it is no wonder; one cannot understand it except by experience.

Besides, it was necessary for our salvation that the Son of God should have been affected in this way. In his death, we must first consider the work of expiation which appeased the wrath and curse of God; this he certainly could not have done unless our sin had been transferred to him. The death, therefore, to which he was subjected had to be dreadful even to him, because he could not have made satisfaction for us unless he had known God's dreadful judgment; we know better the enormity of sin because the Heavenly Father exacted such a dire punishment of his only-begotten Son. Therefore, we must realize that death was not a pleasure or a game for Christ, and that he suffered excruciation to the utmost for our sakes.

And it was not absurd that the Son of God should have been thus troubled. In the act of expiation, the secret divinity of the Son was quiescent and did not exercise its power. Christ in fact put on not only our flesh but also our human feeling; and this he did voluntarily. He was afraid not by constraint, but because he willingly subjected himself to fear. It must be firmly held that his fear was real and not fictitious. But he was unlike the rest of mankind in that, as we have said elsewhere, his feelings were tempered by obedience to the righteous God.

Christ's humanity in feeling has a further value for us. If Christ had not been troubled by the fear of death, which of us would take his example seriously? It is not given to us that we should face death without a troubled mind; so, when we hear that he was not made of iron, we gather our forces and set out to follow him; and the weakness of our flesh which troubles us at death does not hinder us from joining our Leader in battle.

Then the devil taketh him up into the holy city, and setteth him on a pinnacle of the temple, and saith unto him, If thou be the Son of God, cast thyself down; for it is written, He shall give his angels charge concerning thee; and in their hands they shall bear thee up, lest at any time thou dash thy foot against a stone. Jesus said unto him, It is written again, Thou shalt not tempt the Lord thy God.

Again the devil taketh him up into an exceeding high mountain, and

showeth him all the kingdoms of the world, and the glory of them. . . .
Matt. 4:5–8.

It is no great matter that Luke puts this temptation second, while Matthew puts it last. The Evangelists did not arrange their stories exactly in time, but so as to put together, as in a mirror or picture, the main events which are most useful for our knowledge of Christ. It is enough to learn that there were three temptations of Christ. It is foolish to worry our heads over which came second and which third. In this exposition, I shall follow Matthew's text.

It is said that Christ was placed on the pinnacle of the Temple. But the question is whether he was actually lifted up there, or whether this happened in a vision. There are many who assert obstinately that Christ was taken up there, as we say, really and truly; because, they say, it was unworthy of Christ that he should have been subject to delusion at the hand of Satan. This objection is easily disposed of, since it would by no means have been absurd for Christ to have been tempted with God's permission and his own willing subjection [to God's will], provided he did not yield inside himself, that is, in his mind and spirit. And what is said further, namely, that he was shown all the kingdoms of the world, or, as Luke has it, that in the twinkling of an eye he was carried to faraway places, fits best the supposition that all this happened in visions. In a doubtful matter like this, where ignorance does no harm, I prefer to pass no judgment, rather than to provide contentious people with something to quarrel about. It is in fact probable that the second temptation was not continuous with the first, or the third with the second. It may well be that some time elapsed between the first temptation and the second, and the second and the third. This may be so in spite of Luke's saying that Christ rested awhile, which suggests that the time in question was short.

He will charge his angels concerning thee. Satan's malice should not escape us. He misuses the testimony of Scripture, to make the life (Scripture) deadly for Christ, or to turn bread itself into poison. He does not cease using the same trick daily. When the Son of God chose to submit to this trial in his own person, he became an example to all believers, so that they may carefully avoid falling into Satan's snares by a wrong use of Scripture. And without a doubt, the Lord gives our enemy so much leeway, not to put us at our ease and make us lazy, but that we may rather be on our guard. We must be especially careful not to be like those preposterous people who, just because Satan corrupts Scripture, throw it aside as much too doubtful. According to this rule we should stop eating, since there is always danger of being poisoned. Satan does profane the Word of God and twist it around for our undoing; but still Scripture was ordained for our salvation. Shall God's purpose become invalid, just because our own indolence keeps us from using it for our good?

There is no need to argue this point at length. Let us only see what Christ prescribes by his example, which is the rule we are to follow. Does he yield when Satan gives Scripture a wicked twist? Seeing that Satan had armed himself with Scripture, does he let him hold on to it and make away with it? On the contrary, he in turn takes up Scripture, and with it refutes the wicked calumnies which Satan had thrown at him. In the same way, when Satan hides his deceptions under Scripture, or when godless men attack us and try to subvert our faith under the pretext of using Scripture, we should borrow our arms from Scripture alone, and so defend our faith.

Now, even though the promise, *He shall charge his angels concerning thee*, belongs to all the faithful, it applies peculiarly to Christ; because as the head of the church, he has authority over the angels, and they watch over us by his command. Satan was not wrong in using this text to show that the angels were given to Christ as his servants, to protect him and bear him upon their hands. He was wrong in presenting angelic protection as something vague and haphazard; on the contrary, it is promised to the children of God only as they keep to the way which leads to the fulfillment of God's purpose for them. Whatever the force of the phrase *in all thy ways* (Ps. 91:11), Satan wickedly corrupts and mutilates the prophet's words, and both tortures and confuses them when he makes them include any kind of way, however wrong and errant. God commands us to walk in the ways he has set before us, and in this connection declares that his angels shall protect us. When Satan brings up the matter of angelic protection, his intention is to make Christ walk into any danger that comes along; what he says amounts to this: "If you throw yourself at death in defiance of God, his angels will defend your life!"

It is written, Thou shalt not tempt the Lord thy God. Christ answered most aptly that believers cannot hope to receive the promise of God's help except as they humbly let him guide them. We are in no position to rely upon God's promises unless we obey his commandments. Now, we tempt God in many ways. But here *to tempt* is to neglect the means he puts in our hands. This is what men do when they make trial of God's power and prowess, at the same time that they set aside the means provided by God; this is like cutting off a man's hand and arms, and then telling him to do something! In short, whoever desires to experiment with God's power unnecessarily, tempts God by subjecting his promises to unlawful scrutiny.

The devil takes him to a high mountain. As I have said before, we must remember that Satan had this power over Christ's eyes not because of a weakness in his nature, but by a free purpose and permission. Even though Christ's senses were affected and moved by the glory of the kingdoms presented to him, no inward lustful desire pierced his soul; quite otherwise the lusts of the flesh lay hold of us like powerful beasts, and drag us to the things that give us pleasure. Christ had our feelings, but not our unruly appetites. Now, the temptation put before Christ was to seek the inheritance God has promised his children elsewhere than in God. And the daring sacrilege of the devil appears in his seeking to rob God of his empire and to usurp it for himself. "All these things," he said, "are mine; and no one can have them except by my power."

We ourselves have to struggle with the same imposture, which every believer knows within himself, and which we see even more clearly in the whole life of the ungodly. For, even though we know that we owe our security, goods, and comforts to the blessing of God, our senses flatter and bewitch us into seeking Satan's help, as though God were not enough for us. Therefore, the greater part of mankind deny God's authority and sovereignty over the whole world, and imagine that the giver of every good thing is Satan. For, how does it come about that men are universally addicted to evil machinations, to rapine and fraud, if not because they credit Satan with what God alone can do; namely, enriching us by his benediction and according to his good pleasure. They say with their mouth that God gives them their daily bread; but with their mouth only. In fact, they set Satan up as one who dispenses all the riches of the world.

3. Ascension: Examples of Exegesis

Then the disciples went away again unto their own homes. But Mary stood without at the sepulcher, weeping: and as she wept, she stooped down, and looked into the sepulcher, and seeth two angels in

white sitting, the one at the head, and the other at the feet, where the
body of Jesus had lain. John 20: 10–12.

It may well be that when the disciples returned home, they
were full of doubt and hesitation. Although John says that
they believed, it is evident that their faith was not firm. They
had a confused feeling that a miracle had happened; but they
went about as it were in a trance, until something better confirmed them in their faith. It is evident that the sight they saw
was not enough in itself to produce solid faith. What is more,
Christ did not reveal himself to them until they were aroused
from the stupidity of the flesh. When they ran to the sepulcher,
they did indeed give a praiseworthy evidence of their zeal;
still, Christ hid himself from them because their search for him
was much too superstitious.

But Mary stood. Now the Evangelist begins to tell the story
of how, when Christ testified to his resurrection, he appeared to
the women as well as to the disciples. Even though here Mary
alone is mentioned, it seems to me probable that the other
women were with her. It is not rational to suppose that these
other women had fainted out of fear. The writers who take this
view try to escape a contradiction in our story which, as I have
shown, does not exist.

We need not praise the women because they remained at the
sepulcher, while the disciples returned home; for the latter
went home comforted and full of joy, whereas the women indulged themselves in stupid and pointless weeping. What kept
them at the grave was mere superstition, together with the
feelings of the flesh.

And seeth two angels. What wonderful forbearance our Lord
shows toward Mary and her companions in putting up with
their many faults! He does them no small honor by sending
them his angels and then by showing himself to them—an
honor which was denied even to the disciples. Even while the
apostles and the women labored with the same disease, the
stupidity of the former was the less excusable because they had
learned so little from the careful and exact teaching of Christ.
Certainly, it was to shame them that Christ chose to show
himself first to the women.

It is not certain whether Mary recognized the angel or took
him for a man. We know that white garments symbolize
heavenly glory. When Christ revealed his majesty to his three
disciples on top of the mountain, there he also was clothed in
such white garments. Luke says the same thing of the angel who

appeared to Cornelius. I do not deny that Mary might have taken the angel for a man, because Eastern peoples often wore white garments. But the garments with which God adorned his angels were peculiar to them; they were marks by which men might see and recognize them. Besides, Matthew compares to lightning the countenance of the angel who spoke to the women. But still, probably the women's wonder worked only fear; they seem to have stood there struck with stupor and beside themselves.

Moreover, when we read that angels appeared in the visible form of men and clothed in garments, we must remember that this was done to offset human weakness. I have no doubt angels were at times clothed with a body; but as to whether these particular two angels merely appeared to have bodies, that is not the main question, and I shall not settle it. For me it is enough that the Lord gave them a human form, so that they might be seen and heard by the women. They were covered with uncommon splendor, so that they might be distinguished from human beings and show forth what is heavenly and from God.

One at the head, and the other at the foot. The fact that Matthew mentions only one angel does not contradict John's story. Both angels did not speak to Mary at once; this was done by the one who was commissioned for it. There is not much to Augustine's allegory that the position of these angels indicates the course of the future preaching of the gospel, from the place where the sun rises to the place where it goes under. In this place, it is more worth-while to notice the auspices under which Christ ushered in the glory of his Kingdom. When the angels honored Christ's grave [with their presence], they exhibited his celestial majesty. But they did so without abolishing the ignominy of the cross.

Jesus saith unto her, Touch me not; for I am not ascended to my Father: but go to my brethren, and say unto them, I ascend unto my Father, and your Father; and to my God, and your God. John 20:17.

This does not seem to agree with the account in Matthew (28:9): for he writes openly that the women embraced the feet of Christ. Now, since Christ allowed himself to be touched by his disciples, why did he forbid Mary? The answer is easy, if we only remember that Jesus did not repel them until they overdid their desire to touch him. When it was a matter of removing doubt, then surely he did not forbid them. But when he saw that they held on to his feet, he calmed their excessive zeal, and corrected it. They clung to his bodily presence, because they knew only an earthly way of enjoying him. The truth is that Jesus did not forbid them to touch him until he saw their stupid and excited desire to keep him here on earth. Let us note therefore the reason he gave for the prohibition: *for I am not yet ascended to the Father.* By these words, he commanded the women to control themselves until he was received into heavenly glory. Finally, in this way, he pointed out that the purpose of his resurrection was quite different from their fancy about it. He was come to life again not to triumph in the world, but rather to ascend to heaven and to take possession of the Kingdom which had been promised to him; to reign over the church at the right hand of God, by the power of his Spirit. . . .

I ascend unto my Father. With the word *ascend*, he confirms what I have said before. For certainly he rose from the dead not to linger awhile longer on earth, but so that, having entered the heavenly life, he might draw the faithful to him. In short, with this word the apostle forbids us merely to stop with resurrection. He bids us to go forward until we arrive at the spiritual Kingdom, at heavenly glory, at God himself. Therefore this word, *ascend*, is very emphatic; Christ stretches out his hand to his own, so that they may seek their happiness nowhere but in heaven. For where our treasure is, there also must our heart be (Matt. 6:21). Now, Christ declares that he is about to ascend on high; therefore, let us also rise with him, if we would not be separated from him. Furthermore, when he adds that he will ascend, he quickly dispels the sadness and anxiety of his disciples because he was to leave them behind. He wants them to know that by his divine power he will always be with them. *Ascend* indeed implies distant places; but even though Christ is absent bodily, because he is with God, his spiritual power, which works everywhere, shows clearly that he is present with us. Why indeed did he ascend to the Father, except, seated at his right hand, to reign in heaven and on earth? Finally, with this statement Jesus intended to commend the divine power of his reign, so that his bodily absence might not trouble his disciples.

And declared to be the Son of God with power, according to the Spirit of holiness, by the resurrection from the dead. Rom. 1:4.

If you prefer, "designated" to be the Son, etc. (*definitus*). He means that the power of the resurrection, by which he was pronounced the Son of God, was as it were a decree; as in Ps. 2:7, *I have this day begotten thee.* "Begotten" in this verse means actually "made known." Some find in this verse three evidences of the divinity of Christ: his power for working miracles, the witness of the Spirit, and his resurrection from the dead. I prefer to put the three together into one as follows: Christ was designated the Son of God when he rose from the dead, by an open exercise of true heavenly power, which was the power of the Spirit; but the knowledge of this power is sealed in our hearts by the same Spirit. The language of the apostle agrees well with this interpretation. The power with which he was declared, or the power which shone forth in Christ, that is, in his resurrection, was God's own power; and this proves that he was God. The same point becomes clear in another place where Paul confesses that Christ's death revealed him as subject to the infirmity of the flesh, and extols the power of the Spirit in his resurrection (II Cor. 13:4). But this glorious work cannot be known by us unless the Spirit himself impresses it upon our hearts. The very fact that Paul calls the Spirit the Spirit of holiness, shows that in his mind the same wonderful efficacy of the Spirit revealed in the resurrection of Christ from the dead is to be seen in the witness which individual believers know in their hearts. He means that as the Spirit sanctifies, he shows and ratifies the power which he exercised once before in raising Christ from the dead. The various titles which Scripture gives to the Spirit fortify the present argument. For instance, our Lord calls him the Spirit of truth, because he effects truth in believers (John 14:17).

Besides, the power shown forth in Christ's resurrection was his own as well as God's; as is evident from the sayings: *Destroy this temple, and in three days I will raise it up* (John 2:19); and, *No one takes my life; of myself,* etc. (John 10:18). For he did not beg his victory over death (to which he yielded by the infirmity of the flesh) from another, but achieved it by the working of his own Spirit.

Wherefore he saith, When he ascended up on high, he led captivity captive, and gave gifts unto men. (Now that he ascended, what is it but that he also descended first into the lower parts of the earth? He that descended is the same also that ascended up far above all heavens, that he might fill all things.) Eph. 4:8–10.

Because Paul makes this testimony fit his purpose by turning it aside from its original meaning, the wicked accuse him of abusing Scripture. And the Jews go further. They are malicious enough to pervert the natural meaning of this verse, so as to lend color to their calumny that what is said here of God, applies to David and the people of Israel! David, they say, or the people, *ascended up on high*, when, elated by many victories, they were set high above their enemies. But when one weighs carefully what the psalm as a whole says, it becomes clear that the above words apply only to God. The whole psalm is as it were an *epinicion*, a song of triumph, which David sings to God, celebrating the victories given him by God. He makes the recital of his own exploits in this psalm an occasion for commemorating God's own wonderful acts in the deliverance of his people. His aim is to open the eyes of the people to God's glorious power and goodness in the Church. And so, among other things, he says, *He ascended up on high*. When God does not exercise his judgment in an obvious way, the mind of the flesh thinks that he is idle or gone to sleep. So, according to the judgment of men, when the church is oppressed, God himself is brought low. But when he stretches out his arm in vengeance, he is said to arise and ascend to his judgment seat. This way of speaking is common and well known; so the deliverance of the church is called the ascension of God.

When Paul saw that in this psalm David celebrated the triumphs of God with which he wrought salvation in the church, he rightly applied this verse about the ascension of God to the person of Christ. The greatest victory of God took place when Christ, having overcome sin, conquered death, and put Satan to flight, was lifted up to heaven in majesty, that he might reign gloriously over the church. Therefore, there is no reason why anyone should object that Paul's use of this prophecy was contrary to the mind of the psalmist. Since David saw the glory of God in the continuance of the church, it is evident that no ascent of God shall be more victorious and memorable than that which occurred when Christ ascended to the right hand of the Father, to bring to subjection all principalities and dominations, and then to become in eternity the defender and protector of the church.

He led captivity captive. Captivity here is a collective noun for captive enemies. It means simply that the mighty God has overcome his enemies; but this was done more thoroughly in Christ than in any other way. He has overthrown not only the devil, sin, death, and all hell, but also the lust of our flesh, thus by his word making us rebels into an obedient people. On the other hand, he binds his enemies, that is, all the wicked, with chains of iron, and restrains their fury by his power, so that they can do no more than he permits.

The next phrase, *and gave gifts to men,* is especially difficult. According to the psalmist, God receives gifts. Paul speaks of giving gifts, which seems to be quite the opposite of what the psalmist says. Still, this is not absurd. Paul is not interested in quoting Scripture word for word. All he wants to do is get at the real meaning of the passage he mentions. Certainly God received the gifts David speaks of, not for himself but for his people. A little before, the psalm itself had said that the spoils of war had been divided among the families of Israel. Since God received in order to give, even though Paul altered the wording of the psalm he did not depart from its meaning.

At the same time, I am inclined towards another opinion; namely, that Paul changed the word *received* intentionally. When he did this, he intended not to misquote the psalm but to coin an expression of his own which would serve his present purpose. Having quoted a few words from the psalm, with regard to Christ's exaltation, he added that *he gave gifts.* He wanted to show that God's ascent in Christ's person was more excellent than his victories in the ancient church [Israel]. What he does is to compare the lesser with the greater; for after all, when a victor gives freely and bountifully to all his men the spoil taken from his vanquished enemies, his glory is greater than if he gathered it up for himself. The view of others who say that Christ gave us what he received from the Father is forced and has nothing to do with this verse. Thus, in my judgment, the most natural explanation of this passage is that, after quoting the psalm briefly, Paul takes the liberty of adding a phrase of his own, because it is suitable for Christ. The point is that the ascension of Christ is more excellent and wonderful than God's glorious deeds as recounted by David.

Now that he ascended. Now the false accusers belabor Paul again, saying, What frivolous and childish argument is this that forces a figure of speech about the manifestation of divine glory, to apply to the real ascension of Christ! Who does not know, they say, that the word *ascended* is a metaphor? And why infer that he must have first descended? My answer is this. Paul does not here argue like a logician about what follows necessarily or what we may infer from the words of the prophet. He knew very well that what David said of God's ascension was metaphorical. But still, it cannot be denied that God's exaltation indicates a previous humiliation. Paul has a good reason for inferring the descent from the ascent. And when did God come down lower than he did when Christ emptied himself? If God was ever brought down ingloriously, and then ascended with glory, it was when Christ, from the depths of our condition, was received to the glory of heaven.

In short, here we must not look for a careful and literal interpretation of the psalm. What we have is a mere allusion to the word of the prophet. Paul does the same thing in Rom. 10:6, when he turns a passage from Moses to his own use (Deut. 30:12). If there be any doubt about the rightness and propriety of Paul's application of this passage to the person of Christ, it is removed by the evidence of the psalm itself, which is a song in celebration of his Kingdom; because, for one thing, it contains a distinct prophecy of the calling of the nations.

Into the lower parts of the earth. There is no sense in torturing this phrase to make it mean purgatory, or hell. Paul is speaking simply about our condition in the present life. The argument from the comparative *lower* is very weak. What we have here is not a comparison of one part of the earth with another, but of the whole earth with heaven. He means that Christ left his exalted seat and came all the way down into our own deep abyss.

He . . . ascended up above all heavens: that is, beyond the created world. When we say Christ is in heaven, we must not imagine that he is somewhere among the cosmic spheres, counting the stars! *Heaven* means a place far beyond all the spheres, destined for the Son of God after his resurrection. When we speak of it as another place outside the universe, we do so because we must speak of the Kingdom of God using the only language which we have. There are those who claim that no space separates Christ from us, because, they say, *above all heavens* and *ascended into heaven* amount to the same thing! But they forget that whether he be above heavens or in heaven, he is beyond everything under the sun and stars, beyond all the spheres which surround the earth, beyond the whole machinery of the visible world.

That he might fill all things. Since *to fill* often means to accomplish, we may so understand it in this place. When Christ ascended to heaven, he came into possession of the dominion given him by the Father, to rule and direct all things by his power. I think we might arrive at an even more beautiful conception if we put together two ideas which, contradictory though they seem, are in fact perfectly congruous one with the other. So soon as we hear that Christ is ascended, we fancy that he is far away from us; as he indeed is in his humanity or in the body. But Paul reminds us that although he is absent from us bodily, he nevertheless fills all things by the power of his Spirit. Whenever the right hand of God, which embraces heaven and earth, is revealed, Christ's spiritual presence fills all things with the exercise of his boundless power. And this is so, even though, according to Peter, his body is and remains in heaven (Acts 3:21).

Thus, we see that Paul, by indulging in an apparent contradiction, added not a little to the grace of his exposition. Christ, who was before enclosed in a narrow space, ascended to fill heaven and earth. But, did he not do this before? Yes, I admit, he did it before in his divinity. But, after he took possession of his Kingdom, he began to exercise the power of his Spirit in a new way; and in the same Spirit, he revealed his presence among us. As John says: *The Holy Ghost was not yet given, because that Jesus was not yet glorified* (7:39); and again, *It is expedient for you that I go away; for, if I go not away, the Comforter will not come to you* (16:7). In short, when he began to sit at the right hand of the Father, he began also to fill all things.

But he, being full of the Holy Ghost, looked up steadfastly into heaven, and saw the glory of God, and Jesus standing at the right hand of God, and said, Behold, I see the heavens opened and the Son of Man standing at the right hand of God. Acts 7:55–56.

He saw the glory of God. As I said before, Luke means that when Stephen raised his eyes to heaven, immediately Christ appeared to him. But before that he tells us that Stephen was given other than earthly eyes, whose vision enabled him to rise as far as the glory of God. From this we receive the general consolation that God shall be no less with us, provided, leaving the world behind, all our senses seek after him; not that he will appear to us in an external vision as he did to Stephen, but that he will so reveal himself within us as to give us a true knowledge of his presence. And this way of seeing should be enough for us, since, by his grace and power, God not only shows that he is near us, but also proves that he lives in us.

Behold, I see the heavens. God did not intend to have only private dealings with his servant. He wanted to trouble and vex his enemies. For, when Stephen declares openly that he was given this miracle, he offers them a powerful insult. But it may be asked, How were the heavens opened? So far as I am concerned, I judge that nothing was changed as to the nature of the heavens, but that Stephen was given a new sharpness of vision which, overcoming all obstacles, penetrated to the invisible Kingdom of Heaven. For, even if heaven had been torn apart, no human eye could have reached so high as to see it. Therefore, only Stephen saw the glory of God. As to the wicked who stood there, not only was this spectacle hidden from them, but also they were so blinded within themselves as not to perceive the open light of truth. Therefore, he says that the heavens were opened to him, because nothing prevented him from seeing the glory of God. From this it follows that the miracle was wrought not in the sky, but in his eyes. Therefore, we should not dispute about a physical vision, because certainly Christ did not appear to him in a way and order that is natural, but in a new and singular fashion. And, pray tell me, what were the colors of God's glory that they might have affected naturally the eyes of flesh? Therefore in this vision we should consider nothing but what belongs to God. Besides, it is very much worth noting that the glory of God appeared to Stephen not strictly as it was but in so far as a man is capable of seeing it. For the immeasurableness of God's glory cannot be comprehended by the measure of the creature.

4. CHRIST THE KING AND THE KINGDOM OF CHRIST

Nathanael answered and saith unto him, Rabbi, thou art the Son of God; thou art the King of Israel. John 1:49.

It is not surprising that Nathanael knows Jesus as the Son of God because of his divine power. But why does he call him the King of Israel? For, these two things do not seem to be related. But Nathanael is looking deeper. He had heard that Christ is the Messiah; and now he confirms this doctrine which was given [by the prophets], with the further statement that He is the Son of God. Moreover, he reminds himself of the self-evident truth that the Son of God shall appear to become King over God's people. He is therefore right in confessing that the Son of God is also the King of Israel. Faith not only should be fixed upon the essence of Christ (as they say), but should also attend to his mission and power. It avails little to know who Christ is, without knowing also what his will for us was to be and to what end he was sent by the Father. This is why the papists have but the shadow of Christ; they care only to know his bare essence, and neglect his Kingship which consists in his power to save us.

Moreover, when Nathanael calls him the King of Israel, he shows that he is of little faith; because the Kingship of Christ extends to the ends of the world. His faith had not made enough progress for him to realize that Christ was destined to be the King of the whole world, or that the children of Abraham would be gathered together from all parts, so that the whole world might be the Israel of God.

For unto which of the angels said he at any time, Thou art my Son, this day I have begotten thee? And again, I will be to him a Father, and he shall be to me a Son? Heb. 1:5.

Thou art my Son. It cannot be denied that this was spoken of David, but in so far as Christ was in him;[3] therefore, the things we find in this psalm were foreshadowed in David, but manifested in Christ. When David conquered the many enemies surrounding his kingdom and enlarged its borders, there was a foreshadowing of the fulfillment of the promise, *I shall give the nations for thine inheritance.* But how little this was compared with the Kingdom of Christ, which extends from East to West! Again, David was called the Son of God because he was called to do great things. But his glory was a mere spark compared with that which shone forth in Christ, who bore the very image of the Father. Christ alone deserves the singular honor of bearing the name *Son* because the Father has sealed him alone, and no one else, with his image. Therefore, it is blasphemous to give the title *Son* to anyone but Christ.

But the argument of the apostle does not seem to be very strong. He claims that Christ is superior to the angels because he is called the Son. But Christ has this name in common with the princes and all those who are high in power, of whom it is written: *Ye are gods, and the sons of the most high.* Besides, the prophet conferred a greater honor upon the whole people of Israel, when he called them the first-born of God (Jer. 31:9). In fact, in Scripture they are often called *sons.* Again, elsewhere, David calls the angels also sons of God; as when he says, in Ps. 89:6, *Who is like the Lord among the sons of God?* But, the answer to all this is not difficult. The princes are given this name because of their peculiar position; Israel, because by God's grace they were his chosen people; the angels are called sons of the gods figuratively, because they are heavenly spirits and taste of divinity in their blessed immortality. But when David, representing Christ's Person, calls himself without qualification the Son of God, he means something unique, an honor far above that of the princes, or of the angels, or of the whole

3 Literally, he bare the Person of Christ.

people of Israel. But it were most inapt and improper to set Christ above all others as the Son of God, if he had nothing more than they. For the expression *Son of God* sets him apart from the class and number of all other beings. *Since thou art my Son* is spoken to Christ alone, it follows that no angel shares this honor with him.

If again someone takes exception to this argument and says that it raises David above the angels, I reply: It is not absurd that David should be set above the angels, in so far as he is the image of Christ; just as it was not an insult to the angels that the high priest who expiated sins was called a mediator. Neither David nor the high priest received the title for himself; but in pointing to the Kingdom of Christ, each derived his title from Him. The sacraments also, which are in themselves without life, are honored with titles which even the angels cannot claim without blasphemy. Hence it is clear that the argument from the use of the word *Son* is valid.

As to Christ's being begotten, briefly speaking, I take it that in this verse it has to do with his relationship to us. Augustine's subtle reasoning, according to which *today* means in eternity or perpetuity, is frivolous. Of course, Christ is the eternal Son of God, because he is the wisdom of God begotten before time. But this has nothing to do with our verse, which expresses the truth that men know Christ as the Son of God because the Father has revealed him as his Son. Similarly, the *declaration* mentioned by Paul in Rom. 1:4, was, so to speak, a kind of outward begetting. The secret and inward begetting which went before, was beyond human knowledge; it was above our understanding, until God gave us visible evidence of it.

I will be to him a Father. The same is true with regard to this second testimony, which refers to Solomon. Although Solomon was inferior to the angels, yet when God promises to be his Father, he was set apart from the commonality of men. God was to be a Father to him, not as to one of the sons of Abraham, or to one of the princes, but as to one who had pre-eminence over all the rest. The same preference which made him a Son, excluded all others from an equal honor. But now, the context of this verse makes it clear that Solomon is declared the Son, not in himself but as a figure, an exemplar of Christ. The universal kingship here mentioned as destined for the Son, is also said to be a kingdom without end. The kingdom of Solomon, on the contrary, was narrowly bounded; and it was far from being perpetual, since it was divided soon after his death; and a little while after it fell. Besides, in that psalm, the Lord makes a vow, with the sun and moon as witnesses, that so long as they shall shine in the heavens, his Kingdom shall stand. But this does not apply to David's kingdom which collapsed in a short while and finally was utterly destroyed. Further, we may gather readily from many passages in the prophets, that such promises belong to no one but Christ. And let nobody cavil that this is a new invention of ours. For, the Jews called Christ, commonly and usually, the Son of David.

But to which of his angels said he at any time, Sit on my right hand, until I make thine enemies thy footstool? Heb. 1:13.

Again, he exalts the superiority of Christ by another testimony, in order to show the pre-eminence of Christ over the angels.

This verse is taken from Ps. 110, which can be made to apply only to Christ. We know very well from the story of Uzziah's leprosy, that even the kings had no right to act as priests (II Chron. 26:18). Since it is clear that neither David nor the kings who followed him were ordained to be priests, it follows that here we have a prophecy of a new kingship and a new priesthood, in which king and priest were to be one. Besides, the eternal priesthood spoken of in this psalm fits the case of Christ alone.

Now, at the beginning of the psalm, he is put at God's right hand; which means, as I have said, that he is given a position second only to the Father. What we have here is a metaphor which signifies that Christ is the Father's agent and his head ambassador who exercises his power, so that the Father reigns by his hand. No angel was ever honored in this way. Christ therefore is exalted far above the host of angels.

Until I make. Since there never is any dearth of Christ's enemies who set themselves against his Kingdom, the church is always in peril; especially because his foes, who seek to overthrow it, are among the great men of this world; men who both resort to artifice and attack repeatedly with fury and violence. When we look at what is before our eyes, we cannot but conclude that the Kingdom of Christ is about to fall in ruin. But the promise made in this psalm takes away all our fear, because Christ shall not leave his seat [at the Father's right hand] until he has prostrated his last enemy to the ground. There are two things to keep in mind. First, there shall never be quietness for the Kingdom of Christ in this world, because it will always be infested and troubled by its enemies. Secondly, no matter what evils they perpetrate, the enemies of Christ shall not prevail, because Christ sits at God's right hand, not for a time but in eternity. Therefore, all those who do not submit to his sovereignty shall be thrown down and trodden under his feet.

That I may lead forth a people, blind who have eyes and deaf who have ears. Isa. 43:8. (Calvin's wording.)

The brevity of this verse makes its meaning unclear. There are some who translate "I will bring forth the blind and him who has eyes"; that is, both the blind and the seeing, both the deaf and the hearing. Others explain *blind* as those who have eyes, but eyes which are too dim to be able to perceive the secrets of heavenly wisdom. But taking everything into consideration, I prefer to separate the two parts. "I will lead forth the blind, and restore sight to them; I will free the deaf, and they will regain their ears." So the words run: *lead forth the blind, and they will have eyes; the deaf, and they will have ears.*

The content of this verse requires careful consideration. First the people are freed; then eyes and ears are restored to them. The Lord fulfilled this promise when he led his people from Babylon, but the prophecy certainly extends beyond that to the Kingdom of Christ. For in his Kingdom the faithful have been gathered not only from Chaldea, but also from all parts of the earth. This began conspicuously long ago at the time of Peter's first speech (Acts 2:41), when great numbers from different countries joined in one confession of faith. But later others, who seemed wholly alien, joined with the same body and showed themselves sons of Abraham.

Therefore if we seek the full truth of this prophecy we must come to Christ, by whom alone we are delivered from slavery to the devil and confirmed in liberty. He restores eyes and ears to us who were formerly by nature both blind and deaf.

Further we must remember, as I have emphasized rather often, that the return of the people from exile is connected with the restoration of the church accomplished by Christ. For what God began when he brought the people out of exile, he continued and fulfilled in the coming of Christ. So the redemption is one. And hence it follows that the blessing here described cannot be limited to any one short period of time.

And in mercy shall the throne be established; and he shall sit upon it securely in the tabernacle of David, judging, and seeking judgment, and hasting righteousness. Isa. 16:5.

The Hebrews apply the whole verse to Hezekiah, but this interpretation is by no means acceptable. The prophet is describing a greater restoration of the church. (Besides, the Moabites did not suffer punishment in the time of Hezekiah, nor did God's blessing then begin to shine among the Judeans.) What he means is: All the enemies of the chosen people are planning the destruction of the Kingdom which God had promised would be firm forever. But the faithful must not lose courage when they are miserably scattered; they must remember this well-known oracle which attests the continuance of God's Kingdom. And this passage can be interpreted as referring to none other than Christ; although I admit that Hezekiah stands as a symbol of Christ, as did David and his other successors. But all these [men] point us to Christ himself, who alone redeems and leads his people, who alone gathers his scattered remnant.

In this way the prophet recalls the faithful to Christ; it is as if he said: "You know the God whom you serve. He declares himself the guardian of your safety to keep you always secure and unharmed under his protection. And if all things have slid down to disaster, he has promised you a Redeemer under whom a wholly new happiness will rise and prevail. At the very moment of despair the Redeemer of the church will come and restore you to the full flower of freedom. Therefore be perfectly calm and wait for him, even when you see the church poor and scattered."

We must note these words carefully. All other comforts are temporary and illusory unless we depend wholly upon Christ. Therefore if we wish to be blessed and happy let our eyes be fixed upon him. He has promised that we shall be blessed even under the cross; that crucifixion and torture will be the door to a blessed life; that whatever hardships we suffer will end for us with the fullness of felicity.

In mercy. As Isaiah shows, this is no human achievement, but results from the goodness of God who is its sole architect. Therefore we must acknowledge his free favor, and accent the establishment of this holy throne among us as his gift. This the prophet asserts plainly. We should seek no other reason for God's kindness to us except his pure compassion; and truly there is no other cause for it.

Neither honor nor merits (of which surely there are none) can be brought forward as a reason for God's raising again the throne which had fallen through the guilt and the crimes of the people. Quite otherwise, when he saw that those whom he had chosen were lost, he willed to give an example of his infinite goodness. If God is the maker of this throne, by whom can it be overturned? Are the wicked stronger than he?

He will sit firmly in the tent of David. Almost every separate word has its own force, and this little clause is worth careful study. I like the allusion to the tent here because Christ was certainly a man of the common people before he was called to his throne. Also the prophet wishes to give a picture of the church which bears no resemblance to the thrones of kings and princes, and does not glitter with gold and gems. And in addition to presenting the spiritual rule of Christ under a humble and inglorious aspect, he declares at the same time that it will be revealed on earth and among men. For if he had said only that the throne of Christ would be erected, we could wonder if it would be located in heaven or on earth. When he says *in the tent of David*, he shows that Christ reigns not only among angels but also among men. Therefore, we should not think that we must penetrate the heavens to seek him.

The ungodly think that what we proclaim about the reign of Christ is ridiculous; as if it were some phantasm of our own imagination. They wish to see with their eyes something open to their senses. But we have no need to receive any physical sign from him, and are content with his power and goodness.

In firmness (firmly). *'emeth* means sometimes *certainty*, sometimes *truth*. Here the prophet means that Christ's Kingdom will be firm and enduring, even as Daniel (2:44; 7:14) bore witness, and the Evangelist also: *Of his kingdom there will be no end* (Luke 1:33). This permanence distinguishes it from the ordinary kingdoms. For although they are established with great and plentiful resources, they totter or sink by their own weight, so that they are no firmer than images of melting wax.

But Isaiah declares that the empire of Christ, although threatened often by destruction, will endure forever because it will be upheld by God's hand. We must keep his testimony on hand as a weapon against the temptations which arise when Christ's Kingdom is attacked by so many mighty enemies that it seems about to fall. For although the world plots [against it] in every way, and hell itself pours out fire and flame against it, the promise stands.

Who will judge. I take *judge* (*shaphat*) as "govern"; as if the line ran "who will govern." We often see a magnificent throne without an occupant; and it often happens that kings are either figureheads or cattle, so that they are without good judgment, or prudence, or wisdom. But on this throne, the prophet says, will sit one who truly fulfills the office of Governor. Then he makes a further addition to assure us that Christ will be our protector. For when he attributes *justice* and *righteousness* to him, he displays the royal banner under the protection of which Christ receives us and which he will not allow to be violated. And so long as we give ourselves to faith in him, with calm and quiet minds, he will not permit the wicked to injure us with impunity.

The word *hasten* is used to teach us that our reward will be swift and prompt; and this speed must be set against our impatience. For he never seems to us to bring aid quickly enough. But when we are tormented with fervent longing, let us remember that we suffer from impatience because we do not give room enough to his Providence. When to our carnal mind he seems slow, he is really fitting his acts of judgment to the time which he best knows. Let us then submit to his will.

He will judge among many peoples and accuse (or *blame*) *strong nations afar off; and they will beat their swords into plowshares and their lances into sickles. They shall not lift the sword, nation against nation, and they will no more be accustomed to war.* Micah. 4:3. (Calvin's wording.)

Here the prophet describes the fruits of the teaching of God's word. God will recall all peoples to gentleness, so that they will strive to promote brotherly peace among themselves and will lay aside all desire to inflict injuries. As he said before, the church of God can be established in no other way than by the Word. True service of God cannot be begun, nor can it endure, except where God is served by the obedience of faith. Now he shows the goal to which the teaching leads. Those who once lived in mutual hostility and burned with the desire to hurt one another, now, with character transformed, are wholly intent on mutual kindness.

But before the prophet comes to this point, he says *he will judge among many peoples and accuse strong nations.* The word *judge, shaphat,* in Hebrew also means *govern.* God is certainly the subject of the sentence. The prophet is saying that although formerly men did not obey God, they will in the future know him as King and concede supreme power to him. God indeed has always governed the world by his hidden providence and so governs it now. However much the devil and wicked men may rage, however much they boil with their own unrestrained anger, there is no doubt that God checks and curbs their madness with a hidden bridle.

The Scripture speaks in two ways of God's rule. God governs the devil and all the wicked, but not by his Word nor by the Spirit's sanctification. They obey God against their wish and will. God's special rule applies to his church alone, where God by his Word and Spirit turns the hearts of men to obedience, so that they follow him freely and voluntarily. They are thoroughly taught within and without; within, by the inspiration of the Spirit; without, by the preaching of the Word. Then, as Ps. 110:3 says, *your willing people will assemble*. Such is the Kingdom of God, which the prophet here describes.

God *will judge*, not as he now governs the whole world, but in a special way he will subject the faithful to himself so that they desire nothing so much as to surrender themselves wholly to him. But because men must be subjugated before they offer such submission to God, the prophet has added in plain terms *He will convict* (or *accuse*) *many people*. And this addition must be carefully noted, because from it we learn that our inborn pride is too great for anyone, unless mastered by force, to be ready to be God's pupil. The teaching by itself would congeal in the great corruption of our nature, if God did not convict us, that is, unless he prepared us beforehand by force and violence. Now we see the prophet's wisdom in including correction in God's rule. The verb *yakach* means sometimes "remonstrate with," "accuse," sometimes "*convict*." In any case, it here implies the wickedness and perversity of our flesh, since even the best of men never surrender themselves to God until they are subdued. Subdued how? Truly by God's use of force in their correction.

Such are the beginnings of the reign of Christ. The prophet speaks here of *strong peoples* to glorify that reign and to illuminate it by his words. We see here the power of the teaching of the Word, because, after receiving its correction, strong men offer themselves without any hesitation to be ruled by God. The correction is very necessary, but God does not use external force nor any armed soldiers when he wishes to subdue his church. And yet he gathers in it strong men. The power of the teaching is therefore undeniable. For among men, where there is strength, there also is assurance and pride, and afterwards rebellion. But the Word, without any external aid, corrects men's obstinacy, and we see that God works in an unbelievable way when he gathers his church.

There is certainly no doubt that this passage must refer to the Person of Christ. Micah speaks of God without specific mention of Christ, because Christ had not yet been manifested in the flesh. But we know that God's rule of the world and the submission of the peoples of the whole earth to him had its fulfillment in Christ. Also we have affirmed that Christ is true God, for he was not called his Father's servant like Moses or the other prophets. He was supreme King of his church.

But before I come to the fruits of Christ's reign, the phrase inserted here, 'ad rachoq, must be noted. Both length of time and distance of place can be so expressed. The Targum of Jonathan[4] takes it as length of time, because God accuses people through the ages. But I have no doubt that the prophet wished to include far-separated regions; as if he said, God would be King not of one people only: his Kingdom would be extended to the farthest ends of the earth. Therefore he will *convict nations afar off*.

Then the prophet describes the consummation: *They will beat their swords into plowshares and their lances into sickles.* I have already stated briefly his meaning. He speaks of the great change which will come when the nations have been taught the Word of God. Then all will strive to devote their work and their kindly acts to their neighbors. When he talks of *swords* and *lances,* he shows with few words that men have always been prone to unjust violence until they were tamed by the Word of God. Such a change would be impossible while every man followed his own nature. There is no one who does not want his own private comforts; so insatiable is man's greed. Therefore, when all are so intent on gain, when each one is blinded by his self-love, cruelty bursts out from this evil source. Men cannot cultivate peace among themselves, because each one wishes to be first, and snatches everything for himself. No one yields willingly. Thence come disagreements, and from disagreements, wars. This the prophet knows. Yet he adds that as the result of Christ's teaching those who had before then been bristling

---

[4] The Targums are Aramaic translations of the Hebrew Old Testament. Such translations were first made orally in the synagogues to convey the meaning of the Hebrew text to the Aramaic-speaking congregations (cf. Ezra 4:7; Neh. 8:7). Later, written translations were made. That of Onkelos on the Pentateuch is a very literal and exact translation; but the Targum of Jonathan on the Prophets is an edifying paraphrase rather than a translation. It was probably written in the first century A.D., although the tradition of interpretation which it represents is much older.

brutes would become tame. *Therefore they will beat their swords into plowshares and their lances into sickles. They will not*, he says, *draw sword, nation against nation, and they will practice war no more.*

This puts more clearly what I said before. The gospel of Christ will be like a signal of peace for the nations. When a battle standard is displayed, the soldiers gather for the fight and their ardor is kindled. Micah ascribes the opposite result to the gospel of Christ. It will recall men, formerly bent on evil-doing, to a desire for peace and concord. When he says *they will not draw swords, nation against nation*, he shows, as I have said, that where Christ does not reign men are wolves to men. Each one would gladly devour all the others.

By nature, men rush blindly to attack one another, and the prophet says this madness can be corrected, so that wars cease and men refrain from doing injury, only when Christ is made their teacher. For by the word *lamad*, he means that in general men are always struggling with one another and are always ready to inflict injuries unless they change their natures. Whence is gentleness born? Truly from the teaching of the gospel. This passage is memorable because we learn from it that the truth of the gospel has not reached us, unless mutual love and friendliness prevail among us, and the desire to do kindness.

And although today the pure gospel is preached among us, yet if we consider how little each one of us practices brotherly love, we shall rightly be ashamed of our negligence. Daily God declares himself reconciled to us in his Son. Christ bears witness in this law of love that he is [the giver of] peace with God. He offers himself for us, so that we may willingly and quickly be brothers to one another. And we desire indeed to be enrolled as sons of God; we desire to enjoy the reconciliation won for us by the blood of Christ. But meanwhile we tear at one another; we sharpen our teeth; our minds are wholly ruthless. If we wish to prove ourselves disciples of Christ we must heed this part of his teaching and each one of us strive to help his neighbors.

Now this cannot be done without opposition from the flesh; for we are prone to love ourselves and to seek too much our own private advantage. We must shed these immoderate and hurtful emotions of self-interest, if brotherly love is to take their place. We are warned here that it is not enough to refrain from doing injury; a man must be helpful to his brothers. The prophet could have said simply "they will break their swords and lances and refrain from inflicting further damage." But he does not say merely this; he adds, *They will turn* (or *beat*) *their swords*

into plowshares and lances into sickles. That is: when they have
ceased doing evil, they will desire to concern themselves with
acts of kindness. So Paul (Eph. 4:28) urges those who steal to
steal no more and also to work with their hands to serve others.
Therefore unless we want to help our brothers' need and to offer
them our aid, we are only half converted. Many people are not
cruel, they rob nobody, they give nobody reason to complain;
but they live for themselves and enjoy a useless leisure. This
idleness the prophet indirectly condemns when he speaks of
plows and sickles.

But the question may be raised: How has this been fulfilled
by Christ's coming? The prophet is not describing here the
state of the church at any time; he is showing what Christ's
Kingdom will be like at the end. Moreover we know that when
the gospel was first preached, the whole world was more
savagely embroiled in war than ever before; and now, although
in many places the pure gospel is preached, disagreements and
quarrels do not cease. We see greed, ambition, covetousness
flourishing; and from them arise both dissensions and bloody
wars. Yet it would seem to be an absurdity for the prophet to
speak this way about the reign of Christ, if God did not mean to
execute in reality what was predicted. I answer, the reign of
Christ had already begun when God wished the gospel to be
preached everywhere, and today it is still in progress and not
yet complete. Consequently what the prophet describes here
does not yet appear before our eyes. And because the number of
the faithful is small and the majority of men despise and reject
the gospel, robbery and evil deeds do not cease in the world.
Do you ask why?

The prophet speaks of Christ's followers. He shows the fruit of
the teaching. And truly it bears fruit wherever it takes good
root. But the teaching of the gospel takes root in hardly one out
of a hundred. We must look at the amount of progress. For in so
far as any man has taken hold of the teaching of the gospel he
becomes gentle and desires to help his neighbors. But since we
still carry around with us in our flesh the remains of sin, and a
perfect knowledge of the gospel does not exist in us, it is not
strange that no one has rid himself wholly of the unrighteous
and stupid desires of his flesh.

Hence it is easy to see how limited is the imagination of those
who on the basis of the gospel wish to remove the use of the
sword from the world. We know how the Anabaptists have
clamored that the whole political order is the enemy of Christ's

Kingdom; as if the Kingdom of Christ were bound up in one doctrine—there shall be no use of force. This teaching would indeed hold, if in this world we were angels. But as I have said the number of the faithful is small and therefore it is necessary that the rest of the crowd be restrained by a forcible curb. For the sons of God are intermingled with great, savage beasts, or with wolves and false men. For some are openly rebellious against God and others are hypocrites. Therefore the use of the sword will continue until the end of the world.

Now we must notice under what circumstances our prophet was speaking. Isaiah used the same words, and it is probable that Micah was Isaiah's disciple. For although they held their prophetic office at the same time, Isaiah was the elder. But Micah was not ashamed to follow Isaiah and to borrow words from him. Nor was he so concerned for his own importance that he had to produce everything himself. He conformed to what Isaiah had done, and repeated his words exactly, showing the agreement between himself and God's illustrious servant, in order to give the teaching greater authority. We recognize his humility when he gave no thought to ill-natured and spiteful men who might say: "What! He's only repeating somebody else's words." He cared nothing for such slander, and was content to affirm faithfully what God commanded.

The words *afar off* are not in Isaiah, but otherwise the two passages agree.

Behold the days will come, saith the Lord, and I will raise up for David a righteous Branch, and he will reign as king and act wisely (or *prosper*). *He will do judgment and righteousness on the earth.* Jer. 23:5. (Calvin's wording.)

The prophet confirms what he has just said about the restoration of the church. For it would not have been enough to promise shepherds who would faithfully perform their duty, if that one Shepherd on whom God's covenant was founded had not been assured to them. For, the fulfillment of every good for which men can hope must be sought in him.

It is usual for all the prophets, whenever they want to give the people hope of a happy future, to declare the coming Messiah. For in him have always been all the promises of God, now and forever, amen. This appears more clearly in the gospel; but the faith of the fathers could be complete only when they turned their thoughts to the Messiah. For apart from Christ, the fathers could not have had assurance of the love of God, or sure evidence of his kindness and fatherly goodness. This is the reason the prophets set Christ before men's eyes when they wish to inspire good hope in the distressed, who would otherwise be overcome by their sorrow and yield to despair.

We should notice how often the prophets do this, so that we may realize how cold God's promises would be to us, how they would hang in the air or vanish completely if we do not turn our minds to Christ, and seek in him the answer we shall find nowhere else.

There follows: *He will act wisely* (or *prosper*), *and will establish righteousness and judgment on the earth. Shakal* has both meanings, "act wisely" and "prosper," but the prophet seems to be speaking of just judgment rather than of good success, because the two clauses should be read together: "The Messiah will act wisely and then establish righteous judgment." He apparently means that Christ will be endowed with both wisdom and a spirit of right and justice, and so will fulfill all the requirements for a good and perfect king. And the first necessity is wisdom; for honesty is not enough in a king (indeed even among private citizens it gets only moderate praise); if he lacks intelligence, his honesty is of little use. Therefore the prophet here praises Christ for his true wisdom and then speaks of his love for justice and right.

These words are not adequate for honoring Christ. But the figure is taken from human experience; and it is true that the first gift of kings is wisdom, the second integrity. We know that Christ is often compared to earthly kings, or the picture of an earthly king is drawn for us to help us see Christ. For God adapts himself to our dull capacity. Since we cannot comprehend the unthinkable justice or wisdom of Christ, God brings us by easy steps to the knowledge of him by giving us a shadow of him in these similes. . . .

But the difference between the justice of Christ and the justice of other kings must be thoroughly understood. Those who rule well among men can exercise justice and judgment when they try to give every man his just due, by restraining the boldness of the wicked and protecting the good and harmless. This is all that can be asked of earthly kings.

But Christ is altogether different. Not only is he wise to perceive what is best and right, but also he endows his servants with wisdom and insight. He not only does judgment and justice by defending the harmless and aiding the oppressed, by helping the poor and checking the wicked; but also *he establishes justice* in regenerating us by his Spirit. And, *he establishes justice* further by putting a bridle on the devil.

Now we see what I meant when I said that we must attend to both Christ's unlikeness and his likeness to earthly kings. His unlikeness is exceedingly great; yet the comparison has value for us.

And on that day, Israel will be, with Egypt and Assyria, a third blessing in the midst of the earth. For the Lord of hosts will bless saying, Blessed be my people Egypt, and Assyria the work of my hand, and Israel my inheritance. Isa. 19:24–25. (Calvin's wording.)

Isaiah ends the promise with the addition that there will certainly be a blessing for Egypt and Assyria as well as for Israel. Earlier God's grace was in a sense limited to Israel, because with them the Lord had entered into a covenant. For the Lord had extended *his cord* to Jacob, as Moses and David say (Deut. 32:9; Ps. 147:20). *He hath not so dealt with every nation and revealed to them his judgments.* The blessing of God dwelt in Judea alone.

But the prophet says this blessing would in the future belong also to the Egyptians and the Assyrians. Under these names he includes all nations. He specifies these two, not to honor them, but because, since they had been continual enemies of God, they seemed the most alien and the farthest from hope of favor. God had earlier adopted only the sons of Abraham; he now wished to be called the Father of all nations without distinction.

The third. The interpretation of some that Israel will have third place does not please me. For since the Hebrew word is feminine, it ought to be joined to *barakah*, blessing. This blessing is to be understood as an example or mirror of all blessings.

Because he will bless. The repetition serves to explain the preceding. The prophet teaches that by God's free kindness, Assyria and Egypt will be united and associated with the chosen people. He means, "Although this title belonged only to Israel, it will be given also to other nations whom the Lord shall adopt for his own." There is a mutual relation between God and his people. They whom God by his own mouth names a holy people rightly call him their God. And this public naming is now extended to Egyptians and Assyrians.

But although the prophet meant to unite distant nations with the Jews, he differentiates their appropriate positions with suitable labels. By calling the Egyptians the people of God, he means that they will share the distinction with which God had formerly honored the Jews alone. By calling the Assyrians the work of his hands, he distinguishes them by the praise suited to God's church. We have said elsewhere that the church is called τὸ ποίημα of God (Eph. 2:10), or *his work*, because the faithful are remade by the Spirit of regeneration and bear the image of God. The prophet means by *the work of God's hands*, not that we were first created by God, but that we who are separated from the world and are made new creatures, are transformed for a new life. As we well know, nothing in that new life is to be ascribed to us; for we know it all to be God's work.

Israel he honors with its own unique privilege. Because it is God's inheritance, it keeps the right and honor of the first-born among its new brethren. Certainly God's covenant, which he first made with them, gave to them a priority which not even their own ingratitude could erase.

IV

The Christian Life

THE TEXT

1. SALVATION

For God so loved the world that he gave his only-begotten Son, that whosoever believeth in him should not perish but have everlasting life. John 3:16.

Here Christ presents us with the cause and as it were the fountain of our salvation, so as to remove all doubt; for our minds cannot come to rest in tranquillity unless they arrive at the free love of God. Since we are not to seek the ground of our salvation anywhere but in Christ, we must try to find out where he came to us from and why he was offered up to be our Savior. This verse distinctly teaches both truths: faith in Christ means life to all men, and Christ had this life because God loved mankind and would not let it perish. This sequence must be carefully noted. When it is a question of the source of our salvation, we must consider the inborn and wicked ambition of our nature, which traps us into the devilish fancy that we deserve to be saved. Therefore we imagine that God is good to us because he judges us worthy of his favor. But Scripture praises everywhere his pure and unmixed mercy, which does away with all merit.

By this text, Christ means to do nothing else than establish the love of God as the ground of our salvation. When we try to go beyond this, the Spirit himself slams the door in our face; he teaches us by Paul's mouth that God's love is founded in his own will and purpose (Eph. 1:5). And it is obvious that Christ spoke as he did so as to turn men's attention from themselves to the mercy of God alone. God does not declare that he was led to deliver us because he found us worthy of such a blessing. On the contrary, he attributes the glory of our deliverance solely to his love. This appears more clearly from the added statement: the Son was given to men that they may not perish. Therefore,

192

unless Christ rescues the lost, all are doomed to eternal ruin. Paul expresses the same thing in terms of temporal sequence: We were loved while we were enemies because of sin (Rom. 5:10). For surely, where sin reigns, there is only the wrath of God which carries death with it. It follows that mercy alone reconciles us to God and, in so doing, restores us to life.

The above may seem to conflict with many testimonies of Scriptures that Christ is the ground of God's love for us, since apart from him they present God as hating us. We must remember what was said before: the secret love with which our Heavenly Father embraces us, being his eternal purpose for us, takes precedence over all other reasons for our deliverance. But it is true that the grace which God wanted to show us, and by which we are moved to the hope of salvation, appeared with the reconciling work of Christ. Since sins are of necessity odious to God, how can we maintain that God loves us freely, unless an offering has been made for these same sins which are offensive to him? Hence, before we receive any knowledge of God's Fatherly good will for us, the blood of Christ must intercede for us and restore us to God's favor. Besides, as we were formerly told that God so loved us as to give up his Son to die for us, so it is immediately added that in a strict sense faith should look to Christ alone.

He gave his only-begotten Son, that whosoever believeth in him should not perish. Faith looks to Christ rightly when it sees in him the heart of God overflowing with love. Faith rests upon the death of Christ as upon a firm and solid support, and finds in it the only surety of salvation. *Only-begotten* is emphatic, commending to us God's love in all its fervor. And because it is hard for men to be persuaded of God's love, he removes all doubt by saying, We are so dear to God that for our salvation he did not spare his only-begotten Son. Since, therefore, God has testified to his love for us so sufficiently and abundantly, anyone who is not content and still doubts offers no small insult to Christ, as though he were someone who was killed by accident. Rather, we ought to reconsider that since God had the highest regard for his only-begotten Son, our salvation must be very precious to him, because he was willing to pay for it with the Son's death.

That whosoever believeth in him may not perish. What a praise of faith, that it delivers us from eternal destruction! Christ means clearly that even though we are born for death, by faith in him we are offered a sure deliverance from it; therefore, we ought not to fear the death which still awaits us. And now he adds a universal call, inviting all men without exception to share in life, and leaving unbelievers without an excuse. The word *world*, in the previous phrase, has the same significance. Even though there is nothing in the world worthy of God's favor, he shows himself gracious toward the whole world, and he invites all men without exception to faith in Christ, which is nothing less than entering into Life.

On the other hand, let us remember that while life is promised in Christ to all who believe, only a small part of the people are believers. Christ is indeed presented to all, but God opens the eyes of the elect alone, and enables them by faith to seek after him. The wonderful effect of faith is also seen in our receiving Christ from the Father, who has in Christ truly freed us from the punishment of eternal death, and made us heirs of eternal life; for by the sacrifice of his death, Christ has expiated our sins; and now nothing keeps God from acknowledging us as his sons. Since therefore faith embraces Christ, together with the efficacy of his death and the fruit of his resurrection, it is no wonder that by faith likewise we obtain the very Life of Christ.

It is not yet quite clear as to why and how faith gives us life. Is it because Christ himself regenerates us by his Spirit, so that the righteousness of God may live and flourish in us; or is it because, purged by his blood, by God's free forgiveness, we are accounted righteous before him? Of course these two go together. Still, when it comes to the certainty of salvation, we must hold to it that we live because God loves us, and that freely; this he shows by not imputing our sins to us. Sacrifice is here mentioned because by it sin, curse, and death have been abolished. As I have already explained, the two clauses put together in this verse mean that, having lost life, we recover it in Christ. In this wretched state of mankind, ransom comes before salvation.

As the Father hath loved me, so have I loved you: continue ye in my love. John 15:9.

There is much more in this verse than is commonly believed. Those who think that he is here speaking of the eternal and secret love of the Father, philosophize beside the point. It was rather Christ's purpose, in effect, to deposit in our laps a sure pledge of God's love toward us. The abstruse question of how God in eternity loved himself in the Son has nothing to do with this verse. The love in question here has to do with us, because it is as the Head of the church that Christ testifies to God's love for him. Any man who tries to find out how God loved Christ, apart from his office as Mediator, gets caught in a labyrinth, without path or exit. Let us therefore fix our eyes on Christ, because it is in him that we see the pledge of God's love clearly exhibited. For, God poured his love upon him, so that it might flow from him to the members of his body. This is also the significance of the title, *the beloved Son,* in whom the will of the Father is satisfied; and we must consider the purpose of this love, which is that God in Christ may be well pleased with us. Therefore, we must not look at God's love from afar off or in a mirror. Christ was loved by the Father not in and for himself alone, but that he might with himself unite us with the Father.

Continue ye in my love. Some explain these words to mean that Christ enjoined his disciples to love one another. Others explain it better when they say that they refer to the love with which Christ loves us. He in fact bids us live always in the joy of the love with which he once and for all loved us, warning us not to deprive ourselves of it. For many reject the grace offered them, and many throw away what they have in their hands. So then, once we are beneficiaries of the grace of Christ, let us see to it that we do not fall away from it through our own fault.

It is foolish to infer from the above words that, without the help of our constancy, God's grace avails nothing. I do not concede that the Spirit asks no more from us than what is within our ability. Rather, he shows us where we must turn when we lack the strength to obey him. When we hear Christ, in this verse, exhort us to perseverance, we must not rely on our own energy and industry; we must rather pray him who commands us to confirm us in his love.

For the Holy Ghost was not yet given, because that Jesus was not yet glorified. John 7: 39.

We know that the Spirit is eternal. But the Evangelist denies that the grace of the Spirit which was poured upon men after the resurrection of Christ was manifested in public while Christ was in the world in the form of a humble servant. He draws a similar contrast between the New Testament and the Old. In the New Testament, God promises his Spirit to believers as though he had never given him to the fathers. But of course the disciples had already received the first fruits of the Spirit; for where is faith from except from the Spirit? The Evangelist does not deny the presence of the Spirit among the godly before Christ's death; he only says that it was not so conspicuous and striking as after [the resurrection]. This then is the highest adornment of the Kingdom of Christ, that he rules over his church by his Spirit. He came to a proper and solemn possession of his Kingdom when he ascended to the right hand of the Father. No wonder then that the full revelation of the Spirit was deferred until that time.

But there is one question left. Does the Evangelist mean here the visible graces of the Spirit, or that true regeneration which is the fruit of adoption? I answer that the Spirit, which was promised with the coming of Christ, was seen in visible gifts as in a mirror; but here we have to do with the power of the Spirit by which we are born again in Christ and become new creatures. If now we are left on earth, poor, dry, and almost empty of spiritual goods, while Christ sits on the right hand of the Father glorious with the majesty of empire, it is because our faith is too puny and we are too slow [to rise to him].

He who heareth my word, and believeth in him who sent me, hath eternal life . . . hath passed from death to life. John 5:24.

Certain later Latin copies have changed *passed* into *shall pass*. But they have done this out of ignorance and rashness; not knowing what the Evangelist meant, they have presumed to do more than what was right. The Greek word is not in the least unclear. There is nothing wrong about saying *has passed from death*, because the children of God even now have in them the incorruptible seed of life, by which they are called and sit with Christ, by faith, in heavenly glory. Thus they have the Kingdom of God established firmly within them (Luke 17:21; Col. 3:3). Even while their life is hid, they nevertheless by faith do not fail to possess it. Even while they are besieged by death, they have peace because they know that Christ defends them adequately, and that they are safe. The state of the believers in this life is such that they always carry about the stuff of death in themselves. But the Spirit who lives in them is Life itself, and will at the end destroy what is left of death. Paul was right in saying that death shall be the last enemy to be destroyed (I Cor. 15:26). But obviously this verse has nothing to do with the coming full destruction of death, or with the ultimate complete manifestation of Life. The point here is that though life in us is only begun, Christ announces it to the believers as their sure possession. Thus he removes the fear of death from them. And this is not surprising, since they are united with (*insiti sint*) him who is the inexhaustible Fountain of Life.

Jesus said to her, I am the resurrection and the life; he that believeth in me, though he were dead, yet shall he live. John 11:25.

This is the exposition of the second clause. It tells us that Christ is the Life, because he will never let the Life he has given us be destroyed, and will on the contrary preserve it till the end. What would happen to us if we, who are flesh and weak, having received the Life, should be left to our own strength? Therefore, if Christ is to finish what he has begun, it needs be that we continue in Life through the power of Christ himself. Believers are said never to die because their souls, born again of an incorruptible seed, enjoy the indwelling of the Spirit of Christ, who gives them Life without ceasing. While the body is subject to death because of sin, *the Spirit is Life because of righteousness* (Rom. 8:10). The fact that the outer man decays from day to day does not hurt the believers' true Life. It even helps its growth, because the inner man in turn is renewed day by day (II Cor. 4:16). What is more, death itself is in its way an emancipation from bondage to death.

And I give unto them eternal life, and they shall never perish, neither shall any man pluck them out of my hand. John 10:28.

We have this matchless fruit of faith that, by Christ's command, we live with confidence and safety when we are gathered in his fold. At the same time let us keep in mind the support which makes this confidence firm; for he testifies that he has our salvation *in his hand* and will remain its faithful guardian. And as though this were not enough, Christ says that his disciples shall be defended by God's power. This is a striking passage. We are taught that the salvation of all the elect is as certain as that God's power is invincible. Besides, Christ was not beating the air. He wanted to give them a word of promise and to fix it deeply in their minds. Therefore, we must understand this statement of Christ as showing that the salvation of the elect is sure and firmly established. We are besieged by powerful foes; and we are so weak that every moment might well be our last. But because our salvation is in the hands of One who is greater, who is mightier, than all, we ought not to tremble as though our very life were in peril.

From this we gather further how insane is the trust of the papists which rests on free will, on one's own virtue and the merit of works. Far differently, Christ teaches his own that they must think of themselves as in a forest, surrounded by a host of robbers, knowing not only that they are unarmed and open prey, but also that they carry the stuff of death around with them. Hence, if they would live in safety, they can do it only by confidence in God's protection. The only reason for security is that our salvation is in God's hand. Our own faith is unfirm and we ourselves tend greatly to waver. But God who has taken our salvation into his hands is mighty enough to scatter all the weapons of our foes with one puff of his breath. The most important thing we can do is to turn our eyes to this [power of God], if we are not to be overcome by the fear of temptations. For Christ wanted to show us how the sheep are enjoying peace and quiet even while they wander among wolves.

And he said unto them, Ye are from beneath, I am from above; ye are of this world, I am not of this world. I said therefore unto you that ye shall die in your sins, for if ye believe not that I am he, ye shall die in your sins. John 8: 23 – 24.

Since they did not deserve instruction, he wanted to confound them with a curt reproof. So, in this place, he declares that they reject his teaching because they absolutely abhor the Kingdom of God. Under *world* and *below* he includes whatever men have by nature, and brings out the difference between his gospel and the sharpness and penetration of the human mind: the gospel is heavenly wisdom, but our minds are of the earth. No one, therefore, is fit to be Christ's disciple unless he is refashioned by his Spirit. And faith itself is so rare in the world because by nature all men, except those he lifts up by a special grace of his Spirit, are turned against Christ and estranged from him. *If ye believe not that I am he, ye shall die in your sins.*

The lost have no way of recovering salvation except by going to Christ. *That I am* here is emphatic, because it includes all that Scripture says of the Messiah and all that it bids us to hope in him. He is talking primarily about [his work in] the restoration of the church, which exists by the light of faith, and the righteousness and new life which grow from it. Some of the ancients have interpreted this passage as having to do with the divine essence of Christ. But in this they are wrong, because he is speaking of his office [or work] in our behalf. This statement is worthy of special notice. Men are always ignoring the evils which surround them. Even when they have to admit their peril, they neglect Christ and look all around for some other useless remedy. The fact is that unless we are extricated by the grace of Christ, we remain subject to the violence of a whole mass of innumerable evils.

For me to live is Christ, and to die is gain. Phil. 1:21.

In my judgment, interpreters so far have given a wrong translation and exposition of this passage; for the distinction they make is that, to Paul, Christ was life, and death gain. I, on the other hand, take Christ to be the subject of both the phrases in this statement, so that he is said to be gain in life and in death. (It is common in Greek to imply the word πρός without using it.) This interpretation, besides being less forced, goes better with what went before and expresses our faith more fully. Paul affirms that it makes no difference to him, and is the same thing, whether he lives or he dies, because having Christ, he is the gainer either way. And certainly, it is Christ alone who makes both our life and our death blessed; otherwise, if death be misery, life is no better. Hence without Christ, there is little to choose between life and death. On the other hand, if Christ be with us, he will bless our death equally with our life; and we shall look ahead to both with hope and gladness.

Which he wrought in Christ when he raised him from the dead and set him at his own right hand in the heavenly places. Eph. 1:20.

The Greek word is ἐνέργησεν, whence comes ἐνέργεια. In Latin you might say: According to the efficacy which he effected. My translation means the same, and is not as awkward.

However, here Paul rightly enjoins us to consider the power of Christ; for, so far, its presence in us is hidden, and *God's power is perfected in our weakness* (II Cor. 12:9). How are we ahead of the children of this world, except that our situation seems to be worse than theirs? Even though sin does not reign in us, it is still there. Since death itself is working in us, the blessedness we have by hope is totally hidden from the world; for the power of the Spirit is something flesh and blood knows nothing about. Meanwhile, we are exposed to a thousand distresses, and more than all other men are become objects of derision.

Hence, Christ alone is the mirror in whom we are able to see the glory which is altogether blurred in us who live in weakness under the cross we ourselves bear. Since it behooves us to raise our minds on high, to believe in righteousness, blessedness, and glory, let us learn to turn them to Christ. For we now live subject to the dominion of death; but he, having been made alive again by power from heaven, even now has life and dominion. We labor in servitude to sin; and besieged by a thousand afflictions, we are engaged in a dreadful warfare (I Tim. 1:18); he on the other hand, being seated at the right hand of God, has received all government in heaven and on earth, and triumphs wondrously over his foes as he defeats and overthrows them. We bite the dust, covered with contempt and ignominy; to him is given a name which fills men and angels with reverence, and makes devils and godless men grovel in fright. Here we are impoverished, so poor that we lack everything we need; he on the other hand has been appointed by the Father to possess all blessings and to dispense them according to his good pleasure. In view of all this, we shall be the gainers if we turn our minds to Christ, so that in him, as in a mirror, we may contemplate the wonderful treasures of divine grace and the infinite greatness of God's power, all of which we can hardly discern at present in our own lives.

Yet a little while, and the world shall see me no more; but ye see me: because I live, ye shall live also. John 14:19.

He continues to speak to his disciples of his special favor toward them, which should have been enough to mitigate and even take away their sorrow. "When I go away," he says, "and the world no longer sees me, I shall no less be still with you." If we are to rejoice in such secret vision of Christ, we must not judge his presence or absence with the eyes of the flesh. We must rather be intent upon discerning his power with the eyes of faith. Thus it is that Christ is always present to the believers and seen by them in the Spirit, even though they are bodily far from him.

Because I live. This may be taken in two ways. It may simply confirm what went before, or it may go with the next phrase, which says that the believers shall live because Christ lives. I accept the former alternative, even though we may also learn from it that we live because Christ lives. Christ points out why it is that his disciples shall see him, while the world shall not: Christ cannot be seen except in the spiritual life which the world does not possess. No wonder the world does not see Christ, for it is blind because of death. But no sooner does a man begin to live by the Spirit than he is given eyes with which to see Christ, because our life flows from the life of Christ as from its source. Otherwise, we have no life. We in ourselves are dead, and the life we boast is a most awful death. Therefore, when it comes to obtaining life, our eyes must be upon Christ, and his life must be given us by faith. So it is that we receive confidence that, while Christ lives, we are safe from the peril of destruction. For it remains an immovable truth that while he is alive the members cannot be dead.

Then said the Jews unto him, Now we know that thou hast a devil. Abraham is dead, and the prophets; and thou sayest, If any man keep my saying, he shall never taste of death. John 8:52.

The reprobate who keep on with their stupidity are not touched by promises, whether small or great. Hence they can neither be led nor drawn to Christ. Some think that the Jews slandered Jesus and twisted his words around when they spoke of tasting death, because they had not heard him saying anything of the sort. But I think this objection is flimsy. I rather think that the Hebrews meant the same thing by *tasting death* and *seeing death*. Both expressions meant simply "to die." Of course, to apply the spiritual teaching of Jesus to the body is to interpret it falsely. No believer shall see death, for he is born again of an incorruptible seed. Even though believers die, being united with Christ their head, they shall be not snuffed out by death. Their death is simply a transition to the Heavenly Kingdom; the Spirit dwelling in them is Life because of righteousness, and what is left of death in them is consumed. Those who are carnal know nothing about freedom from death except in an obviously physical sense. And this disease is much too common in this world, since many have only contempt for the grace of Christ, which they judge merely by the senses of their flesh. If we do not wish the same blindness to affect us, let us arouse our minds, so that they may discern spiritual life in the midst of death.

And when all things shall be subdued unto him, then shall the Son also himself be subject unto him that put all things under him, that God may be all in all. I Cor. 15:28.

Will God be all in all also in the devil and the ungodly? Far from it, unless perhaps we choose to accept "to be" as meaning to be known and openly be seen. If so, the statement would mean: "Since now the devil is at war with God, since the wicked confound and confuse the order established by him, since we see an infinity of scandalous deeds with our own eyes, it is by no means clear that God is *all in all*. But when Christ executes the judgment commanded him by God, and overthrows Satan and all the wicked, then in their destruction the glory of God shall be revealed. The same may be said of powers which are sacred and legitimate in themselves, for they now prevent, in their way, God's appearing to us rightly and as he is in himself. But then, God shall be *all* in the sense that he shall reign alone and directly in heaven and earth, and will therefore be in all; not only *in all* persons, but in all creatures."

Now, this is a pious interpretation, and since it agrees well enough with the apostle's purpose, I am willing to accept it. However, there would be nothing wrong in taking this verse as having to do with believers, in whom God has already begun his Kingdom and shall then perfect it, so that they shall cleave to him completely.

Both these interpretations in themselves are sufficient refutation of those who pretend that this verse proves their wicked deliriums. Some imagine that God shall be *all in all*, in that all things shall vanish and become nothing. But Paul's words mean only that all things shall be brought back to God as their only beginning and end, and shall thus be bound firmly to him. Others infer from this verse that the devil and all the wicked shall be saved, as though the fullness of God would not be more striking in the destruction of the devil than if he made him his associate and equal. We see therefore with what impudence such madmen torture Paul's statement when they use it to establish their blasphemies.

2. THE CHRISTIAN WARFARE

But let us, who are of the day, be sober, putting on the breastplate of faith and love, and for a helmet the hope of salvation. I Thess. 5:8.

Paul adds this in order that he may shake us the better out of our torpor. He calls us as it were to arms, to impress upon us that it is no time for sleep. He does not, indeed, mention war. But when he bids us to arm with a breastplate and a helmet, he is in fact calling us to warfare. It goes without saying that anyone who expects a surprise attack must rouse himself and keep watching. Having warned us to be watchful while we have the truth of the gospel for light, he now stirs us up with the argument that we have a battle to fight with the enemy, and that it is much too dangerous to be doing nothing. We know that soldiers, who may ordinarily be rather loose-living fellows, when they are near the enemy and in danger of being killed, avoid getting drunk or any other way of "having fun" so that they may watch and be wary. So, since Satan is always breathing down our necks, and is ready and scheming to plunge us into a thousand perils, we ought to be no less watchful and on our guard.

Some interpreters are much too clever in their handling of the pieces of armor mentioned by the apostle. This verse is quite different from Eph. 6:14, where Paul by "breastplate" means "righteousness." Here it is enough to understand that the whole life of Christians is like a perpetual warfare, since Satan never stops attacking and troubling them. It is therefore necessary to be prepared for resistance; and of course we are warned that we had better be well armed against such a powerful enemy. However, Paul does not in this place go into detail about the armor we must have; he merely mentions two pieces, the breastplate and the helmet. But he leaves out nothing a man needs for this spiritual warfare. For anyone who is provided with faith, hope, and love has all the weapons he needs.

Stand fast in one spirit, with one mind striving together for the faith of the gospel, and in nothing terrified by your adversaries: which is to them an evident token of perdition, but to you of salvation, and that of God. Phil. 1:27–28.

In the second place, he commends to the Philippians an indomitable spirit, that they may not be confounded by the fury of their enemies. At that time the fires of savage persecution blazed almost everywhere, because Satan fought with all his force to prevent the inauguration of the gospel; and the more Christ exercised the grace of his Spirit, the greater was the impotent rage of Satan. The apostle, therefore, enjoins the Philippians to stand firm and not to be perturbed.

Which is to them an evident token of perdition. This is the proper meaning of the Greek, and those who translate as "cause" have no good reason for doing so. When the wicked strive against the Lord, they engage in a preliminary battle which anticipates their ultimate ruin; and the greater the outrage they do against the godly, the more they are bent on their own perdition. Of course, Scripture does not teach us anywhere that the afflictions which the godly suffer at the hands of the godless become the cause of their salvation. Paul calls afflictions *evidences* or *proofs* [of salvation] in another place also (II Thess. 1:5). Instead of the word ἔνδειξιν, which we have here, there he uses the word ἔνδειγμα. It is, therefore, a singular comfort that the attacks and troubles we suffer at the hands of our enemies are visible evidences of our salvation. Persecutions are for God's children the seals of their adoption if they bear them with courage and a calm spirit. The ungodly, on the other hand, produce a token of their condemnation; they hit their foot against a stone which shall be their downfall.

And that from God. This is put here as the last clause, so that it may, with God's grace, mitigate the bitter taste of the cross. It goes against nature to see in the cross a sign or proof of salvation. In fact, the cross and salvation seem to be contraries. Therefore, Paul asks the Philippians to consider that God turns those things which make for our misery into occasions of well-being. In this way, he shows that enduring the cross is a gift of God; for it is certain that everything which is for our good is God's gift to us. "To you," he says, "it is given not only to believe in Christ, but also to suffer for him. Therefore your very sufferings are witnesses to the goodness of God, because in them you have a real evidence of your salvation." If only we were convinced deep in our hearts that persecutions are among God's blessings, what progress we should make in the knowledge of divine truth! What is more certain than that the highest honor which grace bestows upon us is that we suffer reproach, or prison, or troubles, or tortures, or even death itself, in his name? For so it is that he decorates us with his medals. And yet there are many who would tell God to take such gifts away, rather than embrace with grateful hearts the cross offered to them. But so much the worse for our stupidity!

For unto you is given in behalf of Christ not only to believe on him but also to suffer for his sake. Phil. 1:29.

He is wise to join faith inseparably with the cross, for in this way the Philippians are taught that they have been called to faith in Christ to the end that they may endure persecution in his name. In other words, their adoption could no more be separated from the cross than Christ could be severed from himself.

Thou therefore endure hardship as a good soldier of Christ. No man that warreth entangleth himself with the affairs of this life: that he may please him who hath chosen him to be a soldier. II Tim. 2:3-4.

It was very necessary to add this second warning. For, anyone who offers to obey Christ, must be ready to endure hardship; there is no perseverance without patience in enduring evil. Therefore he adds, As becomes a soldier of Christ: which means that anyone who is in the service of Christ is a soldier, and that such soldiering consists not in doing evil but in patiently bearing it.

It is absolutely necessary for us to think these things over. How many people we see every day who throw their spears away, people who had passed themselves off as good soldiers! And why does this happen, except because they cannot get used to the cross? In the first place, they are so soft that they cannot stand the thought of battle. Secondly, their idea of the warfare is to get into an [immediate] fight with their enemies. They cannot bear to learn what it is to possess their souls in patience.

He continues with the simile from warfare. Strictly speaking, at first he spoke of a "soldier of Christ" in a metaphorical sense. Now he definitely compares military warfare with the spiritual warfare of the Christian man. Military discipline requires that, as soon as a soldier puts himself at the disposal of a general, he leaves his home and every business behind, and thinks of nothing except the warfare to which he is committed. So also we, if we are to give ourselves wholly to Christ, must break away from all the entanglements of this world.

By *the affairs of this life* he means the care of maintaining a home and other ordinary occupations. The farmers leave their farming, and the merchants their shops and their business until they have served their term as soldiers. So also, whoever wants to fight under Christ must lay aside all the involvements and preoccupations of the world, so that he may apply himself wholly to the warfare. In short, let us keep in mind the old proverb, *Hoc age*; this do: which means that in doing our holy duty nothing should hinder our zeal and attention. The common translation, "No one who fights for God," etc., corrupts the whole meaning of what Paul has in mind.

Then answered Peter and said unto him, Behold, we have forsaken all, and followed thee; what shall we have therefore? And Jesus said unto them. . . . Every one that hath forsaken houses, or brethren, or sisters, or father, or mother, or wife, or children, or lands, for my name's sake, shall receive a hundredfold, and shall inherit everlasting life. Matt. 19:27–29.

Peter tacitly contrasts himself and the other disciples with the rich man whom the world had turned away from Christ. Since they led a life of privation and wandering, and suffered insults and sundry vexations, without hope of a better future, he asks rightly whether it was for nothing that they had left behind everything they had and had devoted themselves to Christ. It was absurd that when they had been despoiled by the Lord, they should not receive back more than they had lost.

But then, what were all those things they had left behind? Being poor and low-class folk, they did not even have a house to leave behind; hence, their boasting was nothing less than ridiculous. Our own experience shows that people commonly overestimate the things they do in the way of duty before God. There are people who were hardly more than beggars under the papacy; and now they go around arrogantly, complaining that they have made great sacrifices for the sake of the gospel. However, there was some excuse for the disciples who, although they did not possess splendid fortunes, lived by the labor of their hands, and were no less happy in their homes than people of great riches. And we know that humble people, who are used to a quiet and decent life, find it harder to be torn away from their wives and children than those who are driven by ambition, or thrown this way and that by the winds of prosperous fortune. Of course, unless there was some reward waiting for the disciples, they had been foolish to change their way of life. Still, although one might excuse them on that ground, they were wrong to demand a taste of triumph before their warfare was finished. When annoyance at the delay of our reward creeps upon us, and lures us to impatience, let us first learn to consider the consolations with which the Lord reduces the bitterness of the cross in this world, and then let us raise our spirits to the hope of heavenly life. Christ's answers make these very two points.

And whosoever shall leave. After having raised their minds to the hope of the future life, he offers them comforts for the present life, and fortifies them for bearing the cross. God does not allow his people to be grievously afflicted, at times even to the point of forsaking them, without making up for their sufferings with his help. Jesus does not say this to the apostles only; he takes the occasion to address his words to all believers in general. The point is that those who willingly give up all for the sake of Christ, have their chief reward in heaven; and yet, even in this life, they are happier than if they had kept everything.

However, it does seem that the hundredfold compensation provided them is not in line with the facts. For in most cases, those who have been deprived of their parents, or children, or other relatives, wives who are widowed and those stripped of their fortunes, all because they have borne testimony to Christ, do not recover their losses; on the contrary, in exile, lowly and forgotten, they struggle bitterly with poverty and hardship. To all this I answer: When we consider God's grace with which he relieves the miseries of his own, we must confess that it is to be preferred to all the riches of the world. For while the unbelievers flourish, they do not know what is waiting for them on the next day; therefore, they must always live in turmoil because of perplexity and fear; neither can they enjoy the smile of fortune without, one way or another, stupefying themselves. Meanwhile, God gives his own a glad heart, so that to them the little they enjoy is worth much more than if without Christ they were affluent with an abundance of riches. I interpret *with persecutions* added by Mark as follows: Christ means that even though the godly are always persecuted in this world, and live as though the cross were tied to their back, still, the condiment of God's grace is so sweet that it exhilarates them, and makes their condition more desirable than the luxuries of kings.

[I] now rejoice in my sufferings for you, and complete that which is behind in the afflictions of Christ in my flesh for his body's sake, which is the church. Col. 1:24.

The apostle had previously claimed for himself the authority which was his by virtue of his calling. Now he is concerned that the Colossians do not detract from the honor due him as an apostle because he had been in bonds and was persecuted for the sake of the gospel. For, Satan uses these occasions to bring contempt upon the servants of God. Further, the apostle encourages them by his example not to be terrified by persecutions; and he reminds them of his zeal, so that his words may carry more weight. Nay more, he settles the matter with an appeal to his love for them, and asserts that he is joyful and only too willing to suffer affliction for their sakes. Someone will ask, "But where is this joy from?" It is from the fruits which [his labors] have produced. "It is pleasant for me to be afflicted for you, because I do not suffer in vain." In the same way, in a former letter to the Thessalonians, he says that, having heard of their faith, he rejoices in all privations and afflictions.

And fill up that which is behind, etc. I take *and* to mean *because*; he says that he is joyful because in suffering he is associated with Christ. He desires nothing more blessed than such fellowship with Christ. He presents all believers in common with the comfort that in all tribulations, especially in those they suffer for the gospel, they share the cross of Christ, to the end that they may rejoice in sharing his blessed resurrection. Nay more, he affirms that in this way what is lacking in Christ's own afflictions is completed. Romans 8:29 says the same thing: "Whom God has chosen, them he has predestined that they may conform to the image of Christ, who is the first-born among the brethren."[1] Moreover, we know that since the Head and the members are united, the name *Christ* sometimes includes the whole body. This is evident from I Cor. 12:12, where, speaking of the church, the apostle finally concludes that being in Christ is like being [a member] in the human body. Therefore, as Christ suffered once in himself, so he now suffers every day in his members; and the sufferings which the Father decreed and appointed for his body are completed [in the church].

There is a second consideration, which ought to encourage and comfort our spirits in affliction: God himself has fixed and appointed by his providence that we be conformed to Christ by enduring the cross, and that our communion with him extend to this very point.

To this, he adds a third reason: that the sufferings of Christ bear fruit not only for the few, but for the church as a whole. He had before said that he suffered in behalf of the Colossians; now he declares more inclusively that the fruit of his sufferings extends to the whole church. Philippians 1:12 also speaks of this same fruit. What other explanation of this verse is clearer, simpler, and less forced? Paul rejoices in tribulation because, as he writes elsewhere, he considers that if Christ's life is to be manifest in us, we must carry about his death in our own bodies (II Cor. 4:10). He says the same in the letter to Timothy: "If we suffer with him, we shall also reign with him: if we die with him, we shall also live with him" (II Tim. 2:11). All will end in joy and glory. Hence, if the members of Christ are to have a symmetry with the Head, they must not reject the state which God himself has appointed for his church. The third point is this, afflictions must be borne to the end willingly, because they are useful to all the godly and promote the well-being of the whole church, by giving a peculiar beauty to the truth of the gospel.

Then they shall deliver you up to be afflicted, and shall kill you: and ye shall be hated by all nations for my name's sake. Matt. 24:9.

Now Christ predicts for his disciples another kind of temptation which shall try their faith; namely, that besides the common

---

[1] Calvin's citation is not correct. He has *elegit* for προέγνω.

afflictions [of man] they shall be hated and detested by the entire world. It is hard enough and sad enough for the children of God to be afflicted without distinction from and together with the wicked and despisers of God, and to be subjected to the same punishments which come upon the latter because of their crimes. It appears the height of injustice that they should be oppressed with the hardship of greater evils which do not touch the ungodly. Just as wheat, after being beaten with a flail together with the tares, is ground under a millstone and crushed, so also God not only afflicts his own with the wicked, but in addition subjects them to a cross which goes beyond what others [have to endure], so that they appear to suffer far greater misery than all the rest of the human race.

Christ here is speaking of the afflictions which the disciples were to suffer for the gospel. What Paul says in Rom. 8:29 is of course true. Those whom God elects, he destines to bear a cross, so that they may conform to the image of the Son. But there Paul means more than persecution at the hands of the enemies of the gospel. Here, on the other hand, Christ is speaking of the kind of cross which the faithful have to carry because of their witness to the gospel; for this makes it necessary for them to incur the hatred of the ungodly, to face their insults and provoke them to fury. He wants to warn his disciples that, as he had explained to them before, the doctrine of the gospel, of which they were to become witnesses and heralds, would at no time please the world or receive its applause. So he prophesies that they will not be fighting with only a few enemies, but that, everywhere they go, nations shall rise against them.

It was monstrous and incredible, calculated to amaze and trouble the strongest minds, that the name of the Son of God should become so infamous and hateful as to create hatred everywhere toward those who honored it. Therefore, Mark says, *take heed to yourselves*; and in this way he brings out the purpose and use of the above warning that they be prepared to endure, lest, being incautious, they be overcome by temptation. It is added further by the same Mark that when the disciples of Christ shall be brought before kings and rulers, it *will be a testimony against* them. Luke puts it a little differently: *This will happen to you in testimony*; but it means the same thing. For Christ says that, where his gospel is defended at the peril of death, there the testimony for it shall be all the greater.

Yea, for thy sake are we killed all the day long; we are counted as sheep for the slaughter. Ps. 44:22.

The faithful here plead for God's mercy, not because they are punished for their own evil deeds, but because they are hated by unbelievers for the name of God.

At first sight, this seems a foolish complaint, and Socrates' answer seems the more admirable when, in answer to his wife's reproach, he said that it was better to die innocent than for his own wrongdoing. Furthermore, the consolation which Christ offered (*Happy are those who are persecuted for righteousness' sake*, Matt. 5:10) appears very different from the words of the psalm. Peter also said the same thing: *Anyone who suffers for Christ's name has all the more reason for joy and thankfulness* (I Peter 4:14).

But I answer that although the best comfort for our sorrow is that its cause is connected with Christ, yet the faithful do not complain to God in vain or wrongly when they say that they are suffering unjustly for his sake. For in this way, they want him to come forward with more vigor as their defender, since it is right that he himself take care of his own glory, when the impious insult and deal cruelly with his worshipers. . . .

It is also right to remind ourselves that the faithful have not been so pure of all stain that God would be unjust in exacting punishment for their sins. But, by his incomparable indulgence, he does bury our sins and subject us to unjust persecution, so that we may glory in bearing the cross of Christ and may therefore be sharers and companions of his blessed resurrection.

This doctrine we must take for our own use. First, we must be ready, after the example of the fathers, to bear calmly any suffering by which our loyalty to the confession of our faith is validated. Secondly, in the deepest shadows of death we must constantly call on the name of God, and we must stand fast in fear of him.

Paul (Rom. 8:23) goes further and asserts that this passage does not merely offer us an example, but describes the perpetual situation of the church. Therefore we are assigned, by God's decree, the perpetual warfare of bearing the cross. At times God spares our weakness by allowing a truce, or a relaxation [of the warfare]. But although swords are not always drawn against us we must, because we are members of Christ, be always ready to share his cross. Let us not then be terrified by the bitterness of the cross, and let us keep this picture of the persecuted church always before us. So long as we are adopted by God in Christ, we are destined for slaughter. If we are to prevent the wearisome weight of the cross or our fear of it from turning us away from our faith, we must keep this thought continually in our hearts. The cup which God pours for us we must drink; no man can be a Christian who does not offer himself in sacrifice to God.

Ye have not yet resisted unto blood, striving against sin. . . . For whom the Lord loveth he chasteneth, and scourgeth every son whom he receiveth. Heb. 12:4, 6.

The apostle goes further and reminds us once again that, even while the wicked persecute us in Christ's name, our warfare is with sin. Christ himself was free from this struggle, because he was clean and unspotted by any sin. In this respect we are unlike him, for sin dwells in us at all times; and our afflictions serve to overcome and rout it.

In the first place, we know that all the evils in the world come from sin; and so came in the beginning death itself. But this is not what concerns the apostle. His point is that the persecutions we suffer are useful to us, because they are medicine for destroying sin. For in this way, God keeps us under the yoke of his discipline, so that our flesh may not play loose with sin. At times he checks our hot blood; at other times he punishes our misdeeds in order that we may afterwards become more careful. Therefore, whether he sets out to heal our vices, or to prevent us from doing evil, as the apostle says, he is training us for the struggle against sin. And when we suffer for his gospel, the Son of God himself honors us with his favor, and does not count our sufferings as punishment of sin. Still we must acknowledge the validity of what the apostle says: When we act against the ungodly in defense of the cause of Christ, we at the same time battle against sin which is the enemy within us. Thus the grace of God is double; he converts the remedy he uses for curing us from our vices into a means of defending his gospel.

Let us remember that the apostle is speaking to people who had thrown away their possessions and suffered many indignities; and had done all that willingly and with joy. And yet, he charges them with indolence because, exhausted while the battle was still in progress, they had not kept up the strenuous march to the end. It is not for us to ask the Lord to discharge us from his army, no matter what fighting we have done. For Christ will have no discharged soldiers, except those who have overcome death itself. . . .

For whom the Lord loveth. The reasoning of this verse seems rather shaky. The Lord afflicts the elect and the reprobate without distinction, and his scourges are evidence of his wrath more often than of his love. So says Scripture, and experience confirms it. And yet, with regard to the believers, it is not surprising that the apostle refers only to the benefit they derive from the troubles they experience. When God punishes the reprobate, he shows himself as a severe and wrathful judge; with his elect, he has no other purpose except to promote their salvation; and this is a demonstration of his Fatherly love. Moreover, since the ungodly do not know that they are governed by God's hand, they think that most of their troubles happen by chance. The ungodly are like a wrongheaded young man, who leaves his father's house and wanders far away; when he all but perishes from hunger and cold and other evils, he admits that he has met the just punishment of his stupidity; by his sufferings, he sees the value of being docile and obedient, but he does not understand that his troubles are the chastisement of his father. So also the ungodly, having alienated themselves from God and his household, do not understand that they are still within the reach of God's hand. Therefore, let us keep in mind that we cannot taste the love of God in our afflictions, unless we are persuaded that they are rods with which our Father chastises us for our sins. Nothing like this occurs to the reprobate, who have the mentality of fugitives from God. This is why it is proper that judgment should begin at the house of God.

Wherefore, even though God's hand falls upon those in his house and those outside, it falls upon the former to show his peculiar care for them. The true solution of our problem is as follows: anyone who knows and is persuaded that he is castigated by God must promptly go on to consider that God afflicts him because he loves him. Since the godly know that God intervenes in their punishment, they have a sure pledge of his good will towards them; for if he did not love them, he would not care about their salvation. Hence the apostle concludes that God offers himself as a Father to all those who endure correction. Those who would rather kick like wild horses, or harden themselves and fight back, are a different sort. In short then, the apostle teaches us that, when God corrects us, he does so only as our Father, provided we yield and obey.

3. The Cross and Persecution

And when forty years were expired, there appeared unto him in the wilderness of Mount Sinai an angel of the Lord in a flame of fire in a bush. Acts 7:30.

It remains to say something of the burning bush. God frequently makes use of a certain similarity among things for giving us signs; and this is the common reason for the sacraments. Besides, nothing could have been more appropriate for confirming the faith of Moses in God's present business with him. Moses knew in what state he had left his people. Although they were a great multitude, they were not unlike a bush. For the denser a bush and the more twigs it has, compactly put together, the more likely it is to burst into flame and the fire spreads most easily to all its parts. Similarly, the band of Israelites was weak and exposed to every kind of harm. This unwarlike multitude, kept down by its own dead weight, inflamed the fury of the Pharaoh until it could burst out with success. A people oppressed by a cursed tyranny is like a pile of wood which has caught fire on all sides. Nothing keeps it from being quickly reduced to ashes, unless the Lord himself sit in the midst of it. Although this story refers to the unusual persecution which was aflame at that time, it nevertheless in a way depicts the perpetual state of the church which is never, in this world, safe and free from affliction. For what are we but food for fire? Countless burning torches of Satan fly around constantly, and set souls as well as bodies on fire; but the Lord himself, by his wonderful and matchless grace, guards and defends us. The fire, therefore, must needs so burn that in this life it reduce us to nothing. But since God dwells in our midst, he keeps us from harm in the midst of our tribulation, as we read also in Ps. 46:5.

And the multitude rose up together against them; and the magistrates rent off their [the apostles'] clothes, and commanded to beat them. Acts 16:22.

When Luke tells us how a crowd gathered together, how some nobodies—in fact jugglers and those who put their bodies on sale, whose sordid ways everybody knows— raised a hue and cry, he reminds us of the world's fury against Christ. Although folly and levity are ever present among the whole population, the amazing power of Satan appears when those who are otherwise reserved and stable suddenly get excited over nothing and join the company of worthless people in resisting the truth of God. Nor did the magistrates themselves show any more restraint. By their gravity, they should have appeased the fury of the populace. They should have opposed violence with energy, and, with their resources, taken the side of the innocent. Instead, they make a disorderly and noisy arrest; and before hearing the truth of the matter, they have the apostles stripped of their clothes and whipped with green rods. Such is the deplorable depravity of mankind that almost all the tribunals of this world, which should be sanctuaries of justice, have been polluted by an impious and unholy assault upon the gospel.

One might also ask, Why were the apostles thrown in prison, when they had already received their punishment? For prisons were established for keeping people in custody, partly for punishment and partly that more might be learned about their case. But it is evident that the servants of Christ are treated with less humanity than adulterers, robbers, and other malefactors of their kind. This gives us a clearer insight into the power of Satan, who incites the spirits of men so that they observe no kind of justice when they persecute the gospel. Still, though the lot of the godly in defense of the gospel is harder than that of the godless in their wickedness, yet theirs is the brighter, because in all the evils which they undergo, they triumph gloriously before God and his angels. They indeed suffer insult and ignominy, but because they know that the wounds of Christ are more precious and carry more dignity in heaven than all the vain and smoky pomps of the earth the more they are wronged and slandered by the world, the more abundant reason they have for glorying. For, if Themistocles[2] used to be so honored by profane writers that they preferred his prison to the seats and courts of magistrates, how much more we should honor the Son of God in whose cause the faithful at all times suffer persecution for the gospel's sake. Besides, even though the Lord allowed Paul and Silas to be inflicted with scourging at the hands of godless magistrates, yet he did not let them suffer shame without turning it into a greater glory. Since the persecutions which go with bearing witness to the gospel are left over for us from the passion of Christ, as our Prince himself converted the curse of the cross to a chariot of triumph, so also he shall adorn the prisons and gibbets of his servants, and

[2] Themistocles (ca. 514–449 B.C.), the Athenian leader in the naval battle of Salamis against Xerxes, was a forceful and imaginative statesman. His checkered career ended in ostracism, and he went to Asia Minor where he was received by the Persians and lived in Magnesia until his death. He was a strong man, but he does not appear to have been a model of virtue. (See Plutarch's *Lives*.)

there they shall triumph over Satan and all the sons of wickedness.

Rending their garments. Since the ancient interpreter[3] had translated this phrase rightly, it was wrong of Erasmus to change it to mean that the magistrates tore their own garments. Luke simply meant to say that when the holy men were beaten, the order of lawful judgment was neglected and that those who laid hands upon them were so violent that their clothes were torn. For it was most alien to Roman custom for magistrates to tear their clothes to pieces publicly in the market place, especially when the matter on hand had to do with an unknown religion, whose protection was no great concern of theirs. But I will not dispute at length about such an obvious matter.

Wherein ye greatly rejoice, though now for a season, if need be, ye are in heaviness through manifold temptations, that the trial of your faith, being more precious than of gold that perisheth though it be tried with fire, might be found unto praise and honor and glory at the appearing of Jesus Christ. I Peter 1:6–7.

Even though the ending of the Greek verb is unclear, the sense of the passage requires that we read *you exult* rather than *exult!* The phrase *in which* refers to the manifold hope of salvation set down in heaven. But Peter does not so much praise as exhort them. His purpose is to teach the benefit we receive when we hope that we shall be saved; namely, the spiritual joy which not only mitigates the bitterness in all evil, but also conquers all melancholy. So, there is more to *exult* than to *rejoice*.

But it appears rather contradictory that the faithful who exult with joy should at the same time be sorrowful, for these are opposite feelings. But they know by experience what words can hardly express: that joy and sorrow go together. However, to settle the matter with few words, the faithful are not blocks of wood that they should be bereft of human sensibility when they meet sorrow, or that they should not be afraid when in peril, or be troubled by poverty, or by the hardships they have to endure under persecution. Therefore, evil does indeed make them unhappy. But faith sweetens their sorrow, so that there is no lack of joy in them because of it. Their sorrow yields to their rejoicing, rather than preventing it. Again, even though joy overcomes sorrow, still it does not abolish it, because it does not deprive us of our humanity. Thus we learn true patience; for its beginning and, as it were, its very root is the knowledge

[3] Jerome.

of God's favor, especially the awareness of the honor he has done us by his free adoption. Anybody who keeps this grace of God in mind has little trouble in absorbing the evils which he endures. For, why is it that we are oppressed by a melancholy spirit if not because we have no taste for the good which is spiritual? Anybody who realizes that the troubles he undergoes have their proper use as trials expedient for his salvation, not only rises above them, but also turns them into occasions of joy.

Ye are in heaviness. Since the reprobate in their turn are not immune to evil, do they not also experience sorrow? Yes, they do. But Peter recognizes that the faithful suffer sorrow willingly, whereas the godless murmur and are perverse enough to battle against God. The godly man suffers as a tame ox bears his yoke or as a horse that is broken submits to the bridle even when put on by a child. God visits the wicked with trouble, even as people bridle a fierce and ornery horse with violent hands: the horse kicks and fights back; but it is no use. Hence, Peter praises the believers because they bear their troubles willingly, and not under compulsion.

He says *now for a season* by way of consoling his readers. For the shortness of time is a mitigation of the evils we suffer no matter how hard they hit us. And we must remember that this present life lasts only a moment.

If need be. The reason for our sufferings is here taken for their cause. The apostle wants to make it clear that God does not make a trial of his people without reason. If God afflicted us without a reason, our burden would be too heavy to bear. Therefore, Peter argues for our comfort on the ground of God's purpose, not that we can always see the reason for our afflictions, but that they occur rightly (so we ought to be persuaded), since they occur at God's pleasure. . . .

More precious than gold. He argues from the lesser to the greater. For, if we prize a corruptible metal like gold so much that, to prove its value, we test it with fire, is it any wonder that God should want to prove our faith, which he prizes much more highly, in the same way? Even though the words of the apostle suggest another interpretation (in that he seems to set no value on gold), he nevertheless compares faith to gold so as to present it as the more precious of the two, and to imply that it is worth the trial to which God subjects it. Besides, the full extent of the meanings of δοκιμάζεσθαι (tried) and δοκίμιον (trial) is not certain. One cannot be sure whether he is speaking of a double testing of gold with fire: once when it is purified of its dross;

and then, when it is tested for judging its quality. Both of these tests apply to faith very well. Much of the impurity of unbelief remains in us. When we are, as it were, purified in God's furnace by various afflictions, the dross in our faith is purged, and the faith becomes pure and clean before God. At the same time it is tested to show whether it be a true or false faith. I accept willingly both these views of the matter, which seem to be justified by what follows immediately in our text. For, since silver is worthless before it is purified, so also our faith receives the honor of a crown before God when it is proved in the proper way.

At the appearing of Jesus Christ. This is added to teach the faithful to keep their spirits high until the end. For now our life is hidden in Christ; and it will remain hidden, and as it were buried, until Christ appears from heaven. The whole course of our lives moves toward the destruction of the outer man; and all the things we suffer are so many anticipations of death. Therefore, if we want to see glory and praise in the midst of our afflictions, we had better fix our eyes on Christ. For the trials, which are so full of reproach and shame for us, are in Christ full of glory. But such glory in Christ is not as yet seen clearly because the day of our consolation has not as yet arrived.

Searching what, or what manner of time, the Spirit of Christ which was in them did signify, when it testified beforehand the sufferings of Christ, and the glory that should follow. I Peter 1:11.

Peter tells his readers that their sufferings had been foretold long before by the Spirit, so that they may endure them with a calm spirit. But there is much more to this statement. He means that from the very beginning God has so ordained and governed the Christian church that the cross has been the preparation for victory, and death the way to life. Such is the clear testimony of Scripture. Therefore, there is no reason why we should be unduly depressed by our troubles, as though they meant our misery, when the Spirit of God himself calls us blessed.

But notice the order. He puts sufferings first, and the glories which are to follow second; and he makes it clear that this order can be neither changed nor reversed. The afflictions come first; and then comes glory. There are two striking thoughts expressed in this sentence: Christians must first suffer many tribulations that they may know the joy of glory; secondly, their sufferings are not evil, because they are bound closely with the glory to come. Since God himself has ordained this conjunction, it is not for us to tear one part away from the other. But it is a rare comfort to us that this situation of ours has been predicted so many ages ago, from which we gather that our coming deliverance from it is no empty promise. Hence we also know that we suffer not by chance but by the solid providence of God. And furthermore, we acknowledge that the prophecies are as mirrors, which in our very tribulations present us with an image of heavenly glory.

Of course, Peter says that it is Christ's own sufferings that were foretold by the Spirit; but he does not separate Christ from his body. Therefore, we must not limit the sufferings in question to Christ's own person. We must rather begin with the Head, that the members may follow him in their order. As Paul says, we must conform to him who is the first-born among his brethren (Rom. 8:29). Hence, Peter is speaking not of something peculiar to Christ, but of the universal situation of the church. We have a better confirmation of our faith in that he invites us to consider our own sufferings in relation to Christ: because in this way, in our relationship to him, we discern better the connection between death and life. It certainly is right and fitting that in this sacred union, the Head should suffer daily in his members. For in this way his sufferings are completed in us, and his glory in turn is fulfilled in his members. More is said about this in Col. 3 and I Tim. 4.

Beloved, think it not strange concerning the fiery trial which is to try you, as though some strange thing happened unto you; but rejoice, inasmuch as ye are partakers of Christ's sufferings, that, when his glory shall be revealed, ye may be glad also with exceeding joy. I Peter 4:12–13.

There is a great deal said about afflictions in this epistle. We have explained the reason for this elsewhere. However, we must notice that sometimes when he calls the believers to patience, he speaks in general of the common ills which infest human life; here, on the other hand, he speaks of the evils which the faithful suffer for Christ's name. In the first place, he reminds them that they must not be surprised [by affliction], as by something sudden and unexpected; that they must meditate upon the cross for a long time, in order to be prepared to bear it when the occasion arises. Anyone who has chosen to go to war under Christ will not become panicky when he meets persecution; he will rather bear it with patience as one who knows all about it. Therefore, if we would have presence of mind when persecutions rush upon us and overtake us, we need to be accustomed in good time to diligent meditation upon the cross.

Moreover, he makes two statements to show that the trial of the cross serves a useful end: by it God proves our faith, and we thus become companions of Christ. In the first place, let us keep in mind that the trial which proves our faith is most necessary. We should therefore be only too glad to obey God when he provides for our own salvation. But our chief comfort should be sought in the society of Christ. Therefore, Peter not only forbids us to be surprised when he puts the cross before us, but also bids us to be joyful. It is indeed a matter for joy that by means of persecution God makes proof of our faith. But it is a far-surpassing joy that the Son of God puts us in a class with himself, to lead us with himself to a blessed participation in the glory of heaven. We must take it as axiomatic that if we bear the dying of Christ in our flesh, his own life shall appear in us. The wicked also have their many troubles; but because they are separated from Christ, they get nothing in return except the wrath and execration of God. So it is that they are soon swallowed up by melancholy and terror.

This then is the whole comfort of the men of faith: they are Christ's associates, that they may in time come to have a share in his glory. So, we must always consider that the way is from the cross to the resurrection. But since this world is a labyrinth where no escape from evil is in sight, Peter turns our eyes to the future when the glory of Christ shall be revealed. What he means is that we must not spurn the day of his revelation because it is now hidden, but we must live in expectation of it. He sets before us a double joy: one which we now have in hope, and another which shall be complete at the coming of Christ. Because the first is mixed with sorrow and sadness, it is the latter which he connects with exultation. It is not good sense to be dreaming in the midst of tribulation of a joy which shall rid us of all trouble. But the consolations of God do temper our experience of evil so that, while we suffer, we have joy.

For the eyes of the Lord are over the righteous, and his ears are open unto their prayers; but the face of the Lord is against them that do evil. And who is he that will harm you, if ye be followers of that which is good? But and if ye suffer for righteousness' sake, happy are ye, and be not afraid of their terror, neither be troubled. I Peter 3:12–14.

It ought to be enough to take the sting out of whatever evil we suffer that we are under the eyes of the Lord and that in his

own good time he will come to our help. The sum of the matter,
therefore, is that the well-being which he speaks of depends
upon God's protection. For, if the Lord did not keep watch
upon his own, they would be like sheep exposed in advance to
wolves for destruction. And if the slightest trouble makes us cry
out, or if we are kindled so quickly to fury and burn with a
desire for vengeance, it is doubtless because we neither take to
heart that we are under God's care, nor acquiesce in his help.
We are taught patience in vain, unless our spirits be first
imbued with the teaching that God cares for us and will come to
our aid in his good time. If we are persuaded that God wills to
defend the cause of the righteous as a Father, our first and
single-minded concern becomes to be innocent of evil; and then,
when we become beset and troubled by the unjust, we flee to
God's protection. The apostle's purpose in telling us that the
ears of the Lord are open to our petitions is to move us to persevere in prayer.

But the face of the Lord. With this phrase Peter points out that
since the Lord is our vindicator, the godless shall not be permitted to flourish forever in their insolence. At the same time,
he threatens that if we take it upon ourselves to defend our lives
against the wicked, we shall have God himself against us. But,
it may be objected, experience teaches us far otherwise; for the
more just a man is, and the more he loves peace, the more he is
vexed by the wicked. To this I answer, No one follows justice
and peace so far that he does not sometimes, some way, sin in
this matter. But we must observe above all that in this life we
are promised nothing beyond what we need for doing our duty.
Hence, our peace with the world is often turned into trouble, in
order that our flesh may be subdued for obedience to God;
hence, whatever causes us trouble, nothing should be a loss to
us [but it should contribute to the same end of obedience].

And who is he, etc. He again confirms the above with an argument derived from common experience. It happens often that
the wicked pick a quarrel with us, or that they are cut to the
quick by us. We may fail to put ourselves out to win their favor;
for the truth is that anyone who keeps being kind is able to
soften hearts which are otherwise like iron. This same truth is
set forth by Plato in the First Book of *The Republic*: στάσεις γάρ
που ἥ γε ἀδικία καὶ μίση καὶ μάχας ἐν ἀλλέλοις παρέχει. ἡ δὲ
δικαιοσύνη ὁμόνοιαν καὶ φιλίαν. "Injustice provokes seditions and
hatreds and quarrels; but justice, concord and friendship."
However, even though this happens commonly, it is not always

so. No matter how much the children of God try to pacify the
wicked with goodness, and to show kindness toward all, they
are nevertheless often attacked without any just cause. Therefore, Peter adds: *If ye suffer for righteousness' sake.* . . . His point in
short is that the believers try to obtain in this life a state of
tranquillity, more by being good than by being violent and
quick to avenge. And then, if having left nothing undone toward
peace, they still suffer, even in this they are happy, for they
suffer for righteousness' sake. This last phrase is a far cry from the
judgment of the flesh. But it is not a rash statement of Christ;
and Peter himself does not repeat it rashly when he takes it
from the mouth of the Master. For God will ultimately come
forth as our liberator; and he will establish openly what at
present seems unbelievable: that the miseries which the godly
bear with patience are in truth rich with happiness. To *suffer
for righteousness' sake* means not only to be subject to some privation or discomfort in espousing a good cause, but also to suffer
injustice, as happens when a man who fears God and does no
evil finds that those around have turned against him.

*For it is better, if the will of God be so, that ye suffer for well-doing,
than for evil-doing. For Christ also hath once suffered for sins, the just
for the unjust, that he might bring us to God.* . . . I Peter 3:17-18.

For it is better. This phrase qualifies not only the next sentence,
but also the whole passage. Peter has spoken of the confession
of faith, which at that time was a perilous affair. He now adds
that it is much better for them to bear privation in defense of a
good cause, and so to suffer unjustly, than to be chastised for
their own infamy. But this encouragement is understood when
we ponder it inwardly, rather than by much talk around it. We
read often in profane writers that, when we suffer evil and must
needs go through with it, a good conscience is help enough.
This sounds very courageous. But it still is true that the spirit is
strong only when it looks to God. Therefore he adds the con-
ditional phrase *if it be God's will.* By these words he tells us that
when we suffer any evil unjustly it comes about not by accident,
but rather, and surely, by the will of God. And he assumes and
confesses that God neither wills nor appoints anything except
for the best of reasons. Hence, the believers have this comfort in
their miseries, that God knows all about it; they know that it is
God who leads them to the scene of contest, in order that under
his auspices they may show forth their faith.

For Christ also. It is another comfort that, if in our afflictions we have a good conscience, we suffer after the example of Christ: and in so doing, we are blessed. And at the same time the apostle proves, from the purpose for which Christ died, that it is not fitting for us to be chastised for doing evil. He reminds us that Christ suffered to lead us to God: and what does he mean except that by the death of Christ we have been so consecrated to God that we are to live and die to him! There are then two parts to this statement. The first is that we are to bear persecution with equanimity, since the Son of God himself shows us the way; the other is that, since by the death of Christ we have been set aside for obedience to God, we are to suffer not because of our misdoings, but for righteousness' sake.

But now someone may bring up the question, Is it not true God chastises believers when he allows them in some way to be afflicted? I answer that God often inflicts upon believers the punishment they deserve. And this Peter himself does not deny. But he reminds us what a great comfort it is to have our cause bound up with God! We shall see in the next chapter that those who are persecuted for righteousness' sake are not being punished by God for their sins. We shall also consider in what sense they are called innocent.

Yet if any man suffer as a Christian, let him not be ashamed: but let him glorify God on this behalf. I Peter 4:16.

After having forbidden Christians to hurt or do any harm so that they may not, like the unbelievers, arouse the world's hatred by their evil-doing, he now bids them to thank God when they suffer persecution in the name of Christ. Certainly, it is no ordinary kindness on God's part that he not only has freed us and exempted us from the common punishment of sins, but also calls us to an honorable warfare, in which we may suffer exile or privation, or insults, or even death itself. It is therefore plain ingratitude to God that, when persecutions come upon us, we murmur or cry out, as though some grave injustice were being done to us; we ought rather to count it gain and favor from God.

V

Faith

THE TEXT

1. ASPECTS OF FAITH

Behold the elation (or, as others translate, *whoever fortifies himself*), *his soul is not upright within him; but the just shall live by his faith.* Hab. 2:4.

This verse is to be connected with the previous one. The prophet wants to emphasize that when all sorts of temptations beset our minds, we can do no better than rely upon the Word of God. He does not present us with a new teaching; he tells us once again that our only solid and certain security lies in the promise of God, and that we must seek no other door to safety when we suffer under all the attacks of Satan and the world.

The two clauses present opposites. All who try to provide their own security will always be turning anxiously in all directions, and can have no peace of mind. The second clause is the logical consequence of this: we shall find quiet nowhere except in faith.

The first clause is interpreted in different ways. Some think that *'uppᵉlāh* is a noun and take it as "loftiness." This meaning does not fit badly, and I do not hesitate to accept it as the more correct. The Hebrews called the citadel *'ōphel*, and those who say that the name is derived from the verb *'āphal* "to go up" are correct. (Those who think the root means "strength" are wrong.) Others misinterpret the verse as meaning that the unbelieving are seeking a citadel where they may defend themselves. But this makes little difference to the main point.

However, some interpreters differ more seriously and disagree as to substance. They put the predicate for subject and the subject for predicate, and get from the prophet's words: "Whoever lacks peace of mind seeks a citadel for himself in which he

223

may rest safely or make himself strong." Others take it: "Whoever is proud and thinks himself well fortified will always have a troubled mind." This latter interpretation pleases me more, but I myself keep to the meaning of the word 'uppᵉlāh, and I think the prophet said, "Where there is elation of mind, there will be no tranquillity."

However, we must first see what those who interpret differently are aiming at. They say that the unbelieving, who are perverse and refractory, are always seeking a place to loiter safely, because they are suspicious of everyone; and further that they do not look to God, but try to find in this world some way of warding off all calamities and dangers. That is what they think.

But as I said, the prophet is rather stating the penalty of all unbelievers; he means that, when they torment themselves, they only get what they deserve. This gives us a better antithesis. And the prophet's teaching is more suggestive when we say that God imposes a due penalty on unbelievers by allowing them to be pulled in all directions and by letting their minds be troubled with hidden torments. When the prophet says that no peace of mind exists among those who think they have protected themselves well [by their own efforts] he knows that they are their own torturers, because they heap upon themselves many troubles, griefs, and anxieties, and are always upset and confused by their many different schemes. They decide first on one thing; then they prefer another. The Hebrews used the term "right-minded" to describe those who agree on some one thing and stand quiet. When uneasy thoughts drive people in various directions, then they say "the mind is not right in us." We should keep to the plain sense of the prophet's words. . . .

Then follows *but the just will live in faith.* I have no doubt that the prophet here sets faith over against all the safeguards with which men blind themselves in order to neglect God himself and to avoid asking aid from him. Because men put themselves in subjection to earthly things, and rely upon the falsehoods in which they trust, the prophet here ties life to faith. But faith, as we know and as I shall later explain more fully, depends upon God alone. Therefore, *to live by faith* means to abandon voluntarily all the defenses which so often fail us. One who knows himself destitute of all protection will live in his faith if he seeks whatever he needs from God alone; if he disregards the world and fixes his mind on heaven.

Since *'amunah* in Hebrew is "truth," some take it here as

"integrity"; as though the prophet had said that a righteous man had more protection in his own honesty and clear conscience than the sons of this world have in all the fortifications in which they take such pride. But these interpreters chill and dilute the prophet's meaning because they do not understand the power of justification, which is free and by faith, which alone gives us our security. It is certain that the prophet meant here by the word 'amunah the faith which takes from us all arrogance and sets us naked and helpless before God, to ask from him alone the safety which otherwise would be beyond our reach. . . .

All unbelievers desire to make themselves secure, and they strengthen themselves with whatever they think can help them. But what does the just man do? He brings God nothing of his own, for man takes hold of faith by prayer alone; faith is not in our own hands. He who lives by faith does not have life in himself; he flees to God because he does not possess it. The verb here is in the future tense to show that life in faith will be lasting.

Now we must come to Paul who used this prophet's witness to teach that salvation is not from works but solely from God's mercy and therefore from faith (Rom. 1:17). Paul seems to have twisted the words to his own purpose, and even beyond what their sense will bear. For the prophet was here speaking of the present life, and he made no mention of heavenly life. As we have said, he was testifying to the faithful that God would be their liberator, and so he was encouraging them to be patient. Then he added that the just will live by his faith, even though he have no other help, and seem to be completely exposed to all the blows of fortune, of the wicked, and even of the devil. Anyone may well ask what this has to do with the eternal salvation of the soul. Paul seems too subtle when he drags this passage into a discussion of free justification by faith.

But we must keep firmly to this principle: All the benefits God confers upon the faithful in this life are for the strengthening of their hope that they shall inherit eternal life. However freely God acts in our behalf, our situation will still be miserable if our hope is restricted to earthly life. Therefore, as often as God aids us in this world and declares himself our Father, he wishes to turn our minds to the hope of eternal salvation. Equally, when the prophet says that men of faith shall live, he does not shut that life within narrow limits; he does not say that God will watch over us for two or three days (that is, for a few years); he goes much further and declares that we shall be truly and solidly blessed. Even if this whole world perishes or keeps changing for the worse, men of faith shall yet endure in firm and real safety. When Habakkuk promises life to the faithful in the future tense, there is no doubt that he goes beyond the bounds of this earth and promises them a life which shall be better than the one they had in this world where it is beset with so many calamities. Besides, the brevity of life here shows that too much of it is not desirable.

We conclude therefore that Paul used the words of the prophet wisely and properly as support for his own teaching. Surely the just live by faith alone, and there is no salvation for the soul apart from God's mercy. . . .

Yesterday we compared Habakkuk's statement that we shall live by faith with the teaching of Paul who inferred from it that we are justified by faith apart from works. The purpose of life and of righteousness is the same. Our life can be sought nowhere except in the Fatherly kindness of God. Therefore, for us, to live is to be bound to God. And there can be no hope of communion with God when our sins are charged to us. For since God is just, and cannot renounce himself, sin must always be hateful to him. Therefore, so long as he accounts us sinners, we are necessarily hated; and where God's enmity is, there is death and destruction. It follows that no hope of life is left us unless we are reconciled to God. And there is no other way for God to bring us back to his favor except by accounting us righteous. Therefore Paul's reasoning is excellent when he takes us from life to justification. The two are bound together, and are inseparable.

And he believed the Lord, and he counted it to him for righteousness. Gen. 15:6.

None of us would guess, if Paul had not showed it to us, how rich and profound a doctrine this verse contains. It is a strange thing, almost a prodigy, that when the Spirit of God kindles so bright a light, most interpreters grope around with closed eyes, as if in the darkness of night. (I am not counting the Jews whose blindness is obvious.) Even those who have in Paul a most lucid interpreter corrupt this passage so insipidly that, as I said, it must be counted a prodigy. Indeed in all ages Satan seems to have fought more violently against free justification by faith than against any other teaching, striving to extinguish it and smother it.

The words of Moses are, *he believed God, and he counted it to him for righteousness.* First, Moses commends the faith of Abraham by which he embraced the promise of God. Secondly, he adds a eulogy of that faith, saying that because of it Abraham acquired (*adeptus sit*) righteousness before God, and that by imputation. For the verb *hashab*, which Moses uses, stands in relation to God's judgment; so also it is used in Ps. 106:31 where we read that the zeal of Phineas *was counted to him for righteousness.* The exact meaning of the word appears more clearly with the negative. In Lev. 7:18, it is said that iniquity will not be imputed to a man when expiation has been made. See also Lev. 17:4; II Sam. 19:19; II Kings 12:15.

We know that there exist criminals before God to whom iniquity is imputed. Exactly in the same way, God approves as righteous those to whom he imputes righteousness. Therefore Abram was received into the number and rank of the righteous by imputation of righteousness. In order to show distinctly the force and nature of this righteousness, Paul brings us before the heavenly tribunal of God.

Therefore those who twist this passage and interpret it as a description of righteousness, as if it said that Abram was a righteous and upright man, are talking insipid nonsense. The meaning of the text is corrupted no less by those who say ignorantly that Abram attributed to God the glory of righteousness and therefore dared confidently to credit God's promises, knowing him to be faithful and true. Although Moses does not expressly name God in the second clause, the usual mode of speaking in Scripture leaves no ambiguity. Certainly it is no less stupid than presumptuous to give to the words *counted for righteousness* any other meaning than that Abram's faith was accepted by God instead of righteousness.

Yet it seems absurd that Abram was justified because he believed that his offspring would be as numerous as the stars of heaven. For believing in one such promise could not make the whole man righteous. Besides, what earthly and temporal promise could be valid ground for eternal salvation? I answer that the faith which Moses records here is not restricted to one point, but includes the whole promise of God. The promise of seed to Abram was not limited to this verse; it is given also in others where a special blessing is added. Hence we conclude that Abram did not in the ordinary fashion hope merely for descendants, but for offspring in which the world was to be blessed.

Now if anyone stubbornly insists that what was said of the

children of Abram in general is distorted when applied to Christ, in the first place, it cannot be denied that God's earlier promise, to his servant, is now repeated over again in answer to Abram's complaint. But we have said before, and the account as a whole plainly shows, that it was his knowledge of the promised blessing which led Abram to desire seed so greatly. Hence it follows that the promise in this passage cannot be taken by itself, separated from the other promises. To conclude the whole matter, I say that if we are to judge the faith of Abram properly, we must consider all that is involved [in the stories about Abram].

God does not promise to give this or that good thing to his servant, in the way that he scatters benefits upon unbelievers who have no taste of his Fatherly love. He assures Abram that he himself will be gracious to him, and he promises him the enjoyment of his own protection and grace, and the confidence of salvation. A man whose heritage is God does not rejoice in flimsy pleasures, but as though already raised to heaven, he delights in the solid joy of eternal life. Certainly it must be held as self-evident that all God's promises, which are destined for the faithful, flow from God's gracious mercy and are proofs of his Fatherly love and free adoption on which their safety is founded. Therefore we say that Abram was justified not because he snatched at one little word about producing offspring, but because he embraced God the Father. Truly, faith justifies us for no other reason than that it reconciles us to God, and this not by its own merit, but only because as we receive the grace offered to us in the promises and are certainly persuaded that we are loved by God as sons, we also come to possess the assurance of life eternal.

Therefore Paul argues further that he to whom faith is reckoned for righteousness is not justified by works. For the merits of anyone who seeks justification by works are measured by God [before whom they are worthy of condemnation]. We comprehend the meaning of justification by faith when we know that God reconciles us to himself freely. Hence it follows that [concern with] the merit of works ends when justification is sought through faith. For if anyone is to possess righteousness by faith, it must necessarily be given by God and proffered to us by his Word.

To make this more clearly understood, when Moses says that faith was counted to Abram for righteousness, this does not mean that faith was the first cause (what is called the efficient

cause) of righteousness; it was only the formal cause.[1] The
words of Moses mean: "Abram was justified because relying on
the Fatherly kindness of God, he had confidence in God's goodness alone, and not in himself and his merits." We need
especially to understand that faith obtains (*mutuari*) from elsewhere a righteousness which we do not possess. Otherwise Paul
would not oppose faith to works as a way of obtaining righteousness. And the mutual relation between free promise and faith
leaves no room for doubt.

The sequence of time must now be noted. Abram was justified by faith many years after he had been called by God, after
he had left his native land and had become a voluntary exile, after
he had been a conspicuous mirror of endurance and self-control,
after he had devoted himself wholly to holiness, after he had
practiced himself in the spiritual and the external worship of
God and had led an almost angelic life. So it follows that, even
at the end of life, we are brought into God's eternal Kingdom
by justification by faith.

At this point many are grossly deceived. They admit indeed
that the righteousness which is given freely to sinners and
offered to the undeserving is received by faith alone. But they
limit this justification by faith to a moment of time, so that a
man, once at the beginning having obtained righteousness by
faith is afterwards made righteous by good works. Faith is
merely the beginning of righteousness, and as life continues
righteousness consists in works. Those who so interpret the
teaching must be insane. For if the angelic integrity of Abram,
exercised faithfully and consistently for so many years, did not
prevent the necessity of fleeing to faith to find righteousness,
where in the world will be found a perfection which can meet
God's scrutiny? Therefore we conclude from the time sequence
[which I previously mentioned] that justification of works is
not to be substituted for justification of faith as if the latter began
and the former completed justification; but that the saints, so
long as they live in the world, are justified by faith. If anyone objects that Abram had formerly believed God when he
followed his call and committed himself to his instruction and
guardianship, the answer is easy. No statement is made as to

---

[1] Calvin is following Aristotle's classification of causes as material, formal,
efficient, and final. The conventional classroom illustration today is the
pair of trousers of which the cloth is the material cause, the pattern is the
formal cause, the tailor is the efficient cause, and the reception at which
the trousers are to be worn is the final cause.

when Abram first began to be justified by believing God; but this one passage does show in what way he was justified in his whole life. If Moses had spoken thus about Abram's first calling, the objection I have just mentioned (that initial righteousness, but not perpetual, is of faith) would have more color. But when Abram is said to become righteous by faith after having gone through so much, it easily appears that the saints are justified by grace until they die.

I admit indeed that after those who believe are born again, in the Spirit of God, the mode of their justification differs somewhat. For those born of the flesh only, God reconciles to himself while they are empty of all good. When he finds in them nothing except a filthy heap of dreadful evils, he holds them righteous by imputation. But those to whom he has given the Spirit of holiness and righteousness, he clothes with his gifts. But even then, if their good works please God, this must be by his gracious imputation, because something of sin always remains in them.

This truth holds: men are justified by believing, not by what they do. It is by faith they obtain grace: and grace cannot be earned as a payment for works. Since Abram, with all his preeminence in virtue, after a long life of unique service of God, was yet justified by faith, the righteousness of each perfected man consists in faith alone. It is important to say plainly that what is here told of one man must be applied to all men. For Abram was called "father of the faithful" with good reason, and there are not diverse ways of seeking salvation. Paul rightly teaches that what is here described is not the righteousness of an individual man, but true righteousness as such.

Verily, verily, I say unto you, He that heareth my word, and believeth on him that sent me, hath everlasting life, and shall not come into condemnation; but is passed from death unto life. John 5:24.

It is not enough to know his teaching that he came to raise the dead, unless we also know how he liberates us from death. He declares that we obtain life by hearing his doctrine, but as he soon adds by *hearing* he means faith. And faith has its seat not in the ears but in the heart; which gives faith its great power, as we have explained before. But let us always keep in mind what the gospel offers us. It is no wonder that anyone who receives Christ with all his merits is both reconciled with God and freed from condemnation of death; for he who receives the

Holy Spirit puts on a heavenly righteousness and walks in newness of life (Rom. 6:4).

That I may know him, and the power of his resurrection, and the fellowship of his sufferings, being made conformable unto his death. Phil. 3:10.

Here the apostle describes the nature and efficacy of faith, which is the knowledge of Christ; not a general and vague faith, but the faith we have in the power of his resurrection. Since resurrection completes the work of redemption, it presupposes death. But it is not enough to know that Christ was crucified and rose from the dead, unless we know these things in our lives. This is why Paul speaks explicitly of the power of his resurrection. We know Christ in the right way when we experience the meaning of his death and resurrection within us and as they become effective in us. The expiation and obliteration of sins, freedom from condemnation, satisfaction, victory over death, the attainment of righteousness, and the hope of a blessed immortality—all these are ours by the power of his resurrection.

And the fellowship of his sufferings. After he speaks of the righteousness which was received freely by partaking in the resurrection of Christ, he speaks in addition of the actions of the godly, so as not to seem to have advocated an idle faith, having no fruits in our life. And, since the false apostles were so aggressive with their empty ceremonials, he indicates the kind of exercises which God requires his people to pursue. Let, therefore, everyone who has shared in all the benefits which Christ has conferred upon us know that his whole life ought to conform to the death of Christ.

Moreover, we participate in the death of Christ and associate with him in it in a twofold way. The one way is inward, which Scripture usually calls the mortification of the flesh, or the crucifixion of the old man. It is of this that Paul speaks in Romans 6. The other is outward, which is called the mortification of the outward man. Of this, he speaks in the eighth chapter of that epistle, and, if I am not mistaken, also in this place. After the all-inclusive power of the resurrection, he sets before us Christ crucified, so that we may be his followers through tribulations and sufferings. When he speaks of the resurrection of the dead in particular, it is to teach us that before we live, we must die. The faithful ought to meditate upon this, so long as they sojourn upon this earth.

It is our singular consolation that, as members of his body, in all our sufferings we are associated in the cross of Christ; that, as he says elsewhere, through afflictions we are shown a way to eternal blessedness. If we die, we shall live. If we suffer, we shall reign (II Tim. 2:11–12). We must, therefore, be ready to let our whole life be in the image of death, until it issues in death itself, just as the life of Christ was nothing else than an anticipation of death. In the meantime, we have joy in the consolation that the end is eternal blessedness. The death of Christ, therefore, is joined with his resurrection. This is why Paul says that he was conformed to Christ's death, that he might attain a glorious resurrection. The phrase *by any means*, indicates not doubt but difficulty. It is meant to arouse our zeal, because ours is no light skirmish, but a battle against many and great obstacles.

For the Father himself loveth you, because ye have loved me, and have believed that I came out from God. John 16:27.

These words remind us that the only bond which unites us with God is union with Christ. But the faith which unites us with Christ is not something contrived; it grows out of a genuine feeling which is here called *love*. Such faith does not merely believe about Christ; it embraces him with the soul. Therefore, *love* expresses well the power and the nature of faith. Truly, if God begins to love us only when we already love Christ, it follows that our love comes before God's grace, and that the beginning of our salvation is in us. But many passages in Scripture cry out against such a statement. The promise of God is, "I shall make them to love me," and John says, "It is not that we first loved him" (I John 4:10). It is unnecessary to cite many passages. There is nothing more certain than the teaching that the Lord calls a people who are not; that he revives the dead, unites to himself those who are strangers, turns hearts of stone into flesh, and appears to those who do not even seek after him. I reply that the elect, before they are called, are secretly loved by God who loves his own before they exist. But before they are reconciled to God, they are rightly regarded as his enemies, as we read in Paul and elsewhere (Rom. 5:10). We are here said to be loved of God when we love Christ; because when we love Christ, we receive a pledge that God loves us as Father; whereas, before we love Christ, he terrifies us as a hostile judge.

And keep my Sabbaths holy, and they will be for a sign between me and you, for understanding (that is, *that you may understand or know*) *that I am the Lord your God.* Ezek. 20:20. (Calvin's wording.)

The way to keep the Sabbath holy had already been explained. Mere idleness was unimportant. Therefore he repeats *and they shall be for a sign between me and you, that you may know that I am the Lord your God.* God bears witness in these words that if the Jews kept the Sabbath rightly, they would experience the working of his grace, which he wished his Sabbath to represent. For we have said that God wished the Sabbath to be a sacrament of the new birth. He promises the people that his Spirit will work among them if only they do not close the door to him by their own impiety and contempt.

Hence we see that sacraments are never without the power of the Spirit except when men make themselves unfit to receive the grace offered. The papists say of the sacraments that they are effective if we do not interpose the barrier of a mortal sin. They make no mention of faith. For example, if someone without a single drop of faith pushes up to the Lord's Supper, they say he will receive not only Christ's body and blood but also the fruit of his death and resurrection, on the sole condition that he has not committed a mortal sin; that is, if he cannot be convicted of theft or murder. We see in what blindness they are sunk; and this by the just judgment of God.

But by us the mutual relation between faith and sacrament must be steadily maintained. The sacraments become effective through faith; and men's unworthiness does not lessen their effect.

Sacraments always retain their own character. Baptism is the water of rebirth, though the whole world disbelieve. The Table of Christ is the communion of his body and blood, even if there were not the tiniest spark of faith in the world. But we do not perceive [without faith] the grace which is offered to us. And although the spiritual content remains always the same, we neither obtain the effect nor feel the power of the sacraments unless we are careful that our lack of faith does not profane what God has sanctified for our salvation.

But continue thou in those things which thou hast learned and hast been assured of, knowing of whom thou hast learned them. II Tim. 3:14.

He commands Timothy to stay put, even when evil is on the rampage and scatters destruction very far and wide. And surely this is the real proof of faith, that we resist all the machinations of the devil with a tireless constancy; that we be not deflected from the right course by every wind that blows, but remain fixed on God's truth as on a sacred anchor.

Now with the phrase *knowing from whom thou hast learned them,* he tells us we can be certain that the doctrine is true. No one who has been taught a wrong doctrine should hold on to it. On the contrary, if we would be Christ's disciples, we ought to unlearn any doctrine which ignores Christ; wherefore, the beginning of sound instruction in the faith is to reject and forget the whole doctrine of the papacy. In fact, the apostle enjoins Timothy not to keep every doctrine handed down to him, but to use discrimination, and to retain that which he has confirmed as true. Besides, he does not claim that what he himself has taught as a private person should be received as an oracle. He confronts Timothy confidently with his own authority, which was already recognized as evident from the apostle's calling and his faithfulness. Since Timothy was convinced that he was taught by an ambassador of Christ, he understood that the teaching he had received belonged not to men but to Christ.

This passage warns us that as we must be zealous to avoid obstinacy in matters where no certainty is to be had (and to this class belong all the teachings of men): we must be adamant in our constancy only in holding on to God's truth. Besides, we learn here that faith needs to be combined with good sense, to distinguish the word of God from the word of men, so that we may not grab at everything that happens to be within our reach. Nothing is further from faith than lightheaded credulity which embraces and champions senselessly everything, no matter what it is and where it comes from. Above all, the foundation of faith is the knowledge that its author is God.

Then spake Joshua to the Lord in the day when the Lord delivered up the Amorites before the children of Israel, and said in the sight of Israel, Sun, stand thou still upon Gibeon; and thou, Moon, in the valley of Ajalon. Josh. 10:12.

Joshua spoke to the Lord is the literal translation. But some explain this as *before the Lord,* because to *speak to the Lord* whom reverence teaches us to petition humbly seems inconsistent with the humility of faith, and also because Joshua immediately afterwards addressed his words to the sun. However, I have no doubt that in the first clause a vow or prayer is meant, and that the second clause gives evidence of Joshua's faith after he has been heard by God. It would certainly have been an act of rash pride to order the sun to stand still, if God had not granted the favor.

Joshua consults God and petitions him, and when he has been answered, he boldly orders the sun to do what he knows God approves. Such is the strength of the privilege of faith, praised by Christ, which subjugates mountains and seas to its power (Matt. 17:20; Luke 17:6). The more the strength of the faithful is exhausted, the more generously does God transfer his power to them, revealing his own power through that faith which is bound to the Word. Briefly, faith founded upon the Word is transmuted into confident power. So Elijah closed heaven and opened it at his command and brought fire down from heaven (I Kings 17–18). So Christ endowed his disciples with heavenly power so that the elements were subject to them.

Only, it is necessary to be on guard against bursting out with rash commands at one's own will. For this reason, Joshua did not begin to delay and hold back the course of the sun until he was duly informed of God's plan. When it is said that Joshua spoke with God, the words do not properly express the meekness and submission with which a servant of God ought to begin his prayers. Yet they serve to show us that Joshua asked of God the thing he desired and then, after he had prayed, he was the free and brave herald of an incredible miracle which had not yet occurred. He never would have given a command to the sun so confidently in front of all Israel unless he had been sure of his own vocation. Otherwise he would only have exposed himself to shame and humiliation.

Unhesitatingly he shouts his order to the sun and moon to turn aside from the perpetual law of nature. He knows that he is commanding them by the power of God which has been given to him.

For I know whom I have believed, and am persuaded that he is able to keep that which I have committed unto him against that day. II Tim. 1:12.

This is the only refuge of the godly; whenever the world counts them condemned and without hope; it is enough that God approves of them. For, what would be the end if they depended upon men?

This shows how different faith is from opinion. When Paul says, I know whom I have believed, he means that it is far from enough for you to believe unless [your belief rest] on the authority of God, and unless you be certain of what you believe. Faith therefore does not lean upon the authority of men; and as it leans upon God, it knows no wavering. Thus, faith must be joined with knowledge, otherwise it would have no firmness against the countless assaults of Satan. Anyone who possesses this knowledge with Paul knows by experience that it is not for nothing that our faith has been called *the victory that overcometh the world*; or that Christ said, *The gates of hell shall not prevail against it* (Matt. 16:18). I say, The man who remains tranquil in the midst of storms and tempests is one who has the firm knowledge that God has spoken, and will not lie; that he will not deceive, but will certainly perform what he has promised. On the contrary, anyone in whom this truth has not been sealed is swayed endlessly back and forth like a reed.

This passage deserves special attention as a superb statement of the power of faith; it teaches us to glorify God, even in the most desperate situations, by not doubting that he is true and faithful; it also teaches us to be content with the Word, as though God himself appeared to us from heaven. Anyone who is not thus persuaded understands nothing. Besides, let us always remember that Paul does not philosophize in the dark, but testifies to the power of confident hope in eternal life as one who, even at present, knows it.

And I am persuaded that he is able. Since the perils which assail us are at once great and powerful, and often tempt our spirits to distrust, it is necessary for us to go about with the shield that God has power enough to protect us. In the same way, when Christ bids us to be confident, he argues, saying, "The Father, who gave you to me is greater than all" (John 10:29). He thus declares that we are above the reach of peril, because the Lord who has taken us under his protection, abounds in power and is able to repel every assault. Satan does not dare to suggest directly that God is powerless, or that he can be prevented from doing whatever he promises, because our minds abhor such blasphemy against God. But he does deprive us of all sense of God's power, by preoccupying our eyes and our minds with other things. The soul of man, therefore, needs to be purified, not only to taste the power of God, but also to keep tasting it under sundry temptations.

Besides, whenever Paul speaks of God's power we must conceive it as, so to speak, active, or ἐνεργουμένην, as he calls it elsewhere (Col. 1:29). Faith always connects the power of God with the Word, and does not imagine it as something distant, but conceives and possesses it in the inner man. So, Rom. 4:20 says of Abram, "He did not hesitate, or dispute, but gave God the glory, being fully convinced that what he had promised, he was able to perform." And it was life eternal that the apostle trusted in God: which means that we are to put our well-being in God's hand as we put our possessions in the hand of a trustee whom we trust as a faithful man. If our well-being depended upon ourselves, it would be endlessly exposed to peril: it is well, therefore, that we turn it over to such a protector; for then it is safely beyond all peril.

Paul, a servant of God, and an apostle of Jesus Christ, according to the faith of God's elect, and the acknowledging of the truth which is after godliness. Titus 1:1.

I believe we shall interpret this verse rightly if we take the word *and* in the latter half of the sentence as meaning *that is*. Thus the last clause of the verse explains the nature of *the faith of God's elect*, even though what we have here is not a full definition of faith but a characterization of it adapted to the apostle's present purpose. He sets his apostleship apart from error and imposture, by asserting that it contains nothing except truth which is at once evident and certain, and which instructs men in a pure worship of God. But since every word in this verse is weighty, we would benefit greatly if we looked at the whole mosaic, section by section.

In the first place, faith is called knowledge, not as against opinion, but as against the hazy affair invented by the papists: for they have contrived an "implicit faith" with no understanding in it. But when Paul makes this knowledge of truth a proper function of faith, he makes it clear that there is no such thing as faith without knowledge.

And the word *truth* expresses even more clearly the certainty that is essential to faith. For faith is not content with the probabilities provided by our reasonings. Its proper object is the truth itself. Besides, we are concerned not with any truth, but with that truth from heaven which stands in contrast to the vanities proposed by the human mind. Since it is this truth which reveals God himself to us, it alone deserves to go by that name; and so it is honored commonly in Scripture: John 16:13: *And the Spirit shall lead you unto all truth;* John 17:17: *Thy word is truth;* Gal. 3:1: *Who hath bewitched you that you do not obey the truth;* Col. 1:5: *Having heard the word of truth, the gospel of the Son of God;* I Tim. 2:4: *He would have all come to the knowledge of the truth;*

I Tim. 3:15: *The church is the pillar and foundation of the truth*. In short, truth is that right and sincere knowledge of God which frees us from all lies and error. And surely such knowledge should be very precious to us, since there is nothing more miserable than for us to wander around all our lives like dumb cattle.

According to godliness, which follows, puts a special restriction upon the meaning of *truth*; at the same time, it commends the teaching of Paul by its fruit and end, which tends toward nothing else than the right worship of God and the flourishing of pure religion among men. It is thus that he defends his teaching as free from every mark of godless curiosity, as he had done before Felix (Acts 24:10) and then before Agrippa (Acts 26:1). Therefore, it is only right that the godly should be suspicious of and detest all empty questioning which does not make for the building up of the church. The only legitimate recommendation that can be given to doctrine is that it teaches reverence and the fear of God. Thus we are reminded that the best disciple of Christ is one who has made the greatest progress in reverence; and he alone is to be considered a true theologian who builds up the consciences of men in the fear of God.

Which hope we have as an anchor of the soul, both sure and steadfast, and which entereth into that within the veil. Heb. 6:19.

This is an eloquent comparison between an anchor and faith resting upon the Word of God. It is obvious that while we wander in this world, we do not stand on firm ground; on the contrary, we are as in the middle of the sea, tossed about by turbulent waves. The devil does not cease stirring up innumerable storms, which almost overturn and sink our ship, unless we throw our anchor deep in the sea. Our eyes see no harbor anywhere. In whatever direction we look, we see only water, and the waves keep rising with deadly threat. Just as the anchor is thrown into the midst of the waters to some dark and secret place, and while it remains there, it keeps the ship from being broken up by the waves surrounding it—so our hope needs to hold fast to the invisible God. But there is a difference between the anchor and our hope; the former is thrown down into the sea because the earth is at the bottom of it; the latter, on the other hand, is lifted up and soars on high because it finds nothing to hold on to on this earth. For our hope must not cling to the creature, but must find its quietness in God. As the cable tied to the anchor connects the vessel with the earth at a long

distance through the dark waters, so God's truth is a bond
which connects us with himself; and no distance, or foggy darkness, can keep us from clinging to him. When we are thus tied
to God, even when we struggle constantly with storms, we remain beyond the danger of shipwreck. This is why he says that
the anchor is sure and firm. It can, of course, be that the rush
of the waters will pull the anchor off, or break the cable, and
tear the beaten ship to pieces. Such a thing can happen in the
sea. But the power of God which sustains us is different; different is the fortitude of hope, and different the firmness of his
Word.

Which entereth into that. As we have said, unless faith reaches
God, it finds nothing except what is unstable and in flux. Therefore, it needs to penetrate as far as heaven. But since the apostle
was dealing with the Jews, he refers to the old tabernacle, and
says that they should not tarry with the things visible, but should
rather penetrate into the inmost holy places hidden behind the
veil: the old and external copies are to be set aside in order that
faith may rest in Christ alone.

*But let him ask in faith, nothing wavering; for he that wavereth is
like a wave of the sea driven with the wind and tossed.* James 1:6.

Here he teaches first the right way to pray. Since we can
pray only as we are led by the Word of God, it follows that
faith comes before prayer. When we pray, we testify to the
grace which is the promise of God to us: and so testifying, we
have hope. Thus, anyone who does not believe the promises,
has only the semblance of prayer. Thus also we learn what
true prayer is; for as James bids us to ask in faith, he explains
in addition that we are to hesitate at nothing. Faith, therefore,
rests upon God's promises and gives us the certainty that what
we ask for we shall receive; whence it follows that a confident trust
in us goes with the love of God toward us. The word διακρίνεθαι
used in this place means properly to inquire into both sides of a
controversy. He would have us be persuaded that once God has
made a promise there is no room left for doubt as to whether
we shall or shall not be heard.

He who wavers. By an elegant simile, he tells us how God
punishes the infidelity of those who doubt his promises. Such
people are tortured by their own inquietude, for there is no
such thing as tranquillity for our spirits unless they lean upon
the truth of God. He concludes finally that those who doubt
God do not deserve anything from him. This is an excellent

passage with which to refute the impious dogma, accepted as an oracle throughout papal lands, that we should pray in a state of doubt, hardly knowing what will come out of our praying. On the contrary, we hold the principle that the Lord will not hear our prayers unless there is the confident expectation that what we ask for we shall receive. But considering the weakness of the flesh, it is all too true that we are agitated by various temptations, which are engines for the shattering of our confidence in God. Hence, we find no one who is not in fact led by the feelings of his flesh to waver and shake in his boots. But it is the business of faith finally to overcome temptations of this kind; for faith is like a tree which has sunk deep roots; indeed, when the winds blow, it sways and bends, but it is not heaved out of the ground; on the contrary, it remains standing and firm where it belongs.

2. Faith as Faithfulness and Courage

Jesus saith to him, Because thou hast seen me, Thomas, thou hast believed; blessed are they who have not seen and have believed. John 20:29.

Here Christ commends faith on the ground that it does not in the least depend upon sense and carnal reason, but acquiesces in the mere Word of God. Therefore, in this brief definition, he brings together both the power and the essence of faith; namely, that it does not consist in seeing what is before us, but penetrates to the very heavens, so as to believe the things which are hidden from the human senses. For surely we ought so to know God that his truth may be to us αὐτόπιστος (to be believed simply because it is his Word). Faith indeed has its own sight, but it is not fixed on things upon this world and earth. For this reason, it is said to be a demonstration of things invisible and not seen (Heb. 11:1). Paul, also, who contrasts it with sight (II Cor. 5:7) points out that faith, without holding to a consideration of the state of things present, or looking about at things visible in this world, hangs on to the mouth of God; and putting its confidence in the Word of God, it rises above the whole world and casts its anchor in heaven.

Shadrach, Meshach and Abednego answered the king and said: O Nebuchadnezer, we are not anxious with what words we are to answer thee (or *negotiate with thee*). (Others translate it, "It is not right that we should answer thee in this matter"; they say *l* is here,

as often, superfluous.) *Lo, God whom we serve is able to* (that is, *can*)
*deliver us from the furnaces of raging fire and will snatch us from thy
hand, O king. But if not, be it known to thee, O king, that we shall not
worship thy Gods, and we shall not adore the images which thou hast set
up.* Dan. 3:16–18. (Calvin's wording.)

The chief emphasis in this account is upon the unbroken
spirit of the three holy and God-fearing men, when they knew
that they were in imminent danger of death. Although a horrible death was before their eyes, they did not swerve from the
right path but set the glory of God above their own life—even
above a hundred lives if they had had so many and such a
sacrifice were required.

Daniel does not report all their words but selects only a few
in which glows the unconquerable power of the Holy Spirit
who instructed them. The king's threat, *be hurled into the furnace
of fire*, was certainly horrible, and terror before his rage would
have been very natural. For we know how dear life is to us and
what dread of death fills our minds. Daniel has described the
whole situation to make it clear to us that God's servants, when
they are led by the Spirit, have too much courage to yield to
any threats or give way to any fears. They say to the king, "We
need not deliberate." When they say that they *are not anxious*,
they mean "the matter is settled; we have no desire to hold a
consultation about what is expedient or helpful. Not at all. . . .
In so holy a matter no deliberation is possible. We have already
decided that we must not depart in any way from the pure
worship of God." Clearly, the fear of death, however closely
it hangs over them, and however deeply it is ingrained in their
hearts, does not make them deviate a hair's breadth from the
true and right worship of God.

They give two reasons for rejecting the king's proposal. They
say that God has sufficient power and might to rescue them;
and then they add that even if they must die, life is not so precious that they would deny God to prolong it. They declare
themselves ready for death if the king still insists that they
worship the statue.

This passage is especially worth our study. We should note
the first answer which shows us that when we are urged to deny
the true God we must close our ears and do no deliberating.
For we begin to dishonor God when we debate whether it be
allowable for any reason whatever to depart from his pure
worship. How I wish that all men would become so conscious
of the supreme excellence of the glory of God that they would

disregard all else whenever there is any attempt to lessen or hide
God's glory!

But many today have accepted a fallacy. They think either
that they have a right to sit on the fence or that at times it may
be better to swerve temporarily from the true worship of God.
They reason: "There is some good on both sides. . . . Or if I did
not compromise, I might harm others as well as myself. If our
ruler had no advisers to counsel moderation, the wicked could
go to extremes and urge him, without restraint, to all kinds of
cruelty. Therefore, it is better to have some middle-of-the-
roaders, who humor the wicked and who keep a watch on their
schemes, so that without open opposition they may by under-
ground means avert danger from the heads of good men." So
they convince themselves that they are doing their bit for God.

Could not Shadrach, Meshach, and Abednego have given
the same kind of excuse? Could they not have thought: "We
have some power to help our brothers. How much greater
barbarities and cruelties would follow if open enemies of
religion replace us! For they would try their best to destroy
from the earth both our race and the memory of our religion.
Isn't it better for us to yield temporarily to tyranny and the
king's harsh decree than to leave our office to be occupied by
raging men who will totally destroy our poor people who are
already in enough trouble?" They could have found plenty of
excuses for their faithlessness if, to avoid danger, they had bent
their knees before the golden image. But they did not.

As I have said, God's right remains unviolated only when we
adhere unquestioningly to his service and are convinced that
no consideration is important enough to permit us to make it
lawful for us to deviate in the slightest degree from that course
of action which he commands by his word and which he requires
of us. . . . Why do we live except to serve God's glory? If we
lose our purpose in living for the sake of life—that is, if we desire
too much to live in the world—we set aside the purpose of life.

When the three declare that God is able to save them, but if
not, they are ready for death—they reveal a truth which ought
to raise our hearts above all temptations. Since our life is dear to
God, he himself, if he wishes, can rescue us. Since, then, we have
in God a sufficient protection, let us not try to imagine any
better way of preserving our life than by surrendering ourselves
wholly to his direction and casting all our anxieties upon him.
And we must also consider the second clause. Even if God wishes
to make his glory shine by our death, this would be a rightful

sacrifice, and it should be offered to him. True religion does not flourish in us unless we take our life in our hand, that is, unless we hold it always ready for sacrifice. (I wanted to present briefly today what, if God permits, I shall treat more at length tomorrow.)

By faith, Noah, being warned of God of things not seen as yet, moved with fear, prepared an ark to the saving of his house: by the which he condemned the world, and became heir of the righteousness which is by faith. Heb. 11:7.

It was a wonderful example of courage that, while the whole world did as they pleased, and gave themselves up to pleasure, without fear and without restraint, Noah alone kept his eyes on God's judgment, although it was delayed for a time; and for one hundred and twenty years he went through the weariness and misery of building an ark. All this time he remained adamant, while the godless crowds jeered at him; he never doubted that the world would perish and he would be saved. Yea, he lived in the ark as in the grave. But I need not say more about this; let someone else who can do better expand on it. [It is enough to say that] the apostle attributes this marvelous courage to faith. So far he had been speaking of the faith of the fathers who lived in the first age of the world. But when Noah and his family came out of the Flood, faith became a kind of regeneration. The case of Noah shows that in all ages men neither have been approved by God, nor have deserved his praise, except by faith.

Now, the story of Noah leads to the following considerations: first, that warned of things to come, which he still could not see, he was filled with awe and fear; secondly, that thereupon he built an ark; thirdly, that by building it he condemned the world; fourthly, that he inherited the righteousness which is according to faith. My first point brings out the power of faith best. It always recalls us to the primary truth that faith is the evidence of things not seen; for it is surely the property of faith to see in God's Word the things which are hidden and far beyond the competence of our senses. When Noah was told that after one hundred and twenty years there would be a flood, the length of time involved might have taken away all his fear. Besides, the whole thing was incredible. He saw the unbelievers going ahead, safe and secure, with their life of pleasure. He might have thought that the dreadful news of a flood was an empty threat to terrify the people. But Noah held such respect for the Word of God that he turned his eyes away from the things present, and feared the destruction threatened by God as though it were already happening. The faith he had in God's Word was turned into the obedience to God which was demonstrated in his building the ark.

Now, somebody will raise the question, Why does the apostle say that faith produced fear if it be true that faith is bound to promises rather than to threatenings? It is the gospel, in which the righteousness of God is offered to us for our salvation, that Paul calls the word of faith (Rom. 10:8). It seems therefore wrong to say that by faith Noah was led to fear. I answer, Faith grows properly out of the promises; it is founded in them and rests upon them. Therefore, we say that Christ is the true end of faith, since it is in him that the Heavenly Father has been reconciled to us, and in him all the promises of salvation have been sealed and ratified. However, nothing keeps faith from being fixed upon God and accepting from him every word he speaks. Or, if you would have it put more briefly, it is the function of faith to hear God as he speaks, and to embrace without doubt whatever proceeds from his holy mouth. Thus, faith acknowledges precepts and threats, as well as God's free promises. But since no one manages to obey God's precepts properly and sufficiently, no one is moved to pray that he may be delivered from his wrath, unless he has laid hold of God's gracious promises and knows him as a good Father and the Author of salvation. Therefore, the gospel is called the Word of faith, for it is the principal part of the Word of God; and this is how faith and the promises are related one to the other. Faith attends to the promises of God; but is no less intent upon his threatenings, in so far as it needs to be taught to fear God and to submit to him.

Prepared the ark. Here the apostle points out the obedience which flows out of faith as water from a fountain. The work of building the ark was long and laborious. It might have been hindered by the scoffings of the ungodly, and thus interrupted a thousand times; for there is no doubt that the holy man was pelted with insults on all sides. The very fact that he bore their derision with an unbroken spirit shows the uncommon zeal of Noah's submission to God. But what was the source of this constancy of obedience if not that he rested in the promise of God, which gave him the hope of salvation, and led him to believe in God to the very end? For he would not have had the courage to meet willingly so many troubles, or to overcome so many obstacles, or to stand firm at his task so long, if he had not already trusted in God. Faith alone therefore is the teacher of obedience, while unbelief keeps us from obeying God. And in our own day, the world's unbelief shows itself in a frightful way, for there are few who obey God.

By which he condemned the world. It would be strange to say that Noah by faith condemned the world. The context of this verse hardly bears this out. Therefore, the reference is to the ark. The world is said to have been condemned by the ark in a double sense. Since the building of the ark took so long, it left the wicked without any excuse. Besides, what followed the building of it showed that the condemnation of the world was just. Why indeed did the ark become the means of salvation to one family, if not because by his righteousness one man was spared the wrath of the Lord, and did not perish with the wicked? Had he not been left as a remnant, the condemnation of the world would not have been so conspicuous. By the very example of his obedience to God's command, Noah condemned the perversity of the world. The very fact that Noah was snatched away so marvelously from the jaws of death is proof enough that the condemnation of the whole world was just; for certainly God would have saved it had it not been unworthy of salvation.

Of the righteousness which is by faith. This is the last thing about Noah which the apostle brings to our attention. Moses says that Noah was a righteous man. History does not tell us that the root and reason of Noah's righteousness was in faith. But the apostle testifies to this as a fair inference from the facts of the case; not only because no one obeys God with sincerity unless, after receiving the promises of his Fatherly goodness, he trusts him with his very life; but also because no one can please God without his forgiveness, no matter how righteous his life is according to the rule of God's law. Therefore, it is necessary that our righteousness rest in faith.

By faith, Abraham, when he was tried, offered up Isaac: and he that had received the promises offered up his only begotten son. . . . Heb. 11:17.

The author goes on with the rest of the story of Abraham, and tells of his offering up of Isaac. Here we have an example of singular courage, and we are not likely to find anything like it anywhere. . . .

And he that received the promises. All that was said so far, however deeply it may have wounded Abraham, was a mere prick compared with this trial in which, after he had received the promise, he was commanded to kill his son Isaac. For all the promises were founded upon this: *In Isaac shall thy seed be called* (Gen. 21:12); and without him no hope remained of any good or blessing whatever. Besides, what was at stake here was nothing earthly. It had to do with the everlasting salvation of Abraham; yea, even of the whole world. We can imagine what anguish took hold of the holy man when he realized that in the person of his son the very hope of eternal life was to be extinguished! And yet by faith he escaped such dark thoughts, and did as he was commanded. What a wonderful power it was that enabled him to overcome so many and so arduous obstacles! No wonder that faith deserves the highest praise, since it alone made it possible for Abraham to persevere without defeat.

But here we meet a difficulty which is no small matter. How is it that Abraham's faith is praiseworthy if it was separated from the promise? For, as obedience is from faith, so faith is from promise. Therefore, when Abraham was deprived of the promise, his faith also must have failed. Now, the death of Isaac, as we have said, would have been as it were the collapse of all the promises; since Isaac was no ordinary man, but one who included Christ. This difficulty, which would otherwise not have been easy to deal with, is resolved by the apostle when he adds soon after that Abraham honored God by believing that he could raise his son from the dead. Therefore, he did not reject the promise made to him, but extended its truth and God's power beyond the life of his son; because he did not set the power of God within narrow limits, as though it were tied up to Isaac's death and would become void with it. He held on to the promise, because he did not bind God's power merely to Isaac's lifetime. He was persuaded that it would be active and efficacious in the ashes of a dead Isaac, as it was when he was alive and breathing.

By faith he forsook Egypt, not fearing the wrath of the king; for he endured, as seeing him who is invisible. Heb. 11:27.
This may be said of the first time Moses left Egypt as well as of the second, when he took the people with him; for, he did leave Egypt in a real sense when he ran away from the Pharaoh's house. When the apostle says that Moses left Egypt before the celebration of the Passover, he means the first flight. His adding that Moses *did not fear the wrath of the king* does not invalidate

this view, though Moses himself says that he fled because of terror.

Still, when we consider the early career of Moses, we see that it was when he came out as the champion of the people that he was not afraid. When I consider all the circumstances, I prefer to think that here we have to do with Moses' second departure. It was then that he scorned the wrath of the king, and was so armed with the power of God's Spirit that he often excited the fury of that beast. Such certainly was the energy of his faith that, taking along with him a multitude untrained in warfare, and bearing the burden of many obstacles, he went with the hope that God by his own hand would open a way through the countless difficulties which beset him. He saw a most potent king seized by impotent rage, and knew that he would do his utmost to the very end. But since he knew that he was departing by God's power, he commended the situation to God, and did not doubt that God would in time bring the assault of all the Egyptians to a dead stop.

As seeing him who is invisible. But Moses did see God in the burning bush; besides, it looks as though this point is introduced here improperly and without relevance to the matter on hand. I admit readily that Moses was fortified by his vision, as he set out for the glorious task of delivering his people. But I deny that his vision of God divested him of his bodily senses and put him beyond the perils of this world. Strictly speaking, God gave him a sign of his presence; but he was very far from having seen God as he really is. What the apostle means to say is that Moses endured as though he were lifted to heaven and saw God alone; as though he were beyond intercourse with men, beyond the reach of this life's perils and the struggle with Pharaoh. And yet, he was certainly beset with so many difficulties that he could not but imagine sometimes that God was far away from him; or, at least, that the obstinacy of the king, supported by overwhelming arms, would be impossible to resist effectively. In short, God presented himself to Moses as living, but not so that faith became superfluous. Moses himself, beset by terrors on all sides, turned his whole mind to God. As we have said, his vision helped him to do this; but he saw more in God than was visible by the sign of the bush. His apprehension of God's power absorbed all fear and every peril; leaning upon God's promise, he saw his people, even while they were being oppressed under the tyranny of the Egyptians, as already lords in the Promised Land.

So, we learn first that the true nature of faith is to set God always before our eyes; secondly, that faith has insight into things higher and deeper than those which fall within the scope of our senses; thirdly, that only a sight of God is sufficient to remove our softness and to make us as rocks against the assaults of Satan. It follows that the more indolent and the weaker a man is, the less faith he has.

By faith the walls of Jericho fell down, after they were compassed about seven days. Heb. 11:30.

Before this, he taught us that the yoke of bondage was broken by faith; he now reminds us that by that same faith the people took possession of their inheritance. As they entered the land, they first came up against the city of Jericho; fortified and almost impregnable, it forbade further progress, since they had no means for assaulting it. The Lord ordered that all the fighting men go around it once every day for six days, and seven times on the seventh day. All this going around was childish and extremely ridiculous. Nevertheless, they obeyed God's command; and their labor was not in vain. It ended happily, according to the promise of God. Surely the walls fell down, not because the people shouted and made a big noise, nor because of the din and the clamor of the trumpets, but because the people believed that God would do as he had promised.

The Lord your God, he is God in heaven above and in earth beneath. Now, therefore, I pray you, swear unto me by the Lord.... Josh. 2:11–12.

The image of the faith of Rahab shines clear as in a mirror when, throwing away all idols, she ascribes the rule of heaven and earth to the God of Israel alone. Without question, when [men acknowledge that] heaven and earth are subject to the God of Israel, the fictitious gods of the nations amongst which they distribute the majesty and the power and the glory of God are wholly repudiated. Therefore Rahab was not too highly honored when two apostles referred to her faith.

Certain arrogant and overpunctilious men make a face at this. I wish that they could weigh fairly what it really involves to distinguish the one true God from all fictions and at the same time to exalt his power so highly as to declare that he by his will rules the whole world. Rahab speaks without hesitation and asserts unequivocally that all existing power belongs to the

God of Israel alone, that he rules all elements, orders all things above and below, determines all human affairs.

However, I do not deny that Rahab's faith was not full-grown. Indeed, I freely admit that it was only a germ of faith, not yet sufficient for her eternal salvation. Nonetheless we must recognize that, however small and frail was this woman's knowledge of God, yet when she submitted herself to God's rule, she produced the certificate of her election; and from such submission as from a seed springs the faith which grows to full measure.

Now, swear. Here is another evidence of her faith. She is convinced, relying on no evidence except the promise of God of which she had heard, that the sons of Abraham are the sure possessors of the land of Canaan. She did not think that God favored robbers who were bursting with unjust violence and unbridled lust into the territory of others. She declared rather that the Israelites were coming into the land of Canaan because God has assigned them the rule over it. . . .

The words of Rahab illuminate what the author of the epistle to the Hebrews says of faith: that it is the vision of things unseen. For Rahab lived among her own people in a fortified city; and yet she trusted her own life to half-dead foreigners as if they were already in possession of the land and could kill or save alive whomever they chose. Certainly this willing offering of herself was truly a laying hold of God's promise and a surrender of herself to God's Fatherly care.

By faith the harlot Rahab perished not with them that believed not, when she had received the spies with peace. Heb. 11:31.

Even though at first sight this example, because of the ignoble character of the person involved, may seem less striking and hardly worth mentioning in this series, the apostle used it fittingly and with good reason. So far he had shown that the patriarchs, whom the Jews regarded with honor and reverence, did nothing praiseworthy except by faith; that the most memorable benefits which God bestowed upon them, were the effects of the same faith. Now he teaches that a woman of alien origin, among the dregs of her own people, and even a harlot, was by faith placed within the very body of the church. From this it follows that even those who are placed highest among us have no worth before God except as they are valued according to their faith; that on the contrary those who are hardly given a place among the godless and the reprobate are by faith taken into the company of angels.

And what shall I more say? For the time would fail me to tell of Gideon, and of Barak, and of Samson, and of Jephthah; of David also, and Samuel, and of the prophets. Heb. 11:32.

The apostle was afraid that by giving a few examples, he would be taken to limit the praises of faith to a small number of people. He anticipates this objection and adds that, if he were to mention everybody one by one, there would be no end to his recital. His point is that what he said of the few applied to the whole church of God. He turns first to the period between Joshua and David, when God raised up Judges to govern the people. He mentions four: Gideon, Barak, Samson, and Jephthah.

It was ridiculous of Gideon to go and attack a host of enemies with three hundred men; to make his men shake the pitchers in their hands and engage in an empty ghost play. As for Barak, he was no match for his enemies, and ruled by the counsel of a woman. Samson was a mere farmer, and was used only to the tools of a farmer. What could he have done against proud conquerors whose power had brought the whole populace to subjection? And who would not at first thought condemn the foolhardiness of Jephthah who set himself up as the champion of a people who were already lost? But because they all followed God's leading and, inspired by his promises, took hold of the task enjoined upon them, the Spirit glorified them by his witness.

Therefore, the apostle attributes their every praiseworthy deed to faith, even though there was not one of them whose faith was not lame! Gideon was too slow in taking up arms, and had trouble in daring to commit himself to God. Barak at first shook in his boots, and was forced into battle by Deborah's insults. Samson was so overcome by the coaxings of his concubine that he was senseless enough to betray the safety of the whole people as well as his own. Jephthah, having let himself in for a stupid vow, and being stubborn enough to perform it, cruelly spoiled a splendid victory with the death of his own . daughter. So, in every one of these saints, we meet something which deserves censure. And yet, faith, however deformed and imperfect, is approved by God. Therefore, the wrongs which burden us should neither dishearten us nor break us down, provided only that we follow our calling by faith.

Women received their dead raised to life again: and others were tortured, not accepting deliverance, that they might obtain a better resurrection. Heb. 11:35.

Having recounted instances where God rewarded the faith of the saints with a happy ending, he now presents us with a different situation, in which the godly, reduced to extreme misery, carried on by faith and remained indomitable even to the death. At first it looks as though there were a great difference between these two outcomes of faith. Some enjoyed magnificent victories over their beaten enemies. They were preserved by the Lord through various miracles, and were rescued from death itself in new and uncommon ways. Others, on the contrary, were subjected to outrage. They were spit upon by almost the whole world; were poor and needy, and so hated by everyone that they had to hide in the holes of wild beasts; and in the end they were dragged out and subjected to cruel and inhuman tortures. So, for all one could see, they were abandoned to the arrogance and savagery of the godless, and were altogether without God's help. Their lot, therefore, would seem to have been altogether different from that of the saints mentioned in the earlier parts of this chapter.

Nevertheless, faith reigned in both instances, and in both it was equally effective. In fact, in the latter it shone even more brightly. The victory of faith is more splendid in contempt of death than in a life stretched out to five generations. The glory of faith is more striking in its effects, and is worthy of greater praise, when we endure want, reproach, and utmost difficulty with a calm and constant spirit, than when we are restored to health by a miracle, or enjoy some other benefit from God.

For ye have need of patience, that, after ye have done the will of God, ye may receive the promise. For yet a little while, and he that shall come will come, and will not tarry. Now the just shall live by faith: but if any man draw back, my soul shall have no pleasure in him. Heb. 10:36–38.

He says patience is necessary, not only because we need to endure a while longer until the end, but also because Satan is resourceful in innumerable devices with which to trouble us. Therefore, unless we are taught great patience, we shall be cut down a thousand times before we are even halfway through our course. It is indeed certain that we shall inherit eternal life; and yet, since this life is like an athletic event, we need to strain every muscle until we get to the finishing line. The course itself contains many obstacles and hardships, which not only slow us down, but would even stop us altogether in our race, unless we overcome them with a prodigious fortitude of spirit. Satan is clever enough to put into our heads every kind of disquiet, so as to break us down. In short, Christians would be unable to take two steps unless fortified by endurance. This then is the only way we can steadily go ahead. Without endurance we neither obey God nor receive the promised inheritance, which is here called *the promise.*

For yet a little while, and he that shall come will come, and will not tarry. But endurance is hard for us. Therefore, he reminds us that it will not be for long. Nothing lifts the spirit so well when it is weary as the hope that the end is at hand. As a general encourages his soldiers by saying the battle will not be long, provided they hold on a little longer, so the apostle tells us that the Lord will come shortly and deliver us from all evil, provided we do not go soft and let our spirits fail.

He gives this consolation greater credibility and authority by an appeal to the witness of the prophet Habakkuk, ch. 2:4. But since he follows the Greek version and departs somewhat from the words of the prophet, I shall first explain the latter, and then compare both with what is said by the apostle.

When the prophet had discoursed of the dreadful fall of his nation, and was terrified by his own prophecy, there was nothing left for him to do except, as it were, to leave the world and withdraw to his watchtower. (But our watchtower is the Word of God by which we are directed toward heaven.) Having been placed in his station, the prophet was commanded to write a new prophecy which affirmed to the godly the certainty of their coming deliverance. But since men are importunate, and their precipitate desires make them always judge God as much too slow, even when he is quick, the prophet declares that the promise will be fulfilled without delay; and at the same time he adds, "If there be delay, wait for it." What he says is that, no matter how quickly God fulfills his promises, he seems to us too slow. As the old proverb says: To desire, even haste is delay. Then follow the words: "Behold, he who lifts himself up shall not have a stable spirit, but the righteous shall live by his faith." With these words, he warns that the ungodly, however armed with their defenses, and however confident they be behind their ramparts, shall not stand: because life is not stable except by faith. Let the unbelievers arm themselves as they please; they will find nothing in this whole world that will not perish; therefore, they have to be always in a state of panic. But the faith of the godly never fails, because it leans upon God. This is what the prophet is talking about.

Now the apostle applies to God what the prophet had said of

the promise, and that rightly, since when God fulfills his promises, in a way he reveals himself. There is little difference
between the prophet and the apostle as to the heart of the
matter. I say that when the Lord stretches forth his hand to
help us, he himself comes. The apostle follows the prophet in
saying, "In but a short while"; because God does not defer his
help any longer than fits his purpose. Unlike men, God does
not dally in order to deceive and fail us. He knows the time of
opportunity, and does not let it pass by without coming forth
to our help at the right moment. The apostle says: *He that shall
come, will come; he will not tarry.* There are two parts to this
sentence. The first says that God will come, because he has
promised; the second, that he will do it at the right time, and
not later.

And now, the righteous shall live by faith. He means that endurance is born of faith. And this is true, because we shall never
be equal to our contests except as we are sustained by faith; as
John says truly in other words, Our victory which overcomes
the world is by faith (I John 5:4). So it is that we rise on high;
so we bound over the obstacles of this life, over its sorrows and
troubles; so we have quietness in the midst of storms and tempests. Thus, the apostle's whole point is that all those who are
righteous before God shall live by faith. And the future tense
of the verb *to live* indicates that life by faith shall be life without
end. Let the reader look up Rom. 1:17 and Gal. 3:11, where
the apostle cites this same verse from the prophet.

*Now faith is the substance of things hoped for, the evidence of things
not seen.* Heb. 11:1.

Whoever made this verse the beginning of chapter eleven did
wrong in breaking up the continuity of our text. As the apostle
has said, his purpose is to show the need for patience. He has
already quoted the testimony of Habakkuk, that the righteous
shall live by faith. Now, he shows further that faith can be
separated from patience no more than from itself. His argument
goes as follows: We shall never attain the goal of salvation,
unless we learn patience; because the prophet teaches that the
righteous shall live by faith. But faith calls us to a destiny which
is far off. Therefore, there is no faith without patience. Hence,
the syllogism includes the minor proposition: faith is the substance of things hoped for. It is wrong to think that here we
have a full definition of faith. The apostle does not speak of
the whole of faith, but of that aspect of it which fits his

present purpose; namely, that it is always bound up with patience.

Now let us consider his words. He calls faith the *hypostasis* of the things hoped for. We of course know that we hope for things not in our hands and still hidden from us, or at least for things we expect to enjoy at some other time. The apostle teaches us here the same thing that Paul does in Rom. 8:24, where the latter says that we hope for what we do not see, by which he implies that we must wait for it with patience. Thus, the apostle warns us that we must exercise faith in God not for things present but for things about whose fulfillment we are in suspense. And this paradox is not without its beauty. Faith, he says, is the *hypostasis*, that is the prop, or the place we have, on which we may plant our foot; but the prop for what? I answer, For things not in our possession, things which are not under our foot, which are in fact even beyond the grasp of our minds.

The same applies to the second clause, where he speaks of *the evidence*, or demonstration, of things not seen. But demonstration has to do with things that are seen; it is used commonly with regard to things open to our senses. Thus faith and demonstration apparently do not go together. And yet they do go together very well; for the Spirit of God demonstrates to us the things hidden to us and quite beyond the kind of knowledge which depends upon the senses. We are promised eternal life, but we are dead; we are told of a blessed resurrection, but we are in a state of corruption; we are pronounced righteous, and yet we are dwelling places of sin; we hear that we are happy, and yet we are buried under countless miseries; we are promised riches of every kind of good, but are exceedingly hungry and full of thirst; God cries that he will come to us quickly, and yet to our own cry he seems to be deaf. What would become of us if we were not upheld by hope and if our minds did not escape the darkness of this world through the bright light of God's Word and his Spirit? Faith, therefore, is said rightly to be the reality (*subsistentia*) of the things we affirm in hope, and the evidence of the things we do not see. It does not displease me that Augustine sometimes translates *evidence* as "conviction," because it is true to the apostle's meaning. But I prefer to render it as "demonstration," because this is less forced.

3. FAITH AS HUMAN ACT

And behold, a woman, which was diseased with an issue of blood for

twelve years, came behind him, and touched the hem of his garment.
Matt. 9: 20.

The Evangelist makes it clear that the issue of blood had
lasted continually for twelve years. She had neglected no
remedy, and had even spent everything she had on doctors.
The glory of the miracle shines all the more brightly, because
an incurable disease was cured suddenly by the mere touch of
a garment; and this was obviously not a human accomplishment. However, we must not generalize from the woman's
notion that if she touched Christ's garment she would be immediately healed, because it came to her under a special impulse
of the Holy Spirit. We know how superstition presumes thought-
lessly and stupidly to play at imitating the saints. But those who
try to follow a unique example without the command of God,
moved by their own fancy rather than by the Spirit, are not
imitators; they are apes.

It is even possible that the faith of this woman was mixed
with some sin and error, which Christ was generous enough to
endure and ignore. Certainly, when afterwards her conscience
troubled her, so that she feared and trembled, her doubting,
which was the contrary of faith, was without any excuse or
justification. Why did she not rather go straight to Christ? If it
was reverence that kept her back, why did she not trust his
mercy, which alone was to be her help? And why was she afraid
of giving offense if she really believed in his kindness?

And yet, Christ acknowledged her faith with high praise. And
this agrees with my previous statement that God deals kindly
and gently with his people; that even though their faith be
mutilated and sickly, he accepts it, without holding against
them the sin and defect which run through it. Therefore, the
woman came to Christ as guided by faith. When she clung to
the garment, instead of asking Christ to heal her, the force of
her thoughtless zeal pushed her somewhat off the right way,
as soon became especially evident when she made her ven-
ture with such doubt and perplexity of spirit. Even though
her behavior was enjoined by the Spirit, it still remains a fixed
rule that we must not allow special cases like this to cause us
to waver in our faith. Faith needs to be bound directly to the
Word of God; for, according to Paul, *faith cometh by hearing, and
hearing by the Word of God* (Rom. 10: 17). And this is a useful
warning, that we may not dignify every opinion, picked up one
way or another, with the title of faith.

But the ship was now in the midst of the sea, tossed with waves: for the wind was contrary. Matt. 14:24.

Readers will find my exposition of this story in my commentary on John 6. Here I shall be brief. When Christ permitted his disciples to be tossed about for a while during a dangerous storm, he intended to fix their attention upon the wonderful help which he provided for them. For the adverse wind began to blow about midnight, or a little before. But Christ came only at the fourth watch, or at the earliest, three hours before sunrise. By this time their faith was shaken by terror even more than their arms were tired by rowing. In this predicament they were sorely in need of their Master's presence; and yet, when they saw him, they were seized with a gross stupor, as though they had seen a ghost.

For this reason Mark says that their heart was blinded and they did not understand about the loaves; for that miracle might have taught them well enough that there was no lack of divine power in Christ for helping them, and that he cared for them and would come to their aid when they needed him.

Therefore they are rightly condemned for feebleness of spirit in forgetting the power of God which they had seen the day before and which should have been still right before their eyes. They were surely blameworthy to have been struck with such stupidity that they had failed to profit from the earlier miracles they had witnessed. But they are reproached mainly for their blindness, which wiped out of their minds the memory of so recent and striking an event, or rather for their failure to acknowledge the Deity of Christ which had been obvious when he multiplied the bread.

But straightway Jesus spake unto them, saying, Be of good cheer; it is I; be not afraid. And Peter answered him and said, Lord, if it be thou, bid me come unto thee on the water. Matt. 14:27–28.

Since Christ is not known as a deliverer until he comes forward as one, it is by his Word that he invited his disciples to know him. Besides, he set forth his own presence among them as the real basis for the trust to which he called them. It is as though he said that, since they know he is there, they have solid ground for good hope. But since terror had already taken possession of their souls, he took them under his care, to keep their dread from hindering or destroying their confidence. Of course, he did not expect that they would be emptied of all fear and filled instead with sheer joy. He sought to break down the strength of their fear, that it might not crush their faith. Whereas the voice of the Son of God is deadly to the wicked, and his presence terrifying, its effect upon believers, as described here, is altogether different; it makes our inner peace and living faith triumph within our hearts, so that we may not succumb to the fretting of our flesh. If we are alarmed and agitated blindly and precipitously, it is because we are ungrateful enough and wicked enough not to take up the shields of God's countless benefits, which, properly wielded, would fortify us against all evil. Now, even though Christ appeared in good time for help, the tempest continued to rage, so that the disciples might be roused to rest their hope and expectation in his grace. From this we know that the Lord often delays the deliverance, which he has in the palm of his hand, for some good reason of his own.

And Peter answered him and said, Lord, if it be thou, bid me come unto thee on the water. The condition which Peter lays down shows that his faith is still immature. *If it be thou,* says he, *bid me come!* But he had already heard Christ speak! Why then does he, doubtful and perplexed, argue with him? Such a rash desire burst out of him because his faith was both little and feeble. He should have estimated himself rightly, and prayed for an increase of faith sufficient to lead and guide him across seas and over mountains. As it was, he was trying to fly without wings; or, without having the voice of Christ firmly in his heart, he desired to turn the water under his feet into solid land. And even though Peter's zeal was doubtless good at its source, yet, since he overdid it and so corrupted it, it is not worthy of praise.

But Peter soon began to pay for his rashness. Let his example teach believers to avoid too much haste. When the Lord calls, we should of course run. But anyone who overreaches himself will find out, from the unhappy consequences, what it means not to know one's limit. Yet, it may be asked, why did Christ comply with Peter's wish? For, in so doing, he seems to have approved of it. The answer is easy. God often helps us better by denying us what we ask of him; and at other times, he is indulgent with us, so that we may see our folly by experience. It happens every day that God, by giving his faithful people more than they need, trains them for sobriety and modesty in the future.

Thus, Christ's dealing with Peter on this occasion was profitable to him and to the other disciples; and it is profitalbe for us today. The power of Christ appeared to better advantage in the person of Peter when, rather than walk upon the water by himself, he took Peter along with him. In this way, Peter understood, and the others saw plainly, that when he did not rest in and lean upon the Word of God with a solid faith, the secret power of God, which had previously solidified the waters, disappeared. Nevertheless, Christ dealt kindly with him and did not let him go under and perish. Both of these things happen to us: as Peter began to sink, when fear seized him, the passing and the unstable thoughts of the flesh soon make us lose our foothold when we should be firmly occupied with our calling. Meanwhile, the Lord deals kindly with us in our weakness, and stretches his hand out, that the water may not suck us in altogether. But we should notice that Peter, seeing the unpleasant and unhappy effect of his temerity, throws himself upon the mercy of Christ. And we also, even while we are receiving our overdue punishment, should seek help from him, unworthy as we are, that he may bring us help in our misery.

And immediately Jesus stretched forth his hand, and caught him, and said unto him, O thou of little faith, wherefore didst thou doubt? Matt. 14:31.
While Christ was kind enough to save Peter, he did not justify his behavior. The weakness of his faith is properly rebuked. But one may ask, Is every kind of fear an evidence of defect in faith? For, Christ's words seem to imply that, where there is faith, there is no place for doubt. I answer that the doubt which Christ condemns is the precise opposite of faith. It is possible for a man to doubt when there is no Word from God to give him certainty. But Peter's case was quite different. He had received Christ's command and experienced his power; and yet, letting go of such a double mainstay, he fell prey to a fear which was at once foolish and perverse.

Then said Martha unto Jesus, Lord, if thou hadst been here, my brother had not died. But I know that even now, whatsoever thou wilt ask of God, God will give to thee. Jesus saith unto her, Thy brother shall rise again. Martha saith unto him, I know that he shall rise again in the resurrection at the last day. John 11:21–24.
She begins with a complaint, even though in this way she tells him shyly what she wants. What she means is: "If you had been here, you could have snatched my brother from death. You can do it even now, because God denies you nothing." But speaking in this manner, she gives vent to her feelings more than is proper to a believer. I admit that these words were

spoken partly by faith; but I submit that they were mixed with a confused feeling which pushed her to speak improperly. For, what is the ground of the confidence which leads her to assume that if Jesus had been there, her brother would not have died? Surely, it was not based on a promise of Christ. It must therefore be that she was rash enough to follow her own wishes rather than yield to Christ. It is [the nature] of faith to attribute all goodness and power to Christ; but it is alien to faith that she believed more than she has heard from Christ. We must recognize that the Word and faith agree the one with the other, so that we dare not presume to invent more than the Word of God allows. Besides, Martha was far too attached to the physical presence of Christ. It follows that her faith was mixed and confused with excessive desire; not being free from superstition it could not shine with full brightness. Hence her words exhibited only a few sparks of faith.

Your brother shall rise again. The kindness of Christ is amazing. He simply ignores Martha's faults, which we spoke of above, and promises her more than she dared ask openly and in so many words.

I know that he shall rise again. Here Martha's lack of courage is evident because she weakens Christ's words. We said above that she went too far when she devised a hope out of her own desires. And now she falls into the opposite error; when Christ stretches out his hand to her, she draws back with trepidation. This is why we should avoid both errors. On the one hand, we should not fill ourselves with hopes which, being empty of God's Word, are like so much wind. On the other hand, when God opens his mouth to us, he should not find our hearts closed and shut firmly against him.

VI

Providence

THE TEXT

1. PROVIDENCE AND HUMAN ACTION

The Lord is my shepherd, I shall not want. . . . Ps. 23: 1–4, 6.

God gently draws us to himself by his good gifts to us, giving us a taste of his sweetness as our Father; but nothing is so easy for us as to forget him when we are enjoying peace and comfort. We ought then to attend most carefully to the example set for us by David. David, raised to a king's throne, possessing ample wealth and great honors, testifies in the midst of the pleasures of his court that he remembers God and is mindful of the benefits which God has conferred upon him. He makes of them ladders by which he may climb nearer to God.

By the metaphor of the shepherd, he praises God's care; he means that God's care for those who are his own is like the solicitude of a shepherd for the sheep intrusted to him. In the Bible, God often assumes the title and role of shepherd, which we must recognize as a special sign of his love for us. Such a mode of expression is humble and undemanding and should make a deep impression upon us, since God for our sake is willing to stoop down and, by such a wonderfully gentle and intimate invitation, entice us to him, so that we may rest safely and quietly under his protection.

But it must be noted that God is shepherd only of those who are conscious of their own needs and weakness, and who feel the necessity of his guidance; for it is they who willingly remain in his flock and submit themselves to his leading. David, who excelled in power and possessions, acknowledged freely that he was a sheep, so that he might have God for his shepherd. What then would become of us, whose floundering proves our wretchedness, if we did not remain under the guidance of this same Shepherd?

Moreover, we must not forget that our greatest happiness is to have God's guiding hand stretched out to us, and to live under its shadow, so that his providence may watch over our safety.

He leadeth me beside the still waters. By *still waters* David meant waters that flow gently, because swift torrents are not suitable for sheep to drink from, and often they are even dangerous. . . . David here says once again that the Heavenly Shepherd overlooks nothing which might take away from the happiness of those under his care. . . . God in no way fails his faithful ones; he sustains them with his own power, feeds and strengthens them, and keeps them from all harm, so that they journey in comfort on smooth roads.

He leadeth me in the paths of righteousness. This means easy and plain paths. Since he continues with his metaphor, it would be out of place to understand this as referring to the direction of the Holy Spirit. David has said that God supplies him liberally with all he needs for this life; and he now adds that God protects him from all trouble.

Yea, though I walk through the valley of the shadow of death, I will fear no evil, for thou art with me; thy rod and thy staff, they comfort me. The faithful who dwell safely under God's hand are nevertheless exposed to many perils. Keeping the same metaphor, David compares God's care in guiding the faithful to the shepherd's rod and staff. When a sheep is walking in a dark valley, only the shepherd's presence keeps it safe from the attacks of wild beasts or from other accidents. David was not boasting of his own fearlessness; but was rather saying that he would walk boldly wherever his shepherd led him. And now that God reveals himself to us in the person of his only-begotten Son, as our Shepherd, more brightly than he did of old to the fathers under the law, we do not honor his protection properly unless we keep our eyes fixed upon it and by so doing trample upon all our trepidations.

Surely goodness and mercy shall follow me all the days of my life; and I will dwell in the house of the Lord forever. Whence was this confidence that God's kindness and mercy would be with him forever, if not from the promise by which God confines his benefits to those who believe, lest they be devoured by those whose palates have no taste for such benefits? For when David said earlier that in the shadow of death itself his eyes would be intently fixed on the providence of God, he showed well enough that he did not depend on things external; nor did he judge God's favor by his bodily senses. When all earthly aids failed, his faith remained, because it rested solely on the Word of God.

The last words of the psalm show clearly that David did not confine himself to the pleasures or comforts of this earth, but kept his gaze on heaven as the ultimate end of everything else. He says plainly that for him the culmination of all the good [gifts] from God is *to dwell in the house of the Lord.*

Blessed is the people whose God is the Lord, and the people whom he hath chosen for his inheritance.

The Lord looketh from heaven, and he seeth all the sons of Adam.

A king is not kept safe by the size of his army, nor will a giant be saved by his great strength.

A horse is a vain thing for safety; neither shall he deliver by his great strength.

Let thy compassion be upon us, O Lord, according as we hope in thee. Ps. 33:12, 13, 16, 17, 22. (Calvin's wording.)

. . . It is of little use to talk of the stability of God's purpose if we do not relate it to ourselves. Therefore the prophet declares that those whom God takes under his guardianship are blessed because God's purpose is not hidden from them, for it is seen in action in the safety of the church. And so we understand that it is not those who consider God's power coldly and with indifference, but those who apply it to their own immediate need, that have a right knowledge of God as the Pilot of the world.

Indeed, when the psalmist says, "If the Lord is our God," he points to the Lord as the fountain of divine love toward us, and tells us that we have no happiness except in him. In this way, he includes in one phrase everything we could ask for if we are to live a happy life. God's care for our safety, keeping us warm under his wings, providing for our needs, counting us worthy of his help in time of peril—all this is grounded in his adoption of us. And in order to keep anyone from thinking that so much good comes from our own prowess and industry, the psalmist specifies that it flows from the fountain of free election which makes us God's people.

Men corrupt this verse senselessly when they transfer to men what the prophet ascribes to God. As if men chose God for their inheritance! I admit that it is by faith that the true God is distinguished from idols; but we must hold fast to the following principle: There would be no communion between him and us if he did not first come to us with his grace.

The Lord looketh from heaven. The psalmist continues the same theme. The conditions of men do not come about by chance. God directs in hidden ways all that takes place. Therefore, the psalmist praises the watchfulness of God so that we may learn to see God's invisible providence with the eyes of faith. For although the evidences of his care are continually before our eyes, the greater part of mankind is blind, and invent a blind chance to match their blindness. The more bountifully and richly God pours out his kindness upon us, the less we turn our minds to him; we keep them instead fixed on what happens to us from the outside.

The prophet castigates the indignity which men offer to God; for no greater wrong can be done to him than to shut him up to stay idly in his heaven. That is like burying him in a grave! For how would God be living if he saw nothing and cared for nothing? Further, by the term *royal throne*, the prophet shows how absurd and stupid it would be to divest God of mind and intelligence. For he means that heaven is not a palace for idle pleasures, as the Epicureans imagine, but a king's seat of government from which God exercises his empire in all the realms of the world. But if God has set his seat in the sanctuary of the heavens in order to rule the universe, it follows that he by no means ignores earthly affairs, but controls them with the highest reason and wisdom.

A king is not kept safe, etc. A man's life is safe not by his own power, but by the grace of God. Kings and giants are mentioned because they think they are exempt from the common lot of men and believe themselves beyond the reach of javelin or arrow. If some misfortune occurs, they expect to find an easy escape. Intoxicated with confidence in their own ability, they are hardly able to remember that they are mortal; and their pride is strengthened by the foolish admiration of the crowd who are astounded at their might. But if the resources of a king do not give him security, and a giant does not escape by his strength when danger comes, it is futile for any ordinary man to depend on earthly riches and forget God's providence. For nothing can be more miserably precarious than the position of both the strong and the weak unless they rely on God's protection.

In the next verse, by the use of synecdoche (a part for the whole), the word *horse* means every kind of earthly assistance. Of course, kings are not armed with swords for nothing; and horses are not useless; nor are any of the wealth and resources, which God supplies to men to guard their lives, without value when they are rightly used. But the more the majority of men are surrounded with fortifications, the farther they go from God and falsely imagine that their wall is impregnable. God rightly confounds such insanity. So it is that the flood of God's gifts is often without effect; because the world, separating them from their Author, deprives itself of his blessing.

Let thy compassion be upon us.

The psalm closes with a prayer, which the prophet offers in the name of all the faithful, asking that they may know they have not relied on God's goodness in vain. In prescribing this rule of prayer by the mouth of the prophet, the Spirit teaches us that the door of God's favor is opened when we do not seek and hope for safety elsewhere. Meanwhile we draw our sweetest comfort from the certainty that our hope will never crack up while we are still on our way; nor do we need to fear that God will not extend his compassion toward us until the end.

And fear not those who kill the body, but cannot kill the soul; but rather fear him who can destroy both soul and body in Gehenna. And yea, I say to you, fear him. Are not two sparrows sold for a farthing? And not one of them shall fall to the ground without your Father. Matt. 10:28, Luke 12:5, Matt. 10:29. (Calvin's wording.)

Christ is perfectly right when he urges his disciples to despise death, because human beings created for heavenly immortality should treat this mutable and perishing life as so much smoke. The heart of the matter is this: if the believers consider to what end they were born, and what their condition now is, they will have no reason for clinging anxiously to this earthly life. However, these words have a still fuller and richer meaning; for Christ teaches us that the fear of God is dead in people who fear tyrants so much that they fail in their confession, that a brutish stupidity reigns in the hearts of those who fear death so much that they will not even hesitate to give up altogether confessing their faith. . . .

For this reason, Luke repeats emphatically: *Yea, I say to you, fear him.* We must understand Christ to say that, when we succumb to the fear of man, we show no respect for God; that when, on the contrary, we show proper reverence to God, victory is easy and in our hands, and no human power can pull us away from our duty. Besides, the experience of every age teaches how necessary it is for ministers and for believers in general to be warned about this danger, because there never was a time when men did not rise up in fury against God, and did not set themselves to crush the gospel. Not all men have equal power to put

the fear of death into the believers; still, the majority of men
are possessed with the ferocity of a Cyclops, which springs forth
when opportunity arises. Besides, the devil often gets hold of
giants, whose very looks would throw the servants of Christ
down lifeless, were they not taught to be hard and immovable
by this teaching.

Moreover, since fearing God and not fearing men go together,
it is stupid and wrong to pay attention only to the latter point.
On the contrary, as we have said before, Christ set a devout and
holy fear of God in opposition to a perverse fear of men, which
takes us away from the right way, as the only remedy for it.
Otherwise, there would have been no point in his saying that, if
we fear God who is Lord over soul and body, we ought not to
fear men who have power only over the body. When Christ
admits that men have the power to kill, he does so only by way
of concession. God holds the bridle of the wicked loose; and
they, puffed up by confidence in their own power, will dare
anything. They strike at shaky souls, and act as though nothing
could stop them. But futile is the insolence of the wicked which
makes them fancy that they can do as they please with the life
of believers. For, all the while, God holds the reins; and when it
pleases him, he checks their attack, however fierce and violent.
And yet they may be said to have the power to kill by God's
permission, because often they are able to go strong and give
vent to their fury. . . .

Are not two sparrows, etc. Now Christ goes on to declare, as I
have already hinted, that no matter how mad the tyrants may
be, they have no power even over the body. Therefore, those
who fear the cruelty of men, as though they were without God's
protection, are fools. In the midst of perils, we have this second
comfort that, since God is the keeper of our lives, we may safely
rely upon his providence. It is really an insult to God, not to
place our lives at the disposal of him who has honored us with
his protection. Christ extends the providence of God to all
creatures in common, and so argues by way of synecdoche (from
the whole to the part), that God exercises a particular care over
us. There is nothing cheaper than a sparrow (two were sold for
a penny; or as Luke has it, five for two pennies), and yet God's
eye is upon it, and nothing happens to it by chance. Will he
then who looks after sparrows neglect to watch over the lives of
men?

Moreover, we must notice two things. Christ defines the
providence of God very differently from those who, not unlike

the philosophers, admit that somehow the world is under divine government, and yet imagine the workings of providence in a confused way, as though God paid no attention to individual creatures. Christ, on the other hand, declares that every single one of God's creatures is under his hand and care, and that nothing happens by chance. In this way, he firmly opposes the will of God to chance, without however affirming the fatalism of the Stoics. It is one thing to find necessity in a context of a chain of many causes; it is quite another to see the world, as a whole and in its individual parts, as subject to the will of God. I confess there is a certain operation of chance in the nature of things considered in themselves; but I say that nothing occurs merely by the wheels of blind fortune, because the will of God reigns over all that happens.

In the second place, we must not look at God's providence after the manner of curious and silly people. It must be to us the ground of our strength, and an invitation to call upon God. When Christ tells us that even the hairs of our heads are numbered, he does it not to arouse us to empty speculation, but to teach us to rest in God's Fatherly care, which he exercises in behalf of these frail bodies of ours.

Him, being delivered by the determinate counsel and foreknowledge of God, ye have taken, and by wicked hands crucified and slain. Acts 2:23.

The chief purpose of Peter in mentioning the death of Christ is to establish faith in the resurrection all the more fully. It was well known among the Jews that Jesus had been nailed to a cross. Therefore, that he rose again would have been a token and evidence of the wonderful power of God. Meanwhile, in order to prick their consciences with a sense of sin, he says that it was they who killed Jesus, not that they had crucified him with their own hands, but that his death had been requested by the people with one voice. Although many of those who heard Peter had had no direct part in that godless and cruel wickedness, he was right in blaming them for it, because all of them had defiled themselves either by silence or by unconcern. There was no place for any pretense of ignorance, because God had already set Jesus before them. Peter thus prepares them for repentance by convicting them of sin.

By the determinate counsel. Here he meets a scandal which arises because it seems absurd at first sight, that this man whom God had adorned with such powers should have afterwards been

subjected to every kind of insult and allowed to suffer an ignominious death. Because the cross of Christ is at first so dis-
turbing to us, Peter declares that it did not occur by chance, or
because Jesus had no power to set himself free, but because it
had been ordained by God. For, only the knowledge that the
death of Christ was ordained by the eternal purpose of God cut
off in advance all occasion for foolish and depraved cogitations,
and prevented people's minds from taking offense at it. One
thing is certain: that God makes no rash or vain decision.
Whence it follows that he had a just reason for willing that Christ
should have suffered. Such knowledge of God's providence
enables us to take the right step toward understanding the purpose and benefit of Christ's death. For, the counsel of God confronts us with the truth that the Righteous One was delivered
to death for our sins, and his blood was our ransom from death.

This then is a notable statement of the providence of God,
teaching us that our life as well as our death is governed by it.
Luke is indeed speaking about Christ; but in him we have a
mirror of the universal providence of God which extends to the
whole world, and shines especially upon us who are members of
Christ.

In this place, Luke sets forth two things: God's foreknowledge
and his sure decree. Although first in order comes foreknowledge
(since God contemplates what he will ordain before he ordains
it), Luke puts it after God's counsel or decree, to teach us that
God neither wills nor decrees anything without having long
before directed it to its proper end. People often make rash
decisions because they decide quickly. Therefore, when Peter
wants to point out that God's counsel is not without reason, he
couples it with his foreknowledge. Now, we need to distinguish
between these two with some discernment, because many have
fallen down at this point. Passing by the counsel of God with
which he directs the whole world, these people grab at his
mere foreknowledge. Hence arises the common distinction according to which, even while God foresees everything, he lays
no constraint upon his creatures. Of course, it is true that God
foresees this or that which is in the future. But Peter teaches us
that what befell Jesus was not only foreseen by God, but also
decreed by him. From this we learn a general truth about God's
providence, one that appears in the government of the world as
a whole, no less than in the death of Jesus: it belongs to God,
not only to know the future, but also to ordain by his will whatever he wants to be done. Peter made this second point when he

said that Jesus was delivered by the sure and determinate counsel of God. Wherefore, the foreknowledge of God is other than the will of God by which he rules and regulates all things.

Some whose discernment is sharper admit that God not only foresees but also regulates with a nod everything that is done in this world. At the same time, however, they imagine a vague direction, as though God lets go of the bridle and allows his creatures to follow the rule of their own natures. They say that the sun rules by God's will, because in giving us light it does the duty enjoined on it by God in the beginning. They think that a free will of this kind is left to men, because their nature is capable of a free choice between good and evil. But those who think in this manner imagine that God is sitting idly in heaven. The Scriptures speak very differently, and defend God's control over particular events and over the several actions of men. But we must consider the purpose of Scripture in teaching us this doctrine; and we must at the same time shun all the mad speculations with which we see people carried away. The intention of Scripture is to exercise our faith, that we may know we are protected by God's hand, and that we may not be subject to harm from Satan and wicked men. . . .

By the hands of the wicked. Peter seems to suggest that the wicked did God's will. From this follows one or the other of two absurdities: either that God does evil, or that whatever wickedness men may perpetrate, they do not sin. As to the second statement, I answer that even though the wicked carry out what God himself has ordained, obeying God is the last thing they do. For obedience comes from a willing disposition, and we know that the purpose of the wicked is inspired by something far different. Besides, nobody but one who knows God's will obeys him. Obedience depends upon a knowledge of the will of God. But God has revealed his will to us in the law. Therefore, they only obey God whose deeds fulfill the demands of the rule of the law, who, therefore, submit themselves willingly to its authority. But we see none of this in the wicked, whom God drives hither and thither without their knowing it. Therefore, let no man say that they are to be excused because they obey God. We must seek the will of God in his law; but the wicked seek to resist God with everything in them.

I deny the other statement, that God does evil, because it suggests that God is disposed to wickedness. We must judge wickedness in the light of the purpose which governs a man's action. People who perpetrate theft or murder sin in that they are thieves and murderers; for they do these things with a wicked purpose. God, who makes use of men's wickedness, must not be put in the same class with them; he must be seen in a far different light; because when he sets out to punish one man, and to exercise another in patience, he never deviates from his nature, which is perfect rectitude. Thus, when Christ was delivered by the hands of wicked men, and crucified, it was done by the consent and decree of God. But the treachery in the matter, which as such is evil, and the murder in it which was a great wickedness, must not be attributed to God.

And the Lord said, Shall I hide from Abraham that thing which I do, seeing that Abraham shall surely become a great and mighty nation, and all the nations of the earth shall be blessed in him? Gen. 18:17–18.

When God proposes something as though it were doubtful, he does so out of kindness to men; for he had already decided what he would do. Here he intended to make Abraham pay close attention to the reasons he gives for the destruction of Sodom.

God gives two reasons for wanting to reveal his purpose before it was fulfilled: first, because Abraham was worthy of the privilege of the superior honor; second, because it would be useful and fruitful in the education of posterity. This in brief is the scope and value of this revelation.

One reason, as I said, why God wished his servant to know beforehand of his terrible vengeance upon Sodom was to honor him with special gifts. God has always shown this same kindness to the faithful; and he even increases it, heaping new and fresh blessings upon the earlier ones; and so it is that he deals daily with us. What ground is there for the innumerable favors he constantly bestows upon us except that he cannot refrain from expressing his Fatherly love with which he has enfolded us; and in doing this, he honors himself and his own gifts in us? For what except his own free gifts does he reward with his kindness? The origin of his kindness was in himself, not in Abraham's merits; nor does the blessing of Abraham flow from any other fountain except God.

Moreover, we learn from this passage, what experience also teaches, that it is the special privilege of the church to know the meaning of the judgments of God and their direction and purpose. God does indeed prove himself a just judge of the world by inflicting punishment on evil men. But because all things seem to happen by accident, God enlightens his sons by his Word, so that they may not walk blindly like unbelievers. So, in the past, when he stretched out his hand to smite all the world, he confined his holy oracle to Judea; that is, when he was ready to bring distresses and misfortunes upon the nations, he declared himself as their author by his prophets and to his chosen people alone. . . . Let us then be mindful that God, having begun to be good toward us, continues unwearied until, having blessed us in every way, he completes our salvation. Having once adopted us and enlightened our minds by his Word, he keeps the torch of the Word blazing before our eyes, that we may in faith keep our minds upon the judgment and punishment of evil which the impious confidently ignore.

Therefore the faithful ought to be well informed on the known history of all times, to be able to judge according to the Scripture the various calamities which befall the wicked, privately and in public. While Sodom was unharmed and enjoying its pleasant luxuries, the Lord announced to his servant Abraham that it would soon perish. There was then no doubt that it perished not by chance but by the act of God. . . . We must accept the same conclusion in other cases; for although God does not foretell the future to us, he wishes us to be eyewitnesses of his acts and to propound their causes wisely. We are not to be deceived by false vision like the unbelievers, who "seeing, see not" and turn their backs to their true goal.

O Assyrian, the rod of my anger, and the staff in their hand is my indignation. Isa. 10:5.

What follows is intended so to announce the coming punishment as to mitigate the sorrow of the faithful with some word of comfort. Therefore greater emphasis is given to the doctrine that whatever the evils perpetrated by the Assyrians, they will be a temporary discipline from God, and that when the unbelievers overdo their insolence, they will finally be put in their places.

Hoi is sometimes an exclamation of pain, sometimes a call for attention; and sometimes it has the sense "woe to," as the ancient interpreters translated it here. But in this passage it can only mean either that the Lord is calling the Assyrians, or that he is assuming the role of a mourner because he has to punish his people at the hand of the Assyrians. But when I look more closely at the whole passage, I prefer the interpretation that God is calling the Assyrians as though they were armed for battle by his own command.

The prophet had already proclaimed that the Assyrians would be upon them; but hypocrites feel so secure that the fear of God never troubles them, before they can see his scourge or until they actually feel its blows. This is why God now summons the Assyrians with "Come," just as a judge calls an officer and orders him to bind a criminal, or commands the executioner to put him to death. So the Lord calls the Assyrians to inflict punishment by their hand.

And the staff. This can refer to the Assyrians, and the clause can be understood as a repetition of the preceding in slightly different words. But I find here a difference in meaning. First, the Assyrians are called "the rod of God's wrath"; second, the swords and weapons with which they are equipped are equated with the anger of God, as though the prophet had said, "God according to his will is using the Assyrian instead of ax or sword as executor of his wrath," and then had added, "Although they may wear swords, what you should fear is [not their weapons but] God's anger against his people." The point is that whatever strength the enemy may have comes from God's anger, and that the enemy would not move a finger unless God roused him by a hidden prodding against the nation He intended to destroy. God calls *the staff* which they hold in their hand his "anger" to make it clear to the Jews that the apparently blind attacks of their enemies are directed by heavenly providence.

I disagree with some interpreters who would turn *beyadam* (in their hand) to "in their place" or "in their land." That is too forced. The point is that God calls the Assyrians as the servants of his wrath, for by their hand he will exact due penalty for the crimes of his people. Therefore, he declares that his anger is all the might they possess.

This teaching has two purposes: first, to terrify the wicked by letting them know that God's threats to destroy them are not empty words, and to show them the reason they are to be punished. These words, therefore, had much more force to rouse from their indifference the wicked who had laughed at all the former threatenings of the prophets.

Secondly, this teaching had also no small value when the Assyrians began to harass the people. For then, in the midst of the disaster, the Jews could see that it was not purposeless, nor happening by accident, for it had been predicted by the prophets.

Someone will object, Why did God when He had first said that the Assyrians were the rod of his anger, afterwards call *their staff* his *indignation?* But we must put it, "The Assyrian is my anger, and the staff which he carries is the staff of my indignation." But so long as we understand what the prophet means, we should not stop anxiously over words. He calls men "the rod of God's anger" because God uses them like a rod; he calls the weapons of men God's "indignation," because they are not directed by men's own will but are the evidence of God's anger.

These words of the prophet are most pertinent today, because they forbid us to think that the wicked burst forth unrestrained wherever their lust drives them; for they are guided and checked by a bridle, so that they will accomplish nothing against God's will. Hence we must conclude that God acts by the hand of the wicked. But here we must think and speak soberly, for there is need to distinguish wisely and carefully between the work of God and the work of men.

There are three ways in which God acts through men. First, all are moved and exist through him; from which it follows that all human actions proceed from his goodness. Second, he acts in a special way when he moves the wicked as seems good to him. Although nothing is further from their thoughts, he uses their work so that they mutually destroy one another and perish, or so that he may discipline his own people by their hand. This last is the prophet's point in this place. Third, God guides men by his sanctifying Spirit; but this way belongs only to the elect.

So whether tyrants, or robbers, or any others injure us; or when foreign nations rise up against us, always, among turbulent and confused commotions, the hand of God sheds his light upon us, to keep us from imagining that anything happens by chance.

Therefore also now, saith the Lord, turn ye even to me with all your heart. . . . Joel 2:12.

After announcing the terrible judgment, the prophet shows that his purpose was not simply to inspire terror, but rather to bring the people back to their right minds. But this he could not do unless he gave them the hope of forgiveness. I have said many times—and indeed the whole Bible proves it—that men cannot be brought back to the right way unless they receive the hope of God's compassion. For despair makes men more obstinate and doubles their wickedness, rather multiplies it a hundredfold.

For when a man who has done wrong despairs, he hurls

himself wholly into the gulf of wickedness without any restraint whatever. Therefore the prophet now describes the kindness and compassion of God in order gently to lead the people to apply themselves to repentance.

So now it was not you that sent me hither, but God. . . . Gen. 45:8.
This is an especially significant passage, for it teaches us that the true course of events is never disturbed by the wickedness and malice of men; that, on the contrary, God directs men's confused and turbulent movements to a good end. Also it shows us how we ought to think of God's providence and how we are to profit from it. When curious men debate over it, they not only muddle and pervert everything by ignoring its purpose, but also concoct whatever absurdities they can to insult God's justice. Their effrontery even makes some pious and modest men wish they could bury this part of our doctrine. For as soon as it is proclaimed that God holds the government of the whole world and that nothing is done without his assent and command, those who feel too little reverence for the mysteries of God burst out with various questions which are not only frivolous, but also pernicious.

However, in our desire to stop such profane intemperance, we should be very careful not to be satisfied with a crass ignorance of truths which are not only revealed by the Word of God but are also very useful for us to know. Good men are ashamed to confess that nothing which men undertake is accomplished unless God wills it, for fear unbridled tongues will clamor either that God is the author of sin, or that no blame is incurred by impious men since they are only following God's purpose. Although there is no way of refuting this sacrilegious madness, we should be content to detest it, and meanwhile hold firmly to the clear witness of Scripture, whatever men may invent. Amid all the shoutings of men, God directs men's plans and efforts from heaven, and finally accomplishes by their hands what he himself has decreed.

Good men who fear to expose the justice of God to the slanders of the impious take refuge in the distinction that God *wills* some things to be done and only *permits* others. As if, without his will, any freedom of action would be possible for men! If he had merely *permitted* Joseph to be carried to Egypt, he would not have ordained him as the instrument for saving the lives of his father Jacob and his sons; and this is what is said here explicitly. A statement like our text would be meaningless if evil things which God afterwards turns to a good end were done only by his permission, and not by his intention and will.

I know that on men's side there are evil deeds which are done out of sheer perversity. Moreover, since the doers are inherently sinful, they must be accounted wholly guilty. But God works through them in a wonderful way, so that he produces pure justice out of impure corruption. How he acts is hidden and too high for us. And it is not strange that lusting flesh rebels against it. But for this very reason we ought to avoid attempting to restrict heaven's great height to our narrow vision. Therefore let it be a fixed point that even while men's passion runs high and rushes uncontrollably hither and thither, God remains supreme over all and by his hidden bridle directs their motions wherever it seems to him good.

At the same time we must also hold that God's action is distinct from man's, so that his providence is free from all iniquity, and his decrees have no affinity with the wrongdoings of men. A most beautiful illustration of this truth is presented to our eyes in this story. Joseph was sold by his brothers for no other reason than that they wanted him somehow destroyed and out of the way. The same act is ascribed to God, but with the very different purpose of providing the house of Jacob with food in time of famine and beyond their every hope. . . . Hence it is clear that, although God at first seems to act as do wicked men, in the end their crime is a far cry from his wonderful justice. . . .

But we also see that men are no less criminal because God, contrary to their expectations, transforms the end they seek in their wickedness to a good and happy outcome. . . . Certainly we must hold that men's deeds must be valued not by their issue, but by whether they failed to do their duty, or acted contrary to God's command, or went beyond the limits of their vocation. When a man neglects his wife and children, and does not labor to provide for their necessities, even though they do not die unless God so wills, this in no way excuses the brutality of the husband and father who deserts them when he ought to be their helper. Therefore people with a bad conscience gain nothing by pushing forward the providence of God as a screen for their misdeeds.

But I ask you to note again, How often God resists the malice of those who desire to harm us, not only resists but also turns their evil efforts to our good! Thus he mitigates the afflictions of our flesh and gives us a calm spirit and greater peace.

And he said: Cursed be Canaan; a servant of servants shall he be unto his brethren. Gen. 9:25.

It is strange that Noah curses his grandson and passes over in silence Ham who committed the crime. The Jews give God's favor as the reason and say that God had so greatly honored Ham that the curse was shifted to his son. But that is a foolish conjecture. I am sure that the punishment was transferred to posterity to make its severity all the more obvious; for God was giving clear testimony that he did not consider the punishment of one man alone to be sufficient, and that therefore the curse had to include his descendants and continue in force through the ages. Meanwhile Ham himself was certainly not exempted; God made his judgment heavier by including his son with him.

Now another question arises. Why did God single out from among Ham's many sons one man in particular for the blow? But here we must not allow too much range to our curiosity. We should keep in mind, it is not without reason that the judgments of God are called an unfathomable abyss. It is not fitting that God, before whose tribunal we must all finally stand, be subjected to our judgment—or rather to our foolish temerity. God chooses as he pleases some, to make them examples of his grace and long-suffering; he destines others for a different purpose, to be proofs of his anger and severity. Here human minds are blind; yet each one of us, knowing his own failure, should learn to praise God's justice rather than hurl himself by insane audacity into the deep abyss.

The curse of God included the whole seed of Ham. But he singled out the Canaanites by name as cursed above all others. We know that this judgment was from God, for it was afterwards validated by the event. Noah was a man and did not know what was to happen to the Canaanites; but in such obscure and hidden matters he spoke as the Spirit directed his tongue.

There is still another difficulty. The Scripture teaches that the sins of men are punished to the third and fourth generation; and yet [our text] seems to depict the punishment of God's wrath as reaching to ten generations. I answer: Scripture does not prescribe a rule which God himself may not transgress, as though he were bound not to punish beyond four generations. We must see grace and punishment as combined and so understand that, while God justly punishes our crimes, he is still more inclined to mercy. Meanwhile, let us admit that he is free to extend punishment as far as it seems good to him.

Servant of servants. This Hebrew phrase means that Canaan will be the lowest among slaves, or that his situation will be worse than common slavery. But does not the lightning bolt of this stern and terrible prophecy seem a harmless joke, since the Canaanites were [at the time it was written] outstanding, in power, riches, and resources? Where then was their slavery? I answer: First, God's threats need not be fulfilled immediately; but they are never empty or ineffective; second, God's judgments are not always visible to our eyes or recognizable by our physical senses. The Canaanites threw off the yoke of slavery which was divinely imposed upon them and even grasped an empire for themselves. But although they had their time of arrogance, they were never in God's sight free.

In the same way, when the faithful are unjustly oppressed and tyrannically harassed by the wicked, their spiritual liberty before God is not destroyed. God promised to his servant Abraham dominion over the land of Canaan, and condemned the Canaanites to destruction. We must be satisfied with this as proof of God's justice.

One more point. The pope asserts that he utters prophecies. Well, so did Caiaphas. I do not wish to appear to deny all his claims; and I freely admit that the title[1] with which he adorns himself was dictated by the Holy Spirit. May he like Canaan become *servant of servants.*

And he said, What hast thou done? The voice of thy brother's blood crieth unto me from the ground. Gen. 4:10.

God shows, first, that he knows men's deeds even when no one complains or accuses; second, that human life is too precious to him for him not to punish the shedding of blood; third, that he takes the faithful under his care not only when they are alive but also after they die.

Earthly judges for the most part doze unless an accuser appeals to them. But even when the wounded are silent, their very injuries cry out to God to pronounce the penalty. It is a wonderfully sweet comfort to good men who are harassed unjustly to hear that the evils they endure silently go before God of their own accord and demand vengeance. Abel was silent when his throat was cut (perhaps he was killed some other way), but after his death the voice of his blood was more eloquent than the

---

[1] The title of the pope, "Pius Episcopus, servus servorum Dei," has been used since the time of Gregory the Great, in the sixth century. It is the regular heading of papal bulls at the present time.

plea of any orator. Thus, men may stifle or silence [the cry of the innocent]; but they cannot prevent God from judging a cause which the world considers buried. This consolation richly nourishes our endurance. When we learn that nothing of our right is lost, we bear our injuries with moderation and steady minds. The soul's calm silence raises an effective cry which fills heaven and earth.

Nor does the teaching of this verse apply to this life alone. We not only know ourselves safe under God's protection amid the innumerable dangers with which we are surrounded, but are also lifted up to the hope of a better life. It clearly follows that those who live under God's protection are safe after they die.

The people therefore that stood by, and heard it, said that it thundered: others said, An angel spake to him. John 12:29.

It was truly monstrous that the multitude was so stupid as to remain unmoved by so open a miracle. Some were so hard of hearing that what God so distinctly uttered they took for a confused sound. Others who were less dull made little of the majesty of the Voice of God, and said it was merely an angel who spoke. But men do the same today. God speaks plainly enough in the gospel, and there reveals such power and energy of the Spirit as ought to shake the heaven and the earth. But for many its doctrine is lifeless as though it were from mortal men; to others the Word of God is confused and barbarous, no different from thunder.

But the question arises, Did that voice sounding from heaven come in vain or without benefit to anyone? I answer that what the Evangelist says of the whole crowd was true only of a part. There were others besides the apostles who had a clearer insight of the matter. The Evangelist wanted to point out briefly what is common in this world: namely, that most people hear but do not understand when God speaks with a clear and loud voice.

2. PROVIDENCE AND GOD

He hath blinded their eyes and hardened their heart. John 12:40.

This passage is from Isaiah (6:9; cp. Matt. 13:14), where the Lord warns the prophet at once that his labors of teaching will only end in making the people worse. First then he says, "Go and tell these people, When you hear, you hear but do not understand." He means, "I send you in order that you may speak to the deaf." Then he adds, "Harden the people's heart";

by which he means that he intends his Word to issue in the punishment of the wicked; that he will make them totally blind, and they will plunge into a deeper darkness. Right as well as formidable is the judgment of God when he darkens the mind of men with the very light of his Word, so that they are bereft of all sense. By means of their only light, he covers them with a gross darkness!

However, we must note that the Word of God does not blind men by its own proper working. Nothing could be more absurd than that there should be no difference between truth and lies, or that the bread of life should act as deadly poison and medicine make a disease worse. When life is turned into death, we must blame men's evil for it. Besides, we must observe that God himself sometimes blinds the minds of men by depriving them of understanding and judgment; sometimes he does it through Satan and false prophets, whose lies make the people mad; sometimes he does it by his ministers, as when the doctrine of salvation is harmful and even deadly to the hearers. This is why, when the prophets fulfill their task of teaching faithfully, they ought to commend the fruit of their labors to the Lord. If they do not succeed, they should not quit, or lose their temper. Let them be satisfied to know that God approves of their labor; that although the savor of their doctrine does men no good, and the wicked turn it into a source of death to themselves, it is as Paul testifies, good and pleasing before God (II Cor. 2:15).

Because the carnal mind is in enmity against God; for it is not subject to the law of God, neither indeed can be. Rom. 8:7.

Paul now proceeds to prove what he had said by adding that nothing but death can issue from all the effort of the flesh, because it struggles in enmity to the will of God. The will of God is the rule of righteousness; whatever does not agree with his will is unrighteous; and if unrighteous, it is at the same time deadly. When God is set against us, it is vain to expect life; for his wrath must directly and inevitably be followed by death, which is vengeance wrought by his wrath. And now let us remember that in all things the will of man is opposed to the will of God. For we differ from God as depravity differs from rectitude.

For . . . to the law of God. This is the explanation of the previous sentence. It tells us how it comes about that all the thoughts of the flesh strive against the will of God. The will of God is attacked only where he reveals it; but it is in the law that God tells us what pleases him. Therefore those who would try to find out rightly whether they conform with God, must judge all their purposes and concerns by the norm of God's law. Even though nothing in this world is active except as directed by God's secret providence, it is an intolerable blasphemy to pretend that therefore nothing happens except by his approval, as some frenzied people cavil in our day. What folly it is, to seek the distinction between rectitude and iniquity, which the law places before our eyes so openly and distinctly, in the deep labyrinth of secret providence! As I have said before, the Lord has his own hidden counsel by which he disposes of everything in the world. But since it is incomprehensible to us, let us have sense enough to keep away from undue curiosity in prying into it. In the meanwhile, it remains true and settled that nothing pleases him except righteousness, and that we cannot judge our own deeds rightly except by the law of God, which testifies without deception to what pleases and what displeases him.

Nor can be. And now look at the faculty of free will, which sophists cannot praise highly enough! With these words Paul affirms certainly and explicitly what they detest with open mouths: that it is impossible for us to bring our powers into subjection so as to obey the law. They throw at our faces that the heart is able to bend itself one way or another, provided only that it is aided by an impulse of the Spirit; that the choice between good and evil is free and in our hand, provided the Spirit comes to our help: so that to choose or to refuse is up to us. They also invent good impulses by which we set ourselves spontaneously to obey the law. Paul, on the contrary, tells us that our hard heart is bulging with irrepressible outrage [against God] and will not by its own nature bend down to put on the yoke of God. Nor does he argue about this or that part of us; but rather, speaking in general, he puts together all the impulses which rise up from within us in the same bundle. Therefore far be the free will of heathen philosophy from the Christian heart! Let everyone know himself as the servant of sin, which he in fact is, that he may become free by the grace which he receives from Christ's own hand. To glory in any other freedom is the greatest stupidity.

But evil men and seducers shall wax worse and worse, deceiving, and being deceived. II Tim. 3:13.

It is the worst of trials that godless men wax great and strong with their sacrilegious audacity, and the blasphemies and errors they perpetrate. Paul says elsewhere that Isaac was troubled not by the sword of Ishmael but by his taunting (Gal. 4:29). We may gather from this verse that the writer did not point to one particular kind of persecution, but spoke in general of trials which the children of God must endure when they contend for the glory of their Father.

I spoke, a little before, of how evil men shall grow worse and worse. The apostle predicts not only that they will offer obstinate resistance, but also that they shall succeed in harming and corrupting others. One good-for-nothing fellow can always tear down more than ten faithful teachers can build, no matter how hard they try. There is no scarcity of the tares sown by Satan and infesting the good earth. No sooner are some false prophets put down than others pop up in all directions.

Now, wickedness has this power not because lies are by nature more effective than truth, or because the devices of the devil are superior to the power of God's Spirit, but because men have a spontaneous inclination toward vanity and error, and will embrace much too readily whatever suits their fancy. Therefore by a just retribution of God, they become blinded and captive slaves to the pleasure of the devil. This is the principal reason for the effectiveness of the pestilence of ungodly teachings. And considering the ingratitude of men, it is right that this should be so. Therefore, godly teachers should take to heart the warning to be prepared for constant warfare, not to break down because it is long and drawn out, or succumb before the impudence and insolence of their adversaries.

There were present at that season some that told him of the Galileans, whose blood Pilate had mingled with their sacrifices. And Jesus answering said unto them, Suppose ye that these Galileans were sinners above all the Galileans, because they suffered such things? I tell you, Nay, but except ye repent, ye shall all likewise perish. Luke 13:1–3.

This passage is extremely helpful to us, because it is almost an inborn disease with us to be hard and severe in judging others, while we treat our own misdeeds as mere trifles. Thus it happens that not only do we deal too sharply with the sins of our brothers, but also, when things go wrong with them, we condemn them as infamous and reprobate people. Meanwhile, so long as God's hand is not heavy upon us, we sleep safely with our sins, as though we enjoyed God's favor and friendship. In this way, we are doubly guilty. For, when God chastises someone under our very eyes, he does it so as to warn us of his judgments, in order that each one of us may learn to examine himself and to weigh the punishment he himself deserves. And if he spares us for a time, by his kindness and mercy he invites us to repentance. It should be far from us to use the time allowed us as an occasion for sloth.

The point Christ makes is that those who suffer hardship at the hands of others are not the worst of men; and his purpose is to condemn our depraved judgment which turns us habitually against those who are afflicted by some calamity, and to root out that self-indulgence with which everybody treats his own self. God exercises his judgments freely, in his own way and order, so that some receive their punishment immediately, whereas others are allowed for a while to enjoy their ease and pleasure in peace. Christ is here teaching us that whatever calamities occur in this world, they are testimonies to the wrath of God; and from this we learn that unless we avert God's wrath we shall be destroyed.

The occasion which led to this exhortation was the statement of some people that Pilate had mixed human blood with the blood of sacrifices. They meant to bring contempt upon these sacrifices, because they were accompanied by such a chastisement. It is likely that this outrage was inflicted upon the Samaritans who had turned aside from the pure worship of the law. The Jews, therefore, were quick to applaud themselves while they condemned the Samaritans. But our Lord turned the matter into something else. Because the Jews hated and condemned the whole people of the Samaritans, he asked them if they thought the wretched few who were murdered by Pilate were so much more wicked than the rest. In other words, he said, "It can be no secret to you that the whole land of the Samaritans is full of ungodliness; and yet many who are worthy of punishment are still safe and sound." He must indeed be a blind and depraved judge who thinks that where there is affliction there must be sin. It is not true that the most wicked are dragged for punishment first. God chooses to punish a few out of a multitude, so that through them he may condemn the rest and fill them with the terror of his vengeance.

After having spoken of the Samaritans, Jesus turns to the Jews themselves. He points out that in those days eighteen people had been crushed to death by the fall of the tower of Jerusalem. He denies that these people were wicked above all others, and argues that their death ought to fill everyone with fear; for, if God had made them an example of his justice, it was not likely that the rest would be able to escape from his hand, even though for a while they were being left alone. Christ does not discourage believers from attending to God's judgment; but he does ask them to do it rightly by beginning with their own sins. . . .

And his disciples asked him saying, Master, who did sin, this man, or his parents, that he was born blind? John 9:2.

First, since Scripture testifies that all the troubles of humanity arise from sin, whenever we see anyone in misery it naturally occurs to us at once that his distress is a punishment inflicted by the hand of God. Thus we err in three ways. First, few judge themselves as severely as they do others. If my brother meets adversity, right away I see the judgment of God in it. When God chastises me with an even heavier rod, I shut my eyes to my sins. But in passing judgment, a man ought to begin with himself; he ought not to spare himself more than others. If we would be just in this matter, we ought to be quicker to discern evil in ourselves than in others. Secondly, excessive rigor is wrong. No sooner do we find someone meeting disaster at God's hand than we jump to the conclusion that it is because God hates him. We turn his faults into crimes and almost despair of his salvation. On the contrary, we so belittle sins in our own case that we hardly see as little faults what we ought to confess as gross wickedness. In the third place, we sin by freely casting off as damned those whom God is trying with a cross.

It is true, as we said above, that all misery arises from sin. But it is also true that God afflicts his own for various reasons. Now, God does not avenge certain crimes in this world, but postpones punishment to the next, to deal with them all the more severely; conversely, he often deals severely with his faithful people, not because they have sinned greatly, but in order to mortify the sin of the flesh. At times he overlooks their sins; he tries their obedience and trains them in patience. Take the case of Job, who suffered more calamity than other men; God was not concerned with his sins. His purpose was rather to make a better trial of Job's faith through his various afflictions. Therefore, the interpreters who attribute all suffering indiscriminately to sin are fools—as though all were punished equally, or as though in afflicting men, God had regard only to each man's desert!

Jesus answered, Are there not twelve hours in the day? If a man walketh in the day, he stumbleth not, because he seeth the light of this world. John 11:9.

This verse has been explained in various ways. Some are of the opinion that men's minds are changeable, and seize every hour upon a new and different purpose; but nothing could be further from what Christ meant. This view would hardly be worth mentioning except that it has become a common proverb. Let us be content with the right and simple meaning of this verse. First, Christ borrows the simile from day and night. When a man walks in the dark, it is not strange if he knocks against something, or goes astray, or even gets lost. But when the sun shines and shows the way, he walks in safety. Now, the calling of God is like the light of day, which keeps us from hitting something or going astray. Whoever obeys the Word of God and does not go ahead except by his command, has a Guide and Director from heaven; and with this confidence, he sets on his way with courage and security. Now, as we learn from Ps. 91:11, anyone who walks in God's ways has angels for protectors and is safe under their guidance, so that his feet do not strike a stone. Therefore, Jesus, fortified by this confidence, goes ahead boldly into Judea without fear of being stoned. There is no danger of going astray when God, acting as our sun, directs our way.

This verse teaches us that, if a man lives by his own wits, without God's calling, he will wander and get lost all his life. Those who think they are very wise, and neither inquire of God nor receive his Spirit to govern all their actions, are blind and grope in the dark. There is only one right way: to hold on single-mindedly to our divine calling and to have God always walking ahead of us. This firmly established rule of life, which we must follow with perfect confidence, leads straight to a successful outcome because God does not rule our lives except for our well-being. And it is essential for us to realize that, as soon as the faithful move one foot in order to follow God, Satan comes forward with a thousand obstacles, and presents them with all sorts of perils, all with the one purpose of contriving to obstruct our way. Nevertheless, the Lord kindles his light and invites us to go ahead; we must walk with courage even though our way may be filled with many deaths. This we must do because God never bids us to go ahead without at the same time fortifying us with his promise; and the promise gives us our firm certainty that if we remain under his authority, he will bring us to a good and blessed end. This is our chariot; anyone who rides in it is never weary and cast down. Even though the obstacles on our way are so great that we could not overcome them in our own vehicle, we always find our way out with the wings which are given us, until we arrive at our destination; not because nothing adverse happens to believers, but because the very evils they meet are helps which bring them to salvation.

Then they sought to take him: but no man laid hands on him, because his hour had not yet come. John 7:30.

They did not lack the will to do him harm, or even the zeal to do it. They also had the power. Why then with all this were they helpless, as if they were bound hand and foot? The Evangelist answers that it was because Christ's hour had not come, by which he means that God's own protection guarded him against their fury and violence. And at the same time, he faces and removes the offense of the cross; because when we hear that Christ was subjected to death not by the will of men but as destined for such a sacrifice by the decree of the Father, we are no longer disquieted. And from this we may infer a general truth, that as we live day by day the hour of our death is in God's hand. It is hard to believe [but true] that, although subject to so many accidents, exposed to evil in the hands of so many lurking men and beasts, and liable to so many diseases, we are nevertheless safe from all peril until God is ready to call us. Our part is to struggle against our own lack of trust. First, let us hold on to the truth here taught us, then next to the goal set before us, and finally to the exhortation which follows: Casting all our cares on God, let each one of us fulfill his vocation without allowing fear to turn him aside from his duty. And let no man go beyond God's purpose for him. For, it is not right that a man trust the providence of God apart from God's own will for him.

But when Phineas, the son of Eleazar, the son of Aaron, the priest, saw it, he rose up from among the congregation and took a javelin in his hand. Num. 25:7. (The Harmony.)

Phineas' courage is celebrated because, while others did nothing, he was fired with holy zeal and leaped forward to inflict punishment. The inaction of the others is tacitly condemned, although their tears merit praise. But since their grief almost stupefied them, their virtue was not free from fault. Certainly, when the unbridled license of the people burst forth like waves from a stormy sea, it is not strange that the courage of good men broke down, or lay prostrate and feeble; and the more glorious was the zeal of Phineas who did not hesitate to oppose so many wicked criminals, raging with their own passions.

Someone may object that he exceeded the bounds of his vocation because he snatched a sword to slay, although he was not armed by God. But the answer to this is ready. Vocation is not always restricted to its ordinary duties, because God sometimes gives his servants new and unusual roles. As priest, Phineas was not charged with punishing crime; but he was especially called to do so by God's instigation and he was under the command of the Holy Spirit.

This incident ought not to be taken as an example from which to draw a general rule. God is free to appoint his servants to whatever special tasks he pleases; and his approval is enough evidence that he himself has called. We conclude without question that Phineas was under divine direction, because God declared that the deed pleased him. And this is repeated in Ps. 106:31. But if anyone in a private capacity begins in an excess of zeal to punish a like crime, he cannot plead Phineas' example unless he is truly convinced of his own heavenly commission.

We must not forget Christ's answer when his disciples wished to follow the example of Elijah and call down fire on those who had not received them: *You know not of what spirit you are* (Luke 9:55). If our zeal is to be approved by God, it must be tempered with spiritual wisdom and ruled by God's authority. The Holy Spirit must lead us and dictate to us what is right.

Our Father who art in heaven, hallowed be thy name. Thy kingdom come. Matt. 6:9–10.

When we set out to pray, there are two things we must seek above all: first, that we may have access to God, and secondly, that we may rest in him with full and solid confidence, knowing his Fatherly love for us and his unbounded kindness; that he is ready to hear our prayers; and above all that he is spontaneously ready to come to our help. Christ calls him *Father*, and with this title, gives us sufficient ground for confidence in him. But because we trust God only in part because of his goodness, he next commends to us God's power. When Scripture says that God is in heaven, it means that God is sovereign over all things; that he holds the world and all that is in it in his hand; that his power sustains all and his providence orders all. So, David himself says in Ps. 2:4, "He who dwells in the heavens, shall laugh at them"; and in Ps. 115:3, "Our God is in heaven; whatever he wills, he does."

In other words, when God is said to be in heaven, it is not meant that he is inside it; we must remember the words, "Heaven of heavens do not contain him" (II Chron. 2:6). This expression sets him apart from all creatures, and warns us that no mean and earthy thoughts about him should enter our minds, because he is higher than the whole world. So, Christ, above all, wanted to establish the disciples' trust in God's goodness and power; because unless our prayers are rooted in such faith, they do us no good. What stupidity and mad arrogance it would be to invoke God as Father, unless we are accepted as his children in the Body of Christ! It follows that we pray rightly only when we come to God trusting in the Mediator.

Hallowed be thy name. Now what I have said becomes clearer. In the first three petitions we are bid to subordinate our self-regard to the glory of God; not because the glory of God has no bearing upon our salvation, but because the majesty of God deserves to come before all other considerations. It is well for us that God reigns and that all honor is his due; for no man is aflame with the desire to glorify God, unless, forgetting himself, he elevates his mind to seek God who is high and lofty. Moreover, there is a close connection and likeness among these three petitions. Where God's name is hallowed, there is his Kingdom; and the principal mark of his Kingdom is that his will be done. When we consider how cold we are, and how slow to choose the greatest goods for which we are here commanded to pray, we see how needful and useful it is that these three petitions be thus distinguished one from another.

To hallow the name of God is simply to honor him as is his due, so that men shall not think or speak of him without the highest homage. The opposite of *to hallow* is *to profane*, which happens when men forget his majesty, or fail to render him the reverence and honor he deserves as God. Now, the glory by which God is hallowed [among men] emanates from and depends upon men's common knowledge of his wisdom, goodness, righteousness, power, and every other excellency of God. Of course, God is never without his holiness; but men do obscure it with their ill will and wickedness, and violate and corrupt it with their unholy contempt. The sum of this petition, therefore, is that the glory of God may shine in the world and be duly celebrated among men. Religion is most alive and vigorous when men confess that all God's works are right and worthy of praise, full of wisdom and altogether righteous. For, so it is that men embrace his Word with the obedience of faith, and approve of his pleasure and his works. But the faith by which we yield to God's Word is as it were our signature by which we acknowledge that God is faithful (John 3:33); whereas, unbelief and contempt of his Word is the greatest possible dishonor to God.

These words spoke Jesus, and lifted up his eyes to heaven. . . . John 17:1.

John's present account of how Christ prayed with eyes raised to heaven indicates his uncommon zeal and ardor. With this gesture, Christ testified that in spirit he was in heaven rather than on earth; that, having left the society of men behind, he was in communion with God. He looked up to heaven, not because God, who fills heaven and earth, is in it, but because it reveals his majesty in a special way. Besides, by asking us to raise our eyes to heaven, he exalts the Deity of God above all his creatures. For this same reason, it is well to raise our hands up while we pray. Human nature being lazy and slow, and the mind being drawn downward toward earthly things, men need such goadings, rather such chariots, that they may rise to God. Besides, if we would imitate Christ, let us beware that there be no more in outward act than in the mind. Let the inner disposition move the eyes, hands, tongue, and all we have.

The behavior of the publican who cast his eyes down does not contradict [the action of Christ spoken of in] this verse. Even though he was cast down with shame over his sins, his humility did not prevent him from being confident as he prayed for forgiveness. It was proper of Christ to pray in a different way, because he had no reason for shame. David, himself, prayed with eyes up, or down, according to the occasion.

VII

Election and Predestination

THE TEXT

1. ELECTION

Malachi—introduction.

Next comes the book of Malachi. Many imagine him to have been an angel, for we know that an angel is called *mala'k* in Hebrew. But it is easy to see what an absurdity that idea is. At that time, God did not send angels to announce his oracles, but used the regular ministry of men. And since the *i, yod*, is added at the end of the name, as is usual in proper names, we may conclude that Malachi was the man's name. But I readily admit that there may have been a reason for the name which today escapes us. I am more ready to agree with others who say that he was Ezra and that Malachi is a second name given him because God had called him for a splendid and magnificent work.

But whatever the fact may be, he was certainly one of the prophets and we can assume with reason that he was the last. In the end of the book he urges the people to stand fast in the pure teaching of the law; and this he does because thereafter God was not to continue sending a succession of prophets as he had done before. . . . Now I come to his words:

The burden of the word of the Lord to Israel by the hand of Malachi. Mal. 1:1.

Those who explain *massa'* as simply another word for prophecy are mistaken, as I have said elsewhere. Not every prophecy is called a *burden*. Further, whenever the word is used, some impending judgment of God follows, and it is clear enough from Jeremiah (23:36) that the word was generally detested. Godless people, when they wanted to insult the prophets, used to say as a common proverb, "This is a burden,"

288

implying that you could expect nothing from prophets but
threats and terrors; that it was better to shut one's ears and to
avoid all prophecies as omens of evil. Malachi's teaching is
properly called a *burden*, because, as I have said and explained
more fully elsewhere, it was necessary to summon the people to
God's judgment court, on account of the infamy which was
once again rampant and had to be stopped. Therefore he says
that God's judgment is upon them. . . .

Hand, as we have seen, means *service*. It means that this
teaching is from God, with Malachi as the intermediary. The
prophet is bringing nothing of his own; he is faithfully reporting
as God, the author [of the prophecy], has commanded him.

*I loved you, saith the Lord. And you said, How didst thou love us?
Was not Esau Jacob's brother? saith the Lord. And I loved Jacob, and
Esau I held in hatred. . . . A son honoreth his father, and a servant his
master. And if I am a father, where is my honor? And if I am a master,
where is my fear? saith the Lord of hosts.* Mal. 1:2–6. (Calvin's
wording).

I am compelled to read all these verses together because
otherwise the meaning of the passage would not be clear. God
is here remonstrating with a perverse and ungrateful people who
doubly deny him his right since they neither love him nor fear
him. He rightly claims the name and position of both Father
and Lord. When the Jews show him no reverence, he reproaches
them for denying him a father's right; and when there is no fear
of him, he accuses them again because they do not recognize
him as Lord, although they cannot elude his authority. But
before he comes to the accusation, he shows that he is both Lord
and Father. And above all he shows that he is a father, in that
he has loved them freely. . . .

God could have appealed to the Jews on other grounds.
Even if he did not love them, they were bound to him by his
sovereignty. However, here God is not speaking of his universal
love toward the whole human race. He is reproaching the Jews
because, having been freely adopted by him as a holy and
special people, they had forgotten his honor and despised him
and had paid no heed to his teaching. When, therefore, God
says that he loved the Jews, we can see that in this way he wants
to convict them of ingratitude because they have spurned the
singular favor by which he had honored them alone, rather
than to convince them of his universal Kingdom to which all
men are subject.

God could have said to them: "I created you and I am your father who feeds you. The sun shines daily upon you and the earth bears its fruits. In fact I hold you bound to me by the innumerable benefits I confer upon you by my kindness." God could have dealt with them in that way; but as I have already pointed out, he preferred to bring before them the free adoption of Abraham's seed. The disloyalty of the Jews was all the more intolerable because they were rejecting an incomparable favor. For God had raised them above all nations not because of any merit or worth of their own, but because he was pleased to do so.

The prophet begins by saying that *God loved the Jews* in order to make them realize that their scorn for God's teaching was the worst possible response to his love. This is the first point.

Next, it is obvious that he is indirectly reproaching their ingratitude when he makes them say, *How didst thou love us?* With this God implies, "If you should say, or rather, should ask, In what way have I loved you? my answer is, Truly in that I set aside Esau and chose your father Jacob, although they were brothers. . . ." We see, as I mentioned above, that the prophet reminds the Jews of the free covenant to leave them no excuse for their wickedness in repaying God so badly for his special grace toward them.

He does not accuse them because they were created like the rest of mankind, or because God has given them the light of his sun, and provided them with food out of the ground. He says that if they have been set above other peoples, it is not by their own merit but because God had seen fit to choose their father, Jacob. The prophet could have named Abraham; but since Jacob and Esau were both descended from Abraham, with whom God had made his covenant, God's gracious favor was the more conspicuous in Jacob. First, God chose Abraham alone, and put the other families of mankind aside. Then, out of this one family whom God had adopted, one man was chosen and the other rejected.

The point is not merely that Esau and Jacob were brothers. We must notice other facts which the prophet does not state because everybody knew them. . . . All the Jews knew that Esau was the first-born, and that it was contrary to nature for Jacob to obtain the first-born's right. . . . But Jacob was divinely chosen and his brother, the first-born, was rejected.

If we seek the reason for this, we shall not find it in a difference of root or origin. The two men were brothers; and even before they came out of their mother's womb, God had already declared by oracle that Jacob would be the greater of the two. So we see that the primary source of every good we find in the descendants of Abraham was derived solely from the free love of God. Indeed Moses says often, Not because you excelled other nations, or were more numerous, did God honor you with so many kindnesses, but because he loved your fathers (Deut. 7:7). The Jews were continually warned not to look for the reason for their adoption elsewhere than in God's free favor. He had seen fit to choose them; this alone was the source of their security.

After having briefly recalled the benefits which should have filled the Jews with shame, the prophet comes to his main point, which is, as I said above, that God declares himself defrauded of his right in two ways: the Jews neither revere him as Father nor fear him as Lord. He could indeed, by right of creation, call himself both Father and Lord, but I have already explained that he refers rather to their adoption because God's grace is the more striking when he out of all mankind chooses some few to be his own people. . . . Those whom he honors with such an election he binds to himself with a most holy chain; and if they desert him, there is no excuse whatever for their treachery.

Since we now understand the prophet's purpose and the aim of the whole reproof, it remains to adapt his teaching to our own use. We are not descendants of Abraham or of Jacob, according to the flesh; but God has given us sure evidence of his adoption, which singles us out from other peoples whom we in no way excel. Clearly, then, if we do not respond to God's call, we are found no less guilty than the Jews. I am touching on this briefly now, to point out that this teaching has no less importance for us today than it did for the Jews at that time.

Although the method of our adoption differs from that which affected one seed or one family, it is true of us as it was of them that we are raised above others not by our own worth but because God has freely chosen us for his people. Since he has so chosen us, we belong to him, more especially because he has bought us by the blood of his Son. By granting us participation in his inestimable grace through the gospel, he has made us both sons and servants. Therefore, unless we honor him as Father and fear him as Lord, the same (and no less) ingratitude will be found in us as was found in that ancient people.

Today I dealt with the main points of this passage in a summary way; tomorrow I shall speak of election, as the text itself requires. It was necessary to discuss first the prophet's purpose, which I have done. Next I will treat single topics more fully so far as necessary.

Prayer

Grant, Almighty God, who hast not only given us life in common with all men in this world, but hast also separated us and illuminated us by the Sun of Righteousness, thine only-begotten Son, in order to lead us into the inheritance of eternal salvation, grant I beseech thee that since we have been rescued from the darkness of death, we may ever attend to that heavenly light by which thou guidest and invitest us to thyself. May we walk as children of light, and never wander from our holy calling, but continually go forward in it, until we shall at length reach the goal which thou hast set before us, so that we may put off the uncleanness of the flesh and be transformed into that ineffable glory of which we have now the image in thine only-begotten Son. Amen.

Yesterday we explained the purpose of Malachi the prophet. ... But to appreciate the justice of his remonstrance, first, we must consider under what obligation we are to God, because he created us as men, in his own image and likeness, for he could equally well have created dogs and donkeys instead of men. We know that Adam was made of the earth as were the other animals, and therefore as to body there was no real difference between men and the dumb beasts. God is said to have breathed the breath of life into men, but we should not take this as the Manichaeans dream about it, as though men receive their souls by way of *transplantation*. (By using this word, they teach that the human soul is of the substance of God.) Moses on the contrary means that the human soul was created out of nothing. We are born by generation, but our origin is clay. Still, there is something special in us, a creation from nothing which is the soul. We see, therefore, that we differ from the beasts only because God by his gracious favor willed to create us men. Therefore, if we do not worship him, he has every right to charge us with ingratitude, since we were created in his image for this very purpose.

This passage, however, has to do with the special favor of

God in taking the seed of Abraham to himself. As the Song of
Moses declares, All peoples belong to God; and yet he has
thrown a rope and separated Israel for himself (Deut. 32:9).[1]
With the whole earth under his dominion, he pleased to choose
one family as his own.

If we look for a reason for this, we shall not find it in men. All
men alike were created out of the earth, and all had souls
created from nothing put into their bodies. If this be so, we see
that when God gives precedence to one race over others, the
distinction among them must have its source in his gracious
favor. . . . The prophet speaks here of the third step in election,
by which God set apart a branch of Abraham's descendants.
But we must keep in mind the first step, by which mankind was
bound to God in a special way, because while he could have
created them donkeys and dogs, he chose to form them after
his own image. The second step was his choice of the race of
Abraham, although his power extended over all peoples without exception. . . . In the third stage, to which Malachi refers,
we must note that, having promised to be the God of Abraham
and his seed, God distinguished also between the sons of Abraham, rejecting some, taking others for his own. This is emphasized by Paul in the ninth chapter of Romans. . . .

Now upon the third step follows a fourth. From the sons of
Jacob, God chose whom he would, and rejected others. The
Scripture is full of statements like the words of Moses (Deut.
9:6), "I did not choose you from other nations because of your
virtue, for I knew that you were a rebellious people, stiff-necked
and obstinate." Even while God knew the perverse spirit of this
people, he chose to reveal in them an example of his wonderful kindness. Therefore, we must not look for the cause of their
adoption outside of God.

But if the election of Abraham, Isaac, and Jacob was a free
act of God, we must conclude that the individuals whom God
singles out from the whole body are freely chosen. And so I
come to the fourth step. . . . For when many who are descended
from Jacob according to the flesh are rejected no less than Esau,
it is clear that when God elects individual men his choice is
governed by his free favor and pure compassion. This is the
line of argument which the apostle follows in the letter to the
Romans.

It seems harsh to many to think that God chooses some and

---

[1] Calvin's paraphrase bears little verbal resemblance to anything in Deut.,
ch. 32, although the main point is made in the Song.

rejects others, and does not consider men's worth, that by his own free will he chooses whom he pleases and moreover rejects others. But what is this scruple except a desire to call God to order and subject him to their judgment? We must return to the first step. If it is unreasonable for God to choose one of two men and reject the other, how can we defend God's justice in creating a donkey and a man—if it needs defense? For as I said the bodies of donkeys and men come from the same clay. And all of a donkey's strength and energy he possesses because he was so created by the secret life-giving power of God. As for man's soul, although it is immortal, it is also a creation from nothing. Now let these good critics explain what wrong they think is done to God, and how he is slandered by the statement that the salvation of men depends on God's will to reject some and choose others. For, if they wish to satisfy human judgment, they have the same problem in the universal election of men and beasts at their creation.

As we have said, there is no real difference among men, except in their hidden election. Some theologians would make foreknowledge the mother of election, and that very foolishly and childishly. They say that some men are chosen and others rejected by God, because God, from whom nothing is hidden, foresees of what sort each man will be. But I ask, Whence comes virtue to one and vice to the other? If they say, "From free will," surely creation was before free will. This is one point. Besides, we know that all men were created alike in the person of Adam. . . . And what does this mean except that the condition of all who come from the one root is the same?

I am not discussing "special gifts." I admit that if our nature had not been corrupted and we all had the same assurance of blessedness, we would be endowed with a variety of gifts. . . . But since in Adam all are sinners, deserving of eternal death, it is obvious that nothing but sin will be found in men. Therefore, God's foreknowledge cannot be the reason of our election, because when God [looks into the future and] surveys all mankind, he will find them all, from the first to the last, under the same curse. So we see how foolishly triflers prattle when they ascribe to mere naked foreknowledge what must be founded on God's good pleasure. . . .

When Moses prays to God not to break his covenant with Abraham, God answers, "I will have compassion on whom I will have compassion." What does he mean? He means that the reason for God's keeping some for himself and rejecting others is to be sought nowhere but in God himself. When he says, "I will have compassion on whom I will have compassion," the repetition may seem empty and dull; but it is in reality emphatic. . . . The reason for compassion is compassion itself.

At that time, Jesus answered and said, I thank thee, O Father, Lord of heaven and earth, because thou hast hid these things from the wise and prudent, and hast revealed them unto babes. Even so, O Father, so it seemed good in thy sight. Matt. 11:25–26.

It is certain that he gave thanks to the Father on their behalf and for their sakes, so that they might not be offended because the church appears so lowly and mean. We are always looking for splendor, and nothing seems more absurd than that the Heavenly Kingdom of the Son of God, the glory of which is celebrated with such magnificence by the prophets, should consist of the dregs and nobodies of low-class peoples. And surely it is an amazing counsel of God that when he had the whole earth in his hands he chose his people out of the contemptible folk, rather than out of the upper classes who might have brought the name of Christ greater credit through their own excellencies. But here Christ sets his disciples apart from the proud, from the high and mighty, so that they will not dare to despise the mean and obscure condition of the church with which he himself is well pleased and happy. Besides, in order to suppress more effectively the curiosity which is constantly creeping into people's minds, he goes beyond the realm of cause and effect, and contemplates the secret judgments of God, in order to lead others to wonder at them with him. Even though God's judgment shows him certainly to be of a mind quite different from our own, our pride is nonetheless insanely blind if we cry out against God's judgment while Christ who is our Head bows his head to it and adores it. But let us consider further the statement, *I acknowledge to thee, O Father.* With these words, he testifies to his acquiescence in the decree of the Father, which accords so ill with the mind of man. There is here a hidden contrast between the praise which he renders to God and the malicious calumnies, and even the insolent barkings, of the world. It is clear that he glorifies the Father, because even though he is the Lord of the whole world, he has preferred babies and simple folk to those who are wise. Now, in this context, it is not without significance that he calls the Father *the Lord of heaven and earth.* In this way he declares that the distinction between the wise who act as blind men, and the uncouth and ignorant who embrace the mysteries of the gospel, depends on nothing else than the will of God. There are many other passages of this kind, where God shows that those who attain salvation are the ones whom he himself has chosen freely; for he is the Creator and Fashioner of the world, and all nations are his own.

This verse is impressive in two respects. The fact that not all receive the gospel is not due to the impotence of God, who could readily make all creatures submit to his empire. Secondly, that some arrive at faith, while others remain stupefied and obstinate, is due to his free election. He draws some to himself and passes others by; and in so doing, he himself distinguishes among men, whose situation by nature is the same. It is for his own glory that he elects little children rather than the wise. The flesh is much too zealous to set itself up. If clever and learned men were to have an advantage, then everybody would assume that faith is acquired by human skill, or industry, or knowledge. There is no other way in which the mercy of God can stand out more clearly than in God's way of choosing; for thus it becomes evident that men come to God empty-handed. Therefore, it is right that the wisdom of men should be overthrown; because in this way it will not obscure the glory of God's grace.

But someone will ask, Whom does Christ call the wise, and whom, little children? Experience teaches us clearly that not all those who are ignoramuses and uncultivated men receive the light and believe; and not all who are prudent or literate are left to their blindness. Therefore, they who are here called prudent and wise are those who, inflated with the devil's own arrogance, cannot bear to hear Christ speaking to them from his own height. And yet, as we are taught by the example of Paul whose fierce zeal was overcome by Christ, it is not always the case that God reprobates those who have too high an opinion of themselves. And when we go down and look at the uncultivated crowd, we find that the majority of them are poisonously mean, and left for destruction together with those who are great men and noble. . . . Christ is the master of the humble, and the first principle of faith is, "Let none be wise in his own eyes." But what matters is not the willingness of men to become like children. Rather, Christ's discourse enlarges upon the grace of the Father, who does not disdain to go down to the weak, and to pull the paupers out of their filth. . . .

Even so, Father. These words remove every excuse for the

kind of unlawful nosiness which always pleases us. Nothing is
more difficult for God than to draw out of us an unquestioning
acceptance of his will as rational and just. He teaches us often
that his judgments are a deep abyss; and still we are impetuous
enough to plunge headlong into its depths. And when anything
does not suit us, we growl and murmur against him; and many
break out in open blasphemy. Against all this, God has laid
down the rule that we accept whatever pleases him as right.
Sober wisdom is precisely this, that one good pleasure of God
is more than a thousand reasons. Christ certainly could have
brought out many reasons for the distinctions God makes
among the people. But, satisfied with God's good pleasure, he
did not search further into God's calling children rather than
others to salvation; nor did he ask why God wills to fill his
Kingdom with these sheep and nobodies. It is evident from this
that people rage against Christ himself when they raise a hue
and cry upon hearing that by the will of God some are freely
chosen and others are rejected; they do it because they cannot
bear to let God have his way.

*Then shall the King say unto them on his right hand, Come, ye
blessed of my Father, inherit the kingdom prepared for you from the
foundation of the world.* Matt. 25:34.

. . . Christ does not invite the believers to possess the Kingdom as though they were fit for it by their own merits. He says
explicitly that it shall be given to the heirs (of God's promise).
He has also another purpose in saying these words. Since the
life of the godly is nothing but an exile full of sorrow and misery,
so that the earth itself can hardly bear them; since they are
hard pressed by want, and are covered with shame and other
afflictions—the Lord testifies to them of a Kingdom all ready
for them, so that with fortified and buoyant spirit, they may be
able to overcome these odds against them. For it is no common
inducement to patience that men be persuaded with certainty
that they are not walking in vain. Therefore, if our souls are not
to be cast down by the pride of the godless in which they now
exult before our face; if our hope is not to be turned into despair
by the troubles we undergo—we must always keep in mind our
inheritance in heaven, which depends not upon doubtful con-
tingencies, but was prepared for us by God before we were born.
This I say to each one of the elect, for it is he whom Christ calls
the blessed of the Father. It is no contradiction that here we
read *from the foundation of the world,* and elsewhere, *before the*

creation of heaven and earth. Here Christ is not fixing the exact time when the eternal inheritance was destined for the sons of God. He rather calls us back to the Fatherly care and protection of God which embraced us before we were even born; he confirms the certainty of our hope by reminding us that all the turbulent agitations of this world shall not have the force to make our lives sway and come down in ruins.

What then? Israel hath not obtained that which he seeketh for; but the election hath obtained it; and the rest are blinded. Rom. 11:7.

Since the elect alone by God's grace are drawn away from destruction, it follows that those who are not elected, in the nature of the case, remain in their blindness. With regard to the rejected, Paul means that those who are left aside by God have the principle of their ruin and damnation from themselves. The Scriptural proofs which he puts together, from not one but several places, when examined in their proper context, do not seem to serve his purpose; for in all these passages, the scourges of God, such as blindness and hardening, are visited upon those who are already wicked. Paul, on the other hand, is trying in this place to prove that the blinded are not those who deserve it through their wickedness, but those who have been rejected of God before the creation of the world.

Let us untie this knot briefly as follows: the source of wickedness which in itself provokes the wrath of God is in the perversity of natures which God has left alone. Therefore, it is not without reason that, according to Paul, such natures proceed from the eternal rejection of God as fruit from the tree or a river from its source. It is true that the godless are punished by God justly with blindness because they are wicked. But if we look for the source of their ruin, we must ultimately come to this, that being cursed by God, all that they do, say, or intend, only furthers and increases their curse. Yet, the cause of eternal rejection is so hidden that there is nothing left for us to do but to be amazed at the incomprehensible mind of God, as will appear finally from the conclusion of this passage. It is stupid, as soon as an immediate cause is mentioned, to make this an excuse for trying to deny the ultimate cause which is hidden from our view; as though, because God condemns the corrupt and depraved seed of Adam, and then repays individuals with the reward of their crimes, according to their deserts, God had not freely ordained, before the Fall of Adam, what seemed good to him for the whole human race.

What shall we say then? That the Gentiles, which followed not after righteousness, have attained righteousness, even the righteousness which is of faith. Rom. 9:30.

Nothing seemed more absurd and less congruous [with justice] than that the Gentiles, who cared nothing for righteousness and wallowed in the debauchery of the flesh, should have been called to partake in salvation and obtain righteousness, and that the Jews, on the contrary, who gave themselves wholeheartedly to doing the works prescribed by the law, should have been deprived of every reward due to the righteous. Paul states this amazing paradox boldly so that he may temper its bitterness with the reason he gives for it: namely, that the righteousness which the Gentiles acquired was by faith, which depends not upon human worth but upon the mercy of God. The zeal with which the Jews plied the law was preposterous, because they sought to be justified by their works; they strove after what no man can attain. What is more, they stumbled at Christ, who alone opened the way by which we obtain righteousness.

In the first part of this verse, the apostle intended to exalt the marvelous grace of God; he looks for the reason behind the call of the Gentiles nowhere except in that God deigned to embrace those who were unworthy of his favor. He speaks particularly of that righteousness without which there is no salvation. But by saying that this righteousness consists in faith, he means that the righteousness of the Gentiles is effected by the free act of God which reconciles them to him. For, if anyone fancies that their own faith prepared the Gentiles for regeneration by the Spirit, he is far from what Paul is talking about. It could not have been true that they had attained what they did not even seek after, unless God had freely taken hold of them while they themselves were lost and wandering, unless God had offered them a righteousness which they could neither have pursued nor practiced, because they were ignorant of it. Whence it must be noticed that the Gentiles were made fit for righteousness by faith, because God had anticipated their faith with his grace. And if it is by faith that they first aspired after righteousness, it was by faith also that they followed it. Thus faith itself was an element in grace.

Woe unto thee, Chorazin! woe unto thee, Bethsaida! for if thy mighty works, which have been done in you, had been done in Tyre and Sidon, they would have repented long ago in sackcloth and ashes. Matt. 11:21.

Since Tyre and Sidon, being nearby, were infamous for their godlessness, their pride, debauchery, and other vices, Christ draws this comparison between their works and those of the Jews, so as to pierce more deeply into the hearts of his countrymen. There was not one among the latter who did not blame the people of Tyre and Sidon for their wicked contempt of God. Therefore, Christ intensified his curse greatly when he said that there was more hope for repentance in those godless places than in Judea itself.

However, to avoid thorny questions about the secret judgments of God, let us hold that this discourse of our Lord is intended to apply to the common mentality of men. By comparing the people of Bethsaida and their neighbors with those of Tyre and Sidon, he is not arguing that God foresaw what these or those would do; he is simply stating what the latter would have done, so far as one can see from the facts of the case. The corrupt ways of their cities and their unbridled profligacies could be explained as due to ignorance, because they had not heard the voice of God, and no miracles had been performed to bring them to their senses. On the other hand, the cities of Galilee which Christ upbraids had shown a more than iron obstinacy, which had led the people to witness a multitude of miracles without learning anything from them. In short, the words of Christ mean nothing except that, in malice and incurable contempt of God, Tyre and Sidon were surpassed by Bethsaida and Chorazin.

And yet, we are in no position to bring a case against God, because, neglecting some from whom more might have been hoped for, he revealed his power among those who were worse and altogether hopeless. God is just when he destines for perdition those who are not worthy of his mercy. Who is to blame God with injustice, because he withholds his Word from some and allows them to perish, whereas he seeks others out in various ways and calls them to repentance to make the latter all the more inexcusable? Therefore, knowing our weakness, let us learn to contemplate this high matter with reverence. We must not tolerate in the least the pride and ill-humor of those who cannot bring themselves to pay the tribute of praise to God's righteousness, except in so far as their mind can grasp it, who spurn with disdain those mysteries which they should in justice adore, because the reason for them is not obvious.

For the Scripture saith unto Pharaoh, Even for this same purpose have

I raised thee up, that I might show my power in thee, and that my name might be declared throughout the earth. Rom. 9:17.

Now he comes to the second part, which is the rejection of the ungodly. Since this seems to be quite absurd, the apostle not only tries to make it plainer than ever that God is without blame in his willing to reject (*reprobando*), but also shows the excellence of his wisdom and justice. Therefore, he makes use of the witness of Ex. 9:16, where the Lord asserts that it was he who had stirred up Pharaoh and that his purpose in so doing was to give evidence of his invincible arm, which he did when he overcame and overthrew Pharaoh, who was obstinate enough to make a great show of resisting the power of God. There is no power of man which can stand up under the power of God, much less break it down. God used Pharaoh as an example.

Wherefore, there are two things to be considered: first, the predestination of Pharaoh to destruction, which must be referred to the just but hidden counsel of God; and secondly, its purpose, which was to declare the name of God. It is the latter that Paul wants primarily to bring out. If God's purpose in hardening Pharaoh's heart was to declare his name, it is wicked to construe this work of God as unjust. Considering its purpose, it was quite the contrary.

Since many interpreters pervert this passage by trying to soften it, let us notice in the first place that the Hebrew word for *stir up* means *appoint*. God wanted to show that in spite of Pharaoh's obstinate resistance, He would make his people free: not only that He had foreseen the Pharaoh's obduracy and was ready with the means of restraining it, but that He himself had ordained it, with the purpose of establishing a shining evidence of his own power. . . .

But let no one imagine that the Pharaoh acted by an ordinary and indefinite prodding from God. We must keep in mind the particular reason and purpose in this matter. This verse means that God not only knew what Pharaoh would do, but also destined his deed for the special use of declaring God's glory. It follows that it is futile to quarrel with him, as though he were bound to give a reason for his ways. In fact, he presents himself to us and, anticipating our objection, declares that the reprobate appear by his providence, so that by them he may glorify his name among the people.

For who hath known the mind of the Lord? or who hath been his counselor? Rom. 11:34.

Therefore, since we are utterly incapable of exploring the secrets of God with our own faculties, we are admitted to a certain and clear knowledge of them by the grace of the Holy Spirit. And if we are to follow his guidance, where he puts us, there we ought to stop and there as it were put down our foot. And if anyone sets out to know more than God has revealed, he shall be overwhelmed by the infinite brightness of his inaccessible light. We must be sure to bear in mind the distinction I made above, between God's secret counsel and the will of God revealed in Scripture. Although the doctrine of Scripture is too high for human ingenuity, still believers are not excluded from access to it when they follow the guidance of the Spirit with sobriety and reverence. But the secret counsel of God is something else. It is so deep and so high that no exploration can attain to it.

For there shall arise false Christs, and false prophets, and shall show great signs and wonders; in so much that, if it were possible, they shall deceive the very elect. Matt. 24:24.

This is added to fill the faithful with fear, and so to make them more watchful and on their guard. For, when false prophets are given unbridled freedom and allowed to flourish, and when they are even given power enough to deceive, the careless are readily caught in the net of their frauds. Christ therefore calls and arouses his disciples to stay at their posts. Besides, he admonishes them not to be troubled when they see the strange spectacle of many all around abducted into error. As he invites them to be watchful, so that Satan may not come upon them in their sleep, he adds ample ground for confidence and peace by promising them that by the help and protection of God they shall be safe against all the snares of Satan. Therefore, no matter how weak and slippery the condition of the godly, here they shall find a firm support upon which to stand, for it is not possible that those who have the Son of God as their faithful protector should fall away from salvation. It is not that they have at their disposal arms enough to resist the armaments of Satan, but rather that they are Christ's sheep, whom no one shall be able to snatch away from his hands (John 10:28). But we are not to forget that the stability of our salvation is not in us but in the secret election of God.

2. PREDESTINATION

And this is the will of him that sent me. . . . John 6:40.

Having said that he had a mandate from the Father to watch over our salvation, Jesus now sets down the way of salvation, which is obedience to the gospel of Christ. He had touched on this earlier; now he explains what he had left obscure. Since God wills that his elect should be saved by faith, and ratifies and executes his eternal decree in this manner, anyone who is not content with Christ, and pries into eternal predestination, takes it upon himself to be saved apart from God's counsel. Divine election is in itself hidden and secret. The Lord reveals it to us in the calling with which he honors us.

Those who seek their or others' salvation in the labyrinth of predestination, while they move out of the way of faith set before them, are insane, By such absurd speculation, they even try to do away with the power and effect of predestination. For, if God elected us for faith, take away faith, and election itself is mutilated. It is in fact wicked to break up the continuity and order of God's counsel, with its beginning and its end. Moreover, since election carries calling with itself and is inseparable from it, and since it is by calling us that God makes faith in Christ effective in us, our call should be to us sufficient evidence of our salvation as though it were his seal cut into us. For the witness of the Spirit is none other than the sealing of our adoption. Therefore faith is strong enough proof of God's eternal predestination. It is a sacrilege to inquire further, because he who refuses simply to accept the testimony of the Holy Spirit, offers him insult with injury.

According as he hath chosen us in him before the foundation of the world, that we should be holy and without blame before him in love, having predestinated us unto the adoption of children by Jesus Christ to himself, according to the good pleasure of his will, to the praise of the glory of his grace, wherein he hath made us accepted in the beloved. Eph. 1:4–6.

The ground and first cause of our calling, as well as of all the good things we receive from God, the apostle presents as the eternal election of God. Therefore, if anyone asks why God has called us to share in the gospel, why he honors us with so many blessings every day, why he opens heaven itself before us, we must always come back to this same principle: that clearly, before the foundation of the world, he has elected us. But, from the time of election itself, we gather that it is free. For, how could we have possessed worth, or how could there have been merit in us, before the world itself was created? It is a childish cavil devised by sophistry to say, "We were not chosen because we were worthy, but because God foresaw that we would be worthy!" For we are all lost in Adam. Unless God himself had by his election redeemed us from ruin, there would have been nothing but ruin to foresee. . . .

In the second place, he confirms that our election is free by adding *in Christ*. For if we are chosen in Christ, the reason for our election is outside of us; that is, our Heavenly Father has included us in the body of Christ, not because he saw that we are worthy of it, but by the favor of adoption. For, if as he says we are chosen in Christ, it follows that we in ourselves are unworthy of our election.

That we should be holy. Here he considers the proximate, not the ultimate, purpose of election. For it is not absurd that the same thing should have two objectives. For instance, the purpose of a building is that it be a house. But this is the proximate purpose: the ultimate purpose is that it be used as a home. We touch upon this in passing because Paul speaks constantly of another purpose, which is the glory of God. There is no contradiction here. Our sanctification is subordinate to the highest end of election, that is, the glory of God. Moreover, this leads us to conclude that sanctity, innocence, and every virtue among men, is the fruit of election. Therefore once again, with this phrase [as he has chosen us], Paul expressly sets aside every thought of merit. If God foresaw something in us worthy of election, Paul would have said the contrary of what we read in this place; which is, in effect, that a holy and innocent life comes from the election of God. For, how does it happen that some men live a godly life in the fear of the Lord, and others prostitute themselves to all manner of wickedness? Certainly, if we are to believe Paul, there is no other reason for this except that the latter follow their own disposition, whereas the others are elected for holiness. Surely, the cause does not come after the effect! Therefore, as Paul testifies, election, which is the cause of good works, does not depend upon men.

Besides, this verse means that election does not give men any occasion for license. Impious people blaspheme, saying; "Let us live as we please. We are safe. For, if we are elect, it is impossible that we should perish." But Paul protests that it is vicious to separate the holiness of life from the grace of election; because those whom God elects, he also calls and justifies. On the other hand, the long-standing inference made from this

verse, by Catharists, Celestines, and Donatists,[2] that we can be
perfect in this life, is without any weight whatever. Perfection
is the goal toward which we strive throughout the course of our
lives, and do not attain until the race is done. Where are the
men who abhor the doctrine of predestination and run away
from it as from a dreadful labyrinth, who consider it not only
useless but downright harmful? [Let them come forward!] On
the contrary, no other part of our doctrine is more useful, provided we treat it in a judicious and sober way, as does Paul,
whose use of it invites us to consider the infinite goodness of
God and moves us to gratitude. This, therefore, is the true fountain from which we are to draw the knowledge of the mercy of
God. Even if men should evade all other arguments, election
shuts their mouths, so that they neither dare nor can claim anything for themselves. But let us remember for what purpose
Paul here argues about predestination, so that we may not dispute from other points of view, and thus fall into dangerous
errors. . . .

Who has predestined us. What follows is a further and greater
commendation of the grace of God. We have already said why
it was that Paul impressed so zealously upon the Ephesians the
gratuity of their adoption, and the eternal election which pre-
ceded it. Since there is in truth no other place in which the
mercy of God is declared with such magnificence, we must
begin with a close look at this passage. Here the apostle presents us with three causes of our salvation, and he soon after
adds a fourth; the efficient cause is the good pleasure of the will
of God; the material cause[3] is Christ; the final cause is the

---

2 Catharists (Cathari) was a name given to members of various heretical
   sects of the Middle Ages, including the Albigenses and the Bogomils. They
   were dualistic and ascetic and in many ways resembled the earlier Manichaeans. Their leaders were known as the Perfect, who were supposedly
   free from all the sins of the flesh and had become the dwelling of the Holy
   Spirit.
   The Donatists were a schismatic church originating in North Africa at the
   time of the Diocletian persecution. They believed that the sacraments
   were valid only when administered by clergy who had remained wholly
   faithful to their trust.
   Celestines. Calvin probably meant not the Benedictine Order founded by
   Pope Celestine V in 1294, but an extreme group of the Spiritual Fran-
   ciscans, who took the name in gratitude for the permission to live as hermits
   given them by the same pope. They were persecuted after his abdication
   and continued under the ban of the Roman Church until 1466.
   All three groups assumed the possibility of perfection in this life.
3 Aristotle's classification of causes. See note 1, Chapter V.

praise of God's grace. Let us now see what he says of each of these.

To the first belongs the following complex of ideas: God in himself, by the good pleasure of his will, has predestined us for adoption, and has, by his grace, received us to his favor. In the word *predestine* we must again notice the sequence. We did not exist when we were predestined; hence, our merit also was non-existent! Therefore, the cause of our salvation could not have been from us, but was from God alone. Paul, still not satisfied, adds *in himself*, which in Greek is εἰς αὐτόν and means the same as ἐν αὐτῷ. By this he means that God did not look for a cause outside himself, but predestined us because it was his will to do it. But this is still clearer from what follows: *according to the good pleasure of his will.* The word *will* would have been enough for Paul's purpose; it is the word he used habitually to contrast the will of God with all other causes by which men commonly think they can induce God to act. But to avoid all ambiguity, he adds *good pleasure*, which expressly sets aside all notion of merit. Therefore, in choosing us, the Lord does not consider what kind of people we are, neither is he reconciled to us because of our worth. The only ground of our reconciliation is his eternal good pleasure by which he predestines us (for holiness). Why then are the sophists not ashamed of confusing matters with alien considerations, when Paul forbids with such zeal any concern except for God's good pleasure? . . .

Meanwhile, he presents Christ, whom he calls "the beloved," as the material cause of eternal election as well as of the love now revealed in him. Thus we are to know that the love of God is poured out upon us through Christ; for he is well beloved, so that he may reconcile us to God. And immediately Paul adds the highest and ultimate purpose of election, which is that we glorify God by praising his wonderful grace toward us. Anyone, therefore, who obscures the glory of God, puts himself in the position of striving to subvert the eternal purpose of God. . . .

We know that all things work together for good in them that love God, to them who are the called according to his purpose. For whom he did foreknow, he did also predestinate to be conformed to the image of his Son, that he might be the first-born among many brethren. Moreover, whom he did predestinate, them he also called; and whom he called, them he also justified; and whom he justified, he also glorified. Rom. 8: 28–30.

Now we know. From the preceding he now concludes that the bitter things of this life, far from hindering our salvation, rather help us on our way. It is no objection that Paul uses the illative particle (δέ, *autem*), because it is nothing new for him to use adverbs in a confusing way. In any case, with this conclusion, he anticipates an objection. The sensibility of the flesh cries out, saying that God does not hear our cry and troubles keep forever coming the same old way. This is what concerns the apostle. He says that, even though God does not do away with the troubles of his people as soon as they occur, he does not really forsake them. He has a wonderful way of turning the hardship they experience into a means of their salvation. If anyone prefers to read this sentence by itself, as a new argument, taking Paul to mean that we must not be troubled and bitter about hardships which in fact are helps toward our salvation, I do not object. However, there is nothing obscure about Paul's meaning. Even though the elect and the reprobate are liable without distinction to the same evils, there is a great difference between the sufferings of the two; for, by means of afflictions, God trains the faithful and oversees their salvation.

But we must recognize that here Paul is speaking only of adversities. What he is saying is that, whatever comes to believers, even if it be harm as the world sees it, God intervenes in their behalf; and the outcome shows that it was useful for them. Even though it is true, as Augustine says, that by the guiding providence of God even the sins of believers, instead of harming them, serve rather the purpose of their salvation—this has nothing to do with this passage, which concerns rather the cross. . . .

To them who according to his purpose. This phrase seems to be added as a correction, in order to keep one from thinking that the good fruit which the faithful gather from their adversities is due to any merit in their love for God. For we know that when it comes to salvation, men are all too inclined to begin with themselves, and to fancy that they have gone ahead of God's grace with preparations of their own. This is why Paul teaches that those whom he calls true worshipers of God have already been elected by him. Surely this is why the sequence in this passage is brought to our attention. We are to know that all things which issue in the salvation of the saints depend upon the free election of God as their first cause. Certainly, Paul intends to show that believers do not love God before they are called by him, as in another place he points out that the Galatians were known of God before they knew him (Gal. 4:9). Indeed, for Paul it is true that afflictions further the salvation of none except those who love God. But equally true is the statement of John that we begin to love God only when he precedes us with his own unmerited love. . . .

The word *purpose* clearly excludes everything that might be imagined as devised among men. Thus Paul denies that the causes of our election can be sought anywhere except in the hidden good pleasure of God. This is even clearer in the first chapter of Ephesians and the first of II Timothy, where the contrast between God's purpose and the righteousness of man is expressly and clearly stated. However, no doubt when Paul here says explicitly that our salvation is founded upon the election of God, he does so in order to go on to the next point, which he adds immediately: namely, that our sufferings which conform us to Christ have been obviously appointed for us by the same heavenly decree as our election, so that our salvation might be connected necessarily with carrying the cross.

For whom he had foreknown. He then shows, by the sequence in election, that all the sufferings of the faithful are nothing but the way in which they are led to conform to Christ; and he has already testified that such conformity is essential to the Christian life. Therefore, we are not to be sorrowful, or to suffer with heavy hearts or in bitterness, unless we would despise the election of the Lord by which we have been foreordained for life, or unless we cannot bear to have in us the image of the Son of God which prepares us for his heavenly glory. The foreknowledge of God, therefore, which Paul mentions here, is not a mere knowing beforehand, as some ignorant people imagine in their stupid way. It is rather the act of adoption, by which God has always distinguished his children from those who are reprobate. In this same sense, Peter says that believers have been elected for the sanctification of the Spirit according to the foreknowledge of God. Whence, those mentioned above reason foolishly when they infer that God has elected those whom he foresaw as worthy of his grace. Peter does not flatter the believers, as though each one of them owed his election to his own merit. On the contrary, by recalling them to the eternal counsel of God, he denies that they are worthy of God's grace. So, Paul here repeats with other words what he had said about God's purpose elsewhere. It follows that God's knowing the elect rests upon his own good pleasure, because he foreknew nothing outside of himself which led him to will the adoption of sons. He marked some for election according to his own good pleasure.

The verb προορίζειν, which some translate as *to predestinate*. must be understood in the context of this passage. Paul means no more and no less than that, by God's arrangement, those who are adopted must bear the image of Christ, that they must conform to *the image* of Christ, and not merely to Christ. In this way he teaches that in Christ God has put before us a living and visible example, who must be imitated by all God's children. In short then, free adoption in which our salvation consists is inseparable from that other decree which demands that we carry the cross [of Christ]; because no one who does not first conform to the only-begotten Son of God can inherit the heavenly life. . . .

And those whom he has predestined (praefinivit), them he has also called. He now proceeds step by step to establish with a clearer argument the truth that, if we are to be saved, we must conform to the humiliation of Christ. He teaches us that our call, and our justification, and finally our glory, are bound up with our association with the cross and cannot by any means be separated from it.

To make sure that the reader understands the mind of the apostle better, it is well to repeat and remind him of what I have stated before: that the word *predestinate* refers not to election but to that decree or purpose of God by which he has ordained that his own bear the cross. In teaching that they are now actually called, he brings out that God has not kept his purpose concerning them hidden in his own hands, but has rather laid it open that they may submit to the rule imposed upon them with a calm and good-tempered spirit. For, calling is here distinguished from hidden election as coming after it. Now, someone may object that a man cannot ascertain for himself what destiny God has appointed for him. The apostle answers that God himself has testified openly concerning his secret counsel through our call. This testimony of God is given truly not only through external preaching, but also through the accompanying power of the Spirit. Here we have to do with the elect, whom God does not so much compel with an outward voice as draw to himself from within.

Justification may rightly be extended to the uninterrupted continuance of God's grace, from our calling to our death. But since, throughout the epistle, Paul uses this word for the free imputation of righteousness, there is no necessity for turning aside from this meaning of it. The real purpose of Paul is to show that we stand to gain much more through suffering than by avoidance of it. For what is more to be desired than that by reconciliation with God our miseries should not any longer signify a curse, or lead us to destruction?

Therefore, he adds immediately that those who at the present time are weighed down by the cross shall be glorified, that they shall lose nothing by the bitter trials they now suffer. Although so far our Head alone is glorified, we already discern in him somewhat the inheritance of life eternal; his glory brings us such assurance of our own coming glory that it is right to regard our hope as the equivalent of a present possession.

We may add that Paul, following the Hebrew style, puts his verbs in the past tense instead of the present. But certainly there is no doubt that he is speaking of a continued action. What he means is: those whom God now exercises under the cross, according to his purpose, are at the same time called and justified, in the hope of salvation; even while they are humiliated, they suffer no loss of glory. Even though their present miseries disfigure their glory in the sight of the world, yet before God and the angels it shines without diminution.

Who hath saved us, and called us with a holy calling, not according to our works, but according to his own purpose and grace, which was given us in Christ Jesus before the world began, but is now made manifest by the appearing of our Savior Jesus Christ. . . . II Tim. 1:9–10.

This gift of grace, of which Paul reminds us, is nothing other than the predestination by which we are adopted to become sons of God. With regard to this matter, I have wanted to bring to the attention of my readers that often God is said to give his grace when we perceive its effect. But here Paul is speaking of it [grace] as God has had it from the beginning. . . .

But is now made manifest. Notice how properly he ties up the faith we have through the gospel with the secret election of God, and assigns to each its proper place. Now, God calls us through the gospel because he has set himself to the purpose of saving us, not suddenly and without forethought, but from the beginning in eternity. And now Christ has appeared for our salvation, not because he has just received the power to save us, but because before the foundation of the world this grace had been bestowed upon him for our sakes; but this we know by faith. The apostle is wise to connect the gospel with the most ancient promises of God; otherwise it would be treated with contempt as a novelty. But someone will say: "Was grace concealed from the fathers who lived under the law? For if it is revealed only with the coming of Christ, it follows that formerly it was hidden." I reply that Paul is speaking of the full revelation of the grace upon which depended also the faith of the fathers. Therefore, nothing is detracted from them. Hence Abel, Noah, Abraham, Moses, David, and all the godly, obtained the same salvation with us, because they put their trust in this manifestation [in Christ]. Therefore, when he says that grace appeared to us with the revelation of Christ, he does not exclude the fathers from communion with that grace, because their faith made them partakers with us of this same appearance. For Christ was yesterday as he is today (Heb. 13:8). But he did not manifest himself, by his death and resurrection, before the time appointed by the Father. The faith of the fathers was turned toward this manifestation, as is also ours, as to the one common pledge and fulfillment of salvation.

In the hope of eternal life (or, *according to the hope) which God, who cannot lie, promised before the times of the ages (ante tempora saecularia).* Titus 1:2. (Calvin's wording.)

Which God promised. Because Augustine understood eternity as prior to the temporal ages, he troubled himself a great deal about the eternity of times, and finally explained eternal times as preceding all antiquity.

Although I do not reject this exposition, when I weigh everything properly, I am forced to take a different view of the matter: that eternal life was promised to men many ages ago, not only for those who lived at that time, but for our generation as well. It was not only for Abraham that God said: "All the nations shall be blessed in thy seed" (Gen. 22:18); it was also for all those who came after. And this is not inconsistent with the first chapter of II Timothy where, in another sense, salvation is said to have been given "before the times of the ages" (*pro tempora saecularia*). Nonetheless the word means the same thing in both places. Now, since the Greek word αἰών means the series of times which follow one another from the beginning till the end of the world, we understand Paul to say in the letter to Timothy that salvation was given or ordained for the elect of God before the times began to flow. But in this place we have to do with God's promise. Here *all ages* is intended not to take us beyond the creation of the world, but to tell us that many ages have gone by since the promise of our salvation.

If anyone prefers, in short, *the times of the ages* may be taken to mean the ages themselves. Since salvation was given by the

eternal election of God before it was promised, in the passage
in Timothy it is said to have been given before *all* ages; there
the word "all" is implicit. But here, "the times of the ages"
means nothing but that the promise is older than the long
succession of the ages, because it began forthwith at the creation
of the world. In the same sense, Paul teaches in Rom. 1:2 that
the gospel which was to be published with the resurrection of
Christ from the dead, had been promised by the prophets in
the Scriptures. ...

VIII

Ethics and the Common Life

THE TEXT

1. WORSHIP AND ETHICS

I beseech you therefore, brethren, by the mercies of God, that ye present your bodies a living sacrifice, holy, acceptable unto God, which is your reasonable service. Rom. 12:1.

Paul has so far dealt with the things necessary for the building of the Kingdom of God: namely, for our righteousness to call upon God alone; to seek our salvation from his mercy alone; and to recognize that the sum of all good is found and is offered us daily in Christ alone. He now rightly proceeds with the formation of our conduct. If it be true that the soul is, as it were, regenerated for a heavenly life through a saving knowledge of God and Christ; and if our life itself is formed and shaped by the holy exhortations and precepts of God—it is futile to search zealously for the elements of a good life unless it is first established that the source of all righteousness among men is in God and Christ, that is, in the resurrection of the dead. Here is the difference between Christianity and philosophy. However splendidly and with whatever great and praiseworthy inventiveness the philosophers discourse on the subject of morals, yet their ornate and striking precepts are after all splendid superstructures without a foundation; for, having omitted the first principles, they present us with a mutilated teaching, not unlike a body without a head. And papal teaching is not very different; for although the papists say something in passing about faith in Christ and the grace of the Holy Spirit, it is clear that they are much nearer to the heathen philosophers than to Christ and his apostles. As the philosophers, before they set down the rules of morality, discuss the ultimate good, and inquire into the source of all the virtues, from which they draw and derive all the duties of men; so, also, Paul lays down the

313

first principle from which flow all the elements of a holy life, that the Lord has redeemed us for no other purpose than that we may consecrate ourselves and all our members to him. . . .

That you present your bodies. Therefore, the principal requirement for doing good works is for us to understand that we are consecrated to the Lord; and from this it follows that we must cease to live to ourselves, and devote all the actions of this life to obedience to him. Thus, there are two things to consider: first, that we are the Lord's; secondly, that we ought for this reason to be holy; for it is an indignity to the holiness of God that anything should be offered to him unless it first becomes holy. Granted this, it follows that our whole life should be an exercise in holiness and that we would not be free from sacrilege if we lapsed into uncleanness; for sacrilege is nothing else than to profane what is consecrated.

Throughout this passage, Paul uses his words with great propriety. To begin with, he says that we are to offer our bodies as a sacrifice to God; this implies that we are not a law to ourselves, but have come entirely under the power of God; which can mean nothing else than that we must renounce and thus deny ourselves. Then, adding two adjectives, he tells us what kind of sacrifice this ought to be. *Living* signifies the nature of our immolation before God; that is, the destruction of our former life, by which we shall be quickened to a new life. By *holy*, as we said before, he designates the quality of the sacrifice offered to God; for a sacrifice is valid only if it has already been sanctified. The third adjective (*acceptable*) reminds us that our life is shaped rightly when by our sacrifice we seek to please God. He offers us a rare consolation when he teaches us that, when we devote ourselves to innocence and holiness, our labor is pleasing and acceptable to God.

By *bodies* Paul means not only bone and skin, but our whole being; he uses the word *bodies*, which is a part of a man to signify the whole of him, for the members of the body are the means by which a man acts; but he demands of us integrity not only of the body, but also of the soul and spirit (I Thess. 5:23). In bidding us to present ourselves, he alludes to the Mosaic sacrifices which were presented at the altar, as it were in the sight of God. But still, he shows us beautifully that we should promptly lay hold of God's commandments and obey them without delay.

So we learn that mortal men err miserably and wander blindly, unless they set themselves to worship God. Thus we also know what kind of sacrifice Paul recommends to the Christian church. Since we have been reconciled to God by the sacrifice of Christ alone, by his grace we all have been made priests, that we may dedicate all we have to the glory of God. . . .

Wherewithal shall I come before the Lord? . . . He hath showed thee, O man, what is good; and what doth the Lord require of thee, but to do justly, and to love mercy, and to walk humbly with thy God? Micah 6:6–8.

Now the prophet assumes the people's role and asks what it is that he ought to do. But he answers the question by citing the law, and so deprives them of the excuse of ignorance. This he does in the hope that they may be induced to confess their guilt.

He hath shown thee what is good. He refutes the hypocrisy with which Jews deceived themselves. It is as if he had said: ". . . When you go to God with your prayers, you pretend a great zeal for piety. But your religion is nothing but an impudent lie. You do not sin out of ignorance or error, but out of sheer mockery of God. Why? For the law teaches you clearly enough what God demands of you. Does it not tell you well enough the nature of true communion with God? But you close your eyes to the teaching of the law, and pretend that you are ignorant of it. But all this is childish. For God has already told you what is good: *to do justly, to love mankind and to walk humbly with your God. . . .*"

Now let us consider the prophet's counsel. When he begins, *With what shall I come before God?* we are to understand that God has come down as if to meet men in a court of law. When men go to law with one another, there is no good cause which the other side cannot obscure with caviling and technicalities. But the prophet shows that when God himself brings them to trial, their evasions only make them ludicrous. This is one point. For another, the prophet shows how deeply hypocrisy is rooted in the hearts of all men, and how they always paint themselves with false colors, and want to do it even before God. Why is it that men are determined not to present themselves [honestly] to God or to walk uprightly? Why are they always looking for a deception? Why? Not because they doubt what is right and are deceived without knowing it, but because they connive and deliberately look for a subterfuge for their errors. Of course men readily fall into errors when they have no taste for what they are taught and refuse to bring God a true integrity of heart. Hence, it is clear that the whole world is without excuse in its superstition. . . . So it is that there is no pretext or escape for anyone who tries to please God with ceremonies and other impertinences. . . .

In our own day we know well enough, and if our eyes are open, common experience shows us clearly, that the wicked who have no real and sincere relation to God, exhibit great anxiety and pretend to be wholly intent upon worshiping God correctly. But they run off in all directions and seek innumerable bypaths, to avoid being forced to present themselves before God. Now we see how such pretense can be exposed; God has already shown in his law what he approves and what he demands of men.

The teaching of the law should be to men like a torch, directing their steps. . . . If anyone asks questions about the road when he already knows it, he really wants to stay where he is and be spared the trouble of moving his feet. God had shown the way by which the Jews were to come to repentance and faith. Their duty was to *walk*. And they irreverently mocked God when they assumed that his judgment was satisfied if they performed the external ceremonies.

Now when the prophet says *do justly*, *seek mercy* (or *kindness*) *and walk humbly before God*, it is clear enough that the first two points refer to the second table of the law. . . . Nor is it strange that he begins with the duties of love of neighbor. For although the worship of God has precedence and ought rightly to come first, yet justice which is practiced among men is the true evidence of devotion to God. The prophet therefore names here justice and compassion, not because God omits the first essential of religion, his worship, but because he is here defining true religion by its manifestations. Hypocrites connect all holiness with external ceremonies. God requires something very different; for his worship is spiritual. And because hypocrites can pretend great zeal and great concern in external prayer to God, the prophets examine the life of men in a different fashion. They ask whether men deal with others justly and kindly, whether they are innocent of all deceit and violence, whether they practice justice and compassion. Our prophet follows this rule when he says the law requires men to practice justice with one another, and then to busy themselves in acts of mercy. Afterwards he adds what is really the prior demand, *walk humbly with God.*

There is no doubt that the name of God is more precious than the whole world, and therefore the worship of him ought to be counted of more value than all the duties by which we exercise our love for our fellow men. But the prophet, as I said, was not scrupulous about keeping this order and preferred to show by what actions men can prove that they really fear God and keep his law.

Then he speaks of the worship of God; and it is worth noting that he says, to walk with God, men must be humble. Here he condemns all pride, all confidence in the flesh. For who everclaims anything at all for himself walks with God, turning his back to Him. The true way to walk with God is to surrender ourselves wholly, making ourselves as nothing. The beginning of worshiping God and glorifying him is to think humbly and modestly of ourselves.

For none of us liveth to himself, and no man dieth to himself. For whether we live, we live unto the Lord; and whether we die, we die unto the Lord: whether we live, therefore, or die, we are the Lord's. For to this end Christ both died, and rose, and revived, that he might be Lord both of the dead and living. Rom. 14:7–9.

He now confirms the previous verse by arguing from the whole to the parts; since our whole life must be devoted to the glory of God, it is no surprise that our particular acts throughout our life should be done before him. So then, a Christian's life is ordered rightly only when he keeps his eyes upon the will of God. Since you should relate everything you do to his will, it is wrong to undertake anything at all which you know will displease him, or anything which you are not convinced will please him.

To live to the Lord, here, does not mean, as it does in chapter 6, verse 8, to come to life by the working of the Spirit. It means rather to be ready for his will and the nod of his head, and to place all things at the disposal of his glory. We are not only to live but also to die in the Lord; that is, we are to die as well as live by his will; and for this he gives the best of reasons: whether we live or we die, we are his; from which it follows that in life and in death we are under his authority.

This teaching is open to a wide application; for in this way God asserts his power over life and death, so that everyone may accept his condition as under his yoke; for it is only just that God should assign to every man his own place, and how he is to spend his life. In this way, we are not only forbidden to undertake anything without God's authority, but we are also enjoined to endurance under all trouble and privation. When our flesh shrinks before adversity, let us keep in mind that if a man, who is neither free nor a law to himself, refuses to depend upon the good pleasure of his Lord, he subverts justice and right order alike. So then, this is the rule for living and dying which has been given us: when God prolongs for us a life which is continually full of bitterness and exhaustion, we must not yearn to get away from it before our time; on the other hand, if he calls us away suddenly in the flower of our youth, we should always be ready to go.

For to this end Christ died. This confirms the above argument. It proves that we ought to live and die to the Lord, by adding that whether we live or we die, we are in Christ's power. He now shows how rightly Christ asserts his power over us, since he acquired it at a great price; for, by his death for our salvation, he obtained a power which he exercises beyond our death; by his death and resurrection, he is worthy that we should, in our dying as well as in our living, serve the glory of his name. *Rose and lived again,* furthermore, means that by the resurrection he partakes of a new mode of life, and that since this life of his, which he now has, is unchangeable, his dominion over us is to be eternal.

He who loveth his life shall lose it; and he that hateth his life in this world shall keep it unto life eternal. John 12:25.

He that loveth his life. Christ adds exhortation to teaching. If it is by death that we bear fruit, when God mortifies us we should bear it with patience. Since he opposes the love of life to the hatred of it, we should understand what it is to love and hate life. Anyone who desires the present life so much that he will not let go of it except by force is said to love life. Anyone who despises life so much as to be willing with courage to go to his death is said to hate life. Life should not be hated as such, because it is regarded rightly as among God's chief blessings. Still, believers should be willing to lay it down when it keeps them from Christ, just as a man who is in a hurry to go somewhere will throw a troublesome and unwieldy burden off his shoulder. In short, it is not in itself wrong to love this life, provided we walk its course with our eyes upon our ultimate end. We love life rightly when we remain in it according to God's intention for us, and are ready to leave it according to his will: in a word, when as it were we carry it in our hands and offer it to God as a sacrifice. Anyone who is unduly attached to this world loses his life; that is, he hurls it to everlasting ruin. . . .

Whoever is attached to this world deprives himself of heavenly life, to which we cannot be heirs unless we live as strangers and sojourners in this world. Hence it is that anyone who is too anxious for his security in this world is an alien to the Kingdom of God, or the true life.

He that hateth his life. I have already pointed out that this is said relatively; we ought to spurn life, in so far as it keeps us from living to God. If meditation on the heavenly life came first in our hearts, the world would not be able to keep us back. . . . Anyone who does not turn his eyes to heaven has not learned how to take care of this life.

And be not conformed to this world; but be ye transformed by the renewing of your mind, that ye may prove what is that good, and acceptable, and perfect will of God. Rom. 12:2.

World has many meanings; here it refers to men's attitudes and moral behavior. Paul forbids us, with good reason, to conform to them. Since the whole world lies in wickedness, if we would put on Christ, we must put off everything that is of man [or the world]; and to remove all doubt, he asks us on the contrary to be transformed into a newness of mind. We find such contrasts often in Scripture; there is no room left for doubt on this point.

Now, consider seriously what kind of newness it is that is required of us. We are not to be renewed merely in our flesh, or, as the Doctors of the Sorbonne[1] interpret "flesh," in the lower part of the soul, but rather in our minds, which is the best part of us, and according to the philosophers, the ruling element in us; for they call reason ἡγεμονικόν, and fancy it as a queen of wisdom. But Paul shames it off its godly throne, and bidding us to put on a new mind, reduces it to nothing. However much we flatter ourselves, the word of Christ is still true, that every man who would enter the Kingdom of God must be born again; for, in mind and heart, we are altogether alienated from the righteousness of God.

That ye may prove what is the will. Here we have the purpose

---

[1] Sorbonne—the original name of the University of Paris, founded by Robert de Sorbon in 1256. The university, where Thomas Aquinas had taught, was in the sixteenth century a citadel of Catholic orthodoxy, and its theologians defended it zealously against the Lutheran heresy.

for which we are to put on a new mind; we are to say good-bye
to all our own counsels and considerations, and to those of all
men, so that we may attend only to the will of God, who alone
possesses true understanding and wisdom. But if we can prove
what is the will of God only by the renewing of our mind, we
can see how far gone we are in our enmity to God.

The additional adjectives in this verse are meant to commend the will of God to us, and to turn us to it with greater
eagerness. If our perversity is to be kept within bounds, it is
necessary to realize that righteousness and perfection which
truly deserve praise belong to the will of God alone. The
world invents its own good works and persuades itself that they
are good. But Paul declares that good and right according to
the world are to be judged by the commandments of God. The
world praises and finds pleasure in its own devices; Paul on the
other hand affirms that nothing is pleasing to God except what
he himself has commanded. In seeking perfection, the world
backslides from the Word of God and goes after new inventions;
Paul fixes perfection in the will of God, and shows that anyone
who goes beyond it imagines falsehood and falls into delusion.

But he that glorieth, let him glory in the Lord. II Cor. 10:17.
This statement is made to avoid the impression that Paul's
glorying was an empty boast. So, he brings himself and others
before the judgment of God, and says that only those of whom
God approves have the right to glory. Besides to glory in the
Lord does not mean the same thing as it does in the former
epistle (I Cor. 1:31) and in Jer. 9:24. In these latter passages,
it means to know God as the Author of all good, and to ascribe
every good to his grace, so that men will not exalt themselves,
but glorify God alone. Here, on the other hand, it means to let
God alone be the judge in our glorying, and to consider all
other judgment as worthless. Some people rely upon human
opinion and weigh themselves in the balance of popular judgment; others are deceived by their own arrogance. Paul commands us to seek only the glory which comes from pleasing the
Lord, by whose judgment we all stand or fall.

Even the pagans say that true glory consists in an upright
conscience. Now, this is true, but it is not the whole truth.
Since all men are blinded by too much self-love, we are not to
be satisfied with our own judgment of our deeds. We must keep
in mind what Paul says elsewhere: that even though he is not
aware of anything [wrong] in him, he is not therefore justified

(I Cor. 4:4). What then? Let us remember that judgment is reserved to God, who [alone] declares it concerning us; therefore, we are in no position to plead our own cause. This is confirmed by what follows. For, it is not the man who commends himself that is approved. It is easy for men to be deceived by a false conviction; and it happens every day. Therefore, putting all else aside, let us aspire to be approved by God: let us be satisfied by his approval alone, which should mean more to us than the plaudits of the whole world. Someone (Cicero[2]) has said that one good word from Plato was equal to a thousand. But we are not concerned with the judgment of men, as to who is worth more than another; we have to do with the judgment of God, whose it is to turn all human pronouncements upside down.

Now Peter sat without in the palace; and a damsel came unto him saying, Thou also wast with Jesus of Galilee. But he denied before them all. . . . And again he denied with an oath, I do not know the man. . . . Then he began to curse and to swear, saying, I know not the man. And immediately the cock crew. And Peter remembered the word of Jesus. . . . And he went out, and wept bitterly. Matt. 26:69–75.

This story of Peter's fall is a clear image of our own weakness, and his repentance is given us as an unforgettable example of the goodness and mercy of God. This one man's story contains a teaching which is extremely useful for the whole church. It instructs those who stand faithful to watch and fear that they may not fall; and it lifts up those who have fallen with the hope of forgiveness.

In the first place, let us notice that Peter showed poor judgment in entering the high priest's court. It was, of course, an act of devotion; it was his duty to follow the Master. But since he had already been warned of his coming defection, he should rather have hidden himself in a corner, so as to avoid an occasion for sin. So, it happens often to believers that, while seeming to do something virtuous, they throw themselves in the way of temptation. Therefore, we ought to pray to the Lord that he hold us back with the rein of his Spirit, so that we may

---

[2] 106–43 B.C. Roman statesman and philosopher who was regarded very highly during the Renaissance. He belonged to the New Academy and was deeply imbued with Stoic ethics. His more famous writings are "On the Supreme Good," the "Tusculan Disputations," "On the Nature of the Gods," "On Duties" (*de Officiis*). He was also a great stylist and was eagerly emulated during the Revival of Learning.

not charge ahead on our own, and be punished right off. Besides, we should pray that, when we propose to do something, we may not fail before we have started, or at a later time; that he may supply us from heaven with the fortitude to finish what we have begun. The knowledge of our own weakness ought not so to unnerve us that we will not go when God calls us. Still, it ought to restrain our rashness, and prevent us from attempting what is beyond our calling. Also, it ought to move us to pray that God, who has led us to begin well, may give us the grace to persevere.

A damsel came unto him. We see here that it takes less than a great struggle, or a big army and many guns, to overpower a man. Any man who is not upheld by the hand of God is soon knocked down by a slight wind or the uproar made by a falling leaf. Peter certainly had as much courage as the rest of us. He had already given evidence of an uncommonly high spirit, even though combined with a preposterous audacity. Still, he denied the Master; not because he was being dragged before the tribunal of the high priest, or because his enemies were upon him to kill him with violent hands, but because he was terrified by the voice of a woman. But he had a little while before fancied himself a soldier fighting to the death! Let us remember therefore that our strength, far from being equal to standing up under powerful attacks, fails in the mere shadow of a battle. But in this way, God works the just reward of our own unfaithfulness; he disarms us and strips us of all power. Thus it is that, when we set aside the fear of God, a mere nothing fills us with trepidation. If Peter had had a living and solid fear of God, he would have been an invincible fortress. As it was, being naked and unarmed, he was frightened while he was still a long way from peril.

He denied before them all. Peter's crime is all the greater because he did not shrink from denying his Master before a whole crowd of witnesses. The Spirit states this fact purposely, so that, when faced with a crowd of people, we may hold on to the confession of our faith. For, if we deny Christ in the presence of the weak, and they are struck by our example, and give way, we become destroyers of human souls, so far as it lies within our power. When we cheat Christ of the witness we owe him in the presence of the godless who have contempt for God, and are enemies of the gospel, we expose his sacred name to ridicule by everybody. Finally, as bold and free confession builds up all the believers, and puts the unbelievers to shame, so equally public defection in the church brings with it ruination of faith and disgrace upon sound doctrine.

It is worth noting that Peter, when he was unable to slip out with a simple denial, doubled his crime by adding an oath; and a little later, under harder pressure, he even stooped to cursing. From this we gather that once a sinner falls, he is immediately forced to go from bad to worse. Thus, those who begin with a mediocre offense thereafter hurl themselves headlong into the most frightful wickedness, which would at first have filled them with horror. And this is the just vindication of God that, after we deprive ourselves of the aid of the Spirit, he permits Satan to exercise his violent dominion over us; and Satan, having first subdued and held us in bondage, throws us around, now in one direction, now in another. But this happens chiefly when we deny our faith; because, when a man through the fear of the cross turns aside from confessing the gospel in its purity, and finds that he still cannot satisfy his enemies, he goes further and denies openly with an oath what he did not have the courage to confess.

Moreover, it is to be observed that in one moment Peter defaulted three times: which shows how unstable we are and how disposed to fall when pushed by Satan. Certainly, a mere nothing will make us fall unless God holds us up with his outstretched hand. When the energy of the Spirit of grace became dead in Peter, he was ready to deny Christ a hundred or a thousand times, no matter who came by and questioned him about his Lord. But, though he was vile enough to fall three times, the Lord spared him; He stopped the tongues of his enemies, so that they did not bury him under their attacks. Thus, it is necessary that Satan be bridled every day; otherwise, he would overwhelm us with endless temptations. For, he never stops attacking us with his numerous weapons. If God were not on our side, knowing our weakness, and breaking the force of his [Satan's] fury, we would have to battle with a whole array of overwhelming temptations. Hence, we ought to celebrate the mercy of God in this matter, because he allows our enemy only a hundredth of the force he would like to use in his assault upon us.

Then he began to curse. By this third denial, Peter's unfaithfulness towards the Master reached the limit. Not satisfied with an oath, he went on to curse, consigning his body and soul to destruction. He calls on God himself to curse him, if he knows Christ; which is as much as saying, "May I perish to hell if I have anything to do with the salvation of God." Therefore, we ought to admire the goodness of Christ all the more, because he raised his disciple up from such a deadly ruin and healed him. Besides, this passage shows us that when a man falls through the weakness of the flesh, and denies knowing the truth, he does not necessarily blaspheme against the Spirit. Of course, Peter had heard from the mouth of the Lord himself what a treachery it is to deny him before men, and what horrible judgment before God and the angels awaited those who in cowardly fear of the cross abandon the confession of faith. Moreover, it is not for nothing that a little while before Peter himself had preferred death as well as torment to denial of Christ. Now, knowing all this and in spite of previous warning, he rushes headlong to deny his Lord! And still, and after all this, he is forgiven. It follows that he sinned not by any incurable malice but through weakness. He would have been more than willing to pay Christ the debt of godly duty, had not fear put out even the sparks of right feeling.

And Peter remembered. Luke is our witness that when the voice [of the cock] had sounded, Christ looked at Peter. Mark says that before this Peter paid no attention to the crowing of the cock. Therefore, he needed the look of Christ to bring him to his senses. Every one of us has the same experience. Which one of us does not ignore calmly with heavy ears, not merely the many and different songs of the birds who call us to glorify God, but also God's own voice which sounds clearly and distinctly in the law and the gospel? And such beastly stupidity takes hold of our minds, not only for a day but at all times, unless Christ bless us with his look, which alone converts the heart of man. It is important to note, however, that it was no ordinary look that accomplished this; for Christ had before looked also at Judas, without making him any the better. When Christ looked at Peter, he added the secret power of the Spirit to his eyes, so that, by the rays of his grace, his look penetrated into Peter's very heart. From this let us know that when a man falls he will not even begin to repent, unless the Lord look at him.

2. FREEDOM, LOVE, EQUALITY

Stand fast, therefore, in the liberty wherewith Christ hath made us free, and be not entangled again with the yoke of bondage. Gal. 5: 1.

Here Paul is concerned with freedom from the ceremonies of

the law, which the false apostles prescribed as necessary. But let readers remember that such liberty is but a part of what Christ has acquired for us. How little it would have been had he freed us only from the ceremonies—but a trickle from the fountain! Christ was made a curse: to save us from the curse of the law (Gal. 3:13); to break the power of the law, in so far as under it we were subject to the judgment of God and to the penalty of eternal death; finally, to snatch us from the tyranny of sin, Satan, and death. Thus, when Paul speaks of the ceremonies, he includes under it the law as a whole. But we shall speak of this more fully under the epistle to the Colossians.

Furthermore, upon the cross, Christ obtained our liberty; and, through the gospel, he gives us its fruit for a possession. Paul therefore does well to warn the Galatians not to be entangled with the yoke of bondage: that is, not to let a trap be laid for their consciences. For, when men put an unjust burden on our shoulders, we might be able to bear it; but when they try to enslave our conscience, we ought to resist strongly and to the death. If we let men bind our consciences, we shall be deprived of a priceless good; what is more, we shall have insulted Christ who is the author of our liberty. But what does *again* mean, since the Galatians never did live under the law? It means simply that they are not to act as though they had not been redeemed by the grace of Christ. Even though the law was given to the Jews and not to the Gentiles, apart from Christ both alike were in bondage, and not free.

For, brethren, ye have been called unto liberty; only use not liberty for an occasion to the flesh, but by love serve one another. For the law is fulfilled in one word, even in this: Thou shalt love thy neighbor as thyself. Gal. 5:13–14.

Now Paul warns them against the wrong use of their liberty. In writing on the epistle to the Corinthians, we pointed out that having liberty is one thing, practicing it quite another; liberty belongs to the conscience, and has to do with God; the practice of liberty is an outward matter and concerns not only God but also our fellow men. After having exhorted the Galatians not to let anyone touch their liberty, he now asks them to exercise it properly. He prescribes a rule for its legitimate use, so that they may not turn it into a pretext of, or an occasion for, license. Liberty is not given to the flesh, which ought rather to be held captive under the yoke; it is a spiritual good which godly minds alone are able to exercise.

But by love. He now explains that the way to temper liberty, so that it will not be dissipated through erratic and licentious abuse, is to regulate it by love. But let us always keep in mind that the question is not how we have liberty before God, but how we are to use our liberty among men. A conscience which has integrity will not submit to any kind of servitude; but there is no danger in acting as servants outwardly, or in not exercising our liberty. In short, if by love we serve one another, we shall always be disposed to build up; so we shall not give ourselves up to loose living, but shall rather by God's grace use our liberty in his honor and for the good of our neighbors.

For all the law. There is here an implied contrast between the exhortation of Paul and the teaching of the false apostles. Since the latter insisted solely upon ceremonies, Paul drives home in passing the real duties and practices of Christians. The present commendation of love is intended to make the Galatians understand that it is the chief part of Christian perfection. But we must now ask why all the precepts of the law are included under love; for the law consists of two tables, the first of which enjoins the worship of God and the duties of piety, while only the second has to do with love. It would seem absurd to make a part of the law into the whole of it. Some try to escape this difficulty by saying that the first table also requires nothing but that we *love* God with all our hearts. But Paul is obviously speaking of love *for our neighbors.* We must therefore look for a better solution of our problem.

I recognize that piety toward God comes before love of our brothers; therefore to observe the first table is more precious before God than to observe the second. But since God is invisible our piety cannot be seen by our fellow men. It is true that religious ceremonials were established to give evidence of piety; but men's observance of them was no proof of their godliness; for it often happens that nobody is more diligent and zealous in going through the ceremonies than the hypocrites. God, therefore, wanted to test our love for him by enjoining us to love one another as brothers. For this reason love is called the perfection of the law (not only here, but also in Rom. 13:8): not because it is better than the worship of God, but because it is the convincing evidence of it. I have said that we cannot see God; he therefore presents himself to us in our brothers, and in their persons demands from us what we owe him. So then, the love of the brother grows from nothing but the fear and love of God; it is not therefore surprising that our love for our brother, being the sign of the love of God, even though it is a part of the law, stands for the whole of it, and includes the worship of God. It is certainly wrong to separate the love of God from the love of man.

Thou shalt love thy neighbor. Anyone who loves another will give him his due; he will not hurt or injure him; he will do what is beneficial to all so far as he can. What else does the second table mean? This is what Paul is talking about in Rom. 13:10. Besides, the word *neighbor* stands for all flesh and blood; for, as Isaiah says, we are bound together by a common nature: *Thou shalt not turn away from thine own flesh* (Isa. 58:7). Above all, the image of God ought to be the bond of a holy union among us. Therefore, here there can be no question of friend or enemy: for, no evil in man can destroy his nature.

The phrase *as thyself* means as we are moved by the feelings of the flesh to love ourselves: so it is that God enjoins us to love our neighbor. But the Word of God is perverted and not interpreted when men conclude (as do teachers at the Sorbonne) that the love of ourselves has priority over the love of the neighbor, because it is the norm for the latter. Such people are asses, and have not even a grain of love: for if our own love were the norm for the love of others, then it would be right and holy, and well approved by God. But the truth is that we never love our neighbor with sincerity and according to the will of our Lord, until we turn our own self-love into the right kind of love. Our love of ourselves and the love of our neighbor are contrary and conflicting dispositions; our self-love produces a neglect of and contempt for others; it produces cruelty, and is a fountain of avarice, robbery, fraud, and every other kind of pestilence; it drives us to impatience, and arms us with a passion for revenge. Therefore, our Lord demands that it be converted to [true] love.

Consider, O Lord, how I have loved thy precepts. Ps. 119:159.

. . . When the saints declare their devotion to God, they do not urge upon him their own shining merits; they act by the principle that God, who knows his true worshipers from the profane and wicked, will look with favor upon them because they seek after him with sincerity. To this it must be added that a sincere love of the law of God is a sure sign of our adoption because it is a work of the Spirit. . . .

Here we are also taught that true keeping of the law grows out of love which is offered freely. For God seeks willing sacrifices, and as Moses said, the first principle of right living is to love him. . . . Hence it must not be forgotten that nothing inclines our hearts to love God except his unmerited goodness and his Fatherly love toward us.

Great peace have they which love thy law; and nothing shall offend them. Ps. 119:165.

This peace is rightly judged to be the first foundation stone of a happy life. We have this peace when we act with a tranquil spirit, when we receive God's favor and our hearts are illumined by his Fatherly goodness. Rightly also does the prophet teach that we receive this peace from love of the law, for anyone who depends upon anything else will tremble every time he feels the least breath of air.

The *stumbling block* in the next clause means all the perturbations of the mind by which men labor in misery and are consumed, when they do not rest upon the Word of God but are carried along by their own lust or by the will of men. . . . But from the word *love* we gather that this peace is not acquired by slavish observance of the law, but is obtained by faith; for the law is neither sweet nor alluring to us unless it reveals God to us as Father and quiets our mind with the assurance of eternal well-being.

Thou shalt not steal. Ex. 20:15.

Thou shalt not steal. Deut. 5:19.[3]

Since the goal of the law is love, the meaning of love must be looked for in the law. This is the rule of love: every man must be secure in his own right, and no man must do to another what he does not wish done to himself.

Hence it follows that men steal not only when they secretly take the property of others, but also when they make money

---

[3] Put together by Calvin in his Harmony of the Pentateuch. Calvin's commentary on the last four books of Moses presents the material in the form of a harmony. The work as a whole (four volumes in the Edinburgh edition) is an astonishing achievement. The laws are arranged, with a combination of insight and ingenuity, under the ten laws of the "Two Tablets" of Sinai. Parallel laws are treated together. The fundamental purpose of each command, both for ancient Israel and for the church of Calvin's day, is briefly explained. Calvin's arrangement is primarily topical but the narrative sections are fitted together to present a reasonable sequence of events. The volumes cannot be fairly presented in excerpts, but Calvin's treatment of the law should "be commended" especially to the Biblical theologians of the present day.

by injuring others, accumulate wealth in objectionable ways, or are more concerned with their own advantage than with justice. Consequently all ways of wrongly appropriating the property of others are included under *theft*; for there is no difference between robbery by force and by fraud.

We know how men hide their evil deeds under all kinds of wrappings; and how by dressing them up in false colors they even win praise for them. Slyness and hateful cunning are called prudence. The man who cleverly tricks others, who entraps the simple-minded and in unseen ways oppresses the poor, is called farsighted and cautious. When the world sells vices for virtues and all men indulge in them openly, God wipes off all the cosmetics and declares every kind of unjust gain to be theft. We need not wonder that the judgment of heaven decrees this law, since almost the same teaching is given by the philosophers.

We must remember that a "positive" command, as it is called, is attached to the prohibition. If we merely refrain from all evil-doing, we are far from satisfying God, who has bound men mutually together so that they may strive to help one another to get ahead by counseling and assisting one another. There is not the slightest doubt that God commands generosity, and kindness, and the other duties which give warmth to human society. Therefore, if we are not to be condemned as thieves by God, we must seek our brothers' advantage no less than our own.

Thou shalt not muzzle the ox when it treadeth out the corn. Deut. 25:4.

This verse belongs properly in the supplement [of the law]; but because it adds force to the command, this place seems appropriate for it—especially since Paul, an apt interpreter, explains it as meaning that God requires laborers not to be defrauded of their just pay. In discussing provision for the ministers of the Word, he fits this commandment to their case (I Cor. 9:10). To prevent anyone from applying it to oxen, rather than to men, he adds that God gave it, not because he was concerned about the oxen, but for the sake of laborers.

But it must be remembered that men are required to practice justice even in dealing with animals. Solomon condemns injustice to our neighbors the more severely when he says, *a just man cares well for his beasts* (Prov. 12:10). In a word, we are to do what is right voluntarily and freely, and each of us is responsible for doing his duty. If animals are entitled to their food, much less should we wait for men to plague us before we give men their rights.

The foreign born you shall not oppress nor plunder; for you were foreigners in the land of Egypt. You shall not afflict widows and orphans. Ex. 22:21–22, Lev. 19:33–34. (Calvin's wording.)

Before passing on to other iniquities, I thought it best to insert here the commandment which requires the people to deal justly with all without exception. If no mention had been made of the foreign born, the Israelites would have thought that when they harmed no one of their own race they had discharged their duty. But when God includes guests and resident aliens as well as members of their own families, they know that justice must be practiced always toward all.

And there is need for God to set himself and his guardianship against injury to foreigners. For they have no one willing to incur hatred in their defense, and are the more subject to the violence and oppression of the wicked because they lack the protections possessed by the native born.

Widows and orphans are in the same situation. The woman on account of her sex is exposed to various injuries unless she is sheltered in the shade of her husband. And many people take advantage of orphans as if they were legitimate prey because they have no adviser. But God hastens to bring his help when they are without human aid, and he declares that he will be their vindicator if they are unjustly treated.

In the first passage (Ex. 22:21–23), the law joins orphans and widows with the foreign born; in the second (Lev. 19:33–34) only the foreign born are mentioned. But the principle is the same. All those who are orphaned or otherwise deprived of earthly resources are under the guidance and guardianship of God and are protected by his hand. This ought to restrain the boldness of those who think that their crimes will remain unpunished if no one on earth takes action against them.

Truly no iniquity will remain unpunished by God. But there is a special reason why God declares that he takes the foreign born, the widows, and the orphans as his wards. Where evil is more flagrant, there is more need of potent remedy. . . .

In the second passage, it is said further that they are ordered to love outsiders and the foreign born as themselves. Hence it is clear that the term *neighbor* is not restricted to those of the same blood or to those who are the same sort of people, among whom the need of love is more obvious. *Neighbor* includes the

whole of mankind, as Christ showed in the person of the
Samaritan who took pity on an unknown man and showed
him human kindness when he had been neglected by a Judean,
and even by a Levite.

*Ye have heard that it hath been said, Thou shalt love thy neighbor, and
thou shalt hate thine enemy. But I say unto you, Love your enemies. . . .
That you may be the children of your Father who is in heaven. . . . For
if ye love them which love you, what reward have ye? Do not even the
publicans the same?* Matt. 5:43–46.

It is astonishing that the scribes fell into the absurdity of
limiting the word "neighbor" to those who are friendly. There
is nothing clearer and more certain than that when God spoke
of our neighbor, he meant to include the whole of the human
species. Since everyone is devoted to himself, and people are
separated from others in the pursuit of their private interests,
mutual communication, required by nature itself, is broken.
Therefore, God testifies that any man whoever he may be is
our neighbor, in order to keep us in the bond of brotherly love
with which we are bound one to another by our common
nature; for it is necessary that whenever I see another man,
who is my own flesh and bone, I see my own self. Even though
most men, most often, break away from this holy society, their
depravity does not remove the order of nature; for we must
remember that God himself is the maker of this union. It follows
that the precept of the law which commands us to love our
neighbor applies to all men. On the contrary, the scribes, who
regarded a man as a neighbor on the ground of his attitude
toward them, denied that anyone was their neighbor unless he
showed himself worthy of their love by returning their friendship. This is the mentality common to the children of this
world, who are not ashamed to hurl their hatred at others for
any reason whatever. Love, on the other hand, which the law
demands, has no regard for anybody's merit, and pours itself
alike upon the unworthy, the wicked, and those without gratitude. Here Christ restores to love its true and authentic meaning, and defends it against misinterpretation and reproach.
Once again, what I said before becomes plain: Christ does not
make new laws; he rectifies the wrong interpretations of the
scribes which had vitiated the purity of the law of God.

Love your enemies. This one point contains the whole meaning
of the teaching of Christ about love as stated above; for, anyone who brings his spirit to loving those who hate him will

easily soften his heart against vengeance; he will be patient towards the wicked, and will be all the more ready to help those who are wretched. With this saying, Christ shows us the way and manner in which we are to fulfill the precept. *Thou shalt love thy neighbor as thyself.* For, no man will fulfill this precept, until he gives up the love of himself, or denies himself; until he sees others as bound by God with himself, and so goes ahead to love those who hate him. We learn from these words that the faithful should have nothing to do with revenge: they ought to wipe it out of their souls, so that they not only will be kept from praying to God for it, but will even pray him for the good of their enemies. Meanwhile, they do not fail to commit their cause to God, to let him punish the reprobate; but they still desire to do all they can to restore the wicked to a sound mind, so that they may not perish; and they consider how they may be saved. At the same time, they are comforted and their troubles become bearable when they do not doubt that God is the avenger of obstinate evil and declares himself the protector of the innocent. It is indeed hard, and contrary to the mind of the flesh, to repay evil with good; but we should not make our evil and weakness an excuse: we should rather inquire simply as to what the law of love demands, so that, relying upon the power of the heavenly Spirit, we may battle and overcome our feelings against it.

Monks and similar loud mouths imagined that these are counsels and not precepts, because they judged our duty before God and the law according to human ability. Moreover, having taken it upon themselves and bound themselves to follow these "counsels," the monks were not ashamed to claim perfection. How faithful they were to this title which they claimed, I will not say. But, it is evident that to interpret this saying as a counsel is insipid and preposterous: first, it is an insult to Christ to say that he did not command but only advised his disciples concerning the right; secondly, it is more than silly to make the duties of love, which are derived from the law, optional; in the third place, it is wrong to interpret the words *I say* as *I advise,* because in this place they mean "I warn" or "I command."

Finally, when Christ adds immediately, *that you may be the children of your Father,* he gives us proof beyond any doubt that these sayings are plain commandments and bind us to their obedience. When Jesus declares openly that no one can be a child of God unless he loves those who hate him, who dares to say that we are not under obligation to practice this teaching? It is as though he had said, "Let anyone who would consider himself a Christian love his enemies." It is truly dreadful and monstrous that for three or four centuries the world should have been covered with such thick darkness as not to see that this is an express command, and that anyone who neglects it, is struck out of the number of God's children.

Moreover, we must remember that we are not asked to imitate God in the sense of doing whatever he does. God chastises the ungrateful and often dispatches the wicked out of this world; it is not for us to imitate God in these respects, because the judgment of the world belongs to him and is beyond our competence. His will is that we imitate him as a Father who is good and does good. This has been known not only by pagan philosophers but also by the worst despisers of godliness, who have confessed openly that we are never so like God as when we do that which is good. In short, Christ himself is our witness that the best evidence of our adoption is to do good to the wicked and the unworthy. But this does not mean that our own goodness makes us children of God: the Spirit himself, who is the witness, earnest, and seal of our free adoption, purifies the depraved impulses of the flesh and does away with their aversion to love. From this effect of the work of the Spirit, Christ shows that the children of God are only those who, like him, are generous and kind.

Do not the publicans? Luke calls these people sinners, that is, vicious and wicked men. He does not condemn the work of the publican as such. The publicans were tax collectors. Princes have a right to impose taxes, therefore it is not wrong to collect them. Luke speaks of publicans as sinners because people in their position are usually greedy and grabbing, and even deceitful and cruel; and because the Jews regarded them as instruments of tyrannical injustice. Anyone who thinks from Christ's words that the publicans as such were the meanest people around is mistaken. Christ was speaking to a common prejudice. What he really meant is that there are people who are so bereft of humanity as to pursue their private interests even while they make a show of doing their duty.

But I say unto you, that ye resist not evil: but whosoever shall smite thee on thy right cheek, turn to him the other side. Matt. 5:39.

There are two ways of resisting: first, by warding off evil without violence; second, by retaliation. Even while Christ does not permit his own to meet force with force, he does not forbid them to avoid unjust violence from others. Paul interprets this verse best when he bids us to overcome evil with good, rather than fight with evildoers (Rom. 12:21). But notice that here we have to do with evil and contrasted ways of correcting it. Christ is talking about retaliation as a way of dealing with evil; when he forbids his disciples to repay evil with evil, his intention is to prevent their giving way to their feelings. He extends the rule of patience, so that we shall not only bear present injury with patience but shall also be ready to endure what is to come. The sum of this saying is that the faithful ought to learn to forget whatever evil they are made to suffer; that when hurt they are not to break out in hatred and ill will, or desire to hurt on their part; that the greater the injustice and passion of the wicked grows, and the more infuriating it becomes, the more Christians must be ready for patience and forbearance.

Whoever shall inflict a blow. Julian[4] and his like have raised a stupid cry against this teaching of Christ, saying that it would destroy the foundations of law and legal justice. But Augustine, in the fifth epistle, is both wise and intelligent when he shows that the intention of Christ was nothing else than to create a just and temperate spirit among the faithful, so that, when they are offended once or twice, they do not fail and grow weary. Rightly understood, Augustine is correct when he says that this statement does not lay down a law of external conduct. On the other hand, I think Christ restrains our hands no less than our hearts. Still, when a man is able to protect himself and his own from injury, and that without vindictiveness, these words of Christ do not prevent him from turning aside the force of an assault, provided he does it calmly and without harming the other man.

Of course, Christ did not intend to exhort his people to whet the malice of those who are already on fire with the desire to hurt others: what would offering the other cheek do except provoke them further? It is not up to a sane and honest interpreter to pounce on every syllable like a birdcatcher; he should pay attention to what is in the speaker's mind. Nothing is less becoming to the disciples of Christ than to amuse themselves

---

[4] Julian the Apostate—A.D. 361–363 Roman emperor, who tried to revive a syncretistic form of paganism, made up of mystery religion, polytheism, and Neoplatonic philosophy. He died fighting the Persians in Mesopotamia. Even though he incurred the hostility of the church, he was a great emperor.

caviling about words, when what the Master wants is clear. And in this place, there is nothing obscure about the intention of Christ: one conflict leads to another, and so, during the whole of their life, believers suffer continually many injuries; therefore, with this saying Christ wants to train them to endure every attack, that by being patient they may learn patience.

And he lifted up his eyes and looked, and, lo, three men stood by him: and when he saw them, he ran to meet them from the tent door, and bowed himself toward the ground. Gen. 18:2.

Before Moses comes to the main point, he describes to us the hospitality of the holy man. . . . His hospitality stands out conspicuously because it is no ordinary virtue to aid unknown men from whom no advantage is expected. For in general when men exert themselves for others, they get advantages in return. He who is kind to foreigners and strangers deserves no little praise, since he voluntarily invites as guests unknown men from whom he had received no favors and where there was no hope of mutual benefit.

What then was Abraham's motive? Truly, simply to satisfy the needs of his guests. He sees them weary from their journey; he is sure they are worn out with the heat; he thinks the time of day bad for traveling. And so he desires to comfort and refresh those who are weary. Certainly nature itself dictates that strangers are to be helped as much as possible—unless we are impelled by our self-love to act only for motives of gain. For none more deserve compassion and help than those whom we see bereft of friends and homeland. Among all peoples the law of hospitality was formerly held sacred. And no epithet was more detestable than ἄξενος, *inhospitable*. It is inhuman cruelty in our pride to despise those who flee to us and lack the ordinary means of self-protection.

But it is asked, Was it Abraham's habit to receive all comers equally? For the number would have been too great, and he would have had to feed mobs. I answer that he was a man of sense and exercised discrimination.

And he bowed. This sign of respect was in common use in the Orient. Certain ancient writers have tried to extract a mystery from this clause, and have said that Abraham worshiped the One in Three whom he had seen and that he saw here by faith the three Persons in one God. This interpretation is better ignored, for it is frivolous and open to mockery and insult. We said before that the angels were entertained by the holy man because he wished to do his duty toward men. But God rewarded his kindness, and he was worthy of the reward of having angels for guests. He did not know that they were angels until they revealed themselves at the end of the banquet. It is a humane and polite honor which he pays them.

But [finally] her merchandise and her reward shall be holy to the Lord. It shall not be deposited or laid away, but her merchandise shall be [set aside] for them who dwell before the Lord, that they may eat and be full, and for thick garments. Isa. 23:18. (Calvin's wording.)

This means that we ought to give to our brothers much more bountifully and generously than men are usually in the habit of doing. For men are somewhat grudging in what concerns their neighbors. Few do their duty eagerly and promptly, or give their labor and kindness without calculation. To correct this fault, God praises above all alacrity.

Paul's direction to the deacons to distribute cheerfully must bind us all, and his statement that God loves a cheerful giver (II Cor. 9:7) must be kept in mind. Also we must note the prophet's words that whatever is distributed to the poor is consecrated to God. And in other passages the Spirit teaches that God himself is served by such offerings. God never ordered sacrifices for his own benefit, and he certainly had no need of them. But he established such acts of piety under the law, and now he commands us to give generously and to spend our money for our neighbors. Whatever we spend in their service, he declares, is a fragrant sacrifice, pleasing and acceptable to him.

Hence when we hear our giving so highly praised, we should be kindled to generosity and kindness; and we should know that our hands are by their gifts, consecrated to God.

Blessed are the meek: for they shall inherit the earth. Matt. 5:5.

Christ means people who are kind and gentle: who are not easily provoked when they are hurt; who do not turn ugly when offended; who are ready to put up with anything rather than repay the wicked in kind. When Christ promises such people that they shall inherit the earth, it looks like sheer nonsense. The ones who usurp dominion over the world are those who fiercely repel all injuries; when attacked and wounded, such men have their hands quick for revenge. And experience shows that the milder one is with such people, the bolder and the more insolent they become. This is the reason for the devil's own proverb: "A man must howl with the wolves; for they will soon devour anyone who turns himself into a sheep." But Christ meets the fury and violence of the wicked with his own and the Father's protection; and so, it is not for nothing that he declares the meek lords and heirs of the earth. The children of this age never feel safe unless they are able to take bitter vengeance upon everyone who causes them evil, and thus to defend their lives with hand or arms. But since in truth Christ alone can protect our lives, there is nothing else to do but to hide ourselves under his wings. We have to be sheep, if we want to be counted among his flock. If anyone objects that what we say is against all experience, let him consider: Why is it that fierce people are so uneasy inside as to be their own disturbers? While they live so turbulent a life, even though they may be lords of the earth a hundred times over, having everything, they possess nothing. On the other hand, answering for the children of God, I say, even though they cannot put their feet down on anything they own, they enjoy the earth as a peaceful home. And this is no fictitious possession, because they live on an earth which they know to have been given them by God. Besides, they live under the cover of God's hand in the midst of all the violence and fury of wicked men; even while exposed to all the missiles of fortune, subject to the malice of evildoers, surrounded by all perils, they still live in safety under God's vigilance, and already and in a measure have a foretaste of the love of God for them: and this is enough, until, on the last day, they inherit the world.

And it came to pass, as Jesus sat at meat in the house, behold, many publicans and sinners came and sat down with him and his disciples. Matt. 9:10.

Matthew says that sinners, that is, men of scandalous lives and infamous reputation, came with the publicans. The reason for this is that the publicans, hated and abhorred by the people at large, did not shrink from such company. As a moderate punishment shames and humbles the sinners, harshness drives them to despair, so that putting aside all shame, they abandon themselves to a corrupt life. There was nothing wicked about collecting tribute or taxes; but when the publicans saw that they were rejected as godless and detestable men, they looked for comfort in the company of people who did not despise them; because, being disreputable, they shared their shame. Meanwhile they mixed with adulterers, drunkards, and their kind, even though they were not like them and detested their crimes, because they were driven to it by public hatred and rejection.

Let the brother of less degree rejoice in that he is exalted: but the rich in that he is made low; because as the flower of the grass he shall pass away. James 1:9–10.

Paul, in I Cor. 7:22, while exhorting slaves to bear their lot with a calm spirit, reminds them that they are God's free men, delivered by his grace from the misery of bondage to Satan; he also warns those who are born freemen to remember that they are God's slaves. In the same way, James here calls upon the lowly to glory in this, that they have been adopted by the Lord to be his children; and he has the same advice for the rich, who have been made to see the vanity of the world and have been brought to equality with the poor. He would have the former be content with their humble and mean position; he forbids the latter to be proud. Since it is the highest and incomparable dignity to be admitted to the society of angels, and even to be made companions to Christ himself, anyone who estimates this favor of God justly will look at everything else which comes his way with equal indifference. Therefore neither poverty nor contempt, nor nakedness, nor hunger, nor thirst, will make his spirit so anxious that he will not be able to comfort himself by saying, "Since the Lord has given me what really matters, I must bear the loss of all lesser things with a serene mind." This is how a lowly brother ought to glory in his high dignity: if he be acceptable to God, his adoption alone is enough reason for happiness; he ought not to be too much troubled because his state in this life is less than prosperous.

But the rich in that he is made low. The rich represents a whole class of people. This warning is directed to all those who excel in honor, or nobility, or anything else. To break down the lofty spirits of those who become inflated by prosperity, he bids them to glory in their lowliness or littleness.

As the flower of the grass. If anyone thinks that this is a reference to Isaiah, I do not object too strongly. But I cannot allow that James is quoting the prophet, who was not speaking figuratively of good fortune or of the vanity of the world, but rather of the whole man, no less of his soul than of his body. Here it is a question of the pomp of wealth or possessions. The point is that it is stupid and preposterous to boast in riches which can be lost in one moment. Of course, the philosophers say the same thing; but their song is wasted on the deaf, until men's ears are opened by the Lord himself, and they hear concerning the eternal Kingdom of Heaven. Therefore, when he says *brother*, he means that we have no place for this doctrine until we are admitted to the company of God's children.

. . . Behold, an Israelite indeed, in whom is no guile! John 1:47.

Since this verse gives us a characteristic trait of a Christian man, let us not pass it by too lightly. Truly, we can grasp Christ's thought without too many words if we notice that sincerity here is contrasted with deceit. He calls deceitful those whom Scripture elsewhere calls of a double mind. He attacks not only the crass hypocrisy of "good men" with a bad conscience, but that practiced by men who are so blinded by their wickedness as to lie not only to others but also to themselves. What makes a man a true Christian is integrity of heart before God and toward men.

3. Social Ethics: The Use of God's Gifts

Now is the judgment of this world: now shall the prince of this world be cast out. John 12:31.

Now, the Lord, as though he had already won the battle, exults as victor, not only over fear but also over death itself. He proclaims the issue of his death in magnificent terms, to avoid consternation among his disciples. *Judgment* is interpreted variously as *reformation* and *condemnation*. I agree rather with the former view, with those who say that the world shall be restored to right order. For the Hebrew, *Mishpat*, which is rendered *judgment*, means a state of good order. Now, we know that apart from Christ there is nothing but confusion in this world. Although Christ has already begun to set up the Kingdom of God, his death was the real beginning of a right order and the full restoration of the world!

Song of Ascents of Solomon. Except the Lord build the house, they labor in vain that build it. Except the Lord keep the city, the watchman watcheth but in vain.

It is vain for you to rise up early, to sit up late, to eat the bread of sorrow: for so he giveth his beloved sleep. Ps. 127:1–2.

There is no reason why the Jews should deny that this psalm was composed by Solomon. They assume that the *l* means *in honor of* Solomon, but ordinary usage is against this, since this kind of ascription everywhere denotes authorship.

Why should they insist on concocting a new interpretation when it [the psalm] seems especially appropriate for Solomon, who had much experience in political affairs, and could discourse in the wisdom of the Spirit on matters about which he had expert knowledge?

He emphasizes for a double reason that both the world and the lives of men are divinely governed. First, whenever men succeed in something, their ingratitude leads them to credit it solely to themselves, and God is not given his due honor. To correct this flagrant wrong, Solomon declares that nothing goes well for us except so far as God prospers our actions. Secondly, he intends to repulse the foolish self-confidence of men who, ignoring God and relying only on their own wisdom or strength, dare to start anything that comes to their heads. Therefore, he sweeps away everything which they rashly claim for their own and calls them to humility and prayer to God.

But he does not disparage man's labor or his effort and planning. For any virtue of ours is worthy of praise if we employ it in our zeal for the fulfillment of duty. The Lord does not want us to be like logs of wood, or to sit idle; he expects us to put to use whatever abilities we may have. It is of course true that the heaviest part of our labors comes from God's curse. But even if man's original state of integrity had remained, God would still have desired us to keep busy. Adam was put in a garden to cultivate it. Solomon does not condemn what God approves, and certainly not the labor men undertake gladly at God's command and offer to him as an acceptable sacrifice. But to keep men from being blinded by pride and from grasping at what belongs to God, he warns them that hard work wins success only so far as God blesses our labor.

By *house* he does not mean just the wooden or stone building. He includes in it the whole family economy, as a little farther on by the word *city* he does not mean merely the buildings and the surrounding walls but the common welfare of the whole state. He also is using the part for the whole (synecdoche) when he speaks of *building* and *guarding*. He is making the general statement that whatever effort, wisdom, or industry men expend in looking after a family or in protecting a city will be ineffectual unless God from heaven orders a prosperous outcome. We need to remember often what has just been said. For since blind pride almost fills the minds of men and leads them in contempt of God to an immoderate exercise of their own abilities, nothing is more salutary for them than to be called to order and reminded that whatever they attempt will quickly come to nothing, unless the grace of God alone sustains it and makes it to prosper.

When philosophers dispute about the political state, they cleverly put together everything which seems to apply to the subject. They show acutely the reasons for and the means of establishing a state; and again they describe the faults by which a good state is frequently corrupted. In fact they search out with the greatest skill all that is needed to understand the matter. But they leave out the main point: that however much men excel in wisdom and ability, they cannot accomplish what they undertake unless God takes it in his hand and uses it as his instrument. Who of the philosophers has ever recognized that human politics are only a tool directed by the hand of God? They have made human virtue the prime cause of good fortune.

When men in sacrilegious boldness rush off to found cities and to regulate the state of the whole world, the Holy Spirit rightly exposes such insanity. So let each one of us work as he can in the line of his duty, giving to God the praise for every success we have. For it is altogether wrong to divide the credit as many try to do, giving half to God and claiming the other half for themselves because they have worked so hard. We must prize the blessing of God alone and live under its reign.

But if even our earthly welfare depends wholly on God's good pleasure, with what wings shall we fly to heaven? A man may establish a decent household with a way of life that suits him; men may make good laws and practice justice—but all such achievements are but a crawling on the ground, and the Holy Spirit pronounces them all transitory. Still less to be tolerated is the madness of those who strive to penetrate heaven by their own strength.

From this doctrine we may gather that it is not strange if world affairs are turbulent and confused, if in cities the rule of law is overthrown; if husbands and wives bring bitter and groundless accusations against each other, parents complain of their children, and all men bewail their lot. How many today devote themselves to the service of God in the practice of their own proper calling? How many, puffed up with pride, are not trying constantly to exalt themselves? God justly pays today's sad wage to unthankful men who defraud him of his honor. But if all should humbly submit themselves to God's providence, the blessing which Solomon celebrates would certainly shine bright in every aspect of our life, both public and private.

The verb *'āmāl*, which we translate *labor*, means not just to be occupied in some work but to labor to the point of fatigue and pain. I said that by *watchmen* we must understand not only those stationed at lookouts but all magistrates and judges. Whatever watchfulness they have is a gift of heaven. But we need still another watchfulness—God's. For unless he watches over us from heaven, no human keen-sightedness will be enough to ward off danger.

In vain. Solomon now explains more fully that it is useless for men to wear themselves out with hard work and grow weak with fasting in order to acquire wealth, since wealth also is the gift of God alone. In order to impress them more effectively, he speaks to each man individually: *For you* [he says] *it is vain.* He mentions specifically the two means which are commonly reckoned to contribute most to amassing wealth. For when men do not spare their labor, but consume night and day in business and spend little of what they gain from their labor on their living, it is not surprising that they accumulate riches in a short space of time. But Solomon declares that there is nothing gained by poor living and perpetual labor.

Not that he forbids living economically or getting up early in the morning to work; but he does urge us to prayer, to the invocation of God. And in order to inspire us to gratitude, he says that anything which obscures God's goodness is vanity. For we prosper only when our hope rests wholly upon God; and moreover the outcome of our work will depend on how we pray. But if anyone pushes God into the background and hastens eagerly ahead, his hurried rush will surely end in a fall. The prophet is not advising men to succumb to indolence and to make no plans in all their lives, merely to doze and indulge their inertia; on the contrary, his point is that, when they pursue the tasks divinely imposed upon them, they ought always to begin with prayer and invocation to God, and offer their labors for his blessing.

Bread of sorrow can be explained in two ways: either "he eats by hard and anxious labor" or "he eats with pain," as it happens when miserly and greedy men scarcely taste their bread before they take their hand back from their lips. It makes no great difference which meaning you choose, for the point of the statement is that miserly men gain nothing when they grudgingly defraud their Provider [of invocation and prayer].

Surely he will give to his beloved sleep. This describes exactly the way in which God's blessing on his sons and servants is manifested. For acceptance of the futility of mere human striving would not be enough; the addition of a promise is needed if men are to perform their duties with a sure hope. This clause may be read, *He will give sleep to his beloved* or *He will give through sleep* what the unbelieving vainly seek to gain through their own struggles. The word *ken* is used to emphasize the certainty [of the promise] and to make more convincing what seems unbelievable and unrealistic; as though Solomon were pointing his finger toward God's feeding of the faithful without any anxiety on their part. Indeed, he speaks as if God in his indulgence, were encouraging his servants to be idle. But since we know from the law that men were created to work and since in the next psalm we shall see that farmers are regarded as blessed of God when they eat what their own hands have produced, it is certain that *sleep* does not mean doing nothing but rather the tranquil labor to which men of faith apply themselves in obedient trust.

For what causes the great excitement of unbelievers who never move a finger without making a commotion (that is, without tormenting themselves with useless anxieties), except that they refer nothing that happens to God's providence? But men of faith, even when they spend their whole lives in hard labor, obey God's call calmly and with tranquil minds. Their hands are not idle, but their minds rest quiet in silent faith as if they were asleep.

If anyone object that the faithful often stew in bitter cares and worry about the future when they are hard pressed by the want of everything they need and destitute of all means of support, I answer: If the faith and devotion of the servants of God were perfect, the blessing of God which the prophet here describes would be plainly visible. And as for those who worry too much —that is due to their own sin in not resting firmly upon God's providence. I even add that they are punished more severely than unbelievers, because it is good for them to suffer anxiety for a time, so that they may attain the quiet of this sleep. But meantime God's kindness [to his servants] persists, and shines always in the midst of the shadows [of this world]; for the Lord supports his sons as with sleep.

Now the Spirit speaketh expressly, that in the latter times some shall depart from the faith, giving heed to seducing spirits, and doctrines of devils; speaking lies in hypocrisy; having their conscience seared with a hot iron; forbidding to marry, and commanding to abstain from meats which God hath created to be received with thanksgiving of them which believe and know the truth. For every creature of God is good, and nothing to be refused, if it be received with thanksgiving: for it is sanctified by the word of God and prayer. I Tim. 4: 1–5.

Paul has been busy warning Timothy about many things. Now he brings out the necessity of being prepared to oppose the perils announced by the Holy Spirit as imminent: namely, that false teachers shall appear, who shall hold out mere trifles as doctrines of the faith; who, putting all holiness in outward observances, shall obscure the spiritual worship of God which alone is lawful. And, in truth, the servants of God always had to struggle against the kind of people Paul describes in this place. Since men's nature is prone to hypocrisy, it is easy for Satan to persuade them that the true worship of God consists in ceremonies and outward discipline; men believe this kind of thing and need no teacher to fix their souls on it; then comes the crafty devil and confirms them in their error. So it comes about that through the ages there have been false teachers who have championed a false worship, which has been the burial of true godliness. Next to this pestilence has appeared another, which has turned matters of freedom into things of necessity. So, the world allows itself readily to be forbidden what God himself allows, in order that it may allow itself to transgress the laws of God. . . .

Speaking lies in hypocrisy. This may refer to demons who deceive others at the instigation of the devil. On the other hand, the speakers may be taken to be simply men.

When Paul says that they lie as hypocrites and *their consciences are seared with a hot iron*, he is coming down to particulars. Let us observe also that these two evils go together and that the second grows out of the first. For, people with bad consciences, which are burned into by their wickedness, take refuge in hypocrisy: that is, they put on false colors so as to deceive the eyes of the Lord. What else can they do, when they are busy trying to win the favor of God with the counterfeit of external observances?

The word *hypocrisy* must be defined in the light of the present passage. First, it has to do with doctrine; and then, with the kind of doctrine which perverts the spiritual worship of God into a set of bodily practices, and so corrupts its real purity. Thus, it includes all artificial means of pleasing God and

claiming his favor. In short, all those who go around draped
with a false sanctimoniousness do it by the devil's prodding;
because no one can worship God rightly with outward ceremonies, for true worshipers adore him in spirit and in truth
(John 4:24). Secondly, such ceremony is a useless medicine
with which hypocrites mitigate their miseries, or rather a plaster
by which they hide their wounds without deriving any benefit
from it; but in fact it kills them.

Forbidding to marry. Having given us a characterization of diabolical doctrine, he now presents us with two particular elements
of it: namely, the prohibition of marriage, and of certain
foods. These arise out of hypocrisy which, having set aside
true holiness, seeks to hide itself under alien and false colors.
For people who do not refrain from ambition, hatred, avarice,
cruelty, and the like, try to acquire integrity by abstaining from
things about which God has left us free. Why are men's consciences burdened with laws about marriage and foods, unless
to permit them to seek perfection outside of God's law? This
kind of thing is not done except by hypocrites, who try to cover
over their wickedness with trifling observances as with a veil, so
that they may transgress the righteousness of the heart which is
what the law requires. . . .

Such is the mind of the world that it always dreams of worshiping God with carnal customs, as though God himself were
carnal. In the ancient church, little by little, things went from
bad to worse, until we arrive at the tyranny according to which
it is wicked for priests and monks to enter into marriage, and
under which no man dare eat meat on certain days. Therefore,
we are today far from wrong in applying this prophecy to the
papists, who urge celibacy and abstinence from foods more
forcefully than any precept of God. They think they can escape
by clever caviling, when they twist Paul's words to apply them
against the Tatianists,[5] or Manichaeans,[6] or others like them;

[5] *Tatianists.* Named after Tatian, an Assyrian Christian, these heretics were
infected with Gnosticism and Docetism, and are even better remembered
for their extreme asceticism. They condemned marriage, meat, and wine.

[6] The Manichaeans are especially important in the church because of the
controversy of Saint Augustine with them. These dualists, who derived
their heresy ultimately from Zoroastrianism, had many adherents because
of the neat way they explained the origin of evil in one god and the origin
of good in another. In its Christianized form, this heresy identified the
treason with Ahriman, the evil god, and Christ with Ormazd, the good
god. Flesh was evil, spirit was good. Hence they forbade eggs and milk as
well as meat; they also forbade marriage and bathing.

as though the Tatianists did not have the same means of escape, by throwing Paul's words at the Phrygians[7] and at Montanus[8] who was the founder of that sect; as though the Phrygians themselves could not come forth with the Encratites[9] as the guilty party. However, Paul is not talking about persons but about the principle of the thing. Thus, if a hundred sects were brought forward as having all labored with the same hypocrisy to forbid certain foods, none of them would be any less guilty. It follows that the old heretics are of no use to the papists, as though they alone were to be blamed; the question always is whether the papists are not guilty in the same way. The papists object on the ground that they are utterly unlike the Encratites, and the Manichaeans because they do not absolutely forbid marriage and meats. They say that they enjoin abstention from meats on certain days, and that they require celibacy only from priests, monks, and nuns. But this is a very poor excuse; for they nonetheless identify holiness with such matters: further, they establish a false and corrupt worship of God; finally, they bind consciences with a necessity from which men ought to be free.

In the Fifth Book of Eusebius,[10] there is a fragment from the writings of Apollonius,[11] in which, among other things, the latter reproaches Montanus for having been the first to dissolve marriage, and for having imposed the law of celibacy. He does not say that Montanus prohibited marriage or certain foods to everybody. It is enough that anyone should lay this kind of religion upon the consciences of men, or that he should require the observance of these things as the worship of God. To forbid

---

7–8 Montanus was a heretic of the early second century A.D., from Phrygia in Asia Minor, and his followers were called both Montanists and Phrygians. They received a new dispensation of the Spirit superior to that of Christ or of the apostles, and waited eagerly for the Parousia. They were visionaries and ascetics, forbidding marriage; and during prolonged fastings they forbade wine, meat, fruits, and bathing. This was a heresy which was espoused by Tertullian and left deep marks in the ancient church.

9 Encratites, second-century heretics, believed in the inherently evil character of matter and advocated abstinence from marriage, flesh, and wine. They believed like the Marcionites that the Creator was the inferior God.

10 Eusebius of Caesarea (A.D. 260–340) was a bishop and church historian who wrote the *Ecclesiastical History* which is an indispensable source book for the history of the ancient church (A.D. 325) inclusive of the reign of Constantine. This is a majestic account of the struggle and the triumph of the church of Jesus Christ.

11 Apollonius Claudius, bishop of Phrygia, c. 171, a learned man and opponent of Montanism.

anything that should be left to human decision, whether for everybody or for some, is diabolical tyranny. That this is true of foods will be clear from what follows.

Which God has created. Let us notice the reasoning in this matter: we ought to be content with the freedom which God has given us in the use of different foods, because it is for our use that he has created them. It is the joy of all godly people to know that every food which nourishes them is offered them by the hand of the Lord; that to eat it is pure and lawful. What arrogance it is to take away what the Lord himself bestows upon men! Did the papists create food? Can they void God's own creation? Let us always keep in mind that he who has created food also gave us free use of it, and that men's efforts to keep us from it are in vain. I say that God created food to be eaten, that is, for our enjoyment. There is no human authority which can change this.

But now he adds, *with the giving of thanks*; because we have nothing with which to repay God's generosity except the evidence of our gratitude. And thus he castigates the godless lawmakers with all the greater abhorrence in that they obstruct the sacrifice of praise, which God in the beginning established for our offering, with their own novel and useless enactments. On the other hand, we cannot act with gratitude unless we are sober and temperate; for no one knows the goodness of God if he makes a wicked use of it.

Of them which believe and know the truth. What then? Does not God make his sun to rise daily upon the good and the evil (Matt. 5:45)? Does not the earth, by his command, yield bread to the wicked? Are not even the worst men fed through his blessings? Therefore, his goodness is toward all men, as David sings in Ps. 104:14. But to all this I answer: Paul is here concerned with the right use of God's gifts, and has shown us the way we are to act before God. The ungodly do not share in such integrity before God, because their unclean consciences contaminate everything they touch, as we can see readily from Titus 1:15. Of course, in this sense, and strictly speaking, God has destined the world and all that is in it for his children alone; for this reason it is said that they shall inherit the earth. In the beginning, Adam himself was given dominion over all things on condition that he remained obedient to God. Therefore, when he rose in rebellion against God, he deprived himself and his posterity of this right which was conferred upon him. So, it follows that we are restored to our original dignity only by the benefit we receive from Christ to whom all things are under subjection: and this we receive by faith. Therefore, whatever men without faith get hold of, they rob or steal from others. . . .

For every creature. The use of food must be judged partly from its nature and partly by him who eats it. The apostle argues in both directions. He asserts that food in itself is clean, because it is God who gives it: and that we make a holy use of it by faith and prayer. When he says that the creatures are good, he is speaking of them in relation to man, not with regard to the body or one's health, but to one's conscience. I say this to avoid philosophical hairsplitting beyond the scope of this passage. Briefly, Paul means that whatever comes from God's hand is neither corrupt nor unclean before God, that it is simply for our nourishment; and as such, with regard to conscience, it is lawful. If anyone objects that of old under the law many animals were declared unclean, or that the fruit from the tree of the knowledge of good and evil was fatal to men, I answer: Creatures are called clean not merely because they are works of God, but because they are given to us by his goodness. We must always pay attention to what God himself commands and to what he forbids.

For it is sanctified. This confirms the previous clause which said, *if it is received with thanksgiving.* This is an argument from the contrast between holy and profane. Now we learn how we are to sanctify all the good things which sustain our present life, that is, according to Paul's witness, by the Word of God and by prayer. But we must realize that if the Word is to do us any good, it must be heard by faith. Even though God himself sanctifies all things by the Spirit of his Word (mouth) alone, we cannot know this blessing except by faith. And to this is added prayer, because Christ himself commands us to ask our daily bread from God (Matt. 6:11): and because we must respond to his goodness with thanksgiving.

Paul's doctrine is based upon the principle that there is no such thing as lawful possession, unless our conscience testifies that what is ours is ours by right. And in truth, which one of us would dare call even a grain of wheat his own, unless he learns from the Word of God that he shall inherit the earth? Common sense tells us that by nature the abundance of this world is destined for our use. But, since in Adam dominion over the world was taken away from us, every time we touch a gift of God, it is polluted by our own filth; it is unclean to us, unless God comes to our help, and uniting us with the body of his Son, once again makes us lords of the earth. It is in this way that we come to a lawful enjoyment of all the things God gives us in such abundance. Paul is right in tying up rightful enjoyment with the Word of God, since it alone enables us to regain what we lost in Adam, for, if we are to be heirs of God, we must know him as our Father; and we must know Christ as our Head, if we are to have what is his. From this we gather that all the gifts of God are usurped by us and are unclean to us, unless we know the true God and call upon his name. It is a beastly business when people start eating without prayer, and when they are full, they run out without as much as mentioning God's name.

And they drank and were drunk with him. Gen. 43:34. (Calvin's wording.)

From the end of the chapter we conclude that there was a sumptuous banquet at which they indulged themselves more freely and hilariously than was usual. The verb *shakar*, which is translated *be drunk*, indicates either that they were not accustomed to drinking wine, or that an unusual amount was drunk at this banquet given in their honor. But the word does not necessarily mean drinking to excess (as riotous men interpret it to excuse their own dissipation by the example of the patriarchs), but drinking with honest and free enjoyment. I admit that the word is ambiguous and is often used in a bad sense, as in Gen. 9:21, and similar passages, but in this place, Moses' meaning is clear.

If anyone raises the objection that a frugal use of food and drink is sufficient for the nourishment of the body, I answer: Although food is a proper provision for our bodily need, yet the legitimate use of it goes beyond mere sustenance. For good flavors were not added to food value without a purpose, but because our Heavenly Father wishes to give us pleasure with the delicacies he provides. It is not by accident that Ps. 104:15 praises his kindness in creating wine to cheer man's heart.

But the more kindly God treats us, the more it becomes our duty to be careful to control ourselves and to use his gifts temperately. For we know how unrestrained our appetite is; in abundance it always overindulges itself and it is always impatient of scarcity. In fact, we must keep Paul's rule (Phil. 4:12) and know both how to be in want and how to abound. This means to be on our guard when large quantities are at hand so that we are not tempted to extravagance; and again we must see to it that we endure privation calmly.

Someone will perhaps say that the flesh is much too clever at camouflaging extravagance, and therefore nothing beyond actual necessities should be allowed it. I certainly agree that Paul's requirement (Rom. 13:14) must be observed, and we must not serve our lusts. But what is most important for religious people is to receive their food from God's hand with a quiet conscience. And to do this, we must determine how far the enjoyment of food and wine is allowable.

For the day of the Lord of hosts shall be . . . upon all the ships of Tarshish. . . . Isa. 2:12, 16.
There is no doubt that Cilicia was called Tarshish in Hebrew. Since there was much trade between that nation and the Jews, we find in Scripture frequent references to ships of Tarshish, so named from the Cilician sea on which they sailed. Trading in ships cannot of course be condemned in itself, for the import and export of goods bring no small advantage to men. And especially since God desires the whole human race to be united in mutual service, it is impossible to disapprove of ships as a means of communication. But since abundance increases pride and cruelty, Isaiah here denounces commerce by which a land is especially enriched. Also trade carried on with far-off foreign nations is often replete with cheating and extortion, and no limit is set to the profits.

Isaiah recognizes in the first place that if Jews are to learn to submit themselves to God, they must be stripped of their wealth. He then uses a symbol for their greed and their unjust gains, as he might have held up a bloody sword to announce a murder. The latter part of the verse makes it clearer that the prophet is condemning commerce because it has infected the land with many corruptions. For it too often happens that riches bring self-indulgence, and superfluity of pleasures produces flabbiness, as we can see in wealthy districts and cities [where there are merchants]. Now those who sail to distant places are no longer content with home comforts but bring back with them unknown luxuries. Therefore, because wealth is generally the mother of extravagance, the prophet mentions here expensive household furnishings, by which he means that the Jews brought God's judgment upon themselves by the lavish way they decorated their houses. For with pictures he includes expensive tapestries like Phrygian embroidery and vases molded with exquisite art.
It is indeed certain that morals are corrupted when men are

greedy for such empty diversions. We know that such indul-
gences brought about the end of the Roman Empire. Before
the Romans entered Greece, they practiced a high degree of
self-control; but finally, after Asia was conquered, they began
to grow soft and effeminate. And when their eyes were trapped
with pictures, vases, jewels, and tapestries, their noses with
ointments and perfumes, all their senses at once were overwhelmed. And by copying the luxury of the East, as if it were a
higher culture, they came more and more to squander their
lives in every kind of pleasure.

And Lot, also which went with Abram, had flocks, and herds, and
tents. . . . And there was strife between the herdmen of Abram's cattle
and the herdmen of Lot's cattle. . . . Gen. 13:5, 7.

Now follows an account of the trouble Abram suffered because of his wealth. Certainly he did not want to part from his
nephew whom he loved especially as if he were his own son.
Surely, if he had had a choice, he would have prefered the loss
of his wealth to separation from one whom he regarded as an
only son. But he found no other remedy to stop the quarreling.
Shall we ascribe the difficulty to his own too stern temper or to
his nephew's insolence? I think we should do better to consider
the purpose of God.

There was danger that Abram might become too well
pleased with his own good fortune, just as many men are
blinded by lesser goods. Therefore God seasons the sweetness of
wealth with vinegar and does not allow the mind of his servant
to be too much entranced with it. When a false sense of value
leads us to seek riches more than is right, because we do not
realize how many troubles they bring with them, the remembrance of this story should serve to limit our inordinate love.
And whenever rich men fall into trouble because of their
wealth, they should learn to use the pain it gives them as a
medicine to purge their minds of too great a desire for the good
things of this present life. Unless God in his wisdom tightened
the curb rein wisely, men would leave the right road and would
stumble badly in their pursuit of prosperity.

Again, when we are hampered by poverty, we should understand that God uses this also as a remedy for the secret vices of
our flesh.

In conclusion, let those who have abundance remember
that they are surrounded with thorns, and let them take great
care not to be pricked by them; and let those who have little

and are very much hemmed in know that God planned [their poverty] to keep them from evil and hurtful snares.

Separation from Lot grieved Abram; but it could serve to correct much evil latent in him, and prevent wealth from stifling the ardor of his devotion. If Abram needed such an antidote, we should not wonder that God employs painful checks against our lust for pleasure. He does not always wait until the faithful have actually slipped, but he looks ahead for them. He did not punish Abram, his servant, for avarice or pride; he gave him a preventive medicine to keep Satan from infecting his mind with such sentiments.

And there was strife. What applies to wealth applies equally to large households. Yet we see how ambitiously many men seek to collect a great crowd of servants—as if they wanted to preside over a whole nation. But seeing that Abram's great establishment cost him so much, we should learn to be willingly satisfied with a small establishment, or with none at all if it so please God. It is almost impossible for a house to be filled with many people without its being in turmoil. Experience proves the truth of the proverb, "A crowd is the same as a tumult." If quiet tranquility is an inestimable good, then we should see that our wisest course is to have a small house and to live unpretentiously within our family.

In this example, note carefully what we are advised to avoid if we are to keep Satan from drawing us into conflicts by circuitous devices. For when he cannot inflame us directly with mutual hate, he implicates us in the disputes of others. Lot and Abram agreed well together, but the quarrel which arose among the shepherds involved them against their will so that they were compelled to separate.

There is no doubt that Abram had given strict orders to his servants to keep the peace; but his zeal and effort did not prevent his seeing the flame of discord, kept alight by small fans, blazing in his own home. So it is no wonder that disturbances arise in the church which contains a still larger number of people. Abram had about three hundred servants; Lot's household was certainly little smaller. What then will happen among five or six thousand, especially when the quarrelers are all free men?

We must not let ourselves be upset by these offenses, but equally we must be on guard in every way against the outbreak of fighting. For unless disagreements are stifled properly at the beginning, they will burst into harmful dissensions.

And the squares of the city will be full of boys and girls playing in the squares. Zech. 8:5.

With a different figure the prophet repeats and emphasizes the same point: that boys and girls will be playing on the public squares and in the streets, which they cannot do in the uproar of warfare. For when arms clash, when the sound of the trumpet is heard, when insults from the soldiers of the enemy threaten, everyone keeps his children in the house. Outside it is an ugly and sad business, and almost nobody will be caught on the street. When fear hangs over the whole [city] even the children lose their gaiety. The prophet, then, is promising that Jerusalem will once again enjoy peace, that God will chase the menace of the enemy to a far distance; not that Jerusalem would ever be free from all danger, but that God's defense would give her people security in the midst of many terrors.

This is not the place to argue subtly whether one may play games in peacetimes. The prophet draws his picture from ordinary human behavior; it is indeed an expression of human nature. For we know that when men are not afraid, they relax and enjoy fun. Besides games and silly amusements are proper for children. Therefore all the prophet intended here was to assure the Jews that even though they were struggling with various enemies, they could nonetheless enjoy security and quiet.

And they shall not wear a rough garment to deceive. Zech. 13:4.

This means that they will not be concerned to maintain their prestige and reputation, but will abandon willingly the esteem which they had dishonestly acquired.

This passage shows that prophets wore a coarse and hairy garment. But interpreters are wrong to cite as evidence passages in which a prophet is ordered to put on sackcloth and a garment of goat's hair. For Isaiah in many of his prophesyings wore neither; he did so only when he announced disaster. And Jeremiah was once ordered to go naked.[12] But ordinarily the prophets were content with hairy garments, that is, with ordinary, coarse clothes.

Now although we have liberty in external things, we must practice some moderation. If, for example, I were to teach in a

---

[12] Jeremiah appears to be a surprising slip of memory for Isaiah (ch. 20:2), or for Micah (ch. 1:8); but it is possible that Calvin had in mind Jeremiah's journey to the Euphrates; if the prophet wore only his girdle and buried it there, he certainly returned "naked."

military uniform, good sense would be quick to object. There is no need of a special doctrine to teach decency and ordinary good taste.

The true prophets wore rough garments to show that their lives were as simple and plain as their clothing. But they did not achieve a reputation for holiness by means of their clothes only, as do the monks today who are supposed to be holy because of their cowls and such trumpery. That was not the aim of the prophets; they meant to show by their dress that their only purpose was to serve God, and that they were separated from the world only in order to devote themselves wholly to their ministry.

It was because the false prophets imitated them that Zechariah says *they shall not wear a hairy mantle*—that is, they shall no longer wear prophetic garb. He was not merely condemning the garb worn by the false prophets. Therefore interpreters twist these words from their true meaning when they use them to condemn long gowns or whatever else of the kind displeases their sour minds. The prophet means simply that when pure doctrine shines bright and true religion has won its due honor, then there will no more be a place for false teachers. They will voluntarily leave their positions of honor and will no longer try to deceive uneducated folk. This is what the prophet really means, as he shows clearly when he adds *to deceive*.

So we see that hairy mantles are condemned, because rapacious wolves hide under sheepskins, and foxes infiltrate the fold in disguise. Zechariah is condemning the motive and not the garment.

Jabal was the father of such as dwell in tents. . . . Gen. 4:20.
Moses now reminds us that some good was combined with the evils which came from the family of Cain. For the discovery of the arts, and of whatever is useful and makes our common life more pleasant, is a gift of God which is not to be despised and an achievement worthy of praise. It is indeed surprising that the race which had departed furthest from the right way, surpassed the rest of Adam's descendants in serviceable endowments.

Indeed, I would suggest that Moses specifically enumerated the arts invented by the family of Cain to inform us that Cain was not so cursed by God that he had no gifts to distribute to his descendants. For it is probable that others also were not lacking in talent, and that there was among other sons of Adam no lack of industrious and clever men who busied themselves in inventing and developing the arts. Clearly, here Moses is celebrating what was left of God's blessing, in a people whom we should otherwise regard as sterile and devoid of every other good.

We must therefore recognize that, although the sons of Cain were deprived of the Spirit of regeneration, they were blessed with endowments far from negligible. In fact, the experience of all ages shows us how many rays of divine light have always gleamed among unbelieving nations, and have contributed to the improvement of our present life. And today we see glorious gifts of the Spirit spread throughout the whole human race. For the liberal and industrial arts and the sciences have come to us from profane men. Astronomy and the other branches of philosophy, medicine, political science—we must admit that we have learned all these from them.

No doubt God endowed them so liberally with his excellent favors to give them no excuse for their impiety. But while we are amazed at the riches of his grace which God pours out on them, we marvel much more at the grace of regeneration given us, by which God sanctifies his elect to be his own.

Although the invention of the lyre and of other musical instruments serves our enjoyment and our pleasures rather than our needs, it ought not on that account to be judged of no value; still less should it be condemned. Pleasure is to be condemned only when it is not combined with reverence for God and not related to the common welfare of society. But music by its nature is adapted to rouse our devotion to God and to aid the well-being of man; we need only avoid enticements to shame, and empty entertainments which keep men from better employments and are simply a waste of time.

However, even if you think the invention of the lyre does not in itself deserve much praise, everyone knows how long and how widely people have valued the carpenter's skill.

To conclude—in my opinion, Moses here wished to show that the race of Cain excelled in many important endowments which at once made their impiety inexcusable and were shining witnesses to God's goodness.

Jabal is said to be the father of the people who live in tents because he invented that convenient shelter, and others afterwards imitated him.

And God made two great lights, the greater light to rule the day, and the lesser light to rule the night; he made the stars also. Gen. 1:16.

The greater light. I have already said that Moses is not analyzing acutely, like the philosophers, the secrets of nature; and these words show it. First he sets the planets and stars in the expanse of the heaven. Astronomers distinguish a number of spheres in the firmament and teach that the fixed stars have their own place in it. Moses mentions *two great luminaries.* The astronomers prove with strong arguments that the star Saturn, which seems small because of its distance, is larger than the moon.

All this shows that Moses described in popular style what all ordinary men without training and education perceive with their ordinary senses. Astronomers, on the other hand, investigate with great labor whatever the keenness of man's intellect is able to discover. Such study is certainly not to be disapproved, nor science condemned with the insolence of some fanatics who habitually reject whatever is unknown to them.

The study of astronomy not only gives pleasure but is also extremely useful. And no one can deny that it admirably reveals the wisdom of God. Therefore, clever men who expend their labor upon it are to be praised and those who have ability and leisure ought not to neglect work of that kind.

Moses did not wish to keep us from such study when he omitted the details belonging to the science. But, since he had been appointed guide of rude and unlearned men rather than of the learned, he could not fulfill his duty except by coming down to their level. If he had spoken of matters unknown to the crowd, the unlearned could say that his teaching was over their heads. In fact, when the Spirit of God opens a common school for all, it is not strange that he chooses to teach especially what can be understood by all.

When the astronomer seeks the true size of stars and finds the moon smaller than Saturn, he gives us specialized knowledge. But the eye sees things differently; and Moses adapts himself to the ordinary view.

God has stretched out his hand to us to give us the splendor of the sun and moon to enjoy. Great would be our ingratitude if we shut our eyes to this experience of beauty! There is no reason why clever men should jeer at Moses' ignorance. He is not explaining the heavens to us but describing what is before our eyes. Let the astronomers possess their own deeper knowledge. Meanwhile, those who see the nightly splendor of the moon are possessed by perverse ingratitude if they do not recognize the goodness of God.

4. MARRIAGE

And the Lord God said, It is not good that the man should be alone; I will make a helpmeet for him. Gen. 2:18.

Here Moses explains God's purpose in creating woman. God wished the earth to be populated by men who would live together and create a society. Some may question whether God's purpose included offspring; for the words say only that since it is not well for a man to be alone, a woman had to be created to be his helpmate. But as I understand it, when God took the first steps towards a human society, he intended the others to follow each in turn. We have then a general principle: man was created to be a social animal. Now since the human race could not exist without woman, no bond whatever in human relations is more sacred than that by which husband and wife unite to become one body and one soul. On this point, nature itself taught Plato and others among the saner philosophers to speak with wisdom.

But although God made the statement that it is not good for man to be alone about Adam, I do not restrict it to his single person. I consider it rather a general rule for human living. Therefore everyone ought to take as a precept directed to himself that solitude is not good—except for a man whom God exempts as a matter of unusual privilege.

Many think celibacy furthers their plans and refrain from marriage to avoid trouble. But it is not only worldly people who say that, if a man wants to be happy, he should stay away from a wife. Jerome's book against Jovinian is crammed with petulant insults by which he tries to make sacred marriage hateful and to disgrace it. Let men of faith learn to fight the evil suggestions of Satan with this Word of God, by which he decrees married life for man, not for his ruin but for his well-being.

I will make a helpmeet for him. Why is the verb used here not plural, as it was in the account of the creation of man when it said, *Let us make?* (Gen. 1:26). Some think that the change indicates a difference between the sexes and shows how greatly superior man is to woman. But a different, although not altogether contradictory, interpretation pleases me better. When the human race was created in the person of a man, a dignity common to all humanity was universally conferred with the words *let us make man.* There was no need to repeat this at the creation of a woman, for she was really a supplement to the man. We certainly cannot deny that woman also, perhaps in a secondary way, was created in the image of God. Hence it follows that what was said of man applies equally to woman.

Now when God designates woman as man's helper, he is not giving women a rule to determine their vocation in life by assigning them a special task; he is rather declaring that marriage itself will be man's best help in life. Let us then accept it as a rule of nature that a woman is a man's helper. Of course we know the common proverb that she is a necessary evil, but we ought to listen to the voice of God which asserts that woman was given to man as a companion and partner to help him to live really well.

I confess indeed that in the present corrupt state of the human race, God's blessing as here described is not often seen and amounts to little. But we must keep in mind the reason for this evil. We have perverted the order of nature instituted by God. If man still had today the wholeness which he had in the beginning, God's ordinance would be fulfilled and the sweetest harmony would reign in marriage. For man would look to God; and woman, equally faithful, would be his helper. Being both of one mind, they would cherish an association no less holy than friendly and peaceful. Now because of our own wickedness and corrupt nature such married bliss is for the most part lost or at least is marred by many annoyances. Quarrels arise, and hurt feelings, bitterness, discords, and a great sea of trouble. So it happens that men are often seriously distressed by their wives and think of them as a hindrance.

Yet marriage cannot be so wholly spoiled by man's sin that the blessing with which God hallowed it by his word is entirely abolished and no longer exists. Therefore in spite of the many troubles of married life, which arise from our degenerate nature, there remains a residuum of divine good; in a fire which is almost smothered, some sparks still glow.

From this truth follows another: women should learn their duty, strive by helping their husbands to fulfill God's purpose. And men also ought to consider carefully what they owe in return to half of the human race. A mutual obligation binds both sexes. By God's law woman is given to man as helper, so that he may do his part as the head and leader.

We must observe one more thing. It is not only because of the necessity which we have suffered since Adam's fall that the woman is called man's helper. Even if man had remained obedient and whole, the woman would still have become his helpmate. But now when marriage is also a remedy for lust,

we have in it a double gift from God. But the second is
incidental.

*Because I have known him, therefore he shall teach his sons and his
household after him and they will do justice and right judgment.* Gen.
18: 19. (Calvin's wording.)

He shall teach his sons. This is the second reason why God
wished Abraham to share his counsel. He did not reveal it
without a purpose. The plain meaning of the verse is that
Abraham is told of God's plan because he is to perform the task
of a good father and teach his family. So we infer that Abraham
was told of Sodom's coming destruction not for his own sake
alone, but as a kindness to all his descendants.

Indeed, the scope of God's purpose must be carefully noted.
His will, as made known to Abraham, bound all Abraham's
descendants. Certainly God does not make his will known to us
with the intent that the knowledge of him should perish with us.
He requires us to be his witnesses to the next generation so that
they in turn may hand on what they have received from us to
our remoter descendants. Therefore it is a father's duty to teach
his sons what he himself has learned from God. In this way we
must propagate God's truth. It was not given us for our private
enjoyment; we must mutually strengthen one another according to our calling and our faith.

There is no doubt that the gross ignorance which prevails in
the world is the just punishment of men's indolence. For while
the greater part of the people shut their eyes to the light shed
by heavenly doctrine, many smother it by making no effort to
transmit it to their children. God rightly withholds the precious
treasures of his Word as punishment for the world's indolence.

We must consider particularly the phrase *after him,* which
teaches us that God's care is not limited to our own lives. He
takes measures to provide that his eternal truth live and
flourish after our death and that a holy manner of life continue
on earth when we are dead. Hence we also conclude that
histories which inspire terror in us are worth knowing, since our
carnal confidence needs a sharp stimulus so that we may be
stung to fear God.

Let no one imagine that this kind of teaching does not apply
to him; for when God mentions the sons of Abraham, he means
the whole household of the church. There are perverse and
deluded interpreters who insist that if they terrify consciences
they repel and discourage faith. However, nothing is more

alien to faith than disrespect and sloth; and on the other hand, the teaching which leads men to the fear of God fits most perfectly with the preaching of mercy, for it brings unhappy and hungry men running to Christ.

And they will keep the way of the Lord. With these words Moses shows that the judgment of God is announced not only in order that those who in their stupidity are well satisfied with themselves may be filled with dread, and so be driven to long for the grace of Christ, but also in order that the faithful who are already endowed with fear of God may become more and more practiced in the pursuit of religion. God desires to have Sodom's destruction recounted not only to draw wicked men toward himself by their fear of the same punishment, but also to give to those who have already begun to serve God a better understanding of true obedience. The law contributes not only to the beginning of repentance, but also to our continuing perseverance [in the Christian life].

When Moses adds *that they may do justice and right judgment* he is describing briefly the way of God which he has already mentioned. Although the definition is not complete, yet he briefly indicates by synecdoche the duties of the second table of the law, and shows us what God especially requires of us. The Scripture often draws a description of a good and godly life from the second table of the law; not that love of neighbor is more important than the service of God, but that men can prove their loyalty to God only by living honestly and doing no injury to their neighbors. By the words *justice* and *right judgment*, he includes the kind of equity which gives to each man his due. If one wants to differentiate between the two words, *justice* implies the honesty and kindness which we practice, when we strive to help our brothers in every way and avoid hurting them in any way by fraud and violence. *Right judgment* means that we stretch out our hands to the poor and oppressed, that we see and support good causes, that we work hard to keep the weak from being unjustly hurt. These are the lawful tasks with which the Lord orders his own to keep occupied.

IX

The Church

THE TEXT

1. THE CONDITION OF THE CHURCH

On the next day much people that were come to the feast, when they heard that Jesus was coming to Jerusalem, took branches of palm trees, and went forth to meet him, and cried, Hosanna! Blessed is the King of Israel that cometh in the name of the Lord. And Jesus, when he had found a young ass, sat thereon; as it is written, Fear not daughter of Zion; behold thy king cometh, sitting on an ass's colt. John 12:12–15.

Branches of palm trees. Among the ancients, the palm was a symbol of victory and peace. Moreover, they used palm branches when they invested someone with sovereignty, or when they came as suppliants before a victorious king or general. But these folk carried palm branches as a sign of festive joy at the coming of the new King.

They shouted, Hosanna! and so shouting, they voiced their conviction that Jesus Christ was the Messiah, promised by the fathers of old, their hope of deliverance and salvation. For Psalm 118, from which this exclamation is taken, was written about the Messiah, to the end that the saints might ardently hope for and continually desire his coming, and that they might receive him with reverence when he appeared. Therefore, it is a probable, if not a certain inference, that this prayer was common among the Jews, and was in everybody's mouth. Therefore, the Spirit of God moved these people to address their prayer to Christ; and they thus became his chosen heralds, to testify that the Messiah had come. *Hosanna* is made up of two Hebrew words, which mean, "save, I pray Thee." The Hebrews pronounce it *Hoshia-nna*. The sound of words is often corrupted when transliterated into another language. Yet the Evangelists, who wrote in Greek, purposely kept the Hebrew word, to express properly the fact that the crowd used a solemn

361

form of prayer which had come down from David and was kept by the people of God through the ages for the special and sacred purpose of blessing the Kingdom of Christ. The words which come next, *Blessed is he that cometh in the name of the Lord*, were used to the same end. For this is a propitious prayer for the joyful and prosperous success of Christ's Kingdom, upon which depends the restoration and the happiness of the church of God.

And now we have to untie the knot that in this psalm David speaks of himself rather than of Christ; and this won't be too difficult. We know that a kingdom was established in the hands of David and his posterity, in anticipation of that ever-lasting Kingdom which was to appear in its own time. We do not need to believe that David was thinking only of himself. What is more, the Lord himself sent prophets who turned the eyes of the godly in another direction. Therefore, what David sings about himself is rightly applied to the Redeemer who was to come from his seed. . . .

That cometh in the name of the Lord. We must first understand the meaning of this expression. A man comes in the name of the Lord when he neither rashly pushes himself forward, nor usurps honor under false pretenses, but when he has been called by God, accepts him as the author and the guide of his actions. This eulogy applies to all the true servants of God. A prophet comes in the name of the Lord, directed by the Spirit of God; and delivers to men the pure doctrine which he receives from heaven. So also, a king comes in the name of the Lord, when God governs his people by his hand. But since the Spirit of the Lord rested upon Christ, and since he is the Head of the church, all those who have ever been ordained to rule over the church are subject to him; they are indeed as streams flowing from a Fountain. Christ is said properly to have come in the name of the Lord; not only because he excels all others in authority, but also because God has totally revealed himself in Christ. For in him dwells the fullness of Deity bodily, as Paul says in Col. 2:9; and he himself is the living image of God; in short, he is truly Immanuel. He has a special right to this eulogy, because God manifested himself in him wholly, and not partially as he had done by the prophets. Therefore, if we want to honor God's servants, we ought to start with the Head.

Rejoice, thou barren who didst not bear, rejoice and be glad, thou who hadst no children! For the sons of the widowed are more than the sons of the wife, saith the Lord.

Enlarge the space of your tents and extend your tent cords. Isa. 54: 1–2.
(Calvin's wording.)

After speaking of the death of Christ, the prophet rightly
turns to the church to give us a better understanding of what
Christ's death has done and accomplished for us. There would
be no such understanding if Christ's death were considered by
itself. Therefore we must turn to his body which is the church.
Christ suffered for the church—not for himself.

The same order is followed in the Creed of our faith. After we
confess that we believe in Christ who suffered for us and was
crucified, we continue by affirming that we believe in the
church which, as it were, flowed from his side. So Isaiah, after
speaking of the death, resurrection, and triumph of Christ,
rightly comes down to the church which is never to be separated
from its Head. In this way, each one of the faithful may
learn from his own experience that Christ did not suffer in
vain.

If this teaching had been omitted, the faithful could not
fortify their hearts with the hope of the restoration of the
church. But the congratulation in these verses shows plainly that
when Christ comes forth from death as conqueror, he conquers
not for himself alone, but also to breathe life into his body,
which is the church. . . .

Tents. The metaphor is taken from a kind of dwelling common in that region. The church is compared to tents because
it has no solid structure in the world. It always appears unsettled and wandering, and is moved here and there in various
migrations, as necessity requires. But I am sure the prophet
was also thinking of that earlier liberation of God's people,
when they were led through the desert and lived in tents forty
years. In memory of that liberation, they later held yearly a
solemn feast, according to God's commandment. And as we
have said, the prophets habitually refer to it.

Someone will object that the structure built by the ministers
of the Word is too solid to be compared to a tent. But I answer:
The likeness to a tent refers to the external appearance of the
church rather than to its spiritual or essential (if I may use the
word) existence. The true structure of the church is the Kingdom of God, and this is neither frail nor like a tent in any way.
But in the meantime, the external church is moved here and
there because it has no firm habitation in which it can abide.
It is more solid and stronger than the best-fortified citadels
because, relying on God's unconquerable power, it scorns all

peril. But it is like a tent because it is not supported by earthly resources, wealth, and power.

Next we come to the reason the prophet orders that the *cords* be lengthened to enlarge the tent; obviously because no ordinary sized place was sufficient to hold the people whom God was going to gather from all parts of the world into one church.

Thus saith the Lord, the Redeemer of Israel, his Holy One, to the despicable of soul, to the abominable race, to the slave of masters: Kings will see and princes will stand up and adore, because of the Lord; because faithful is the Holy One of Israel and he who chose thee. Isa. 49: 7. (Calvin's wording.)

Isaiah continues the same theme to enable the people, who are suffering from a heavy disaster, to take hold of the hope of a better future. To strengthen their hope the more, he calls God who promises them deliverance, the *Redeemer* and the *Holy One of Israel*.

Someone will object that this is a contradiction. God is called the Redeemer of the very people whom he has abandoned to oppression. Where is the redemption, where is the holiness, when the people could see that they were wretched and ruined? I answer, The prophet reminds them of their past history as a ground for confidence and hope. Since the Jews were overwhelmed with despair, the prophet protested and argued that the God who had formerly redeemed their fathers was still mighty and still possessed the same power as of old. Therefore, although he had for a time hidden his salvation in order to exercise the faith of the godly, believers were commanded to stand firm with uplifted hearts, because their redemption by God's hand was sure. Meanwhile, it was necessary for them to think thoughts far removed from the experience of the senses.

This passage is important for us, because from it we learn how great is the faith we need when God speaks to us. For his promises are not fulfilled immediately, and he lets us suffer and endure affliction for a long time.

Some translate *bezoh* as "despised," and some as "despicable." I prefer the latter. God adds to the people's misery by declaring that their souls are despicable in his sight. Many who are despised by others are still worthy of honor because they are gifted men; such people do not cease to swell with pride, and they trample down the pride of those who despise them with their own greater pride. But God says here that he himself

despises this people no less than they are despised by their
fellow men. But his purpose in describing the extremity of their
disgrace and misery is to assure them that the time of their deepest humiliation will also be the acceptable time when he shall
bring them his help.

The abominable nation. I see no reason why some change the
number of *nation, goy,* to the plural when the prophet uses the
singular. It is certain that these words are addressed especially
to the race of Abraham.

He adds *serve masters,* that is, "be oppressed by strong tyrants" for *meshalim* means those who have so much strength and
power that it is not easy to escape from their hands.

When God says that *kings shall see,* he speaks magnificently of
the liberation of his people; yet meanwhile he permits them to
be tried in a fiery furnace, to make trial of their patience and
faith. For if what God promised occurred immediately, before
he had even finished speaking, there would be no place for the
exercise of faith.

The repetition in naming the rulers is customary in Hebrew.
We should say "kings and princes shall see; they shall stand up
and adore." The verb *adore* explains *stand up.* (Today we *stand
up* to honor someone.) Briefly, the greatest princes of the world
shall stand up, as they testify that the restoration of God's
people is God's own glorious work, worthy of reverence.

Because he is faithful. This is the reason for the admiration and
honor which the princes show to God. They will come to know
God's faithfulness and constancy with regard to his promises.
Moreover, God wishes to be known as true, not as an abstract
concept, but through the experience of the way he preserves
the people whom he has adopted. Therefore, let us learn that
the promises of God are not to be estimated by our [immedi-
ate] situation, but by his truth. When nothing but destruction
and death hangs over us, let us remember these words by which
God constrained a despicable and contemptible people.

Also, we must realize how great and wonderful is God's work
in liberating the church. Proud kings who think nothing worth
looking at or valuable are compelled to see, to wonder, to be
amazed, and even against their will to reverence God. This new
and unprecedented work of God is especially commended to us,
and our own judgment tells us what and how great it is; for
even if we ignore past history, we know our own liberation from
the miserable tyranny of Antichrist. When we consider our own
situation carefully, it must, in the psalmist's words, seem to us

a dream (Ps. 126:1). God has done a stupendous and incredible work in us who bear Christ's name.

And who hath chosen thee. At the end of the verse the prophet repeats what he had mentioned before, that this people had been set apart by God. But we must realize that election is the beginning of sanctification. This people was God's holy inheritance only because God had of his mere good pleasure thought it good to choose them, therefore [in these words], Isaiah points to the hidden will of God as the source from which sanctification flows. He thus prevents Israel from thinking themselves separated from others on account of their own merit; it is as though he had said, "The Lord who chose you confirmed his choice by his own work in you, and demonstrated it by its effects." In the same way, God's faithfulness must be known in our salvation, and our salvation must equally be ascribed to his election. Meanwhile, let all who desire to share in this great good become a part of Israel, that is, of the church, outside of which there can be neither salvation nor truth.

For behold, in those days, and in the time, when I bring again the captivity of Judah and Jerusalem, then I will also gather all nations, and I will bring them down to the valley of Jehoshaphat. . . . Joel 3:1–2.

The prophet said this when the Jews were an object of hatred to all peoples and were, so to speak, the dregs and filth of the whole world. The enemies of the Jews were as many as there were nations under the sky. And the Jews, seeing the hostility of the whole world, were likely to slip into complete despair. They would think: "Even if God wishes to save us, there are so many obstacles that we are certain to perish. The Assyrians are not our only enemies; we have met still greater hatred from all our neighbors." For we know that the Moabites and Ammonites, Tyrians, Sidonians, Philistines, in fact whatever peoples were in that region, had been most hostile to the Jews. And since all roads to their country were closed [to the exiled Jews], it was difficult for them to imagine any hope except by the inspiration of the Lord himself.

For this reason, the prophet said that God would be the judge of the whole world, and that it is within his will and power to summon all nations. . . .

Moreover he says this summons will occur *in those days and at that time when the Lord brings back the captivity of Judah and Jerusalem.* Christian scholars force this into a prophecy of Christ's coming. But they twist the words away from the sense which the context demands. For there is no doubt that the prophet here spoke of the return [from the exile]. Yet he included [in his prophecy] also the Kingdom of Christ. And as we have said elsewhere, this was a very common and frequent practice. When the prophets testified that God would be the Redeemer of his people and promised liberation from the Babylonian exile, they also led the faithful to Christ's Kingdom as if by a continuous pull toward it.

For what was the restoration [from exile] but the prelude of the true and real redemption truly manifested in the person of Christ? Therefore, the prophet does not speak exclusively of the coming of Christ, nor of the return of the Jewish people; he embraces the whole process of redemption, which had only begun when God led his people back from the Babylonian exile, and continues from Christ's first coming to the Last Day. And when it is said that God will redeem his people, we are not to think this redemption will be a brief and instantaneous act. God will continue to exercise his grace until he has exacted the penalty from all the enemies of his church. . . . In brief, the prophet does not reveal God as a halfway redeemer. God will not make an end until he has finished whatever belongs to the felicity of his church and has perfected it in all things. . . .

Joel is saying: "God will not pour out a thin stream of grace. He will bring full redemption to his people. When the whole world rises against them, he will prevail because he himself will undertake to protect his church and defend the safety of his own." Therefore, those who strive to delay or hinder the restoration of the church will accomplish nothing. God is its vindicator, and he will judge all peoples.

Now we must see why the prophet names the Valley of Jehoshaphat. Many think that valley was mentioned because it had been called the "valley of blessing" (II Chron. 20:26). There, as we know, Jehoshaphat had won a great victory with only a small force, although many peoples had joined together against him. When he had fought against a great army and had conquered marvelously (for his followers were few), the people blessed God there, and the name *Blessing* was given to the place. Therefore, many think that the valley was mentioned here to recall to the Jews' remembrance how wonderfully they had been saved in the past. For the memory of that would surely turn their minds to hope. . . . And this seems to me a probable explanation.

Some locate the Valley of Jehoshaphat between the Mount of Olives and the city; but I do not know how probable that conjecture is. In my judgment, the important point is that the text reminds the people of God's past goodness so as to inspire the faithful in all ages to hope for their own salvation.

Others indeed prefer to interpret Jehoshaphat from the meaning of the root from which it is derived. (And certainly *Jeho-shaphat* means "the judgment of God.") They translate it as "the valley of God's judgment." If you prefer this meaning, I do not object. Certainly the name is appropriate, and even if the prophet is here speaking of the holy king in order to encourage the Jews to follow his example, there is no doubt that he is also referring to the judgment of God or to the verdict he will deliver in favor of his people. For the next words are *I will decide upon them there*; and the verb, like the name, is from the root *shaphat*. Clearly, if the name belongs to the place and was also the name of the king, the prophet wished to enlarge its meaning; it is as if he had said, "When God dwells in the midst of his people, he will call all nations to judgment; and this is what he now wills to declare and establish."

Some twist the passage into a reference to the Last Judgment —but that is violently forced. From that misinterpretation arose the idea that the whole world will gather in the Valley of Jehoshaphat. But we know such mad dreams filled the world when the light of sane teaching was quenched. It is not strange, after the world had so profaned the worship of God, that all men became fascinated with crude absurdities. But when we consider the prophet's purpose, there is no doubt that he names the Valley of Jehoshaphat to give hope to the Jews that God himself will guard their safety. He says frequently that God will live among them; later in this very chapter we read, *And God will live in the midst of you.*

And I fed the flock of slaughter, truly (or *therefore*) *the poor of the flock; and I took for myself two staffs, the one I called Elegance* (or *Beauty*) *and the other I called Cords* (or as some translate, *Destroyers.* This we shall discuss); *and I fed the flock.* Zech. 11:7. (Calvin's wording.)

Here the prophet continues an earlier theme and clarifies what had not been sufficiently explained: namely, that the ingratitude of the people, especially since it was combined with obstinacy, was worthy of death and left no room for pardon. God's Fatherly care had been basely and dishonorably rejected,

as well as the gracious kindness which he had shown to the
people.

God declares that he has *fed the flock*. Others take Zechariah
as the subject; but as I said, God is enumerating the favors
which in time of peace he had conferred on the people until he
saw that they were unworthy of any kindness. We should
remember that the prophet is speaking to the remnant. He is
not here recounting God's ancient favors to Israel, but describing the state of the people after their return from the exile in
Babylon. In an earlier passage, God seemed to entrust this
fraction of the people to Zechariah to feed. But as I have said,
this whole address is intended to make it obvious that all guilt
belonged to the people who had rejected God's kindness and
stubbornly fought against him, leaving no room or entryway
for his mercy. This remonstrance is therefore in the name of God
himself.

Truly the poor. Some translate *because of*. The word *lakhen* may
introduce an explanation, or we may take the phrase to mean
especially the poor. In any case, what the prophet means is that
God had looked after the whole people because he hoped there
were some sheep left who deserved mercy. God says that because he hoped there were some poor little sheep among the
corrupt flock, he did not deem it hard or troublesome to lead
his people as their shepherd. *I fed the flock of slaughter, truly*, he
says, because there were in the flock some poor sheep whom I
was unwilling to desert. I preferred to try everything rather
than abandon one small sheep if there was one in the whole
flock.

He says he took two staffs, one called *no'am*, the other
hobelîm. Those who translate the second "destroyers" do indeed
interpret the Hebrew word literally if we stick to the vowel
points. But since *hebel* and the plural *hᵃbālîm* means "ropes" or
"cords," I have no doubt that the prophet means here "small
cords" or "binding twine." You say, "But the grammar does
not permit that!" As if Zechariah had written the vowel points,
which were not then in use! I know, of course, the great care
with which the ancient scribes worked out the points, when the
language was no longer in ordinary and familiar use. And those
who neglect the points or reject them entirely are certainly
lacking in sense and good judgment. But some right of choice
must be allowed. If we read *destroyers* here, the words make no
sense; and if we read *cords* we alter only the two vowel points,
and not a single letter. Since the context itself requires "cords,"

I am astonished that interpreters have slavishly allowed themselves to be coerced [by two vowel points] and have not seen what the prophet was talking about.

Now the prophet says He took two staffs, but obviously not to do the ordinary work of a shepherd. Any shepherd is content with one crook. (Staff here means a shepherd's crook.) And each shepherd works with his own crook. But here the prophet says that two crooks or shepherd's staffs were needed, because when God leads his people his care of them surpasses that of any human shepherd.

But I leave the rest for tomorrow.

Yesterday we said that the name *ḥᵃbālîm*, by which Zechariah called the second staff, ought not to be translated "destroyers," as do all the Hebrews. God here teaches that he has done everything which can be done by a good and faithful shepherd, and that his people were perishing by their own fault. Now since God himself was discharging the duties of a shepherd, he could not have been carrying a staff for destruction. Besides, it is obvious that the prophet has put this word (*ḥᵃbālîm*) together with the other, *noʿam*. And finally, he says that the staff called *ḥᵃbālîm* was broken to annul the brotherhood between Israel and Judah. What connection is there between "destroy" and "unite"? It is correct therefore to take the name *ḥobelîm* or *ḥᵃbālîm* as "cords."

Now we must see why the prophet names one staff *Elegance* or *Beauty* and the other *Cords*. Some think the *noʿam* stands for natural law and *ḥᵃbālîm* for the law of Moses. And those who translate "cords" (as Jerome rightly does here) think that since the law bound the ancient people to a hard yoke, it was called a rope because it constrained them. Others, like Jerome himself, refer to the words of Moses, *When the Lord cast his cord, he chose a place in Israel*, etc. (Deut. 32:8). And therefore they think that the *cord* stands for "inheritance." But the first interpretation is too farfetched and forced. And at variance with the second is the prophet's use of the word in the plural which is not consistent with *inheritance*. From the context it can be assumed, as we said yesterday, that *cords* are to be understood as *union*. Therefore, the text means that God had fulfilled the office of shepherd towards his chosen people and had prescribed for them the best possible order. This I understand from *noʿam*. For nothing could more perfectly exemplify the beauty of order than the rule of life which God used for Israel. With good reason, therefore, he compares his

shepherd's crook to *Beauty*; as if he said that the rule
had been so perfectly fashioned that nothing better could be
imagined.

For the second staff he takes *Unity* or *Concord*, and this
marked the height of his favor; for he had gathered together
the scattered Israelites that they might once again be one
people. It is true that few from the Kingdom of Israel had returned to their homeland; but it is clear that not all of the
remnant was only from Judah, Benjamin, and the Levites;
there were others mixed in with them. Therefore, the appropriate interpretation of this verse is that God had not only
established a most beautiful order [of government], but had
also added brotherly unity so that the sons of Abraham were
joined together in one spirit and one soul.

Therefore, since theirs was so good a shepherd, their ingratitude was the more shameful and unendurable when they threw
off his yoke and refused to be guided by his staff. Now we see
why the prophet used these words *Beauty* and *Union*, when he
described God as carrying two staffs.

*Its waters will roar and toss tumultuously, and the mountains will be
shaken with its swelling. Selah.*

*The streamlets of her river will make glad the city of God, the holy
place of the tabernacles of the Most High.*

God is in the midst of her; she shall not be moved. Ps. 46: 3–5.
(Calvin's wording.)

To understand the full meaning of this [third] verse, we
should read it with what follows. Although the waters of the
sea roar and roll wildly, and the mountains themselves shake
at the violent impact, the City of God in the midst of such
dreadful turmoil lies happy and calm, content with its narrow
streams. The prophet means that the narrow channel of a small
river is enough to give complete joy to the Holy City, even if
the whole world should quake. I have mentioned before how
useful a teaching this passage contains. Our faith is truly tested
when in a time of great conflict hell seems ready to engulf us.
And here we have pictured for us the victory of our faith over
the whole world, whenever faith rises to conquer all fears amid
confusion and threats of complete destruction. The sons of God
do not find danger laughable, nor do they jest at death; but
in danger they rejoice because they know that God's promised
aid outweighs all the evils which inspire terror. The sentiment
of Horace appears very noble when he says of the righteous

man, conscious of his own innocence:

Si fractus illabitur orbis
Impavidum ferient ruinae.

(When all the bulwarks of the earth crash suddenly to pieces, he will face without fear the falling fragments.) But since no one has ever found a man such as Horace imagines, the words are empty. True courage is founded altogether in God's protection; and those who rely upon God can boast not only that they are unafraid, but that they will be safe and secure when ruin overtakes the whole world.

The prophet says explicitly that the City of God will be happy, although it does not possess a tumultuous sea which can throw its ever-surging waves against the assaults [of its enemies]. All it has is a little river. The prophet is referring to the brook which flowed from Siloah and went past Jerusalem. I have no doubt that he here blames obliquely the false confidence of those who are fortified with earthly resources and dream that they are beyond the reach of hostile weapons. Those who anxiously gather invincible garrisons appear indeed to be able to prevent invasion by foreign enemies, as though they were protected on all sides by the sea; but it often happens that they are overwhelmed by their own weapons as a tempest devastates and submerges an island in a flood. But those who trust themselves to God, although in the eyes of the world they are exposed to all kinds of injuries and have no defense to ward off attacks, nonetheless rest in security. For this reason, Isaiah (8:6) blames the Jews for despising the gently flowing waters of Siloah and seeking for deep and rapid rivers. . . .

In the same way today also, the Spirit encourages and inspires us to the same constancy: to despise the forces of those who march against us in splendor and confidence, to stand tranquil among all commotions and disturbances. Nor need we be ashamed of our nakedness if God's hand is outstretched to preserve us. Therefore, although God's help drips in a small stream like a rivulet, it brings us more of tranquillity than if all the powers of the world were all heaped up together at one time for helping us.

God in the midst of her. Now he shows how great the security of the church is, because God dwells in the midst of it. The verb *will be moved* is feminine in Hebrew and cannot refer to God as if he were going to remain stationary in the future. The statement means simply that the Holy City shall not be moved from its place because God dwells in it and is always ready to bring it help.

But ye shall be named the priests of the Lord. Isa. 61:6.

With these words the prophet shows the people how much more glorious their condition would be than it had been before; he means, "Up to now the Lord has chosen you for his own; but in the future he will honor you with much more splendid gifts, for he will elevate you all to priestly honor." As we know, although the whole people was called a priestly Kingdom, only the tribe of Levi performed the priestly office. The prophet here announces that in the future all will be priests. But this did not become manifest until the reign of Christ, although the restoration of the church began when the people returned from Babylon. At the coming of Christ, all the faithful were honored and exalted with priestly dignity.

We should consider the nature of this priesthood carefully. Animals are no longer to be slain as sacrifices to God; it is human beings that are to be brought as sacrifice—that is, brought to obedience to Christ—as Paul said he did when by the sword of the gospel, he made an offering of the Gentiles that they might obey God (Rom. 15:16).

See then how childishly the papists misinterpret this passage when they use it to prove their own priesthood. Priests are set up by the pope and his followers to sacrifice Christ, not to teach the people. But Christ offered himself as a sacrifice for men's eternal redemption and he alone officiated in that priestly act. He simply orders the fruit of his sacrifice to be brought to us in the teaching of the gospel. Those who usurp his office and wish to repeat the offering which he completed are sacrilegious.

But every one of us ought to offer himself and all his possessions to God in sacrifice, and so to perform his rightful priestly office. Secondly, ministers who are especially called to the office of teaching should use the sword of the Word to make men a sacrifice and to consecrate them to God. True ministers, certainly, are those who try or undertake nothing of themselves, but carry out faithfully and resolutely the commands which they have received from God.

And thou shalt be a crown of glory in the hand of the Lord, and a royal diadem in the hand of thy God. Isa. 62:3.

A royal diadem. He calls the church God's crown because God wishes his glory to shine in us. When we read this, we must see and wonder at the inconceivable goodness of God. For although we are by nature filthy and corrupt and more foul than the mire of the streets, he adorns us bounteously and desires to have us as *the diadem of his Kingdom.*

2. THE MINISTRY

From the Introduction to the Commentary on Isaiah.

It is usual to cover many subjects in discussing the office of the prophet. But no summary (or explanation) of it pleases me better than one which relates the prophets to the law from which they drew their teaching as brooks flow from their source. Since the prophets set the law as the rule for themselves and copied it, they may properly be called and counted its interpreters. There is no separation between the two.

The law contains three most important divisions: first, the teaching of the way of life; second, threats and promises; third, the covenant of grace, founded in Christ and including in itself all special promises. The sections dealing with ceremonies were exercises by which the people were kept to the worship of God and religion, and were appendixes to the first table.

The prophets explained the teaching of the law more extensively than was done in the law itself and interpreted more fully what the two tables covered in few words; and they made clear what the Lord particularly required at the moment. The threats and promises which Moses stated in general, they fitted to their own time and made specific. Finally, what related to Christ and his Kingdom, expressed rather obscurely by Moses, the prophets announced more plainly, bearing fuller and richer witness to the covenant of grace.

If we are to understand the relationship between the prophets and the law, we must discuss the matter in more detail. God established the law itself as the perpetual rule of his church, to be always in the hands of men, and to be followed by all posterity. But he saw the danger that the teaching transmitted by Moses would not be enough for a rude and unruly people. And further, he saw that the people themselves could scarcely be restrained except by a tighter rein. Therefore, since he had forbidden them to consult either magi or soothsayers, either astrologers or observers of animals' entrails, and had required them to be satisfied with his teaching alone, he added the promise that a prophet would never be wanting in Israel (Deut. 18:15).

He did this with the purpose of meeting the anticipated complaint of the people that their situation was worse than that of any of the heathen, for the latter had their divining priests, pontiffs, interpreters of omens, casters of lots, astrologers, soothsayers, and such like, to whom they could go for advice; but they themselves had nobody to help them in case of doubt and uncertainty. To remove every excuse for their polluting themselves with the accursed rites of the nations, God promised to raise up prophets through whom he would disclose his purpose; they would faithfully proclaim whatever he commanded so that in the future the people could not complain of lacking anything.

The promise of *a prophet* is an exchange of number, ἑτερώσις (the singular stands for the plural). For although the passage looks ahead to (*Fr.* applies to) Christ, as Peter clearly, most appropriately and emphatically, interprets it (Acts 3:22), and although Christ is the chief of the prophets and on him all depend in their teaching and to him all with one consent look, yet the words apply also to the other prophets who are included collectively in the singular noun. Therefore, when God promised prophets through whom he would disclose his mind and purpose, he ordered the people to assent to their interpretations [of the law] and to their teaching.

God did not intend the prophets to add anything to the law. They were to interpret it faithfully and establish its authority. So when Malachi (in ch. 4) urges the people to be constant in sincere faith, and orders them to continue in the teaching of their religion, he says, *Remember the law of Moses, my servant, which I commanded him in Horeb for all Israel.* He recalls them to the one law of God and commands them to be content with it. Does Malachi wish the prophets to be ignored? By no means! But since the prophets are dependent on the law, and the law summarily includes everything, his statement is sufficiently inclusive. Those who believe the teaching of the law in its main divisions and devote themselves to them will not neglect the prophets. It is absurd to boast of zeal for the law, when one neglects the divine interpretation of it. So today, many insolent men boast of their zeal for the Word, while they in no way accept the pious counsel and warnings drawn from the teaching of the Word.

When the prophets dealt with morals, they brought forward nothing new; they clarified the things in the law which were wrongly understood. For example, the people thought that when they offered sacrifices and kept the external ceremonies they had done their duty perfectly. For the world measured God by its own notions and worshiped him with material gifts. The prophets condemned this attitude severely and showed that all the ceremonies without sincerity of heart are worthless, that God is worshiped when men call upon him with true faith. Of course the law itself bears sufficient witness to this truth. But it needed to be taught more diligently and oftener brought to the people's attention. Besides, it was necessary to expose the hypocrisy which leads men to cover themselves with the concealing garments of ceremonies. As for the second table of the law, it is from there that the prophets draw when they exhort men to desist from all injury, violence, and fraud. Thus they do nothing else but keep the people to the obedience of the law.

The prophets have a special task with regard to threats and promises. They note specifically, as if with a pointing finger, what Moses stated in general terms. Besides, they have their own vision by which the Lord unveils the future so that they may apply the promises and threats to the immediate need of the people, and bear witness more definitely and certainly to the will of God. Moses threatens, *God will pursue you in battle. . . .* The prophets say, *Behold God will arm the Assyrians against you; he will hiss for the Egyptians.*

Also the prophets are much more clear when they speak of the covenant of grace, and they establish the people more firmly in it. For they always call the people back to it when they wish to comfort them. And they set before them the coming of Christ, who was both the foundation of the covenant and the bond of mutual communion between God and the people. Therefore the whole sum of the promises must be referred to Christ. Anyone who believes this will easily understand what to look for in the prophets and what their purpose was in writing as they did. For the present, it is enough to point it out.

From the prophets, therefore, we should learn how we are to carry out the teaching of the Word. We must imitate them in seeking from the Word advice, judgment, threats, and consolations which are suited to the people in their present situation. For although the revelation given to us is not such that we can presume to predict the future, yet our teaching is valid when we exhibit the judgments of God from the history and example of the ancient people by comparing the ways of men in our time with those of theirs.

For what God formerly punished, he will punish no less today,

since he is forever like himself. Let wise teachers keep this insight if they wish to treat the teaching of the prophets fruitfully.

*And the Lord put out his hand and touched my mouth; and the Lord
said to me, Behold, I have put my words in your mouth.*

See, I have appointed you (or *set you*) *today over nations and
kingdoms.*

*And you, gird up your loins and rise, and speak . . . and fear not
before them.* Jer. 1:9–10, 17. (Calvin's wording.)

Jeremiah is here describing his call so that his teaching may
not be ignored as if it came from a man in his private capacity.
He asserts that he did not come forward of his own accord, but
was sent by God and instructed in his duty as prophet by Him.
He says that for this purpose God put His words in his mouth.

This passage should be carefully studied, since Jeremiah
here describes briefly how anyone who accepts the office of a
teacher in the church ought to decide concerning his call. He
must bring to his work nothing of his own. So Peter also says in
his first letter, *If any man speak, let him speak as it were the oracles of
God* (I Peter 4:11); that is, he should not speak uncertainly as
if he were giving out comments of his own, but he should be
able to speak out confidently without hesitation in the name of
God; just as Jeremiah in this passage demands to be heard
because, as he declares, God has put his words in his mouth.
We can be sure that whatever comes from man's own cleverness
may be ignored. God demands for himself alone the honor of
being heard in his church (as I said yesterday).

Hence it follows that none should be recognized as servants
of God, none should be counted just and faithful prophets or
teachers, unless God is speaking through them, unless they
invent nothing by themselves and teach nothing by their own
will, but preach only what God commands.

For Jeremiah, a visible symbol was added to give greater
assurance of his vocation. However, this is not to be made a
general rule as if it were necessary for the tongues of all teachers
to be touched by God's hand. Here the reality is combined with
the external sign. It is the reality which gives to all the servants
of God the rule not to express their own comments but simply
to transmit, as if from hand to hand, what they have received
from God. It was peculiar to Jeremiah that God stretched out
his hand and touched his mouth to show plainly that the prophet's mouth was consecrated to God. For us, it is enough to
understand clearly how important it is that the tongues of

ministers of the Word are consecrated to God and that they are not to mix their own theories with his pure doctrine. In the person of Jeremiah, God intended to give us a visible sign of this consecration, by reaching out his hand to touch his mouth.

After God has testified that Jeremiah's tongue is consecrated to Him and set apart from common and profane use, God assigns him his authority. *See*, he says, *I have set you over nations and kingdoms*. With these words, God shows the great reverence which he wishes done to his Word, even when delivered by mortal men. There is no one who does not profess that he is willing to obey God, but there is scarcely one in a hundred who welcomes his Word. As soon as it is spoken, men raise violent objections; or if they do not dare to show their fury and hostility, we see how they resist it, some by excuses, some by silence. Therefore the authority which God gives to his Word should be well noted.

God says, *Behold, I have appointed you*, and thus encourages the prophet to be high-minded, to remember his vocation, and not to flatter men slavishly nor comply with their selfish desires. *See*, he says. By this word we should understand that teachers cannot pursue their calling with full vigor unless the majesty of God stands vividly before their eyes. For they can despise whatever splendor and power and pomp they find among men only when they compare them with God's glory. Experience teaches that when we turn our eyes on men, whatever dignity they possess, even though it be small, inspires us with fear.

Why are prophets and teachers sent? Truly to call the whole world to order; not to spare their hearers but to denounce them freely whenever there is need, even to threaten them when they appear obstinate. If the teacher allows himself to be impressed with any sort of superiority in men, he will not dare to offend those whom he thinks distinguished by power or wealth, or by some reputation for wisdom or honor. There is no remedy against such fears, except for teachers to keep God before their eyes and to be assured that he is the author of their words. When their minds are raised to God, they can look down on all human heights and excellencies. This is the purpose of the words God uses, *See, I have appointed you over nations and kingdoms*. Here God affirms that the authority of his Word is so great that it makes subject to itself whatever is high and mighty upon earth —even kings not excepted.

But what God has joined together, man may not separate. It is true that God here exalts his prophets above the whole world, even above kings. But just before, he had said, *Lo, I put my words in your mouth.* Therefore, whoever would claim such great authority for himself must proclaim God's Word and prove himself to be a prophet in reality by injecting no comments of his own into it. ... To conclude—we see from the context that it is not men who are so highly exalted, even if they are true ministers of the heavenly doctrine, but the content of the teaching itself. God here claims supreme authority for his Word, even though its ministers are men, ordinary, despised, poor, and with no superiority in themselves.

I have already explained that our text says this to give courage to true prophets and teachers, and to enable them to oppose kings and people boldly, because they are armed with the power of heavenly doctrine.

Rise and speak. We see that the reason God spoke privately to his servant Jeremiah was to enable him to assume publicly the office of teacher. Hence we conclude that those who are called to direct the church of God cannot be acquitted of guilt if they do not preach sincerely and boldly whatever is commanded them. Therefore Paul says that he is free from bloodguilt because he has spoken from house to house and in public whatever he received from God (Acts 20:26 f.). And elsewhere he says, *Woe to me if I preach not the gospel, for the duty is laid upon me* (I Cor. 9:16).

When God orders the prophet to *gird up* his *loins,* this must refer to the garments worn in the Orient, then as now. Men wore long robes and whenever they began to work, or undertook some hard labor, they used to tuck them up. When God says, *Gird your loins,* he means, "Begin the course which I have enjoined upon you." God requires hard work from his servant, and he is to go at it unhampered. ...

Fear not before them. This exhortation was very necessary since Jeremiah was undertaking a most abhorrent task. He was to act as a herald, and to declare war against his people in the name of God. Jeremiah stated specifically that this calamity was the people's own making, because their obstinacy had been so great that God now refused all leniency. This was a hard word to accept—especially when we remember the great pride of the Jews. They gloried in their holy race and further, as we shall see later, the Temple was in their minds an impregnable citadel, even against God himself. Sent to such a people, the prophet had no small need of being strengthened by God if he was to enter upon his work fearlessly. ...

This passage contains a teaching which is useful to us. From it we learn that courage never fails God's servants when their strength of heart comes from the knowledge that God himself has called them. When their hearts are lifted up by this assurance, God supplies them with indomitable strength and bravery, and they become formidable to the whole world. But if they are inhibited and timid, and shift back and forth, and are influenced by fear of men, God makes them contemptible and causes them to tremble at the slightest breath, and to waste away inwardly.

Why? Because they are not worthy that God should exalt them and reach out his hand to them, and arm them with his weapons, and give them a courage which could frighten both the devil and the whole world.

Truly, I am filled with power by the Spirit of the Lord, and with judgment and courage, to announce to Jacob his crime, to Israel his sin. Micah 3:8. (Calvin's wording.)

Here Micah with heroic courage stands alone against all the false teachers, even though he is met with a multitude of them who, as usual, find their shield in their great number. He says, *I am filled with power by the Spirit of the Lord.* Such confidence befits all the servants of God and prevents them from yielding to the empty and windy boasts of their opponents who are upsetting the whole order of the church.

Whenever God for a time permits pure doctrine to be perverted by false teachers whom he allows to prevail because of their rank or number, we must turn our thoughts to this memorable example and keep our minds unperturbed, our firmness unwavering, and the power of the Holy Spirit indomitable in our hearts. Then we may continue on the way of our vocation and learn how to set the name of God against all human fallacies—provided we know that our obedience to God is approved by him as being faithful.

Therefore, when Micah says that he is *filled with power*, it is evident that he is taking his stand before the eyes of the whole nation, and that alone, by himself, he is challenging a great throng. False teachers were running around everywhere. The devil always has seed enough, when God lets him loose. Therefore their number was not small; yet Micah did not hesitate to come forward. "I myself," he said (for the pronoun *'ānokî* is emphatic); "you despise *me* as only one man (or with a few others); you may imagine that I who serve God am alone. But I myself alone am enough for a thousand, or rather for numbers beyond counting, because God stands on my side, and approves

of my ministry because it is his service. For I offer you nothing
except what he has commanded."

Then he expresses still more confidence by the word '*ūlām*.
Truly, he says, *I am filled*. That word *truly* counters those mag-
niloquent boasts by which false prophets are always winning
fame and glory with the crowd. For Micah means that whatever
they belch forth is empty wind. "You," he says, "are wonderful prophets! You are certainly above the angels if your words
are to be believed. But prove to us that what you boast of is real.
Bring some sign which validates your calling. There is none.
Therefore it follows that you are full of wind and not of the
Spirit. What you boast of, *I* possess."

Undoubtably Micah means that he was endowed with no
common and ordinary power to meet the need of the time. As
God uses the work of his servants, so also he is present with them
and arms them with a stronger defense. When a man is
performing the work of teaching without any great opposition,
an ordinary measure of the Spirit is enough for doing his duty.
But when anyone is drawn into a hard and difficult contest, he
is at once armed by God. We see examples of this daily. For
many simple men who had never tasted learning have been
endowed, when their warfare began, with the Heavenly Spirit so
that they shut the mouths of celebrated teachers who seemed to
be oracles. By such evidence God testifies plainly today that
he is the same God who formerly gave his servant Micah such
rare and incredible power. This is why the prophet says he is
filled with power.

Afterwards he adds *by the Spirit of the Lord*. Here he excludes
every charge of pride and every appearance of claiming something for himself. He declares all to be a divine gift.

Now we must carefully note Micah's situation. Although he
rightly and deservedly claimed the title of teacher, yet he had
nothing to distinguish him from the others in the eyes of the
world. All his opponents had exercised the same office and had
obtained the honor due to it. So much was common to all. But
Micah was either alone or with Isaiah and a few more. And
when he dared to set himself in opposition to the others, we see
that it is not the vocation alone which must be considered. We
know the greatness of Satan's malice as he attacks Christ's
Kingdom. We also know the pride and ferocity of false teachers.
Since both the devil's fury and the pride of false teachers are
well enough known, there is no reason why the faithful should
take bare titles seriously. If the people who lived at that time

claimed, as the papists do today, that they did not possess the discrimination or the judgment to decide between impostors and God's servant, what was to be done? Micah was alone, and the others were very numerous. Besides, the others were prophets or at least had that title and reputation. As I said, this situation is worth considering. The vocation was common to them all. But the others were lying when they pretended to follow it; Micah alone, or with a few others, carried out faithfully whatever God commanded. And Micah alone is counted prophet and teacher.

Finally, the only way the false teachers can make sail against us is by appearing to be endowed with the Spirit of God. But whoever desires to be counted a servant of God and a teacher of the church should have the seal which Micah offers. If he is endowed with the Spirit of God, the honor belongs to God. On the other hand, if a man has nothing to show but the title, anybody can see how trifling a thing that is in God's sight.

Then the prophet adds with *judgment and courage.* By *judgment,* he doubtless means all uprightness; that is a common meaning of the word. Then he adds *courage,* because these two qualities are especially necessary for all ministers of the Word. They must have great wisdom and must hold fast to what is true and right; they must be endowed with inflexible firmness to overcome Satan and the whole world, and not to swerve from their course though the devil mobilize all things against them. We see then what these two words express. First he put *koach, power*; then he put *geburah, courage* or *strength of mind.* By the word *power,* he means in general the gifts with which those who undertake the office of teaching should be endowed. The first requirement of a teacher is general ability. Micah divides the ability of the prophets into two parts: first, wisdom or judgment, and second, courage, so that they may understand what God demands and be effective in teaching. Then they must be firm, so that they may not yield to every breeze, nor be overcome by threats and terrors, nor be swayed back and forth by the favor of the world. They should yield to no seductions. Therefore, courage is added to judgment.

Afterwards he adds *to announce to Jacob his crime and to Israel his sin.* Here we see that a prophet does not seek the favor of the people. To gain favor, it was necessary to flatter with nice words people who sought adulation, the very ones who, corrupted by hatred and malice, had rejected Micah. It would have been necessary for him to please them with soft words; and he does not do it. In one place he says: "They sell their blessings to you and deceive you with the hope of peace. They declare war if their greed is not satisfied. They flatter you because you like it, and you seek teachers who promise you wine and strong drink. But I was sent to you for a different purpose. For God has not committed flatteries to me to make pleasant songs for you; he gave me reproofs and threats. I will therefore publish your sins and will not hesitate to condemn you before the whole world, because you deserve it." Now we understand why the prophet says he was endowed *with courage to announce his sin to Jacob.*

From this we conclude that when we deal with wicked and criminal men, we need the support of heaven's own constancy. And this is the almost universal and perpetual situation of all the servants of God. For those who are sent to teach the world are sent into warfare. It is not enough to teach faithfully what God commands unless we also contend. Although the wicked rise up against us with violence, let us be of a *bronze countenance*, as Ezekiel says (3:8 f.). Let us not yield to their fury, but present to it unconquered constancy. Since our battle is with the devil, with the world and all the wicked, if we wish to do our duty faithfully we need to be endowed with the courage of which Micah speaks. And as I have shown, the servants of God ought to persist in this firmness no matter by what obstacles Satan attempts to delay them or turn them back.

This doctrine should be taught to all the faithful so that they may distinguish wisely between the faithful servants of God and impostors who falsely claim his name. So it is that no one who truly and from his heart desires to obey God shall be deceived. For God will always give a spirit of judgment and discretion. But today unhappy souls are dragged to perpetual ruin, because in fact they shut their eyes, or blink voluntarily, or willingly involve themselves in obscurities, saying: "I cannot judge; I see on both sides learned or famous men, or at least men of some reputation and importance. Some call me to the right, others to the left. Where should I go? I prefer to shut my mouth and my ears." Thus many make ignorance a pretext for inaction.

But we know that when God exercises our faith and tests it our eyes ought to be open. For this purpose it is that he allows dissensions and quarrels to rise in the midst of the church, with some men proposing one thing and some another. When God loosens Satan's rein so that contests of this kind and disturbances are produced in the bosom of the church, we have no real excuse for not following whatever the Lord commands, because he always guides us by his Spirit—only we must not keep hugging our own indolence.

O sword (or *spear*), *awake above my shepherd and above the man who is my associate, saith the Lord.* Zech. 13:7. (Calvin's wording.)

The word '*myth* ('*amith*) some translate "relative," some "kinsman," some "one who adheres to God," because they are sure that this passage can be understood only as referring to Christ. But, as I have already said, they have followed a false principle of interpretation. The Greek translation is τὸν πολίτην, "citizen." Others translate, as does Theodotian, σύμφυλον, that is "relative." Jerome preferred "one who adheres to me."

But '*amith* in Hebrew means "associate," "neighbor," or "close friend," in fact anyone united to us for any reason. I have no doubt that God by this title refers to the pastors of the church, because they are his representatives to the people; and, as we know, the better pastor one is, the nearer he is to God. Similarly, kings and judges who exercise sovereignty are called God's sons. Thus also, pastors are called God's associates because they have a part in God's work of building the church. God is the head Shepherd, but he uses his ministers to carry out his work. They are called his associates, because they are co-workers with God, as Paul also taught. To conclude: the prophet calls the pastors God's associates in the same sense in which Paul called them συνεργούς (I Cor. 3:9).

Therefore I have also made you contemptible and base before all the people, according as ye have not kept my ways, but have been partial in the law. Mal. 2:9.

The prophet ends by saying that the priests glory in the honor of their office without reason, because they have ceased to be priests of God.

Now let us go back to the beginning. Let us have in mind the prophet's purpose in this discussion. He attacks the priests particularly because they wished to reserve for themselves a special privilege which would set them above all criticism, and also because if the priests themselves are not kept in order, ordinary and common men are deprived of true doctrine. There is no doubt that the priests were flattering the people, and attempting to destroy their reverence for the prophets and to put an end to the influence of prophetic teaching. This is why our prophet denounces them so severely. . . . Now that we understand his purpose, it is easy to grasp the meaning of the whole matter.

But before I go further, we should note that in this passage [as a whole] we have a description of true and legitimate priesthood. The prophet does not argue here about the priestly office; he sets before our eyes a living picture which we cannot fail to understand, and from which those who are engaged in a pastor's work may learn what it is that God requires of them.

Here I am omitting what I discussed in the first place: that God meant his priests to be feared; and I have already explained sufficiently that they ought not to abuse their authority as if unlimited power had been allowed them. God does not wish his church to be subjected to tyranny. He wills to be its only ruler, by the ministry of men. . . .

But we must now attend to the words of the prophet: Levi executed his office with good faith and from the heart *because the law of truth was in his mouth, and iniquity was not found in him.* To this we should add the statement which follows immediately after, *For the lips of the priest should keep knowledge* (v. 7). This rule cannot be set aside. Those who are priests or pastors in the church must be teachers. And Gregory wisely applies the above rule figuratively to teaching. We know that little bells were to be fastened on the priest's robe, and Moses says specifically that the priest never walks but the bells tinkle. Gregory, whom I just mentioned, applies this to the matter of teaching. "Woe to us," he says, "if we walk without sound, that is, if we boast of being shepherds and are only dumb dogs. For nothing is more unendurable than to count a man as a pastor in the church who does not speak, and whose voice does not ring out clearly for the upbuilding of the people." This is what a Roman pope said. Let those who boast, proudly and with full mouths, of being his successors at least produce some sound so that we can hear their teaching. But since they exercise all their authority like barbarians, anybody can see how faithful they are in guarding God's covenant!

But I come back to the words of our prophet. He says that this rule, prescribed by God, was not to be broken at man's pleasure, or by any custom. The priest should keep knowledge on his lips. Malachi explains further and shows that the priest is the guardian of knowledge, not to keep it in private for his own benefit, but to teach it to the whole people. He says *they will ask the law at his mouth* (v. 7). This is one point.

Secondly, he restricts the word *knowledge* to the true doctrine which flows from the law of God; for that is the only fountain of truth. . . . Therefore, it is not enough for a man to keep his mouth open and be ready to teach everybody unless what he teaches is the pure doctrine. We see then that it is not just any kind of sermon which is required of priests, but the pure Word proceeding from the mouth of God himself, as is said in Ezekiel (3:17): *You will take the word from my mouth and announce it to them from me.* Here God shows that priests do not have the power and authority to come out with every useless thing that comes into their noddles, or with everything they think is fitting. They will be good teachers just so far as they are God's pupils. . . .

Finally we ought to consider *because the priest is the messenger of the Lord of hosts.* These words may appear designed to honor the priesthood; but the prophet means that the priests have nothing of their own or apart from God. Therefore whatever reverence is due them belongs to God whose ministers they are. As I said, he is reasoning from the above definition, and as if that stated specifically, "Whoever wishes to be counted priest, let him also be a teacher." And at the same time we must also realize that the prophet implies a certain relationship between God and priest, as though he had said, "Priests can take no more on themselves than to be God's interpreters. . . ."

We see, therefore, how much the prophet has included in these few words. First, there is no priesthood without teaching; nor is there any true priest who does not sincerely perform the duty of teaching. Secondly, he shows that God's right and power is in no way diminished when priests preside in the church, since God has assigned that office to them by the same law which also affirms that authority always belongs to God alone. Otherwise, the priest would not be *the messenger of the God of hosts.*

At the same time the prophet requires of priests also sincerity in the performance of their duties. For we know that many apparently excel, and teach eloquently, and even expend much energy eagerly in their work; but some of these are impelled by ambition and others by avarice. Therefore the prophet appends here another rule, that they *walk uprightly* before God: that is, that they do not seek to satisfy men or receive the world's applause, but do their work with a clear conscience.

So I have shown that the prophet sets here an example before us, to show us what God demands of us, whom he has appointed pastors of his church.

And the angel of the Lord bore witness to Joshua, saying: If you walk in my ways and keep my watch, you also will judge (or rule) my house (dwn means judge, but the word is used for any kind of government, therefore rule my house is preside over my temple). And you will keep my porch and I will give you passage among those who stand by. Zech. 3:6–7. (Calvin's wording.)

. . . This whole passage has to do with the glory and worship of God, for it is profaned if it is applied to ourselves. We must especially guard against applying it to the church and its government. For we know how ready men are to divert to their own tyrannical use whatever power God assigns to his church.

Of course God wishes to be heard when he speaks through his servants and those whom he has made teachers. But we can now see how from the beginning of the world ambitious and proud men have used this as a pretext for gaining authority for themselves, and have expelled God from his own dominion. In fact, the regiments of Satan claim for themselves full and unlimited power over all the faithful on the ground that God wishes the priesthood to be honored and prescribes that it rule over his church. Since, therefore, in all ages Satan has misused the glorious praise with which God has honored his church, we must always add the caution as the prophet does here that God had no intention, such as some individual man might have, of exalting men by abdicating his own rank and position. The whole glory of the church is here presented to insure the pure worship of God and the submission of all in the church to God's own dominion—not only of the common people but also of the priest himself. Whatever excellence there may be in the church, God will have everything to be so ordered that he alone is supreme. And this is as it should be.

We now understand the prophet's purpose. And to give this teaching the more weight, he says, *the angel bore witness.* The word he uses is a legal term. A *man bears witness* when he takes a solemn oath that he is speaking the truth. . . . The Holy Spirit intends by this word to make us more attentive, to show us that this is no ordinary matter, and to persuade us to have greater reverence for this command, since God himself introduces it by an oath or something similar. . . .

The angel teaches briefly that priests are not given their pre-eminence to enable them to run riot with their own lusts. The law is interposed to constrain them to do their duty faithfully and to obey God's voice. We see therefore that there are two things which go together: the dignity of the priesthood and the faith shown by God's servants who are called to that office. Those who wish to rule without any restraint prove clearly enough that they are not legitimate priests of God. . . .

But we must also see what is meant by *ways* and *my watch* or *guardianship*. For these certainly belong to the office of the priest. God commands all of us in general to follow where he calls; and what he requires as the rule of living faithfully and rightly is called a *watch* or *guardianship*, because God does not let us wander freely but guards us against errors and shows us what rules we must observe. There is therefore a general guardianship which concerns all the faithful.

But the priestly *watch* is, as I just said, restricted to the priestly office. We know that God does not resign his own Kingship when he elevates men. But he does give them a mandate to be his representatives, and they are truly his vicars when they teach from his Word purely and faithfully; God exercises his Kingship no less because he uses the work of men and employs them as his servants. We see then that God has established the guardianship of the priests [over the church] so that the church may be ruled by the pure Word of God. . . . In short, the pastors of the church rule by divine appointment, but they do not exercise their own domination. They are to govern the churches according to God's own command, so that God himself may guide them by human hands.

I understand by the *keeping* of the *courts* not janitor service but whatever has to do with the worship of God. . . .

Whatever excellence there is in the pastors of the church must not be separated from the service of God. God does not resign his power to mortal men or in any way take away from his own rightful dominion. But he makes men his ministers, so that he alone by their hand may govern his church and he alone have pre-eminence over it. Whence it follows that those who do not do their work with sincerity do not deserve respect. And if they grasp for themselves what belongs to God, they are to be denied the name of priest. They are then nothing but a mask of Satan by which he would deceive the simple folk.

Whosesoever sins ye remit, they are remitted unto them, and whosesoever sins ye retain, they are retained. John 20:23.

Here without doubt the Lord has put together the whole sum of the gospel. Therefore we must not separate the power of forgiving sins from the office of teaching, for in this passage they are tied together. Christ had said shortly before, "As the living Father sent me, so I myself send you." Now, he declares what this embassy means and involves. However, he insists that it was necessary for him to give them the Spirit, so that they would not act of themselves. This then is the principal purpose of the preaching of the gospel: that men be reconciled to God by the free remission of sins, as Paul teaches in II Cor. 5:18, where for this reason the gospel is called the ministry of reconciliation. There is of course much else in the gospel; but what God means to accomplish by it above all is this: to receive men into his favor by not imputing their sins to them. Therefore, if we want to act as faithful servants of the gospel, we must heed this matter most seriously. It is at this point that the gospel differs most from philosophy, since it teaches that the salvation of men is through the free remission of sins. It is from this that flow the other blessings of God: that God illumines and regenerates us by his Spirit, restores us to his image, and arms us with invincible fortitude against Satan and the world. Thus the whole doctrine of godliness and the spiritual building of the church rests upon the foundation that God makes us free from all sins and adopts us to himself [as his sons].

Thus Christ gives his disciples authority to remit sins; but he in no way yields to them what belongs to him. He alone remits sins. This honor, in so far as it is his due, he does not resign to the apostles. He commands them to testify to the remission of sins in his name, so that through them men may become reconciled to God. In short, properly speaking, he alone through his apostles remits sins.

And whosoever sins ye retain. Christ adds the latter clause in order to terrify those who despise his gospel. He would have them know that such pride will not go unpunished. Since the apostles are entrusted with the embassy of salvation and eternal life, they are also to be armed, as the apostle Paul says, with vengeance against the godless who push aside the salvation set before them (II Cor. 10:6). But this consequence of preaching is given last, that its true purpose [the salvation of the hearers] may receive the priority. It is the proper function of the gospel to reconcile us with God. The eternal death of unbelievers which issues from the preaching of the gospel happens not of itself but because of unbelief.

And it came to pass on the morrow, that Moses sat to judge the people: and the people stood by Moses from the morning unto the evening....

And Moses' father-in-law said unto him, The thing that thou doest is not good. Ex. 18:13, 17.

This is a memorable event, and one especially profitable to know. When Jethro saw the government over which God presided and which he adorned with the rare splendor of his glory, he nonetheless criticized it because he found something reprehensible going on. He criticized Moses himself, the greatest of the prophets, with whom alone God spoke intimately, because he had been inconsiderate enough to exhaust himself and the people with too much labor.

Moses' outstanding ability and heroic mind are evident in that he submitted to so many annoyances, endured so many troubles, and, unbeaten by weariness, every day undertook new labors. The greatness of his spirit can never be praised enough. He spent himself freely for a depraved and perverse people; and he did not desist from his purpose although he saw no gratitude for his kindness. . . . Surely, he possessed many virtues, worthy of highest praise. Yet in all that was praiseworthy, Jethro found a fault.

Thus we are warned that in the most excellent deeds of men there is always some defect; and nothing exists so perfect that it is without blemish. Therefore those who are set to rule the people should know that however devotedly they perform their office, their best plan, if it be examined, leaves something to be desired. Not only kings and magistrates, but also the pastors of the church, should know that even when they stretch every nerve to fulfill their duties, there is always something which can be corrected and improved.

Also, it is worth noting that no mortal possesses the maximum of every kind of gift or is capable of undertaking everything at once, however great and varied his talents. For who is the equal of Moses? Yet when he took upon himself the whole responsibility of ruling the people, we find him unequal to the burden.

The servants of God should learn to measure their strength; when they greedily take on too many jobs, they may well crack up. For πολυπραγμοσύνη, "too-much-to-do," is a common disease and attacks most men so violently that it cannot be quickly checked. To keep us all within our limits, let us learn how God has designed and ordered the affairs of the human race, so that each individual is endowed with only a limited amount of gifts, on which depends also the distribution of duties. The world is not lighted by a single ray of the sun; light is produced by all its rays together, as each makes its own contribution at the same time. In the same way God, to keep men in mutual association and good will by a sacred and unbreakable bond, dispenses his gifts variously. He does not raise anyone inordinately above the rest by bestowing on him absolute perfection, and so he binds all men together.

Augustine writes truly that in this story God humbled his servant. And Paul records that he himself was inflicted with the breath of Satan's messenger so that he might not be too much puffed up by the sublimity of God's revelation to him.

And Joseph saw that they [Pharaoh's butler and baker] *were sad. . . . And they said unto him, We have dreamed a dream, and there is no interpreter of it. And Joseph said unto them, Do not interpretations belong to God? Tell me then, I pray you.* Gen. 40:6, 8.

Joseph offers his services in accordance with his vocation. This should be noted, to keep any of us from unconsciously taking more upon himself than he knows God has allowed him. Paul carefully warns us that the gifts of the Spirit are variously distributed, that a different role is assigned to each one of us, and that no one should encroach greedily upon the gift of another or take it for himself. Each individual should rather confine himself to his own vocation and its prescribed limits. Unless such modesty prevails, everything is confused; for God's truth is rashly torn apart by the stupidity of many. Peace and concord are disturbed and in the end no kind of order will be secure. We know that Joseph was safe in promising to interpret the Pharaoh's dream because he knew that he was taught and ordained for this manifestation of God's grace. To this end he was given the gift of interpreting dreams. But he did not try to go beyond what his powers allowed. He did not divine the content of Pharaoh's dreams; and he confessed that it was hidden from him. The case of Daniel was different. Daniel was provided with the spirit of divination to such a degree that he was able to interpret the king's dream when it had escaped the latter's memory. Thus we see that Joseph, who was given only half [as much as Daniel], kept himself within its proper limits.

Moreover, Joseph not only guarded himself from all presumption, but also declared that what he had was the gift of God. He said honestly that of himself he possessed nothing. He did not boast that he was keen or clever, but wished only to be known as the minister of God. Our vanity must be controlled, not only that God alone may be glorified and may not be defrauded of his due, but that the prophets, professors, and others who excel in heavenly gifts may humbly submit themselves to the direction of the Spirit.

Further we should note that Moses says Joseph was sorry for the grief of those who were with him in prison. Men are subjected to misfortunes to keep them from despising others who are in trouble; for sharing misery begets sympathy. Therefore, it is not strange that God trains us by various hardships. For nothing is more becoming for us than sympathy with our brothers who lie despised and weighed down under misfortunes. This sympathy has to be learned by experience because our inborn callousness becomes thicker and thicker with prosperity.

This book of the law shall not depart out of thy mouth; but thou shalt meditate therein day and night, that thou mayest observe to do according to all that is written therein. . . . Josh. 1:8.

The study of the law must be assiduous; because, when it is omitted even for a short time, many errors slip in, and our memory grows rusty. Besides, when continuous study is neglected, many things become strange and difficult to practice. Therefore, God orders his servant to persist in the daily study of the law and never cease to pursue it as long as he lives. Whence it follows that those who show contempt for this study are blinded by their intolerable arrogance.

But why does God forbid the law to *depart from* his *mouth* rather than from his *eyes*? To take *mouth* by synecdoche[1] for *face* is inane. I am certain that the word *mouth* applies primarily to a man who studies not only for himself but also for the benefit of a whole people whose government is his responsibility. So he is commanded to attend to the teaching of the law, in order that when he speaks about it, he may be able to do so with benefit to the people as a whole, as his responsibility requires.

Meanwhile, he is commanded by his own teachableness to give others an example of obedience. For there are many who have the law in their mouths in public, while at the same time they are the worst keepers of it. Joshua is therefore given both commands: to teach others and to conform his own conduct and himself wholly to the same standard.

3. Preaching and Teaching

Lift up your heads, O ye gates; and be ye lifted up, ye everlasting

---

[1] A figure of speech by which the part represents the whole.

doors; and the King of glory shall come in. Who is this King of glory?
The Lord strong and mighty, the Lord mighty in battle. Ps. 24: 7–8.

Since the magnificent splendor by which the Temple was to
surpass the external dignity of the Tabernacle had not as yet
been realized, David here is speaking of the future building of
the Temple. In this way, he is encouraging the faithful to apply
themselves more wholeheartedly and with greater faith to the
ceremonies commanded in the law. God showed no ordinary
kindness when he dwelt among them [giving them] a visible
symbol [of his presence] and wished his heavenly abode to be
seen on earth.

The value of this doctrine ought to be clear to us today;
because it is a sign of the inestimable grace of God toward us
also when, due to the weakness of our flesh, he lifts us up to himself by way of godly practices. For what is the purpose of the
preaching of the Word, of the sacraments, of religious gatherings, and of the whole external order of the church except to
unite us with God? Not without reason does David give such
high praise to the cult ordained by the law, for in the Ark of
the Covenant God offers himself to the faithful and gives them
a sure pledge of his present help as often as men call upon him.

For God does not dwell in temples made with hands, nor
does he find pleasure in external pomp. Yet because it pleased
him to help a rude and, so to speak, childish people to be lifted
up to God by the use of earthly things, David did not hesitate
to propose the building of a splendid temple for the strengthening of their faith. He did this to assure the Jews that the temple
is no empty theater but a place for worshiping God rightly
according to the direction of his Word. He wanted the temple
to stand out before their eyes so that by its effect they might
feel the nearness of God. Hence in short, the Temple which God
had commanded to be built on Mount Zion was meant with
its greater splendor to surpass the Tabernacle, so that by its
brilliance it might be a fitting mirror of the glory and power of
God who dwelt among the Jews. Meanwhile, David himself
burned with the desire for a great temple, and kindled the same
zeal in the hearts of all the pious, so that aided by the rudiments
of the law, they made progress in the fear of God.

Who is the King of glory? These words, which are in praise of
God's power, are meant to teach the Jews that he is not sitting
idly in the Temple but coming in with might to bring help to
his people. The question is twice repeated—which shows that it
is highly emphatic. The prophet plays the role of an astonished

questioner in order to teach the more impressively that God comes clothed with irresistible power to watch over the safety of his people and that under his shadow the faithful are safe.

We have already said that God did not dwell in the Temple as though his immeasurable essence were enclosed in it. But he was present there, with his power and grace, according to the promise given to Moses, *Where I will set the memorial for my name, I will come to thee and bless thee* (Ex. 20:24). This promise was not given in vain, for the faithful know that God truly stands in their midst. They do not look for him superstitiously, believing that he is affixed to the Temple; but with the aid of the outward worship of the Temple, they turn their spirits toward heaven. In truth, whenever the people invoked God in the Temple, by this very act the Ark of the Covenant was no empty or illusory symbol of the presence of God, for God always stretches out his mighty hand to protect the safety of the faithful.

The repetition also warns us that the faithful cannot be too zealous and untiring in their use of this mediation. When the Son of God, clothed in flesh, appeared as *King of glory*, the Lord of Hosts himself entered his Temple to dwell with us, not in a shadowy metaphor, but in reality. Therefore, nothing prevents our boasting that we by his power shall be unconquered. Although today the sanctuary is not on Mount Zion, nor is the Ark of the Covenant the image of God who dwells above the cherubim, our situation is the same as that of the fathers, because the preaching of the Word and the sacraments unite us with God. Therefore, we ought to hold on to these props with reverence, for if we spurn them in ungodly arrogance, it cannot be but that God shall remove himself far from us.

The Lord said to Cain, Why art thou wroth; why is thy countenance fallen? Gen. 4:6.

Moses does not specify *how* God spoke. Whether he [Cain] was presented with a vision, or heard an oracle from heaven, or was warned by a secret inspiration, in any case, he felt constrained by the judgment of God. To drag Adam into this, and to assume that as God's prophet and interpreter he inveighed against his son, is forced and vapid. I understand the aim of various good men, no less eminent for piety than for doctrine, when they play about with such notions. They intend to glorify the visible ministry of the Word and to cut down Satan's sleights of hand which he passes off under the guise of revelation. I admit that nothing is more helpful to the church than to keep pious minds submissive to the authority of preaching so that they may not seek the Word of God in erratic speculations. But in the beginning it is necessary to remember that the Word of God was given in the form of oracles in order that later when administered by human hands it might be held in greater reverence.

I admit that Adam was given the duty of teaching, and I do not doubt that he carefully instructed his children. But the words of Moses are too arbitrarily limited by those who think that God spoke *only* by his ministers.

. . . He cried with a loud voice, Lazarus, come forth. John 11:43.

Christ's divine power is all the more evident in that he did not touch him, but called him with his voice; meanwhile, in so doing, he has commended to us the secret and astounding efficacy of his Word. How indeed did Christ restore life to the dead except by his Word? Wherefore, in reviving Lazarus, he gave us a symbol of spiritual grace, which we apprehend every day by faith, as he shows that his voice gives life.

And as Moses lifted up the serpent in the wilderness, even so must the Son of Man be lifted up. John 3:14.

Here he explains more clearly why he had said that heaven was opened to him alone: it was certainly in order that he might bring to it all who are willing to follow him as their guide. Moreover, he declares that he will appear publicly and openly to all, and will pour out his power upon all men. *To be lifted up* means to be placed in a high and lofty place, so that he may be seen by all. And this occurs by the preaching of the gospel. Some say that this verse refers to the cross; but this explanation does not fit the context and has nothing to do with the subject on hand. The simple meaning of the words is that by the preaching of the gospel Christ is raised up as a standard, so that the eyes of all men may be turned to him, as prophesied by Isaiah (2:2).

Then Jesus said unto them, Yet a little while I am with you, and then I go unto him that sent me. John 7:33.

By these words he testifies that death will not destroy him, that, rather, when he puts off his mortal body, he will declare himself the Son of God by the victory of his glorious resurrection. It is as if he had said: "In spite of all you can do, when I finish the mission enjoined upon me, my Father will receive me into his heavenly glory. Thus after my death I shall not only retain my present state, but shall also enter one far more excellent which is all ready for me." This statement leads us to the larger admonition that, when Christ calls us to the hope of salvation by the preaching of the gospel, he is present with us. It is not for nothing that the preaching of the gospel is called Christ's descent to us (Eph. 2:17).

. . . I speak to the world those things which I have heard from him. John 8:26.

Jesus says that he advances nothing which he has not received from the Father. The teaching of a minister should be approved on the sole ground of his being able to show that what he says comes from God. We know that Christ at this time was in the form of a servant; therefore it is not strange that he demands to be heard because he presented man with God's mandate. Besides, by his example he set down a law for the whole church: namely, that no man ought to be heard except as he speak from the mouth of God. But while he lays low the wicked arrogance of men who force themselves upon others without having the Word of God, he instructs godly teachers who have a single-minded knowledge of their calling and fortifies them with an indomitable constancy, so that, guided by God, they may have courage to defy all mortals.

Then Jesus said unto them, When ye have lifted up the Son of Man, then shall ye know that I am he and that I do nothing of myself; but as my Father hath taught me, I speak these things. John 8:28.

It is true that on the cross Christ erased the handwriting of sin and abolished the condemnation of death, and that in so doing he triumphed over Satan before God and his angels. But it is only by the preaching of the gospel that this triumph at last began to be known by men. We ought to hope that what happened after the cross, namely, his coming out of the grave and his ascension to heaven, shall happen in our own day. For in spite of the fact that the impious are busy contriving how they may oppress Christ by way of his doctrine and his church, he not only rises but also turns their wicked zeal into a means of greater advance for his Kingdom.

But the Comforter, which is the Holy Ghost . . . shall teach you all things, and bring all things to your remembrance, whatsoever I have said unto you. John 14:26.

Isaiah threatens the unbelievers with the punishment that the Word of God shall be to them as a sealed book (Isa. 29:11). But the Lord also humbles many of his own people in the same way. When he does this, we should not reject the Word, but should wait calmly and patiently for his light. Besides, since Christ testified that it was the peculiar office of the Holy Spirit to teach the apostles whom he himself had already taught by word of mouth, it follows that outward preaching is vain and useless unless the Spirit himself acts as the teacher. God therefore teaches in two ways. He makes us hear his voice through the words of men, and inwardly he constrains us by his Spirit. These two occur together or separately, as God sees fit.

But notice how he promises the Spirit will teach. He says the Spirit will suggest or remind. Therefore, the Spirit will not be a maker of new revelations. With this one statement we must refute all the lies which Satan has introduced into the church, with the pretext that they are of the Spirit. Mohammed and the pope have this principle of religion in common: they pretend that Scripture does not contain perfect doctrine, and that they receive a higher revelation from the Spirit. The Anabaptists[2] and the Libertines[3] in our own time derive their mad ideas from the same notion. But any spirit that comes out with some fable got someplace outside the gospel is an imposter, not the Spirit of Christ. Christ promises the Spirit who shall confirm the gospel as the very one who has written and signed it.

Behold the Lord will proclaim to the end of the earth, Say to the daughter of Zion, Behold your Savior cometh. Isa. 62:11. (Calvin's wording.)

When he says *Say to the daughter of Zion,* he leaves us in no doubt that the task of the ministers of the Word and of the prophets whose peculiar work God himself assigns is to promise freedom and security to the church. And we gather that these promises were not restricted to one age only but were to extend to the end of the world. For although a beginning was made by the return from Babylon to Judea, the promise continued in effect to the coming of Christ; for at his coming it was that this

---

2 See Ch. I, note 1.

3 *Libertines*—a pantheistic and antinomian sect whose members called themselves spiritual. There is no evidence that they were a power inside Geneva. Calvin's own enemies were libertines in the sense that they resented the moral and social discipline imposed upon the formerly gay city. (*Opera,* Vol. 7, pp. 145–248.)

prophecy was finally fulfilled and redemption reached its goal. Moreover, the Savior comes whenever the grace of God is proclaimed by the gospel. In short, the prophet is announcing the future day when the voice of God will resound from the rising of the sun to its setting, and will be heard not by one people but by all people. The voice cries, *Behold your Savior comes;* and we know this refers properly to the gospel. Therefore the teachers of the church are commanded to lift up the minds of the faithful with the confidence of the Lord's coming, even though God seems far away from his people. In fact, this promise applies especially to Christ's Kingdom, in which these things are fully and solidly established. Christ has truly revealed himself the Savior of his church.

Of righteousness, because I go to the Father, and ye see me no more. John 16:10.

Of righteousness. Notice the order of Christ's words. He now says that the world is convicted with regard to righteousness. For men do not hunger and thirst after righteousness; on the contrary they reject whatever is said about it unless they are touched by a sense of sin. We must understand, about the faithful especially, that they cannot make progress in living according to the gospel unless first they are humbled; but this does not happen unless they first know they are sinners.

It is the peculiar office of the law to call consciences before the judgment seat of God and to strike them with terror. But the gospel is not preached rightly unless it lead men from sin to righteousness and from death to life. Therefore, we must learn the meaning of the first clause, *of sin*, from the law. But we must here understand *righteousness* as communicated to us by the grace of Christ. So, it is with good reason that Christ makes it to depend upon his ascension to the Father. As Paul is witness (Rom. 4:25), He rose for our justification, and sits on the right hand of the Father, to exercise the dominion given him and thus to fill all things. In short, from the glory of heaven, he covers the earth with the sweet savor of his righteousness. The Spirit proclaims through the gospel that this is the only way we are accounted righteous. After the world becomes convicted of its sin, the Spirit convinces it of true righteousness. When Christ ascended to heaven, he established the Kingdom of Life; and he sits at the right hand of the Father to maintain true righteousness.

And when he is come, he will convict the world of sin and of righteousness and of judgment. John 16:8. (Calvin's wording.)

He will convict the world means that he will not remain enclosed in you, but will send forth his power from you into the whole world. He therefore promises his Spirit who shall judge the world and constrain to an orderly life those who formerly, without reverence or fear, lived in the frenzy of an unbridled license. But let it be clear that he is speaking here not of a secret revelation, but of the power of the Spirit which is manifested in the external teaching of the gospel, and that by the voice of men. But how does it happen that the voice of man penetrates the soul, and working at its very root, finally brings forth fruit, changing hearts of stone into hearts of flesh and renewing the whole man—how, unless this same voice be endowed with power by the Spirit of Christ? Otherwise it would be a dead letter and a mere sound, as Paul teaches beautifully in II Cor. 3:6, where he glories in being a servant of the Spirit because God has worked mightily through his teaching. All this means that the apostles were to receive the Spirit, who would endow them with a heavenly and divine power, and would enable them to exercise authority throughout the world. All this is ascribed to the Spirit rather than to themselves, because they were to have nothing of their own power; they were to be servants and instruments, ruled by the Holy Spirit alone.

By *world*, I understand all those who have been converted to Christ, including the hypocrites and the reprobates. There are two ways in which the Spirit *convicts* men by the preaching of the gospel. Some are affected seriously, so that they bow down readily and assent willingly to the judgment which condemns them. Others, even though convicted, are unable to escape condemnation, because they do not yield from the heart, and will not yield to the authority and dominion of the Holy Spirit. Even though overcome, they rage within themselves; and while confounded, they do not cease to revel in being obstinate. Now we understand how the Spirit was to convict the world through the apostles. God himself stands in judgment through the gospel; and thus it is that men begin to be disturbed in their consciences and to feel the grace of God.

And the Father himself, which hath sent me, hath borne witness of me: ye have neither heard his voice at any time, nor seen his shape. John 5:37.

It is wrongheaded to limit this statement to the voice heard at his baptism. When he says God has testified to him in the past, he means that he has not come forth as somebody no one had ever heard of, because God had already pointed to him in the Law and the Prophets, and given him certain marks which he might bring with him and by which he might be recognized. This means that God testified to his Son when long ago he held out the hope of salvation to the ancient people, or promised the full restoration of the Kingdom of Israel. Therefore, the Jews should have known Christ from Scripture, even before he appeared in the flesh. And now, since they despise and reject Christ, it is obvious that they have no taste for the law; hence Christ's reproach is just. And yet they glory in their knowledge of the law, as if they had never left God's bosom.

After Christ complains that they have not received him, he speaks even more bitterly of their blindness. When he says that they have not heard or seen God, he speaks in a metaphor and means that they are utterly turned aside from the knowledge of God. For as men make themselves known by face and speech, so God speaks by the voice of his prophets, and puts on a visible form in the sacraments, so that he may be known by us according to our own measure. Anyone who does not know God through the living image he himself has given us shows that he only worships a God of his own fabrication. Therefore Paul says that they do not see the glory of God in the face of Christ, because a veil is thrown over their eyes (II Cor. 3:14).

Verily, verily, I say unto you, we speak that we do know, and testify that we have seen. . . . John 3:11.

Some say that *we* above refers to Jesus and John the Baptist. Others say that the plural pronoun has been put in the place of a singular. I myself do not doubt that Christ here speaks for all the prophets of God and for himself as one of them. Philosophers and other windy doctors often force upon us trifles which they themselves have invented. But here Christ vindicates himself and all the servants of God as men who hand down only teaching that is true and certain. God does not send his servants to babble of things of which they are ignorant or doubtful. He trains them in his own school, in order that what they have learned from himself they deliver to others. While with this eulogy Christ declares to us the certainty of his own teaching, he also prescribes the rule of modesty for all his servants. They are not to mouth their own dreams and opinions, or to offer human inventions in which there is nothing solid; on the contrary, they are to be faithful and bear a pure witness to

God. Let everyone attend to what God has revealed to him, and let him not go beyond the bounds set by his faith. Finally, let no man allow himself to speak except as he hears from the Lord.

Whose fan is in his hand, and he will thoroughly purge his floor, and will gather the wheat into his garner: but he will burn up the chaff with unquenchable fire. Matt. 3:12.

In the former verse John dealt with the grace of Christ, so that Jews might turn to him and receive a new life. But now he speaks of judgment, in order to strike the scornful with terror. Since many hypocrites are proud enough to repudiate the grace which Christ offers them, it is necessary to proclaim the judgment which awaits them. For this reason John presented Christ as a dreadful judge toward unbelievers. We also must present our doctrine in this order, and let them know that their rejection of Christ will not go unpunished; they must be aroused from their torpor, and led to fear him as Judge, whom they despised as Savior.

Besides, I have no doubt John intended to teach that Christ would accomplish this judgment by means of his gospel. The preaching of the gospel is the winnowing fan. Before God sifts us, everyone flatters himself that he is wheat. The whole world is in a state of confusion, with the good and the evil thrown together. Hence it is necessary that the chaff be blown away. When Christ comes in our midst with his gospel, when he rebukes our consciences and brings us before the judgment seat of God, then the chaff, which took so much space on the floor, is blown away with the wind. Although the gospel purifies each one of us from chaff, John here compares the reprobate with chaff, and the believers with wheat.

Therefore, since the threshing floor is not the world, as some would have it, but the church, we must consider to whom it is that John speaks. The Jews flatter themselves that they alone were the church, since up to that time they alone were in it. But John tells them that their pride is foolish, since they would soon be thrown out on the threshing floor like so much chaff, and that rightly. He takes a look at the church at that time, which was filled with husks, straw, and other rubbish, and declares that it will soon be purified with the blowing of the gospel.

But how is Christ to separate the chaff from the wheat when there is nothing but chaff in us? The answer is easy. The elect shall be made into wheat; in this way, freed from chaff, they shall be gathered into the barn. This cleansing is begun by Christ, and continued day by day; but its effect shall not be realized fully until the Last Day. For this reason, John turns our minds toward our ultimate end. But we must remember that even now the faithful enter by hope into God's granary which is their real and eternal home. The reprobate on the other hand even now, being under conviction of guilt, feel the heat of the fire which shall at the Last Day become a devouring conflagration. Many have given us subtle discourses about the eternal fire which shall torment the wicked after the Last Judgment. But many passages in Scripture make it plain that the word *fire* is a metaphor. For if the fire is real or as they call it material, so are the sulphur and brimstone mentioned by Isaiah (30:33). Surely, *the fire* is no different from *the worm*; and if, as everybody agrees, *the worm* is a metaphor, we must think the same of *the fire*. To put aside speculations with which silly people weary themselves for nothing, it is enough to hold that such forms of speech were used because of our own crudity. They were intended to convey to us a sense of dreadful torment which we can neither imagine nor express properly with our words.

Have I any pleasure at all that the wicked should die, saith the Lord God, and not that he should return from his ways and live? Ezek. 18:23.

Here the prophet reiterates in different words that God certainly desires nothing more than for those who are perishing and rushing toward death to return to the way of safety. This is why the gospel is today proclaimed throughout the world, for God wished to testify to all the ages that he is greatly inclined to pity. Even to pagans, deprived of the Law and the Prophets, some taste of this truth has always been given. They have often smothered it under many errors, yet we always find them being led by some hidden impulse to seek divine favor. The feeling is somehow ingrained in them that God is merciful to all who seek him.

But God has given clearer witness to this truth in the Law and the Prophets. Moreover, we know in what intimate terms he appeals to us in the gospel when he promises his forgiveness. Indeed, this is the knowledge of salvation: to embrace God's mercy offered to us in Christ. It is in Christ that what the prophet says here is proved to be most true: [We know that] "God does not desire the death of the sinner," because of his own will he comes forth to meet him. Not only is he ready to receive all who flee to his mercy, but he calls to himself with a loud voice those whom he sees cut off from every hope of safety.

We must also notice how God desires all to be made safe, that is, by *turning from their own ways*. God does not wish to save all men by destroying the distinction between good and evil. Before forgiveness comes repentance. How then does he wish all to be made safe? Truly, as formerly through the Law and the Prophets, so also today the Spirit through the gospel condemns the world for sin, by righteousness and judgment (John 16:8). In this way God reveals to men their misery, in order that he may receive them to himself. He wounds that he may heal; he kills that he may give life. We believe and are assured that God does not desire the death of sinners, because he calls all equally to repentance and promises that if they only repent he will be ready to receive them.

Then Jesus said unto them, I go my way, and ye shall seek me, and shall die in your sins; whither I go, ye cannot come. John 8:21.

First, we must consider how the people to whom he speaks sought Christ. If their conversion had been real, they would not have sought him in vain, because he has promised truly that no sooner does a sinner groan over his sin than He shall run to his help. Therefore, Christ means that they have sought after him not by the proper means of faith, but because of a desire to escape the anxiety which is an extreme evil. While the unbelievers want God to look on them with favor, they do not cease to run away from him. God himself declares to us that by repentance and faith we may come to him. But they, hard of heart, turn against God: and broken down with despair, they cry against him. In short, they are so far from seeking God that they will not let him help them, unless he be untrue to himself, which he will never be. Thus it is that the scribes, however impious, were willing to receive the redemption promised at the hand of the Messiah, provided Christ changed himself to suit their own nature. Wherefore by this word Christ denounces all unbelievers and threatens that if they despise the teaching of the gospel, even if they be filled with such anguish as to be forced to cry to God, their howling will do them no good, because as we have said already, *seeking, they do not seek*.

And Abraham took Ishmael his son and all that were born in his house and all that were bought with his money . . . and circumcised the flesh

of their foreskins, in the selfsame day, as God had said unto him. Gen.
17:23.

Moses now praises the obedience of Abraham, because he
circumcised his whole household as he had been commanded.
. . . Two points are worth considering. First, Abraham was not
deterred by the difficulty of the task from offering to God the
sacrifice which he owed. We know that he had a great number
of people in his household. . . . And there was danger of stirring
up a riot in a peaceful community. But relying on God, he
began what was an impossible task. Secondly, we see how well-
ordered his household was. Not only the slaves born in the
house, but also foreigners bought for money, quietly accepted
the pain of circumcision. Obviously Abraham had taken great
pains to train them in their duty. And since he had kept up a
holy discipline, he now received the reward of the care he had
taken. Discipline in easy things prepared the way for something
hard.

Today, when God wishes his gospel to be preached in the
whole world, so that the world may be restored from death to
life, he seems to ask for the impossible. We see how greatly we
are resisted everywhere and with how many and what potent
machinations Satan works against us, so that all roads are
blocked by the princes themselves. Yet each man must perform
his duty without yielding to any impediment. At the end our
effort and our labors shall not fail; they shall receive the success
which does not yet appear.

These things I have spoken unto you in proverbs: but the time cometh
when I shall no longer speak to you in proverbs, but I shall show you
plainly of the Father. John 16:25.

Christ's purpose at this point is to encourage his disciples.
He does not want them to think that his teaching is of little
help to them in their hope of progress toward the better, because
there is so much in it they cannot follow. For, they might have
suspected that Christ did not want to be understood, or that he
was purposely keeping them in suspense. So, he promises them
briefly that his teaching, which might offend them by its obscurity, will become fruitful to them. The Hebrew word *mashal*
at times means "a proverb." The Hebrews called riddles and remarkable sayings also *meshalim* because, like proverbs, they contained similes and figures of speech; and the Greeks called them
ἀποφθέγματα because they are usually ambiguous and obscure.
Christ means therefore that he is speaking to them in figures

and not in a simple and plain language, but that soon he shall speak to them with familiar words, so that his teaching may not be to them perplexing or difficult.

Now we understand what I have already touched upon: namely, that he wants to encourage his disciples to expect further progress, and to keep them from rejecting his teaching because they do not understand it. Unless the hope of some benefit burns and glows within us, zeal for learning must necessarily cool off. Besides, we see clearly that Jesus spoke to his disciples in a simple and even homely style, and not in riddles; but they were so dull that they hung on to his words dumfounded but without understanding a thing. So the obscurity was not in the teaching but in their minds.

And the same happens to us. People praise the Word of God rightly as our very light. But still, our own darkness obscures the Word of God to such an extent that we think we are only hearing allegories. The prophet Isaiah threatened the wicked and the unbelievers, saying that he would be to them as a barbarian and would speak with a stammering tongue (28:11); again, Paul said that the gospel is hidden from those whose minds are blinded by Satan (II Cor. 4:3). So, also, to weak and uneducated people, Christ's words sound so confused as to be unintelligible. Even when their minds are not altogether darkened, as are those of the ungodly, they still are as it were in a cloud. And the Lord allows us for a while to be stupid, so that he may humble us with a sense of our poverty; but he enables those whom he illumines with his Spirit to make such progress as to know his Word and understand it.

The same is true of the next phrase, *the hour cometh*: that is, "the hour will come when I shall no longer speak to you in figures." Certainly, the Spirit did not teach the apostles anything they had not heard from Christ's own mouth. What he did was to fill their hearts with a new light, and thus to drive their darkness away, so that they heard Christ in a new and different way, and understood what he said.

When Jesus said that *he would speak of the Father*, he pointed to the proper goal of his teaching, which is to lead us to the Father in whom alone we shall find our true happiness. But another question remains, Why does he elsewhere say that it is given the disciples to know the mystery of the Kingdom of God (Matt. 13:11), whereas here he admits that he speaks to them in riddles? Why did he in the previous statement distinguish between the disciples and the crowd to whom he spoke in parables? I answer, The apostles were not such ignoramuses as to have no inkling of a notion as to what their Master was saying. Therefore, Christ had reason to distinguish them from crowds who were blind. But when in this place he says that he has spoken to them in allegory, he is turning their attention to the future when his gracious Spirit shall endow them with a new and bright light of understanding. Therefore, both statements are true. The apostles were far beyond those who had no taste for the Word of the gospel. Still, compared to the new wisdom which they were to receive from the Spirit, their knowledge was like that of children at their alphabets.

INDEXES

GENERAL INDEX

COMMENTARY SELECTIONS

BIBLICAL REFERENCES

R. Worley